W9-AVR-738

BARRON'S

H A N D B O O K O F

COMMONLY USED AMERICAN IDIOMS

Second Edition

EDITED BY:

ADAM MAKKAI, Ph.D.

Professor of Linguistics
University of Illinois at Chicago

Eve Kang

3/11/95

BARRON'S

BASED ON:

A Dictionary of American Idioms (Barron's, © 1975)
by Maxine Tull Boatner, Ph.D., and John Edward Gates, Ph.D.
Professor of English, Indiana State University, and
Adam Makkai, Ph.D., Professor of Linguistics,
University of Illinois at Chicago.

© Copyright 1991, 1984 by Barron's Educational Series, Inc.

All inquiries should be addressed to:
Barron's Educational Series, Inc.
250 Wireless Boulevard
Hauppauge, New York 11788

Library of Congress Catalog Card No. 90-48406

International Standard Book No. 0-8120-4614-5

Library of Congress Cataloging in Publication Data

Handbook of commonly used American idioms / edited by Adam Makkai.
    p.   cm.
    ISBN 0-8120-4614-5
    1. English language—United States—Idioms—Dictionaries.   2. Americanisms—
Dictionaries.   I. Makkai, Adam.   II. Title: Commonly used American idioms.
PE2839.H36   1991
423′ .1—dc20   90-48406
                                                        CIP

PRINTED IN THE UNITED STATES OF AMERICA

4 5500 987

Table of Contents

Introduction iv

    What Is an Idiom? iv

    How to Use This Handbook viii

    Part of Speech Labels ix

    Restrictive Usage Labels ix

Acknowledgments xi

Guide to the Parts of an Entry xii

A Handbook of Idioms xv

Introduction

WHAT IS AN IDIOM?

If you understand every individual word in a text and still fail to grasp
what the text is all about, chances are you are having trouble with idioms.
For example, suppose you read (or hear) the following:

> *Sam is a real cool cat. He never blows his stack; he hardly ever*
> *flies off the handle. What's more, he knows how to get away*
> *with things . . . Well, of course, he is getting on, too. His hair*
> *is pepper and salt, but he knows how to make up for lost time by*
> *taking it easy. He gets up early, works out, and turns in early.*
> *He takes care of the hot dog stand like a breeze until he gets*
> *time off. Sam's got it made; this is it for him.*

Needless to say, this is not great literary style, but many Americans,
especially when they converse among themselves, use expressions of this
sort. Now if you have learned the words *cool* to mean 'not very warm,'
cat, 'the familiar domestic animal,' *blow*, 'exhale air with force,' *stack*,
'a pile of something, or material heaped up,' *fly*, 'propel oneself in the air
by means of wings,' *handle*, 'the part of an object designed to hold by
hand'—and so forth, you will still not understand the foregoing sample of
conversational American English, because basic dictionary information
alone will not give you the meaning of the forms involved. An idiom—as
it follows from these observations—is the assigning of a new meaning to
a group of words each of which already has its own meaning. Here is a
"translation" of this highly idiomatic, informal American English text,
into a more formal, and relatively idiom-free English:

> *Sam is really a calm person. He never loses control of himself;*
> *he hardly ever becomes very angry. Furthermore, he knows*
> *how to manage his business financially by using a few tricks*

. . . Needless to say, he is also getting older. His hair is
beginning to turn gray, but he knows how to compensate for
wasted time by relaxing. He rises early, exercises, and goes to
bed early. He manages his frankfurter stand without visible
effort, until it is someone else's turn to work there. Sam is
successful; he has reached his life's goal.

Now if you were to explain how the units are organized in this text, you
would have to make a little idiom dictionary. It would look like this:

to be a (real) cool cat	to be a really calm person
to blow one's stack	to lose control over oneself, to become angry
to fly off the handle	to become excessively angry
what's more	furthermore, besides, additionally
to get away with something	to perpetrate an illegitimate or tricky act without repercussions or harm
of course	naturally
to be getting on	to age, to get older
pepper and salt	black or dark hair mixed with streaks of gray
to make up for something	to compensate for something
lost time	time wasted, time spent in fruitless labor
to take it easy	to relax, to rest, to avoid worry
to get up	to rise from bed in the morning or at other times
to work out	to exercise, to do gymnastics
to turn in	to go to bed at night
to take care of (a need)	to see the needs of, to manage something
like a breeze	without effort, easily
time off	period in one's job during which one is not performing one's services
to have got it made	to be successful, to have arrived
this is it	to be in a position or in a place, or to have possession of an object, beyond which more of the same is unnecessary

Many of the idioms in this sample list can be found in this handbook.
An interesting fact about most of these idioms is that they can easily be
identified with the familiar parts of speech. Thus some idioms are clearly
verbal in nature, such as *get away with, get up, work out, turn in*, etc. An
equally large number are nominal in nature. Thus *hot dog*, "frankfurter in

a bun" serves as a noun. Many serve as adjectives, as in our example *pepper* and *salt*, meaning "black hair mixed with gray." Many are adverbial, as the examples *like a breeze*, "easily, without effort"; *hammer and tongs*, "violently" (as in *they went at it hammer and tongs*). These idioms that correlate with the familiar parts of speech can be called *lexemic idioms*.

The other most important group comprises longer idioms. Often they are an entire phrase, as in our examples *to fly off the handle*, "lose control over oneself," and *to blow one's stack*, "to become very angry." There are many of these in American English. Some famous ones are: *to kick the bucket*, "die"; *to be up the creek*, "to be in a predicament or a dangerous position"; *to be caught between the devil and deep blue sea*, "to have to choose between two equally unpleasant alternatives"; *to seize the bull by the horns*, "to face a problem and deal with it squarely." Idioms of this sort have been called *tournures* (from the French), meaning "turns of phrase," or simply *phraseological idioms*. What they have in common is that they do not readily correlate with a given grammatical part of speech and usually require a paraphrase longer than a word.

The form of these phrase-length idioms is set and only a limited number of them can be said in any other way without destroying the meaning. Consider the idiom *kick the bucket*, for example. In the passive voice you get an unacceptable form, such as *the bucket has been kicked by the cowboy*, which no longer means "the cowboy died." Rather it means that he struck a pail with his foot. Idioms of this type are regarded as *completely frozen forms*. Notice, however, that even this idiom can be inflected for tense; e.g., it is all right to say *the cowboy kicked the bucket, the cowboy will kick the bucket, he has kicked the bucket*, etc. Speakers disagree as much as do grammarians whether or not, for example, it is all right to use this idiom in the gerund form (a gerund being a noun derived from a verb by adding *-ing* to it, e.g., *singing* from *sing, eating* from *eat*), as in *his kicking the bucket surprised us all*. It is best to avoid this form.

The next largest class of idioms is that of well-established sayings and proverbs. These include the famous *don't count your chickens before they're hatched* (meaning "do not celebrate the outcome of an undertaking prematurely because it is possible that you will fail, in which case you will look ridiculous"); *don't wash your dirty linen in public* (meaning "do not complain of your domestic affairs before strangers, as it is none of their business"). Many of these originate from some well-known literary source or come to us from the earliest English speakers of the North American Continent.

Unpredictable meaning is not the only criterion of idiomaticity. Set phrases or phraseological units may also be idiomatic, even though their meanings may be transparent. What is idiomatic (unpredictable) about them is their construction. Examples include *How about a drink? What do you say, Joe?* (as a greeting); *as a matter of fact; just in case; just to be on the safe side,* and many more.

Interestingly, there are also one-word idioms, which occur when a single word is used with a surprisingly different meaning from the original one. Examples include *lemon,* said of an unsuccessful item of manufacture, such as a watch or a car; and *dog,* said of a disappointing date or a tough exam. (*My car is a lemon; my math exam was a dog.*)

Why is English, and especially American English, so heavily idiomatic? The most probable reason is that as we develop new concepts, we need new expressions for them, but instead of creating a brand new word, we use already existent words and put them together in a new sense. This, to a degree, is true of all known languages. There are, in fact, no known languages that do not have some idioms. Consider the Chinese expression for "quickly," for example. It is *ma shang;* translated literally it means "horseback." Why should the concept of "quick" be associated with the back of a horse? The answer reveals itself upon a moment's speculation. In the old days, before the train, the automobile, and the airplane, the fastest way of getting from one place to the other was by riding a horse, i.e., on horseback. Thus Chinese *ma shang* is as if we said in English *hurry up! We must go "on horseback,"* i.e., "Hurry up! We must go quickly." Such a form would not be unintelligible in English, though the speaker would have to realize that it is an idiom, and the foreigner would have to learn it. However, in learning idioms a person may make an incorrect guess. Consider the English idiom, *Oh well, the die is cast!* What would you guess this means—if you didn't know it? Perhaps you might guess that the speaker is resigned to something because of the *Oh well* part. The expression means "An irreversible decision has been made and I must live with it." You can now try to reconstruct how this idiom came into being: The die cast in gambling cannot be thrown again; that would be illegal; whether you have a one, a three, or a six, you must face the consequences of your throw—win or lose, as the case may be. (Some people may know that the phrase was used by Caesar when he crossed the Rubicon, an event that led to war.)

How, then, having just learned it, will you use this idiom correctly? First of all, wait until you hear it from a native speaker in a natural context. Once you have heard the idiom used more than once, and fully understand its meaning, you can try using it yourself. Imagine that you have two job offers, one sure, but lower-paying, and one that pays more, but is only tentative. Because of fear of having no job at all, you accept the lower-paying job, at which moment the better offer comes through, and naturally you feel frustrated. You can then say *Oh well, the die is cast* . . . If you try this on a native speaker and he looks at you with sympathy and does not ask "What do you mean?" you have successfully placed a newly learned idiom in an appropriate context. This can be a rewarding experience. Native Americans often react to foreigners politely, but the natives can definitely tell how fluent you are. A person who uses a bookish, stilted expression and never uses an idiom in the right place might develop a reputation as a dry, unimaginative speaker, or as one who is too pompous. *The use of idioms is, therefore, extremely important. It can strike a chord of solidarity with the listener.* The more idioms you use IN THE RIGHT CONTEXT, the more at ease native Americans will feel with you and the more they will think to themselves, "Look how well this person communicates!" To achieve this evaluation you must scrupulously apply the guidance of the RESTRICTIVE USAGE LABELS. See the paragraph under this heading later in this Introduction.

We will now take a look at some practical considerations for the use of *Handbook of Commonly Used American Idioms*.

HOW TO USE THIS HANDBOOK

This handbook can be used successfully by nonnative speakers of English, students, workers, immigrants—in short, anybody who wants to achieve fluency in idiomatic English. The handbook contains entries of the types mentioned—lexemic idioms, phrase idioms, and proverbial idioms. When a phrase has a special meaning that you cannot decode by looking up and understanding the individual words of which the phrase is composed, then you know you are dealing with an idiom. You may already know some of these idioms or may be able to imagine what they mean. Looking in the book for any of the following idioms that you may already know well will help you to understand how you should use this book: *boyfriend, cop out, wheel and deal, gung-ho, generation gap, idiot box, oddball*.

This handbook is like any other tool: You must familiarize yourself with it and learn how to use it before it begins to work well for you. Study the directions carefully several times, and practice looking up idioms. That way, searching for an idiom and finding it will become second nature to you. If you hear an idiomatic expression that is not in the book, you are likely to develop the ability to track down its meaning after hearing it used for a while. Keep your own idiom list right beside your regular dictionary. If you read a technical text, a novel, or a newspaper article and do not understand an expression, look it up in your regular dictionary first; if you do not find the expression, try this handbook.

How do you find out if this handbook can help you understand a hard sentence? Sometimes you can easily find the idiom, as with *fun house, dog-eat-dog, bottom line*. If not, pick an important word from the most difficult part and look for that. If it is the first word in the idiom, you will find the whole phrase, followed by an explanation. Thus the expression *bats in one's belfry* is listed in this handbook under *b*, the word *bats*. You may, of course, find that the reason you do not understand a particular sentence is not because of any idioms in it; in that case your regular dictionary will be of help to you. Also, there are more idioms than listed in this book; only the most frequently occurring ones in American English are included. British English, for example, or the English spoken in Australia, certainly have many idiomatic expressions that are not a part of American English.

PART OF SPEECH LABELS

Those idioms that correlate with a well-defined grammatical major form class carry a part of speech label. Sometimes, as with many prepositional phrases, a double label had to be assigned because the given phrase has two grammatical uses, e.g., *in commission* can be either adverbial or adjectival. Many prepositional phrases are adverbial in their literal sense, but adjectival in their nonpredictable, idiomatic sense. The letter *v.* stands for verb; it was assigned to phrases containing a verb and an adverb; verb and preposition; or verb, preposition, and adverb. The letters *v. phr.* stand for ''verbal phrase''; these include verbs with an object, verbs with subject complement, and verbs with prepositional phrase.

RESTRICTIVE USAGE LABELS

You must pay particular attention to whether it is appropriate for you to use a certain idiom in a certain setting. Terms labeled *slang* are often picturesque but socially taboo language whose use should be restricted to informal circumstances where unconventional vocabulary might be accepted. *Informal* indicates that the form is used in conversation but should be avoided in formal composition. *Formal* indicates the opposite; this is a form that people usually do not say, but they will use it in an essay or in a speech or lecture. *Literary* alerts you to the fact that the form is bookish or is a quotation; it would be inappropriate for you to use these often. *Vulgar* indicates that you should altogether avoid the form; recognizing it may, of course, be important, since one way to appraise a person is by the language he uses. *Substandard* labels a form as chiefly used by less educated people; *nonstandard* means that a phrase is awkward.

Adam Makkai, Ph.D.
Professor of Linguistics
University of Illinois at Chicago Circle

Acknowledgments

This handbook is the result of the work of many hands. It is based on *A Dictionary of American Idioms,* first published by Barron's Educational Series in 1975, which, in turn, had its source in *A Dictionary of Idioms for the Deaf,* edited by Maxine Tull Boatner, project director, aided by chief linguistic advisor, J. Edward Gates, published in 1969 and copyrighted by the American School for the Deaf. The consulting committee consisted of Dr. Edmund E. Boatner, Dr. William J. McClure, Dr. Clarence D. O'Connor, Dr. George T. Pratt, Jack Brady, M.A., Richard K. Lane, and Professor H. A. Gleason, Jr., of the Hartford Seminary Foundation. Special editors for various subcategories, such as usage, sport terms, etc., were Elizabeth Meltzer, and E. Ward Gilman; Loy E. Golladay helped as language consultant with reviewing and editing. Definers were Edmund Casetti, Philip H. Cummings, Anne M. Driscoll, Harold J. Flavin, Dr. Frank Fletcher, E. Ward Gilman, Loy E. Golladay, Dr. Philip H. Goepp, Dr. Beatrice Hart, Dr. Benjamin Keen, Kendall Litchfield, Harold E. Niergarth, Ruth Gill Price, Thomas H. B. Robertson, Jess Smith, Rhea Talley Stewart, Harriet Smith, Elizabeth D. Spellman, John F. Spellman, George M. Swanson, Barbara Ann Kipfer, and Justyn Moulds. The following have cooperated as simplifiers: Linda Braun, Dr. G. C. Farquhar, Carey S. Lane, Wesley Lauritsen, Nellie MacDonald, Ruth S. McQueen, and Donald Moores. In this new handbook by Barron's Educational Series, a well-known expert on idioms, Dr. Adam Makkai of the University of Illinois at Chicago, has added several hundred contemporary idiomatic phrases to the collection as well as editing the entire text for ease and convenience of reference. Many of these new entries are of the slang character, originating within recent cultural movements; others reflect the popular usage of space technology terms.

Guide to the Parts of an Entry

The following are complete entries as given in this book, for *throw out* or *toss out*, *give up*, *hot water*, *get lost*, and *feather in one's cap*. A guide to the different parts of these entries is given at the left. The order in the outline shows how the different information about the words is presented in this handbook.

Guide

1. ENTRY FORM

The idiom in a basic dictionary form, with a, an, or the or a possessive cut off the beginning, and any words that change left out of the middle.

2. VARIANT

Additional wordings of the same idiom, differing in one or a few words.

3. PART-OF-SPEECH LABEL

Tells you how the phrase is used—like a noun, verb, adjective, adverb, preposition, conjunction, interjection. Some idioms are not used like a single word, but like two or more different parts of speech, or like sentences; these have no part-of-speech label.

4. STYLE LABEL

Tells you whether the phrase is *slang* (used only in very informal situations), *informal* (used only in familiar speaking and writing, not in English compositions, except in dialogue), *formal* (used only in formal writing and speaking, not in friendly talk and letters to familiar friends and relatives), *literary* (used only in stories and poems, for special effects.)

5. SENSE NUMBER

Marks the beginning of one or two or more meanings of an idiom. Each different sense begins with a new number. Closely related senses have letters added to the numbers (e.g., 1a, 1b.).

6. DEFINITION

Tells you the meaning of the idiom. There may be two or more definitions, but they nearly always mean the same thing. They just say the same thing in different words.

Parts of an Entry

[**throw out**]¹ *or* [toss out]² [*v.*]³ [To force to leave; dismiss.]⁶ [*When the baseball manager complained too loudly, the umpires threw him out.*]⁹ [(The umpires ordered the manager to leave the game when he complained too loudly.)]⁹ [**4**]⁵ [To cause to be out in baseball by throwing the ball.]⁶ [*The shortstop tossed the runner out.*]⁸

[**give up**]¹ [*v.*]³ [**1a**]⁵ [To stop trying to keep; surrender; yield.]⁶ [*The dog had the ball in his mouth and wouldn't give it up.*]⁸ [(He wouldn't drop the ball from his mouth.)]⁹ [*Jimmy is giving up his job as a newsboy when he goes back to school.*]⁸ [(He won't keep the job when he goes back to school.)]⁹ [**1b**]⁵ [To allow, permit.]⁶ [*Ford gave up two walks in the first inning.*]⁸ [(Ford allowed two men to walk in the first inning.)]⁹ [**2**]⁵ [To stop doing or having; abandon; quit.]⁶ [*The doctor told Mr. Harris to give up smoking.*]⁸ [(He told him to stop smoking.)]⁹ [*Jane hated to give up her friends when she moved away.*]⁸ [(She didn't want to stop having them for friends.)]⁹ [**3**]⁵ [To stop hoping for, waiting for, or trying to do.]⁶ [*Johnny was given up by the doctors after the accident, but he lived just the same.*]⁸ [(He was hurt so badly that the doctors stopped believing he could live.)]⁹ [*When Mary didn't come by nine o'clock, we gave her up.*]⁸ [(We stopped waiting.)]⁹ [*I couldn't do the puzzle so I gave it up.*]⁸ [(I quit trying.)]⁹ [**4**]⁵ [To stop trying; quit; surrender.]⁶ [*The war will be over when one of the countries gives up.*]⁸ [(When one country stops fighting the war will be finished.)]⁹

A different meaning will be marked by a different sense number.

7. USAGE NOTE
Gives you additional information about the way the idiom is used.

8. ILLUSTRATIVE SENTENCES
Shows one or more ways that the idiom is used in sentences.

9. PARAPHRASE
Gives the meaning of the sentence, or the part of the sentence in which the idiom is; explains the illustrative sentence.

[**hot water**]¹ [n.]³ [*informal*]⁴ [Trouble.]⁶—[Used with *in, into, out of.*]⁷ [*John's thoughtless remark got him into a lot of hot water.*]⁸ [(His remark got him into a lot of trouble.)]⁹ [*It was the kind of trouble where it takes a friend to get you out of hot water.*]⁸ [(It was the kind of jam in which a friend is the best means of getting out of trouble.)]⁹

[**get lost**]¹ [v. phr.,]³ [*slang*]⁴—[Go away!]⁶ [Usually used as a command.]⁷ [*Get lost! I want to study.*]⁸ [(Go away; I want to study.)]⁹ [*John told Bert to get lost.*]⁸ [(John told Bert to go away.)]⁹

[**feather in one's cap**]¹ [n. phr.]³ [Something to be proud of; an honor.]⁶ [*It was a feather in his cap to win first prize.*]⁸ [(It was an honor for him to win first prize.)]⁹ From the medieval practice of placing a feather in the helmet of one who won honors in battle.

Key to Abbreviations:

adj.—adjective	interj.—interjection	prep.—preposition
adv.—adverb	interrog.—interrogative	syn.—synonym
cl.—clause	n.—noun	v.—verb
conj.—conjunction	phr.—phrase	

A Handbook of
Commonly Used
American Idioms

A

about time *n. phr.* Finally, but later than it should have been; at last. *Mother said, "It's about time you got up, Mary."* (Mary got up late, and Mother told her she should have gotten up earlier.) *"The basketball team won last night. About time."* (It has been a long time since the team won a game.)

about to **1** Close to; ready to.— Used with an infinitive. *We were about to leave when the snow began.* (We were ready to leave when snow began to fall.) *I haven't gone yet, but I'm about to.* (I'm almost ready to go.) **2** *informal* Having a wish or plan to.—Used with an infinitive in negative sentences. *Freddy wasn't about to give any of his ice-cream cone.* (He had no plan to give me any.) *"Will she come with us?" asked Bill. "She's not about to," answered Mary.* (She certainly won't come; she doesn't want to come with us.)

above all *adv. phr.* Of first or highest importance; most especially. *Children need many things, but above all they need love.* (They need love the most.)

according to Hoyle *adv. or adj. phr., informal* By the rules; in the usual and correct way; regular. *It's not according to Hoyle to hit a man when he's down.* (It's not fair to hit a man when he's down.) *In quitting without notice, he didn't act according to Hoyle.* (In quitting without first telling the boss, he didn't act by the rules.)

ace in the hole *n. phr.* **1** An ace given to a player face down so that other players in a card game cannot see it. *When the cowboy bet all his money in the poker game he did not know that the gambler had an ace in the hole and would win the money.* (He did not know that the gambler had a hidden high card that would win the game and the money the cowboy bet.) **2** *informal* Someone or something important that is kept as a surprise until the right time so as to bring victory or success. *The football team has a new play that they are keeping as an ace in the hole for the big game.* (They are keeping the play as a surprise to win the game.) *The lawyer's ace in the hole was a secret witness who saw the accident.* (No one knew that the lawyer had a witness who had seen the accident.)

acid head *n. slang, drug culture* A regular user of LSD on whom the hallucinogenic drug has left a visible effect. *The reason John acts so funny is that he is a regular acid head.* (The reason he acts odd is that he is a regular user of LSD, which has had a detrimental effect on him.)

acid rock *n. slang, drug culture* A characteristic kind of popular music in which loudness and beat predominate over melody; especially such music as influenced by drug experiences. *John is a regular acid rock freak.* (John is unusually and excessively fond of hallucinogenic rock music in which beat predominates over melody.)

across the board *adv. phr.* **1** So that equal amounts of money are bet on the same horse to win a race, to place second, or third. *I bet $6 on the white horse across the board.* (I bet $2 that the white horse would win, $2 that he would be second, and $2 that he would be third in the race.)—Often used with hyphens as an adjective. *I made an across-the-board bet on*

1

the white horse. (Equal amounts were bet that the horse would either win or place second or third.) **2** *informal* Including everyone or all; so that all are included. *The President wanted taxes lowered across the board.* (He wanted the taxes of everyone, rich and poor, to be lowered.)—Often used with hyphens as an adjective. *The workers at the store got an across-the-board pay raise.* (Everyone got more pay.)

act up *v., informal* **1** To behave badly; act rudely or impolitely. *The dog acted up as the postman came to the door.* (The dog barked and jumped when the mailman came.) **2** To work or run poorly (as a machine); skip; miss. *The car acted up because the spark plugs were dirty.* (The car ran in a jerky way because the spark plugs needed cleaning.)

add fuel to the flame *v. phr.* To make a bad matter worse by adding to its cause; spread trouble; increase anger or other strong feelings by talk or action. *By criticizing Julia, the father added fuel to the flame of his son's love.* (The father made his son love Julia more when he criticized her.) *Bob was angry with Ted, and Ted added fuel to the flame by laughing at him.* (Ted laughed at Bob and Bob became angrier.)

add insult to injury *v. phr.* **1** To hurt someone's feelings after doing him harm. *He added insult to injury when he called the man a rat after he had already beaten him up.* (He fought the man and also called him bad names.) **2** To make bad trouble worse. *We started on a picnic, and first it rained; then, to add insult to injury, the car broke down.* (On the way to the picnic we were caught

in rain, and then, to make things worse, the car broke down.)

afraid of one's shadow *adj. phr. informal* Scared of small or imaginary things; very easily frightened; jumpy; nervous. *Mrs. London won't stay alone in her house at night; she is afraid of her own shadow.* (She is afraid of all sorts of little things.) *Johnny cries whenever he must say hello to an adult; he is afraid of his own shadow.* (He is so shy that he is afraid to say "hello.")

after all *adv. phr.* **1** As a change in plans; anyway.—Used with emphasis on *after.* *Bob thought he couldn't go to the party because he had too much homework, but he went after all.* (At first Bob thought he couldn't go to the party, but he changed his plan and went to it; he went anyhow.) **2** For a good reason that one should remember.—Used with emphasis on *all.* *Why shouldn't Betsy eat the cake? After all, she baked it.* (Betsy should eat some cake because she baked it. Don't say Betsy can't have any cake; remember, she baked it.)

after one's own heart *adj. phr., informal* Well-liked because of agreeing with one's own feelings, interests, and ideas; to one's liking; agreeable.—A cliché. Used after *man* or some similar word. *He likes baseball and good food; he is a man after my own heart.* (I like him because he likes the same things that I like.) *Thanks for agreeing with me about the class party; you're a girl after my own heart.* (You pleased me by agreeing with me about the party.)

against the grain *adv. phr.* So as to annoy or trouble, or to cause anger or dislike.—Usually follows *go.* *His coarse and rude ways went against the grain with me.*

(His rudeness irritated me.) *It went against the grain with her to have to listen to his gossip.* (She disliked hearing his mean talk.)

against time *or* **against the clock** *adv. phr.* **1** As a test of speed or time; in order to beat a speed record or time limit. *John ran around the track against time, because there was no one else to race against.* (John timed himself with a watch to see how fast he could run around the track.) **2** As fast as possible; so as to do or finish something before a certain time. *It was a race against the clock whether the doctor would get to the scene of the accident soon enough to save the injured man.* (The doctor had to get there as quickly as possible or the injured man might die.) **3** So as to cause delay by using up time. *The outlaw talked against time with the sheriff, hoping that his gang would come and rescue him.* (The outlaw kept talking so his friends would have more time to come and save him before the sheriff could put him in jail.)

ahead of the game *adv. or adj. phr., informal* **1** In a position of advantage; winning (as in a game or contest); ahead (as by making money or profit); making it easier to win or succeed. *The time you spend studying when you are in school will put you ahead of the game in college.* (You will get along better in college than others who have studied less.) *After Tom sold his papers, he was $5 ahead of the game.* (He made a $5 profit.) **2** Early; too soon; beforehand. *John studies his lessons only one day early; if he gets too far ahead of the game, he forgets what he read.* (When John reads his lesson very early, he forgets what he read.)

a hell of a *or* **one hell of a** *adj. or adv. phr., informal* Extraordinary, very. *He made a hell of a shot in the basketball game.* (He made a fantastic shot . . .) *Tom said three hours was a hell of a long time to wait to buy a ticket.* (Tom thought three hours was much too long to wait.) *It left one hell of a bruise.* (It left a severe bruise.)

air one's dirty linen in public *or* **wash one's dirty linen in public** *v. phr.* To talk about one's private quarrels or disgraces where others can hear; make public something embarrassing that should be kept secret.—A cliché. *Everyone in the school knew that the superintendent and the principal were angry with each other because they aired their dirty linen in public.* (They quarreled where anyone could hear.) *No one knew that the boys' mother was a drug addict, because the family did not wash its dirty linen in public.* (The family did not talk to other people about its secrets.)

air shuttle *n., informal* Air service for regular commuters operating between geographically close major cities, e.g., between Boston and New York City; such flights do not require reservations and operate on a frequent schedule. *My dad takes the air shuttle from Boston to New York once a week.* (He uses the commuter air service between those two cities.)

a little knowledge is a dangerous thing *literary* A person who knows a little about something may think he knows it all and make bad mistakes. *John has read a book on driving a car and now he thinks he can drive. A little knowledge is a dangerous thing.* (It would be dangerous for John to try to drive just because he has read about it.)

all along or (informal) **right along** adv. phr. All the time; during the whole time. *I knew all along that we would win.* (I knew it all the time.) *I knew right along that Jane would come.* (I believed during the whole time she would come.)

all at once adv. phr. **1** or **at once.** At the same time; together. *The teacher told the children to talk one at a time; if they talked at once, she could not understand them.* (The teacher could not listen to all the children at once; they should speak one at a time, in turn.) *Bill can play the piano, sing, and lead his orchestra all at once.* (He can do three things at the same time.) **2** or **all of a sudden** Without warning; abruptly; suddenly; unexpectedly. *All at once we heard a shot and the soldier fell to the ground.* (Suddenly we heard a shot and the soldier fell to the ground.) *All of a sudden the ship struck a rock.* (Without warning the ship struck a rock.)

all but adv. phr. Very nearly; almost. *Crows all but destroyed the cornfield.* (They ate nearly all the corn.) *The hikers were all but frozen when they were found.* (The hikers were almost frozen.)

all ears adj. phr., informal Very eager to hear; very attentive.—Used in the predicate. *Go ahead with your story; we are all ears.* (We are very eager to hear your story.) *When John told about the circus, the boys were all ears.* (They were very attentive.)

all eyes adj. phr., informal Wide-eyed with surprise or curiosity; watching very closely.—Used in the predicate. *At the circus the children were all eyes.* (The children were interested in the circus and watched closely.)

all out adv. phr., informal With all one's strength, power, or determination; to the best of one's ability; without holding back.—Usually used in the phrase *go all out.* *We went all out to win the game.* (We tried our hardest to win.) *John went all out to finish the job and was very tired afterwards.* (John used up a lot of energy and was tired out.)

all over adv. phr. **1** In every part; everywhere. *He has a fever and aches all over.* (All parts of his body ache.) *I have looked all over for my glasses.* (I have looked everywhere.) **2** informal In every way; completely. *She is her mother all over.* (She is just like her mother.) **3** informal Coming into very close physical contact, as during a fight or wrestling. *Before I noticed what happened, he was all over me.* (Before I noticed what happened, he was wrestling and tangling with me.)

all right adv. phr. **1** Well enough. *The new machine is running all right.* (The new machine is doing satisfactorily.) **2** informal I am willing; yes. *"Shall we watch television?" "All right."* ("Shall we watch television?" "Yes.") **3** informal Beyond question; certainly.—Used for emphasis and placed after the word it modifies. *It's time to leave, all right, but the bus hasn't come.* (It is certainly time to go, but the bus has not come.)

all right adj. phr. **1** Good enough; correct; suitable. *His work is always all right.* (His work is always satisfactory.) **2** In good health or spirits; well. *"How are you?" "I'm all right."* (How do you feel? I feel fine.) **3** slang

Good. *He's an all-right guy.* (He's a good fellow.)

all right for you *interj.* I'm finished with you! That ends it between you and me!—Used by children. *All right for you! I'm not playing with you any more!* (I'm angry with you and I won't play with you any more.)

all roads lead to Rome *literary* The same end or goal may be reached by many different ways.—A proverb. *"I don't care how you get the answer," said the teacher. "All roads lead to Rome."* (If you get the right answer to the question, it makes no difference how you figure it.)

all set *adj., informal* Ready; completed. *"How are you doing fixing my tire?" Joe asked. "All set," the man answered.* (He says he's ready.)

all shook up *adj. slang* In a state of great emotional upheaval; disturbed; agitated. *What are you so shook up about?* (What is it that disturbs you so?)

all systems go Originally from space English, now general informal usage Everything is complete and ready for action; it is now all right to proceed. *After they wrote out the invitations, it was all systems go for the wedding.* (After they wrote the invitations, everything was in order to proceed with the wedding ceremony.)

all the same *or* **just the same** *adv. phr., informal* As if the opposite were so; nevertheless; anyhow; still. *Everyone opposed it, but Sally and Bob got married all the same.* (Although everyone was against their getting married, Sally and Bob did so.) *Mary is deaf, but she takes tap dancing lessons just the same.* (Although

Mary cannot hear, she is learning to tap dance as if she could hear.)

all the thing *n. phr.* (also **all the rage**) The fashion; the vogue. *Dustin Hoffman was all the rage in the movies.* (He was one of the most popular actors.) *It was all the thing in the late sixties to smoke pot and demonstrate against the war in Vietnam.* (It was fashionable to indulge in the use of marijuana and criticize the foreign policy of the Johnson administration.)

all the time *adv. phr.* **1** *or* **all the while** During the whole period; through the whole time. *Mary went to college in her hometown, and lived at home all the while.* (Mary always lived at home while she was going to college.) *Most of us were surprised to hear that Mary and Tom had been engaged all year, but Sue said she knew it all the time.* (Sue knew it all year.) **2** Without stopping; continuously. *Most traffic lights work all the time.* (The lights that tell the cars when to stop and go work all day and all night.) **3** Very often; many times. *Ruth talks about her trip to Europe all the time, and her friends are tired of it.* (Ruth talks too often about her trip to Europe.)

all the way *or* **the whole way** *adv. phr.* **1** From start to finish; during the whole distance or time. *Jack climbed all the way to the top of the tree.* (He climbed as high as he could go.) *Joe has played the whole way in the football game and it's almost over.* (He has played the whole game till now.) **2** In complete agreement; with complete willingness to satisfy.—Often used in the phrase *go all the way with. I go all the way with what George says about Bill.* (I agree completely.)

Mary said she was willing to kiss Bill, but that did not mean she was willing to go all the way with him. (Mary wasn't willing to do anything that Bill wanted.) *The bank was willing to lend Mr. Jones money to enlarge his factory, but it wasn't willing to go all the way with his plans to build another in the next town.* (The bank wasn't willing to satisfy Mr. Jones by building a factory in another town.)

all wet *adj., slang* Entirely confused or wrong; mistaken. *When the Wright brothers said they could build a flying machine, people thought they were all wet.* (When the Wright brothers told of their plans for a flying machine, people thought they were imagining something impossible.) *If you think I like baseball, you're all wet.* (You are all wrong, if you think I like baseball.)

along for the ride *adv. phr., informal* Being in a group for the fun or the credit without doing any of the work. *He wants no members in his political party who are just along for the ride.* (He wants no members who will not work for the party.)

a lot *n., informal* A large number or amount; very many or very much; lots. *I learned a lot in Mr. Smith's class.* (I learned much in Mr. Smith's class.) *A lot of our friends are going to the beach this summer.* (Many of our friends are going to the beach.)—Often used like an adverb. *Ella is a jolly girl; she laughs a lot.* (Ella often laughs.) *Grandfather was very sick last week, but he's a lot better now.* (Grandfather is much better now.) *You'll have to study a lot harder if you want to pass.* (You must study much harder to pass.)—Also used as an adverb with *more, less,* and *fewer.* *There was a good crowd at the game today, but a lot more will come next week.* (Many more people will come to the game next week.)—Often used with *whole* for emphasis. *John has a whole lot of marbles.* (John has a very large number of marbles.) *Jerry is a whole lot taller than he was a year ago.* (Jerry is much taller.)

and how *interj., informal* Used for emphatic agreement. *"Did you see the game?" "And how!"* (I surely did!) *"Isn't Mary pretty?" "And how she is!"* (She is very pretty!)

and then some And a lot more; and more too. *It would cost all the money he had and then some.* (It would cost all the money he had, and more too.) *Talking his way out of this trouble was going to take all his wits and then some.* (It was going to need more cleverness than he had to explain his way out of this trouble.)

answer for *v.* **1** To take responsibility for; assume charge or supervision of. *The Secret Service has to answer for the safety of the President and his family.* (The Secret Service is responsible for the safety of the President and his family.) **2** To say you are sure that (someone) has good character or ability; guarantee; sponsor. *When people thought Ray had stolen the money, the principal said, "Ray is no thief. I'll answer for him."* (When people thought Ray might have stolen the cash, the principal spoke for his honesty.) **3** Take the blame or punishment for. *When Mother found out who ate the cake, Tom had to answer for his mischief.* (Tom was punished.)

ante up *v.* To produce a necessary amount of money; pay. *Tom and Dick had no money with them;*

so Bob had to ante up the $10 for the pizza. (Bob had to pay the whole bill.)

ants in one's pants   *n. phr., slang*   Nervous overactivity; restlessness. *Jane cannot sit still; she has ants in her pants.* (Jane is a very restless girl. She always likes to do something.) *You have ants in your pants today. Is something wrong?* (You are very nervous today. Are you worried about something?)

apple of one's eye   *n. phr.* Something or someone that is adored; a cherished person or object. *Charles is the apple of his mother's eye.* (Charles' mother loves him more than anything else. She adores him.) *John's first car was the apple of his eye. He was always polishing it.* (John was very proud of his first car.)

apple-pie order   *n. phr., informal*   Exact orderly arrangement; neatness. *The house was in apple-pie order.* (The house was neat and tidy.) *Like a good secretary, she kept the boss's desk in apple-pie order.* (The secretary kept her boss's desk orderly and neat.)

arm and a leg   *n. slang*   An exorbitantly high price that must be paid for something that isn't really worth it. *To get a decent apartment these days in New York you have to pay an arm and a leg.* (You have to pay an exorbitant amount to get a decent apartment.)

armed to the teeth   *adj. phr.* Having all needed weapons; fully armed.—A cliché. *The paratroopers were armed to the teeth.* (They had many things to fight with.)

around the clock *also* **the clock around**   *adv. phr.*   For 24 hours a day continuously; all day and all night. *The factory operated around the clock until the order was filled.* (The factory ran for 24 hours a day until it had filled the order.) *He studied around the clock for his history exam.* (He studied all day and all night for his history exam.)—**round-the-clock** *adj.* *That filling station has round-the-clock service.* (You can go there or telephone for help all day and all night.)

around the corner   *adv. phr.* Soon to come or happen; close by; near at hand. *The fortune teller told Jane that there was an adventure for her just around the corner.* (The adventure would soon happen.)

as it were   *adv. phr.*   As it might be said to be; as if it really were; seemingly.—Used with a statement that might seem silly or unreasonable, to show that it is just a way of saying it. *In many ways children live, as it were, in a different world from adults.* (Children and adults seem to live in different worlds, but it's just because their interests are so different.) *The sunlight on the icy branches made, as it were, delicate lacy cobwebs from tree to tree.* (The ice on the trees seemed to be lacy cobwebs.)

ask for   *v., informal*   To make (something bad) likely to happen to one; bring (something bad) upon oneself. *Charles drives fast on worn-out tires; he is asking for trouble.* (He is likely to have a blowout and wreck the car.) *The workman lost his job, but he asked for it by coming to work drunk several times.* (The workman brought the loss of his job upon himself, because he came to work drunk.)

ask for the moon *or* **cry for the moon**   *v. phr.*   To want something that one cannot reach or have;

try for the impossible. *John asked his mother for a hundred dollars today. He's always asking for the moon.* (John has as little chance of getting $100 from his mother as he has of getting the moon if he asked for that.)

asleep at the switch *adj. phr., informal* Failing to act promptly as expected; not alert to an opportunity.—A cliché. *When the ducks flew over, the boy was asleep at the switch and missed his shot.* (He was not watchful and did not shoot in time.)

as luck would have it *adv. clause* As it happened; by chance; luckily or unluckily. *As luck would have it, no one was in the building when the explosion occurred.* (Luckily, no one was in the building to be hurt.) *As luck would have it, there was rain on the day of the picnic.* (As it happened, it rained on the day of the picnic.)

as soon as *conj.* Just after; when; immediately after. *As soon as the temperature falls to 70, the furnace is turned on.* (When the temperature falls, the furnace goes on.) *As soon as you finish your job let me know.* (Tell me when you finish.) *He will see you as soon as he can.* (He is busy now; he will see you when he is free.)

as the crow flies *adv. clause* By the most direct way; along a straight line between two places. *It is seven miles to the next town as the crow flies, but it is ten miles by the road, which goes around the mountain.* (It is seven miles in a perfectly straight line to the next town, but it is ten miles by the road, which curves around the bottom of the mountain.)

as to *prep.* **1** In connection with; about; regarding. *There is no doubt as to his honesty.* (There is no doubt about his honesty.) *As to your final grade, that depends on your final examination.* (About your final grade, it depends on your examination.) **2** According to; following; going by. *They sorted the eggs as to size and color.* (They classed the eggs according to size and color.)

as well as *conj.* In addition to; and also; besides. *Hiking is good exercise as well as fun.* (Hiking is good exercise and also fun.) *He was my friend as well as my doctor.* (Besides being my doctor, he was my friend.) *The book tells about the author's life as well as about his writings.* (It tells about his life in addition to his writings.)

as yet *adv. phr.* Up to the present time; so far; yet. *We know little as yet about the moon's surface.* (We do not know much yet about the moon's surface.) *She has not come as yet.* (She has not come yet.)

at all *adv.* **1** To or at every place; in every direction or location. *Bob liked to go anywhere at all.* (Bob liked to go to any place he could.) *Mary could find Barbara nowhere at all.* (Mary looked everywhere, but Barbara wasn't in any place she looked.) **2** In any manner; in the smallest amount. *It's not at all likely that Joan will go.* (It is very unlikely that Joan will come.) *It was early March, but the weather was not at all cold.* (The weather was not the least bit cold. It was warm.)

at all costs *adv. phr.* At any expense of time, effort, or money. Regardless of the results. *Mr. Jackson intended to save his son's eyesight at all costs.* (He wanted to save his son's eyesight; it did not matter how much time and money he might have to spend.)

Carl is determined to succeed in his new job at all costs. (He is determined to be successful; he doesn't care how hard he has to work.)

at a loss *adj. phr.* In a state of uncertainty; without any idea; puzzled. *A good salesman is never at a loss for words.* (He can always think of something to say.) *When Don missed the last bus, he was at a loss to know what to do.* (He did not know how he would get home.)

at any rate *adv. phr.* In any case; anyhow. *It isn't much of a car, but at any rate it was not expensive.* (It isn't much of a car, but at least he didn't pay a high price for it.)

at bay *adv. or adj. phr.* In a place where you can no longer run away; unable to go back farther; forced to stand and fight, or face an enemy; cornered. *The dog ran the rat into a corner, and there the rat turned at bay.* (Cornered, the rat turned to fight the dog.) *The police chased the thief to a roof, where they held him at bay until more policemen came to help.* (The police chased the thief to a roof, and held him there at gunpoint until more policemen arrived.)

at cross purposes *adv. phr.* With opposing meanings or aims; with opposing effect or result; with aims that hinder or get in each other's way. *Tom's parents acted at cross purposes in advising him; his father wanted him to become a doctor; but his mother wanted him to become a minister.* (Tom's father and mother gave him opposing advice; his father wanted him to become a doctor but his mother wanted him to become a minister.)

at death's door *adj. or adv. phr.* Very near death; dying. *He seemed to be at death's door from his illness.* (He seemed to be dying from his illness.)

at ease *or* **at one's ease** *adj. or adv. phr.* **1** In comfort; without pain or bother. *You can't feel at ease with a toothache.* (You can't feel comfortable or free of pain.) **2** *or* **at one's ease** Comfortable in one's mind; relaxed, not troubled.—Often used in the phrase **put at ease** or **put at one's ease**. *We put Mary at her ease during the thunderstorm by reading her stories.* (We made Mary forget about the storm and relax.) **3** Standing with one's feet apart and without talking, in military ranks. *The sergeant gave his men the command "At ease!"* (The men did not have to stand stiffly but could relax when they stood in line.)

at fault *adj. phr.* Responsibile for an error or failure; to blame. *The driver who didn't stop at the red light was at fault in the accident.* (The driver who went through the red light was to blame for the accident.) *When the engine would not start, the mechanic looked at all the parts to find what was at fault.* (He looked to see which part was keeping the engine from working.)

at first *adv. phr.* In the beginning; at the start. *The driver didn't see the danger at first.* (He didn't see the danger when he began.) *At first the job looked good to Bob, but later it became tiresome.* (In the beginning Bob thought he had a wonderful job, but after a time he grew tired of doing the same thing again and again.) *There was a little trouble at first, but things soon were quiet.*

(He had a little trouble at the start, but things were soon all right.)

at first blush *adv. phr.* When first seen; without careful study. *At first blush the offer looked good, but when we studied it, we found things we could not accept.* (At first, the offer seemed good, but after careful study we found things we could not accept.)

at first glance *or* **at first sight** *adv. or adj. phr.* After a first quick look. *At first sight, his guess was that the whole trouble between the two men resulted from personalities that did not agree.* (His first guess was that the two men just couldn't get along.) *Tom met Mary at a party, and it was love at first sight.* (He loved her as soon as he saw her.)

at hand *also* **at close hand** *or* **near at hand** *adv. phr.* **1** Easy to reach; nearby. *When he writes, he always keeps a dictionary at hand.* (When he writes, he keeps a dictionary where he can reach it easily when he needs it.) **2** *formal* Coming soon; almost here. *Examinations are past and commencement day is at hand.* (It is almost commencement day.)

at heart *adv. phr.* **1** In spite of appearances; at bottom; in reality. *His manners are rough, but he is a kind man at heart.* (He is really a kind man in spite of his rough manners.) **2** As a serious interest or concern; as an important aim or goal. *He has the welfare of the poor at heart.* (He thinks the health and happiness of the poor are important.)

at large *adv. or adj. phr.* **1** Not kept within walls, fences, or boundaries; free. *The killer remained at large for weeks.* (The killer succeeded in not being caught for weeks.) *Cattle and sheep roamed at large on the big*

ranch. (Cattle and sheep roamed freely over the big, unfenced ranch.) **2** In a broad, general way; at length; fully. *The superintendent talked at large for an hour about his hopes for a new school building.* (He talked all about a new building, not only about getting the money, not only about why it was needed, not only about where it would be built.) **3** As a group rather than as individuals; as a whole; taken together. *The junior class at large was not interested in a senior yearbook.* (Almost no one in the junior class was interested in a senior yearbook.) **4** As a representative of a whole political unit or area rather than one of its parts; from a city rather than one of its wards, or a state rather than one of its districts. *He was elected congressman at large.* (He was elected congressman by the vote of the whole state, rather than by the vote of only one congressional district.) *Aldermen are voted for at large.* (Aldermen are voted for in all wards of the city instead of one alderman from each ward.)

at last *also* **at long last** *adv. phr.* After a long time, finally. *The war had been long and hard, but now there was peace at last.* (The war had been long and hard, but now, finally, there was peace.) *The boy saved his money until at last he had enough for a bicycle.* (He saved his money and after a long time he was able to buy a bicycle.)

at least *adv. phr.* **1** *or* **at the least** At the smallest guess; no fewer than; no less than. *You should brush your teeth at least twice a day.* (It is necessary for you to brush your teeth two times every day and no less.) *At least three students are failing in math-*

ematics. (Three or more students are failing mathematics.) *Mr. Johnson must weigh 200 pounds, at least.* (Mr. Johnson appears to weigh 200 pounds, and probably weighs more.) **2** Whatever else you may say; anyhow; anyway. *It was a clumsy move, but at least it saved her from getting hit.* (It was awkward, but it saved her from getting hit, anyway.) *She broke her arm, but at least it wasn't the arm she writes with.* (Luckily, she writes with the arm that is not broken.) *The Mortons had fun at their picnic yesterday—at least the children did—they played while their parents cooked the food.* (Maybe the parents didn't have fun, but the children had fun, anyhow.) *He's not coming—at least that's what he said.* (Maybe he will come, but he said he would not come.)

at leisure *adj. or adv. phr.* **1** Not at work; not busy; with free time; at rest. *Come and visit us some evening when you're at leisure.* (Come and visit us when you have free time.) **2** *or* **at one's leisure** When and how one wishes; at one's convenience; without hurry. *John made the model plane at his leisure.* (He worked on the plane whenever he felt like working.) *You may read the book at your leisure.* (You may read it slowly without rushing.)

at length *adv. phr.* **1** In detail; fully. *You must study the subject at length to understand it.* (You must study the subject fully to understand it.) *The teacher explained the new lesson at length to the students.* (He explained everything about the new lesson to the students.) **2** In the end; at last; finally. *The movie became more and more exciting, until at*

length people were sitting on the edge of their chairs. (Toward the end the movie made people sit excitedly on the edge of their chairs.)

at liberty *adv. or adj. phr.* Free to go somewhere or do something; not shut in or stopped. *The police promised to set the man at liberty if he told the names of the other robbers.* (The police promised to let the man go free.) *I am sorry, but I am not at liberty to come to your party.* (I cannot come to your party because I have something else I must do at that time.)

at loggerheads *adj. or adv. phr.* In a quarrel; in a fight; opposing each other. *The two senators had long been at loggerheads on foreign aid.* (The two senators had long been enemies about foreign aid.) *Because of their barking dog, the Morrises lived at loggerheads with their neighbors.* (The Morrises were not friends with their neighbors; they quarreled about the noisy dog.)

at odds *adj. phr.* In conflict or disagreement; opposed. *The boy and girl were married a week after they met and soon found themselves at odds about religion.* (They married too soon after they met, and quickly found that they were in serious disagreement about religion.)

at once *adv. phr.* Without delay; right now or right then; immediately. *Put a burning match next to a piece of paper, and it will begin burning at once.* (Right then the paper will begin to burn; in a second it will be hot enough to burn.) *Mother called the children to lunch, and Paul came at once, but Brenda stayed in the sandpile a little longer.* (Paul did not stay in the sandpile after his mother called him; he came when Mother called.

at one fell swoop *or* **in one fell swoop** *adv. phr.* **1** *literary* In one attack or accident; in one bad blow. *The millionaire lost his money and his friends at one fell swoop.* (He lost money and friends in one unlucky happening.) **2** At one time; at the same time. *Three cars drove into the driveway, and Mrs. Crane's dinner guests all arrived at one fell swoop.* (They all came at the same time.)

at one's beck and call *or* **at the beck and call of** *adj. phr.* Ready and willing to do whatever someone asks; ready to serve at a moment's notice. *A good parent isn't necessarily always at the child's beck and call.* (One can be a good parent without always jumping to do a child's bidding.)

at one's door *or* **at one's doorstep** *adv. phr.* **1** Very close; very near where one lives or works. *Johnny is very lucky because there's a swimming pool right at his doorstep.* (The swimming pool is very close to Johnny's house.) *Mr. Green can get to work in only a few minutes because the subway is at his door.* (The subway is near where Mr. Green lives.)

at one's fingertips *adv. phr.* **1** Within easy reach; quickly touched; nearby. *Seated in the cockpit, the pilot of a plane has many controls at his fingertips.* (As he sits in the cockpit, an airplane pilot has many controls where he can touch them easily.) **2** Readily usable as knowledge or skill; familiar. *He had several languages at his fingertips.* (He could speak and write several languages easily.) *He had the whole design of the machine at his fingertips.* (He was thoroughly familiar with the plan of the machine.)

at one's heels *adv. phr.* Close behind; as a constant follower or companion. *The boy got tired of having his little brother at his heels all day.* (He didn't like having his little brother follow him around all the time.) *John ran by the finish line with Ned at his heels.* (John passed by the finish line and Ned was close behind him.) *Bad luck followed at his heels all his life.* (He had bad luck all his life.)

at one's wit's end *or* **at the end of one's wits** *adj. phr.* Having no ideas how to solve a problem; feeling puzzled after having used up all one's resources. *He had approached every friend for help in vain, and now he was at his wit's end.* (He had asked everyone he could think of for help, and now he was unable to think what to do next.) *The designer was at his wit's end: he had tried wings of many different kinds, but none would fly.* (The designer could think of no more ideas; he had tried many kinds of wings without finding a wing that would fly on the new airplane.)

at pains *adj. phr.* Making a special effort. *At pains to make a good impression, she was prompt for her appointment.* (She made a special effort to make a good impression by being punctual.)

at sea *adj. phr.* Not knowing what to do; bewildered; confused; lost. *The job was new to him, and for a few days he was at sea.* (The job was strange at first, and it took him a few days before he knew how to do it.) *When his friends talked about chemistry, Don was at sea, because he did not study chemistry.* (Don did not understand what his friends were talking about.)

at sixes and sevens *adj. phr.* Not in order; in confusion; in a mess. *He apologized because the house was at sixes and sevens.* (He apologized that the house was in a mess.) *Our teacher had just moved to a new classroom, and she was still at sixes and sevens.* (She was still not organized; she did not know on which shelves her things were.) *After the captain of the team broke his leg, the other players were at sixes and sevens.* (They were troubled and did not know what to do without a leader.)

at —— stage of the game *adv. phr.* At (some) time during an activity; at (some) point. *At that stage of the game, our team was doing so poorly that we were ready to give up.* (At that time during the game, we were ready to give up.) *It's hard to know what will happen at this stage of the game.* (It's hard to guess what will happen at this point.) *At what stage of the game did the man leave?* (What was happening when the man left?)

at stake *adj. phr.* Depending, like a bet, on the outcome of something uncertain; in a position to be lost or gained. *The team played hard because the championship of the state was at stake.* (The team could win or lose the state championship. It depended on the outcome of the game.) *The farmers were more anxious for rain than the people in the city because they had more at stake.* (The farmers would lose more than the city people if there were no rain.)

at swords' points *adv. or adj. phr.* Ready to start fighting; very much opposed to each other; hostile; quarreling. *The dog's barking kept the Browns at swords'*

points with their neighbors for months. (The Browns had been quarreling with the neighbors for months because of the dog.) *The mayor and the reporter were always at swords' points.* (The mayor and the reporter were always opposed and ready for a quarrel.)

at the drop of a hat *adv. phr., informal* **1** Without waiting; immediately; promptly. *If you need a babysitter quickly, call Mary, because she can come at the drop of a hat.* (She needs almost no time to get ready.) **2** Whenever one has a chance; with very little cause or urging. *At the drop of a hat, he would tell the story of the canal he wanted to build.* (At any time, he would tell the story of the canal he wanted to build.) *He was quarrelsome and ready to fight at the drop of a hat.* (He was quarrelsome and always ready for a fight.)

at the tip of one's tongue *or* **on the tip of one's tongue** *adv. phr., informal* **1** Almost spoken; at the point of being said. *It was at the tip of my tongue to tell him, when the phone rang.* (I was just starting to tell him, when the telephone interrupted me.) *John had a rude answer on the tip of his tongue, but he remembered his manners just in time.* (John almost gave a rude answer.) **2** Almost remembered, at the point where one can almost say it but cannot because it is forgotten. *I have his name on the tip of my tongue.* (I can almost remember his name.)

at the top of one's voice *or* **at the top of one's lungs** *adv. phr.* As loud as one can; with the greatest possible sound; very loudly. *He was singing at the top of his voice.* (He was singing as loudly as he could.) *He shouted at the top of his lungs*. (He shouted with all his strength.)

at this rate *or* **at that rate** *adv. phr.* At a speed like this or that; with progress like this or that. *John's father said that if John kept going at that rate he would never finish cutting the grass*. (If John cut the grass so slowly, it would take him a very long time to finish.) *So Johnny has a whole dollar! At this rate he'll be a millionaire*. (He will soon be a millionaire.) *"Three 100's in the last four tests! At this rate you'll soon be teaching the subject,"* *Tom said to Mary*. (He said that Mary was learning so much that soon she would know as much about the subject as the teacher knew.)

at times *adv. phr.* Not often; not regularly; not every day; not every week; occasionally; sometimes. *At times Tom's mother lets him hold the baby*. (Sometimes Tom's mother lets him hold the baby.) *You can certainly be exasperating at times!* (Sometimes you are very annoying.) *We have pie for dinner at times*. (We have pie for dinner occasionally, but not every day.)

ax to grind *n. phr., informal* Something to gain for oneself, a selfish reason. *In praising movies for classroom use, he has an ax to grind; he sells motion-picture equipment*. (In urging movies for school use, he wanted his own profit, since his business is motion-picture equipment.) *When Charles told the teacher that he saw Arthur copying his homework from Jim, he had an ax to grind; Arthur would not let Charles copy from him*. (Charles told the teacher about Arthur's cheating because Arthur made him angry; Charles had a selfish reason for doing it.)

B

babe in the woods *n. phr.* A person who is inexperienced or innocent in certain things. *He is a good driver, but as a mechanic he is just a babe in the woods.* (He can drive, but he knows so little about the car that he can't fix it if anything goes wrong.)

back and forth *adv.* Backwards and forwards. *The chair is rocking back and forth.* (The chair rocks backward and then forward. *The tiger is pacing back and forth in his cage.* (The tiger keeps walking from one end of his cage to the other and back again.)

back down *or* **back off** *v., informal* To give up a claim; not follow up a threat. *Bill said he could beat Ted, but when Ted put up his fists, Bill backed down.* (Bill decided not to fight.) *Harry claimed Joe had taken his book, but backed down when the teacher talked with him.* (Harry gave up and confessed that Joe had not taken his book.)

back out *v., informal* To fail to keep a promise; get out of an agreement. *She backed out of her engagement.* (She had promised to marry him, but broke her promise.) *He agreed to help him with a loan, but backed out.* (He agreed to lend him money, but changed his mind.)

backseat driver *n., informal* A bossy person in a car who always tells the driver what to do. *The man who drove the car became angry with the backseat driver.* (The driver became angry with the bossy passenger.)

back to the salt mines *informal* Back to the job; back to work; back to work that is as hard or as unpleasant as working in a salt

mine would be.—An overworked phrase, used humorously. *The lunch hour is over, boys. Back to the salt mines!* (The lunch hour is over. Let's get back to work!) *"Vacation is over," said Billy. "Back to the salt mines."* (After being on vacation, going back to school will be hard work.)

back to the wall *or* **back against the wall** *adv. phr.* In a trap; with no way to escape; in bad trouble. *The soldiers had their backs to the wall.* (The soldiers were trapped and had to fight or give up.) *He was in debt and could not get any help; his back was against the wall.* (He owed money and could not get help; he was in bad trouble.) *The team had their backs to the wall in the second half.* (The team was in trouble and might be beaten.)

back up *v.* 1 To move backwards. *The train was backing up.* (It was moving back.) 2 To help or be ready to help; stay behind to help; agree with and speak in support of. *Jim has joined the Boy Scouts and his father is backing him up.* (His father is helping him to be a good Scout.) *In football the linebacker backs up the linemen.* (The linebacker is behind, ready to help the linemen.) *The principal backs up the faculty.* (He supports and agrees with the teachers.) *Jim told us what had happened and Bob backed him up.* (Bob agreed that Jim's account was correct.) 3 To move behind (another fielder) in order to catch the ball if he misses it. *The shortstop backed up the second baseman on the throw.* (The shortstop ran behind the second baseman so he could catch the throw if the second baseman missed it.)

back-up *n., attrib.* (stress on back) Additional, extra. *The City sent a back-up team of firemen to free the children from the burning building.* (The City sent extra fire fighters.)

bad blood *n., informal* Anger or misgivings due to bad past relations. *(There's bad blood between the Smiths and the Jones; they'll never talk to each other.* (They can't overcome their past differences.)

bad egg *n., slang* A person who is a ne'er-do-well; good-for-nothing; a black sheep; a bum. *The judge sent the bad egg to prison at last.* (He broke the law often and the judge sent him to prison.)

bad-mouth (someone) *v. slang* To say uncomplimentary or libelous things about someone; deliberately to damage another's reputation. *It's not nice to bad-mouth people.* (It isn't nice to make disparaging remarks about others.)

bad news *n., slang* An event, thing, or person which is disagreeable or an unpleasant surprise. *What's the new professor like?—He's all bad news to me.* (I don't like him at all.)

bad paper *n., slang* **1** A check for which there are no funds in the bank. **2** Counterfeit paper money. *Why are you so mad?—I was paid with some bad paper.* (I was given a check that bounced, or a counterfeit banknote.)

bad shit *n. slang, vulgar, avoidable* An unpleasant event or situation, such as a long-lasting quarrel or a grudge preventing two people from approaching each other calmly. *There is just too much bad shit between Pete and Jack; they'll never be friends again.* (There is so much hard feeling between them that they will never cooperate normally.)

bad trip *n., slang, drug culture; also used informally* A disturbing or frightening experience, such as terrifying hallucinations, while under the influence of drugs; hence, by extension any bad experience in general. *Why's John's face so distorted?—He had a bad trip.* (He had a frightening hallucinogenic experience.) *How was your math exam?—Don't mention it; it was a bad trip.* (I had a terrible time while I took it; I think I flunked.)

bag and baggage *adv., informal* With all one's clothes and other personal belongings, especially movable possessions; completely. *If they don't pay their hotel bill, they will be put out bag and baggage.* (They will be put out with everything they own.)

baker's dozen *num., informal* '13' or 'roughly a dozen.' *How many do you want, Ma'am?—Oh, make it a baker's dozen.* (Make it twelve or as near to it, if slightly over, as you can.)

ball game *n., slang, also informal* The entire matter at hand; the whole situation; the entire contest. *You said we can get a second mortgage for the house? Wow! That's a whole new ball game.* (Getting the loan changes the situation entirely in our favor.)

ball of fire *n., informal* A person with great energy and ability; a person who can do something very well. *He did poorly in school but as a salesman he is a ball of fire.* (He is a very successful salesman.) *The new shortstop is a good fielder but certainly no ball of fire in batting.* (He is not a very good batter.)

banana oil *n., slang* Exaggerated flattery; statements that are obviously made with an ulterior motive; bluff; baloney (*slang*). *Cut out the banana oil; flattery will get you nowhere!* (Stop the exaggerated flattery; it has no effect on me.)

bang-up *adj., informal* Very successful; very good; splendid; excellent. *The football coach has done a bang-up job this season.* (The coach led the team through a fine season of games.) *John did a bang-up job painting the house.* (John did a very good painting job.)

bank on *v., informal* To depend on; put one's trust in; rely on. *He knew he could bank on public indignation to change things, if he could once prove the dirty work.* (He knew he could rely on public anger to clean up the mess, if he could get them started by showing the dishonesty.) *The students were banking on the team to do its best in the championship game.* (The students expected the team to do its best.)

barge in *vb. phr., informal* Uninvitedly to appear or to interrupt. *I'm sorry for barging in just like that, but could you tell me where's the nearest exit?* (Apologizes for interrupting, and wants to go out.)

bark up the wrong tree *v. phr., informal* To choose the wrong person to deal with or the wrong course of action; mistake an aim. *If he thinks he can fool me, he is barking up the wrong tree.* (He cannot fool me; I know him too well.) *He is barking up the wrong tree when he blames his troubles on bad luck.* (His troubles come from his own mistakes, not luck.) *The police were looking for a tall thin man, but were barking up the wrong tree; the thief was short and fat.* (The police were hunting the wrong man.)

bark worse than one's bite *informal* Sound or speech more frightening or worse than one's actions. *The small dog barks savagely, but his bark is worse than his bite.* (The small dog sounds mean, but he really is not.) *The boss sometimes talks roughly to the men, but they know that his bark is worse than his bite.* (The boss sounds very angry, but does not threaten or fire the men.) *She was always scolding her children, but they knew her bark was worse than her bite.* (She scolded them but did not punish them very much.)

basket case *n., slang, also informal* **1** A person who has had more than one limb cut off as a result of war or other misfortune. **2** A helpless person who is unable to take care of himself, as if carried around in a basket by others. *Stop drinking, or else you'll wind up a basket case!* (If you don't stop drinking you will become entirely helpless.)

bat an eye *or* **bat an eyelash** *v. phr., informal* To show surprise, fear, or interest; show one's feelings.—Used in negative sentences. *When I told him the price of the car he never batted an eye.* (He was not surprised or upset at the price.) *Bill told his story without batting an eyelash, although not a word of it was true.* (He told his story that he knew was not true, but he was calm and did not show any embarrassment.)

bats in one's belfry *or* **bats in the belfry** *n. phr., slang* Wild ideas in one's mind; disordered senses; great mental confusion. *When he talked about going to the moon he was thought to have bats in his belfry.* (His friends thought he had wild ideas and talked foolishly.)

bawl out v., informal To reprove in a loud or rough voice; rebuke sharply; scold. *The teacher bawled us out for not handing in our homework.* (The teacher gave us a loud scolding.)

bear in the air or **bear in the sky** n. phr., slang, citizen's band radio jargon A police helicopter flying overhead watching for speeders. *Slow down, good buddy; there's a bear in the air.* (You are being observed by a police helicopter.)

bear out v. To show to be right; prove; support. *Modern findings do not bear out the old belief that the earth is flat.* (New facts do not support the old belief that the earth is flat.) *Fulton's faith in his steamboat was borne out.* (Fulton's faith in his invention was shown to be correct.)

bear trap n., slang, citizen's band radio jargon A police radar unit designed to catch speeders. *Watch the bear trap at exit 101.* (At exit 101 there is police radar speed control, so slow down.)

bear up v. **1** To hold up; carry; support; encourage. *The old bridge can hardly bear up its own weight any more.* (The old bridge is hardly strong enough to hold itself up any more.) *He was borne up by love of country.* (Love of country supported his spirits when things looked bad.) **2** To keep up one's courage or strength; last.—Often used with under. *This boat will bear up under hurricane winds.* (This boat will stay afloat even in a storm.) *She bore up well at the funeral.* (She was brave and calm at the funeral.)

bear with v., formal To have patience with; not get angry with. *Your little sister is sick. Try to bear with her when she cries.* (Try to have patience with her when she cries.) *It is hard to bear with criticism.* (It is hard to be patient when others criticize you.)

beat about the bush or **beat around the bush** v. phr., slang To talk about things without giving a clear answer; avoid the question or the point. *He would not answer yes or no, but beat about the bush.* (He talked about other things but did not really answer.) *He beat about the bush for a half hour without coming to the point.* (He talked around the question, missing the point.)

beat into one's head v. phr., informal To teach by telling again and again; repeat often; drill; also, to be cross and punish often. *Tom is lazy and stubborn and his lessons have to be beaten into his head.* (His teacher has to be cross and tell him often.) *I cannot beat it into his head that he should take off his hat in the house.* (I have told him often and punished him, but he still wears his hat in the house.)

beat it v., slang To go away in a hurry; get out quickly. *When he heard the crash he beat it as fast as he could.* (He ran away as fast as he could.)—Often used as a command. *The big boy said, "Beat it, kid. We don't want you with us."* (The big boy told the little boy to go away.)

beat one's brains out or **beat one's brains** v. phr., slang To try very hard to understand or think out something difficult; tire oneself out by thinking. *It was too hard for him and he beat his brains out trying to get the answer.* (He tried very hard to understand.) *Some students are lazy, but others* *beat their brains and succeed.* (Some try much harder than others.)

beat one's head against a wall *v. phr.* To struggle uselessly against something that can't be beaten or helped; not succeed after trying very hard. *Trying to make him change his mind is just beating your head against a wall.* (He is so stubborn that it is hopeless to try to persuade him.)

beat the band *adv. phr., informal* At great speed; with much noise or commotion.—A cliché;—Used after *to. The fire engines were going down the road to beat the band.* (They were going full speed.) *They cheered to beat the band.* (They clapped as loudly as they could.)

beat the bushes *also* **beat the brush** *v. phr.* To try very hard to find or get something. *The mayor was beating the bushes for funds to build a new playground.* (The mayor went to every possible source asking for money.)

beat to *v., informal* To do something before someone else does it. *I was waiting to buy a ticket but only one ticket was left, and another man beat me to it.* (He bought the ticket just before I had a chance to buy it.) *We were planning to send a rocket into space but the Russians beat us to it.* (They sent out a space rocket before we were ready.)

beat to the punch *or* **beat to the draw** *v. phr., slang* To do something before another person has a chance to do it. *John was going to apply for the job, but Ted beat him to the draw.* (Ted applied and got the job before John applied.) *Lois bought the dress before Mary could beat her to the punch.* (Lois bought the dress before Mary could buy it.)

beat up *v., informal* To give a hard beating to; thrash; whip. *When the new boy first came, he had to beat up several neighborhood bullies before they would leave him alone.* (When he first came, he had to fight and beat several tough boys in the neighborhood to gain their respect.)—Used with *on* in substandard speech. *The tough boy said to Bill, "If you come around here again, I'll beat up on you."* (The boy warned Bill not to come there again or he would beat him.)

beauty sleep *n.* A nap or rest taken to improve the appearance. *She took her beauty sleep before the party.* (She took a nap before the party, so that she would look fresh and not tired.) *Many famous beauties take a beauty sleep every day.* (Many famous beauties take a nap every day.)

bed of roses *n. phr.* A pleasant easy place, job, or position; an easy life. *A coal miner's job is not a bed of roses.* (A coal miner's work is very hard and unpleasant.) *After nine months of school, summer camp seemed a bed of roses.* (School was a time of hard study, but summer camp was easy.)

beef up *v., informal* To make stronger by adding personnel or equipment; make more powerful; reinforce. *The general beefed up his army with more big guns and tanks.* (He got more guns and tanks to strengthen his army.) *The university beefed up the football coaching staff by adding several good men.* (The university made their coaching staff better by getting several new men.)

bee in one's bonnet *n. phr., informal* A fixed idea that seems fanciful, odd, or crazy. *Robert Fulton had a bee in his bonnet* *about a steamboat.* (He was stubborn in his idea and people thought it was foolish.) *Grandmother has some bee in her bonnet about going to the dance.* (She has a foolish idea about going to the dance, but she is too ill.)

before one can say Jack Robinson *adv. cl., informal* Very quickly; suddenly.—An overused phrase. *Before I could say Jack Robinson, the boy was gone.* (The boy ran away suddenly.)

beg off *v.* To ask to be excused. *Father told Tom to rake the yard, but Tom tried to beg off.* (Tom tried to get his father to excuse him.) *Mrs. Crane accepted an invitation to a luncheon, but a headache made her beg off.* (She asked to be excused from the luncheon.)

beg the question *v. phr., literary* To accept as true something that is still being argued about, before it is proved true; avoid or not answer a question or problem. *The girls asked Miss Smith if they should wear formal dresses to the party; Miss Smith said they were begging the question because they didn't know yet if they could get permission for a party.* (The girls were trying to plan for a party before the question of permission for a party was decided.) *Laura told Tom that he must believe her argument because she was right; Father laughed and told Laura she was begging the question.* (Father told Laura she thought she had won the argument; but really she had not yet proved she was right.)

behind bars *adv. phr.* In jail; in prison. *He was a pickpocket and had spent many years behind bars.* (He had spent many years in prison.) *That boy is always in trouble and will end up behind bars.* (He may get in bad trouble and be put in jail.)

behind one's back *adv. phr.* When one is absent; without one's knowledge or consent; in a dishonest way; secretly; sneakily. *Say it to his face, not behind his back.* (Say it openly. Do not say one thing when he is here, and another when he is gone.) *It is not right to criticize a person behind his back.* (It is better to tell him what he does wrong.)

behind the eight ball *adj. phr., slang* In a difficult position; in trouble. *Mr. Thompson is an older man, and when he lost his job, he found he was behind the eight ball.* (He found it hard to get another job at his age.) *Not having a car puts Bill behind the eight ball; he cannot get to work.* (There is no public transportation.)

behind the scenes *adv. phr.* Out of sight; unknown to most people; privately. *Much of the banquet committee's work was done behind the scenes.* (Most people did not know what the committee did.) *John was president of the club, but behind the scenes Lee told him what to do.* (People thought John made the decisions, but really Lee did.)

behind the times *adj. phr.* Not in style; still following old ways; old-fashioned. *Johnson's store is behind the times.* (The store is old-fashioned; it looks like stores of 40 years ago.) *The science books of 30 years ago are behind the times now.* (The old science books do not explain new discoveries.) *Mary thinks her parents are behind the times because they don't think a woman should be nominated for President.* (They have old-fashioned ideas about the role of a woman.)

be-in *n., slang; gradually taken over by informal usage* A gathering, often held at some public place in the open, like a park. *We really enjoyed the be-in at the park.* (We had a good time at the open gathering in the park.)

be into something *v. phr., informal* To have taken something up partly as a hobby, partly as a serious interest (basically resulting from the self-realization movement of the late sixties). *Roger's wife is into women's liberation.* (Roger's wife has taken up the cause of women's liberation.) *Did you know that Syd is seriously into transcendental meditation?* (Did you know that Syd practices transcendental meditation seriously?) *Jack found out that his teenage son is into pot smoking and gave him a serious scolding.* (Jack learned that his son has started to smoke marijuana and took corrective measures.)

believe one's ears *v. phr.* **1** To believe what one hears; trust one's hearing.—Used with a negative or limiter, or in an interrogative or conditional sentence. *He thought he heard a horn blowing in the distance, but he could not believe his ears.* (He thought his ears were fooling him.) **2** To become sure of (something). *Is he really coming? I can hardly believe my ears.* (Are you sure he is coming? It is surprising!)

believe one's eyes *v. phr.* **1** To believe what one sees; trust one's eyesight.—Used with a negative or limiter or in an interrogative or conditional sentence. *Is that a plane? Can I believe my eyes?* (Are my eyes deceiving me? Is it really a plane?) **2** To become sure of seeing something. *She saw him there but she could hardly believe*

her eyes. (She saw him, but she could hardly believe that it was true.)

below the belt *adv. phr.* **1** In the stomach; lower than is fair in boxing. *He struck the other boy below the belt.* (He struck the other boy a foul blow.) **2** *informal* In an unfair or cowardly way; against the rules of sportsmanship or justice; unsportingly; wrongly. *It was hitting below the belt for Mr. Jones's rival to tell people about a crime that Mr. Jones committed when he was a young boy.* (It was unfair for the man to tell about something past that makes no difference now.) *Pete told the students to vote against Harry because Harry was crippled and couldn't be a good class president, but the students thought Pete was hitting below the belt.* (They thought Pete was breaking the rules of sportsmanship.)

be my guest *v. phr.* Feel free to use what I have; help yourself. *When Laura asked if she could borrow John's bicycle, John said: "Be my guest."* (Feel free to use it.)

bend over backward *or* **lean over backward** *v. phr., informal* To try so hard to avoid a mistake that one risks making the opposite mistake instead; do too much to avoid doing the wrong thing; *also,* make a great effort; try very hard. *Instead of punishing the boys for breaking a new rule, the principal bent over backward to explain why the rule was important.* (The principal probably wanted to punish the boys for breaking the new rule, but instead he explained pleasantly why the new rule would really help the boys.) *Mary was afraid the girls at her new school would be stuck-up, but they leaned over backward to make her feel at* home. (The girls at the new school tried to make Mary happy instead of leaving her alone.)

bent on or **bent upon** Very decided, determined, or set. *The sailors were bent on having a good time.* (They had only one purpose, to have a good time.) *The policeman saw some boys near the school after dark and thought they were bent on mischief.* (The policeman thought the boys planned to do something bad.) *The bus was late, and the driver was bent on reaching the school on time.* (The driver was determined to go fast and get to the school before classes started.)

beside oneself *adj. phr.* Very much excited; somewhat crazy. *She was beside herself with fear.* (She was so afraid that she did not know what to do.) *He was beside himself; he was so angry.* (He was terribly angry.) *When his wife heard of his death, she was beside herself.* (The news of her husband's death shocked and almost crazed her.)

beside the point or **beside the question** *adj. or adv. phr.* Off the subject; about something different. *What you meant to do is beside the point; the fact is you didn't do it.* (What you meant to do doesn't matter now.) *The judge told the witness that his remarks were beside the point.* (His remarks had nothing to do with the case.)

bet one's boots or **bet one's bottom dollar** or **bet one's shirt** *v. phr., informal* **1** To bet all one has. *This horse will win. I would bet my bottom dollar on it.* (I am so sure he will win, I would bet my last dollar on it.) **2** or **bet one's life** To feel very sure; have no doubt. *Jim said he would bet*

his boots that he would pass the examination. (Jim was very sure he would pass.) *Was I scared when I saw the bull running at me? You bet your life I was!* (You can be sure that I was scared.)

bet on the wrong horse *v. phr., informal* To base one's plans on a wrong guess about the result of something; misread the future; misjudge a coming event. *To count on the small family farm as an important economic factor in the American future now looks like betting on the wrong horse.* (To depend heavily on the future of the U.S. small family farm now looks like misreading the future.) *He expected Carter to be elected President in 1980 but as it happened, he bet on the wrong horse.* (He thought Carter would be elected in 1980, but that was a bad guess.)

better half *n., informal* One's marriage partner (mostly said by men about their wives). *"This is my better half, Mary,"* said Joe. (He is introducing his wife.)

between the devil and the deep blue sea or literary **between two fires** or literary **between Scylla and Charybdis** *adv. phr.* Between two dangers or difficulties, not knowing what to do. *The pirates had to fight and be killed or give up and be hanged; they were between the devil and the deep blue sea.* (Either way, they faced danger.) *The boy was between the devil and the deep blue sea; he had to go home and be whipped or stay in town all night and be picked up by the police.* (He didn't know which to choose, a whipping or arrest.) *When the man's wife and her mother got together, he was between two fires.* (He was scolded by both.)

be up to something *v. phr. informal* **1** To feel strong or knowledgeable enough to accomplish a certain goal. *Are you up to speaking Russian and French besides English at the reception?* (Can you do it?) **2** Intend to do something mischievous. *I am afraid John is up to no good.* (He is about to pull some trick or mischief.)

beyond the pale *adv. or adj. phr.* In disgrace; with no chance of being accepted or respected by others; not approved by the members of a group. *Tom's swearing is beyond the pale; no one invites him to dinner any more.* (Polite people don't invite Tom because his language is offensive.)

bide one's time *v. phr.* To await an opportunity; wait patiently until one's chance comes. *Refused work as an actor, Tom turned to other work and bided his time.* (When Tom couldn't get work as an actor, he supported himself in other ways, and waited for his chance.) *Jack was hurt deeply, and he bided his time for revenge.* (Jack was hurt deeply, and he waited for an opportunity to get even.)

big as life *or* **large as life** *adj. phr.* **1** *or* **life-size** The same size as the living person or thing. *The statue of Jefferson was big as life.* (It was the same size as Jefferson himself was.) *The characters on the screen were life-size.* (The screen was so big that the actors were full size.) **2** *or* **big as life and twice as natural** *informal* In person; real and living. *I had not seen him for years, but there he was, big as life and twice as natural.* (He looked the same as ever.)

big cheese *or* **big gun** *or* **big shot** *or* **big wheel** *or* **big wig** *n., slang* An important person; a leader; a high official; a person of high rank. *Bill had been a big shot in high school.* (Bill had been a leader in student affairs.) *John wanted to be the big cheese in his club.* (John wanted to be the most important member of his club.)

big daddy *n., slang, informal* The largest or most important thing, animal, or person in a congregation of similar objects or persons. *The whale is the big daddy of everything that swims in the ocean.* (The whale is the biggest water creature on earth.) *The H-bomb is the big daddy of all modern weapons.* (It is the deadliest of all modern weapons.) *Joe is the big daddy of our tennis club.* (He is the leader of the group.)

big deal *interj., slang; informal* (sarcastic stress on the word *deal*) Trifles; an unimportant, unimpressive thing or matter. *So you became college president—big deal!* (I am not impressed with the fact that you became a college president.)

big frog in a small pond *n. phr., informal* An important person in a small place; someone who is honored in a small company, school, or city; a leader in a small group. *As company president, he had been a big frog in a small pond, but he was not so important as a new congressman in Washington.* (As company president in a small company he was respected and honored, but in Washington the other congressmen did not know or honor him.)

big head *n., informal* Too high an opinion of one's own ability or importance; conceit. *When Jack was elected captain of the team, it gave him a big head.* (He became conceited. He was full of his own importance.)

big lie, the *n.*, A major, deliberate misrepresentation of some important issue, on the assumption that a bold gross lie is more believable than a timid minor one. *The pretense of democracy by a totalitarian regime is part of the big lie about its government.* (The ''people's government'' gives the people no political choices.)

big stink *n.*, *slang* A major scandal; a big upheaval. *I'll raise a big stink if they fire me.* (If they fire me, I will cause a major scandal or commotion by complaining to the right people.)

big time *n.*, *informal* **1** A very enjoyable time. *I certainly had a big time at the club last night.* (I certainly enjoyed myself at the club.) **2** The top group; the leading class; the best or most important company. *After his graduation from college, he soon made the big time in baseball.* (He was a fine player and soon was in the big leagues.) *Many young actors go to Hollywood, but few of them reach the big time.* (It is hard to become a movie star.)

big-time *adj.* Belonging to the top group; of the leading class; important. *Jean won a talent contest in her home town, and only a year later she began dancing on big-time television.* (Jean danced in programs on the big television networks.) *Bob practices boxing in the gym every day; he wants to become a big-time boxer.* (Bob wants to become a famous fighter in boxing.)—Often used in the phrase *big-time* operator. *Just because Bill has a new football uniform he thinks he is a big-time operator.* (Bill exaggerates his importance.)

big wheel *n.*, *informal* An influential or important person who has power and connections in high places. *Uncle Ferdinand is a big wheel in Washington; maybe he can help you with your problem.* (He works for the government and has good connections.)

bird has flown *slang* The prisoner has escaped; the captive has got away. *When the sheriff returned to the jail, he discovered that the bird had flown.* (When the sheriff returned to the jail, he found that his prisoner had escaped.)

bird in the hand is worth two in the bush Something one has, or can easily get, is more valuable than something one wants and may not be able to get; one shouldn't risk losing something sure by trying to get something that is not sure. *Johnny has a job as a paperboy, but he wants a job in a gas station. His father says that a bird in the hand is worth two in the bush.* (Keep the job you have until you are sure of a better one.)

birds and the bees *n. phr.*, *informal* The facts about sex and birth. *At various ages and in response to questions, a child can be told about the birds and the bees.* (Each child can be told the facts of sex and birth to fit the individual's stage of maturity.)

birds of a feather flock together People who are alike often become friends or are together; if one is often with certain people, one may be their friend or like them. *Don't be friends with bad boys. People think that birds of a feather flock together.* (If you are friends with bad boys and people see you with them often, they will think that you are bad, too.)

birthday suit *n.* The skin with no clothes on; complete nakedness. *The little boys were swimming in their birthday suits.* (They were swimming without any clothes on.)

bite off more than one can chew *v. phr., informal* To try to do more than one can; to be too confident of one's ability. *He bit off more than he could chew when he agreed to edit the paper alone.* (He took on a job that was too hard for him when he agreed to edit the paper without help.) *He started to repair his car himself, but realized that he had bitten off more than he could chew.* (He started to repair his car himself, but soon realized that he didn't know enough to do it.)

bite the dust *v. phr., informal* **1** To be killed in battle. *Captain Jones discharged his gun, and another guerilla bit the dust.* (Captain Jones fired his gun, and another guerilla dropped dead.) **2** To fall in defeat; go down before enemies; be overthrown; lose. *Our team bit the dust today.* (Our team lost.)

bite the hand that feeds one *v. phr.* To turn against or hurt a helper or supporter; repay kindness with wrong. *He bit the hand that fed him when he complained against his employer.* (He was injuring the man he was dependent on.)

bitter pill *n.* Something hard to accept; disappointment. *Jack was not invited to the party and it was a bitter pill for him.* (He felt bad about not being invited.)

black and white *n. phr.* **1** Print or writing; words on paper, not spoken; exact written or printed form. *He insisted on having the agreement down in black and white.* (He wanted the agreement written, not just spoken.) *Mrs. Jones would not believe the news, so Mr. Jones showed her the article in the newspaper and said,* *"There it is in black and white."* (He showed her that the news was printed in the paper.) **2** The different shades of black and white of a photograph. *He showed us snapshots in black and white.* (He showed us pictures that were black, grey, and white, not colored.)

black-and-white *adj.* Divided into only two sides that are either right or wrong or good or bad, with nothing in between; thinking or judging everything as either good or bad. *Everything is black-and-white to Bill; if you're not his friend, you are his enemy.* (You can't be anything in between or different from his friend or enemy.) *The old man's religion shows his black-and-white thinking; everything is either completely good or completely bad.* (The old man judges everything as very good or very bad.)

black out *v.* **1** To darken by putting out or dimming lights. *In some plays the stage is blacked out for a short time and the actors speak in darkness.* (In some plays the lights are turned off for a while.) *In wartime, cities are blacked out to protect against bombing from planes.* (The lights are turned off so bombers cannot find them.) **2** To prevent or silence information or communication; refuse to give out truthful news. *Dictators usually black out all criticism of the government.* (Dictators do not let the people know the facts.) **3** *informal* To lose consciousness; faint. *It had been a hard and tiring day, and she suddenly blacked out.* (She had had a bad day, and suddenly she fainted.)

blast off *v.* **1** To begin a rocket flight. *The astronaut will blast off into orbit at six o'clock.* (He will begin a rocket flight.) **2** *Also* **blast away** *informal* To scold or protest violently. *The coach blasted off at the team for poor playing.* (He gave the team a violent scolding.)

blaze a trail *v. phr.* **1** To cut marks in trees in order to guide other people along a path or trail, especially through a wilderness. *Daniel Boone blazed a trail for other hunters to follow in Kentucky.* (He made marks with an axe and left a path through the woods so others could follow it and not get lost.) **2** To lead the way; make a discovery; start something new. *Henry Ford blazed a trail in manufacturing automobiles.* (Henry Ford led the way in building automobiles.) *The building of rockets blazed a trail to outer space.* (Rockets have started something new in space travel.)

blind alley *n.* **1** A narrow street that has only one entrance and no exit. *The blind alley ended in a brick wall.* (The alley stopped at a brick wall.) **2** A way of acting that is unproductive or mistaken. *John did not take the job because it was a blind alley.* (The job would not lead to a better job.) *Tom thought of a way to do the algebra problem, but he found it was a blind alley.* (Tom's figures did not give the right answer.)

blind leading the blind One or more people who do not know or understand something trying to explain it to others who do not know or understand. *Jimmy is trying to show Bill how to skate. The blind are leading the blind.* (Jimmy does not know how to skate himself, but he is trying to teach Bill.)

blood is thicker than water Persons of the same family are closer to one another than to others; relatives are favored or chosen over outsiders. *Mr. Jones hires his relatives to work in his store. Blood is thicker than water.* (Mr. Jones trusts his relatives and likes to have them working for him.)

blood runs cold *also* **blood freezes** *or* **blood turns to ice** One is chilled or shivering from great fright or horror; one is terrified or horrified. Usually used with a possessive. *The horror movie made the children's blood run cold.* (The movie frightened the children badly.) *Mary's blood froze when she had to walk through the cemetery at night.* (Mary was very scared.) *Oscar's blood turned to ice when he saw the shadow pass by outside the window.* (Oscar was very surprised and frightened.)

blow a fuse *or* **blow a gasket** *or* **blow one's top** *or* **blow one's stack** *v. phr., slang* To become extremely angry; express rage in hot words. *Mr. McCarthy blew a fuse when his son got married against his wishes.* (Mr. McCarthy got very angry when his son married against his wishes.) *When the umpire called Joe out at first, Joe blew his top and was sent to the showers.* (Joe used hot words toward the umpire, who put him out of the game.)

blow in *v., slang* To arrive unexpectedly or in a carefree way. *The house was already full of guests when Bill blew in.* (Bill arrived unexpectedly.)

blow into *v. slang* To arrive at (a place) unexpectedly or in a carefree way. *Bill blows into college at the last minute after every vacation.* (Bill arrives late in a carefree way.) *Why Tom, when* *did you blow into town?* (Why Tom, when did you arrive in town?)

blow one's brains out *v. phr.*
1 To shoot oneself in the head. *Mr. Jones lost all his wealth, so he blew his brains out.* (Mr. Jones killed himself by shooting himself in the head.) **2** *slang* To work very hard; overwork oneself. *The students blew their brains out to get the stage ready for the play.* (They worked very hard to get the stage ready.) *Mary is not one to blow her brains out.* (Mary does not work very hard.)

blow one's cool *v. phr., informal* To lose one's composure or self-restraint. *Faced with the proof of his guilt, the defendant finally blew his cool.* (He could no longer act relaxed and unmoved by the situation.)

blow one's mind *v. phr., slang, informal; originally from the drug culture* **1** To become wildly enthusiastic over something as if understanding it for the first time in an entirely new light. *Read Lyall Watson's book* Supernature; *it will simply blow your mind!* (It will make you see things suddenly in an entirely new light.) **2** To lose one's ability to function; as if due to an overdose of drugs. *Joe is entirely incoherent—he seems to have blown his mind.* (He seems to have overdosed on drugs; he cannot talk coherently.)

blow one's own horn *or* **toot one's own horn** *v. phr., slang* To praise oneself; call attention to one's own skill, intelligence, or successes; boast. *People get tired of a person who is always blowing his own horn.* (They don't like to hear him boasting.) *A person who does things well does not have to toot his own horn; his*

abilities will be noticed by others. (People will notice his successes and praise him to others.)

blow over *v.* To come to an end; pass away with little or no bad effect. *The sky was black, as if a bad storm were coming, but it blew over and the sun came out.* (We expected a storm, but the wind blew the clouds away and there was no storm.) *They were bitter enemies for a while, but the quarrel blew over.* (They were bitter enemies, but later became friends again.) *He was much criticized for the divorce, but it all blew over after a few years.* (People blamed him, but later forgot about it.)

blow the lid off *v. phr., informal* Suddenly to reveal the truth about a matter that has been kept a secret either by private persons or by some government agency. *The journalists blew the lid off the Watergate cover-up.* (They found and revealed the fact that there has been a government cover-up about the Watergate robbery.)

blow the whistle on *v. phr., slang* **1** To inform against; betray. *The police caught one of the bank robbers, and he blew the whistle on two more.* (They caught one man, and he named two others.) **2** To act against, stop, or tell people the secrets of (crime or lawlessness). *The mayor blew the whistle on gambling.* (The mayor started arresting gamblers.) *The police blew the whistle on hot-rodding.* (The police became strict about reckless driving by youngsters.)

blow up *v.* **1a** To break or destroy or to be destroyed by explosion. *He blew up the plane by means of a concealed bomb.* (He destroyed the airplane with a hidden bomb.) *The fireworks factory blew up when something went wrong in an electric switch.* (The factory exploded when an electric switch failed.) **1b** *informal* To explode with anger or strong feeling; lose control of oneself. *When Dad bent the nail for the third time, he blew up.* (He became very angry.) **1c** To stop playing well in a contest, usually because one is in danger of losing or is tired; *especially:* To lose skill or control in pitching baseball. *Our team was behind but the pitcher on the other team blew up and we got the winning runs.* (The pitcher did not pitch as well as he had been pitching.) **2** *informal* To be ruined as if by explosion; be ended suddenly. *The whole scheme for a big party suddenly blew up.* (The plan suddenly collapsed; there was no party.) **3a** To pump full of air; inflate. *He blew his tires up at a filling station.* (He put air in his tires at a filling station.) **3b** To make (something) seem bigger or important. *It was a small thing to happen but the newspapers had blown it up until it seemed important.* (It was not important, but the newspapers had made it seem so.) **4** To bring on bad weather; also, to come on as bad weather. *The wind had blown up a storm.* (The wind had brought a storm.) *A storm had blown up.* (A storm had come.) **5** To copy in bigger form; enlarge. *He blew up the snapshot to a larger size.* (He made a large copy of the snapshot.)

blow-up *n.* (stress on *blow*) A noisy quarrel; an angry fight. *John and Sue had a major blow-up last night.* (They had a big fight.)

boarding house reach *n. phr., informal* Skill at quickly reaching for food that is a long distance away on the table. *John devel-*

oped a boarding house reach while he was away at camp.* (John learned to reach for things at the far end of the table.)

blue in the face *adj. phr., informal* Very angry or upset; excited and very emotional. *Tom argued with Bill until he was blue in the face.* (Tom argued until he was so angry he couldn't talk any more.) *Mary scolded Jane until she was blue in the face, but Jane kept on using Mary's paints.* (Mary talked until she was very much upset.)

bog down *v.* **1** To stop progressing; slow to a stop. *Work on the railroad bogged down because lumber was slow to arrive.* (Building progress stopped.) **2** To engage in unproductive or unsatisfying activities.—Usually used in the passive. *The poet wrote little because she got bogged down in housework.* (She spent her time on housework instead of writing.)

boggle the mind *v. phr., informal* To stop the rational thinking process by being too fantastic or incredible. *It boggles the mind that John should have been inside a flying saucer!* (The story that John has been inside a flying saucer is so fantastic that it is intellectually undigestible.)

boil down *v.* **1** To boil away some of the water from; make less by boiling. *She boiled down the maple sap to a thick syrup.* (She boiled off enough of the water so that the thin sap became a thick syrup.) *The fruit juice boiled down until it was almost not good for jelly.* (The juice boiled away almost too much.) **2** To reduce the length of; cut down; shorten. *The reporter boiled the story down to half the original length.* (He cut the story down to half the first length.) **3** To reduce itself to; come down to; be briefly or basically. *The whole discussion boils down to the question of whether the government should fix prices.* (The question simply is whether the government should fix prices.)

bonehead *n.*, *slang* An unusually dense or stupid person. *John is such a bonehead—small wonder he flunks all of his courses.* (It's no surprise that he fails; he is so dumb.)

bone of contention *n. phr.* Something to fight over; a reason for quarrels; the subject of a fight. *The boundary line between the farms was a bone of contention between the two farmers.* (The line was something the two farmers had always fought over.) *The use of the car was a bone of contention between Joe and his wife.* (They quarreled about using the car.)

bone to pick *n. phr.*, *informal* A reason for dispute; something to complain of or argue about.— Often used jokingly. *"I have a bone to pick with you," he said.* ("I have a quarrel with you," he said.)

bone up *v.*, *informal* Try to learn a lot about something in a short time; study quickly. *Carl was boning up for an examination.* (He was preparing very hard for an examination.) *Jim had to make a class report the next day on juvenile delinquency, and he was in the library boning up on how the courts handle it.* (He was trying to get quickly all the information he could about the handling of juvenile delinquency by the courts.)

bore to tears *v. phr.* To fill with tired dislike; tire by dullness or the same old thing; bore. *The party was dull, and Roger showed plainly that he was bored to tears.*

(Anyone could see that Roger was tired of the party.) *Mary loves cooking, but sewing bores her to tears.* (Mary is not at all interested in sewing.)

born with a silver spoon in one's mouth *adj. phr.* Born to wealth and comfort; provided from birth with everything wanted; born rich. *The stranger's conduct was that of a person who had been born with a silver spoon in his mouth.* (He acted like a person who has always had everything.)

born yesterday *adj. phr.* Inexperienced and easily fooled; not alert to trickery; easily deceived or cheated. Usually used in negative sentences. *When Ruth started the new job, the other workers teased her a little, but she soon proved to everyone that she wasn't born yesterday.* (She showed that she was no fool.) *I won't give you the money till I see the bicycle you want to sell me. Do you think I was born yesterday?* (Do you think you can fool me?)

bottle up *v.* **1** To hide or hold back; control. *There was no understanding person to talk to, so Fred bottled up his unhappy feeling.* (He found no friend, so he hid his unhappiness without telling anyone about it.) **2** To hold in a place from which there is no escape; trap. *Our warships bottled up the enemy fleet in the harbor.* (They trapped the enemy ships in the harbor.)

bottom dollar *n.*, *informal* One's last penny, one's last dollar. *He was down to his bottom dollar when he suddenly got the job offer.* (He had no more money to live on when the new job offer came and rescued him.)

bottom drop out *or* **bottom fall out** *v. phr.*, *informal* **1** To fall below an earlier lowest price. *The* *bottom dropped out of the price of peaches.* (The price of peaches went much lower than it had gone before.) **2** To lose all cheerful qualities; become very unhappy, cheerless, or unpleasant. *The bottom dropped out of the day for John when he saw his report card.* (John became very unhappy when he saw his report card.) *The bottom fell out for us when the game ended with our team on the two-yard line and six points behind.* (Everybody was hoping for a touchdown to tie the score but the game ended too soon, and our hopes were lost.)

bottom line *n., informal* **1** The last word on a controversial issue, a final decision. *"Give me the bottom line on the merger,"* said John. (He wants to know what the final decision is.) **2** The truth with no embellishments. *The bottom line is that Joe is an alcoholic.* (He is an alcoholic, in truth.) **3** The lowest price reached on bargaining. *"$500 is the bottom line,"* said the used car dealer. (He won't sell for less.)

bottom-line *v., informal* to finish; to bring to a conclusion. *Let's bottom-line this part of the project and break for coffee.* (Let us conclude the first part and rest.)

bound for *adj. phr.* On the way to; going to. *I am bound for the country club.* (I am on my way to the country club.) *The ship is bound for Liverpool.* (The ship is going to Liverpool.)

bow out *v., informal* To give up taking part; excuse oneself from doing any more; quit. *Mr. Black often quarreled with his partners, so finally he bowed out of the company.* (Mr. Black was not happy with his partners, so he quit the business.) *While the movie was being filmed, the star got sick and had to bow out.* (Before the movie was finished the star got sick and had to leave the group.) **2** To stop working after a long service; retire. *He bowed out as train engineer after forty years of railroading.* (He retired as engineer after forty years' service.)

box office *n., informal* **1** The place at theaters where a ticket may be purchased just before the performance instead of having ordered it through the telephone or having bought it at a ticket agency. *No need to reserve the seats; we can pick tickets up at the box office.* **2** A best-selling movie, musical, or drama (where the tickets are all always sold out and people line up in front of the box office). *John Wayne's last movie was a regular box office.* (It was an instant sellout.) **3** Anything successful or well liked. *Betsie is no longer box office with me.* (I don't like her any more.)

boyfriend *n., informal* **1** A male friend or companion. *"John and his boyfriends have gone to the ball game,"* said his mother. (John and his friends have gone.) **2** A girl's steady date; a woman's favorite man friend; a male lover or sweetheart. *Jane's new boyfriend is a senior in high school.* (The boy that is Jane's favorite date is a senior.)

boys will be boys Boys are only children and must sometimes get into mischief or trouble or behave too roughly. *Boys will be boys and make a lot of noise, so John's mother told him and his friends to play in the park instead of the back yard.* (John's mother knew that boys playing together would make a lot of noise.)

brain drain *n., informal* **1** The loss of the leading intellectuals and researchers of a country due to excessive emigration to other countries where conditions are better. *Britain suffered a considerable brain drain to the United States after World War II.* (Many outstanding British intellectuals moved to the U.S. after W.W. II.) **2** An activity requiring great mental concentration resulting in fatigue and exhaustion. *That math exam I took was a regular brain drain.* (The math exam exhausted me.)

branch off *v.* To go from something big or important to something smaller or less important; turn aside. *At the bridge a little road branches off from the highway and follows the river.* (A smaller road leaves the highway and goes along the river.) *Martin was trying to study, but his mind kept branching off onto the opening of the fishing season.* (His mind left the lesson and turned to fishing.)

branch out *v.* To add new interests or activities; begin doing other things also. *First Jane collected stamps; then she branched out and collected coins, too.* (Jane collected both stamps and coins; she added a hobby to the one she had.) *John started a television repair shop; when he did well, he branched out and began selling television sets too.* (John made his business larger by selling TV sets too.)

brazen it out *v. phr.* To pretend one did nothing wrong; be suspected, accused, or scolded without admitting one did wrong; act as if not guilty. *The teacher found a stolen pen that the girl had in her desk, but the girl brazened it out; she said someone else must have put it there.* (When the teacher accused the girl of stealing the pen, the girl did not

admit it; she pretended to have done nothing wrong.)

bread and butter *n. phr.* The basic needs of life; food, shelter, and clothing. *Ed earned his bread and butter as a bookkeeper, but added a little jam by working with a dance band on weekends.* (He earned his living as a bookkeeper, but got some extra money by working with a dance band on weekends.)

break down *v.* (stress on *down*) **1** To reduce or destroy the strength or effect of; weaken; win over. *By helpful kindness the teacher broke down the new boy's shyness.* (She lessened his shyness by helpfulness and kindness.) *Advertising breaks down a lot of stubbornness against change.* (Advertising removes much opposition to change.) **2** To separate into elements or parts; decay. *Water can be broken down into hydrogen and oxygen.* (Water can be changed into hydrogen and oxygen.) **3** To become unusable because of breakage or other failure; lose power to work or go. *The car broke down after half an hour's driving.* (Mechanical failure made it impossible to drive the car after half an hour.) *His health broke down.* (His health failed.) *When the coach was sick in bed, the training rules of the team broke down.* (The training rules were not obeyed by the team.)

break-down *n.* (stress on *break*) A collapse of a mechanism, a social structure, or an organ. *The military had to take over because of the total break-down of law and order on the island.* (They had to take over to replace the collapsed civil order.)

break even *v. phr., informal* To end a series of gains and losses having the same amount one started with; have expenses equal to profits; have equal gain and loss. The *storekeeper made many sales, but his expenses were so high that he just broke even.* (The storekeeper's profits were balanced by his expenses, so he didn't make any money.) *If you gamble you are lucky when you break even.* (Most people who gamble lose money, so you are lucky if you win enough to balance your losses.)

break ground *v. phr.* 1 To begin a construction project by digging for the foundation; especially, to turn the formal first spadeful of dirt. *City officials and industrial leaders were there as the company broke ground for its new building.* (City officials and industrial leaders watched the program as the company president turned the first spadeful of earth for its new building.) 2 To begin something never done before. *The school broke new ground with reading lessons that taught students to guess the meaning of new words.* (The school began giving a new kind of reading lesson.)

break in *v.* 1a To break from outside. *The firemen broke in the door of the burning house.* (The firemen forced the door from the outside.) 1b To enter by force or unlawfully. *Thieves broke in while the family was away.* (Thieves forced their way in while the family was away.) 2 To enter suddenly or interrupt. *A stranger broke in on the meeting without knocking.* (A stranger rushed into the room without waiting to get permission.) *The secretary broke in to say that a telegram had arrived.* (The secretary interrupted to say that a telegram had come.) 3 To make a start in a line of work

or with a company or association; begin a new job. *He broke in as a baseball player with a minor league.* (He got his start in baseball with a minor league team.) 4 To teach the skills of a new job or activity to. *An assistant foreman broke in the new man as a machine operator.* (An assistant foreman taught the new man to operate a machine.) 5 To lessen the stiffness or newness of by use. *He broke in a new pair of shoes.* (He wore the new shoes until they were soft and comfortable.) *Breaking in a new car requires careful driving at moderate speeds.* (To lessen the stiffness of a new car means driving it carefully at moderate speeds for the first few hundred miles.)

break into *v.* 1 To force an entrance into; make a rough or unlawful entrance into. *Thieves broke into the store at night.* (Thieves forced their way into the store by breaking open a rear door.) 2 *informal* To succeed in beginning (a career, business, or a social life). *He broke into television as an actor.* (He got a start as a TV actor.) 3 To interrupt. *He broke into the discussion with a shout of warning.* (He interrupted the talk to shout a warning.) 4 To begin suddenly. *He broke into a sweat.* (He suddenly began to sweat.) *She broke into tears.* (She suddenly began to cry.) *The dog heard his master's whistle and broke into a run.* (The dog began to run.)

break off *v.* 1 To stop suddenly. *The speaker was interrupted so often that he broke off and sat down.* (His hearers bothered him with shouts and noise until he stopped speaking and sat down.) *When Bob came in, Jean broke off her talk with Linda and talked to Bob.* (Jean suddenly stopped talking to Linda and started talking to Bob.) **2** *informal* To end a friendship or love. *I hear that Tom and Alice have broken off.* (I hear they have stopped dating each other.) *She broke off with her best friend.* (She ended the friendship with her.)

break one's heart   *v. phr.*   To discourage greatly; make very sad or hopeless. *His son's disgrace broke his heart.* (His son's disgrace made him very sad.) *When Mr. White lost everything he had worked so hard for, it broke his heart.* (Losing his money and his property made Mr. White feel very dejected.)

break one's neck   *v. phr., slang* To do all one possibly can; try one's hardest.—Usually used with a limiting adverb or negative. *John nearly broke his neck trying not to be late to school.* (John tried very hard to get to school on time.) *Mother asked Mary to go to the store when she was free, but not to break her neck over it.* (It was not very important that Mary go to the store. She could do it when she felt like it.)

break out   *v.*   **1** To begin showing a rash or other skin disorder.—Often used with *with.* *He broke out with scarlet fever.* (His skin showed a rash from scarlet fever.) **2** To speak or act suddenly and violently. *He broke out laughing.* (He began to laugh loudly.) *She broke out, "That is not so!"* (She suddenly shouted, "That is not so!") **3** To begin and become noticeable. *Fire broke out after the earthquake.* (Fires began and grew worse.) *War broke out in 1812.* (War began in 1812.) **4** *informal*   To bring out; open and show. *When word of the victory came, people began breaking out their flags.* (People got out their flags and hung them up to be seen.) *When Mr. Carson's first son was born, he broke out the cigars he had been saving.* (He opened a box of cigars and gave them to his friends to celebrate.)

break the ice   *v. phr., informal* **1** To conquer the first difficulties in starting a conversation, getting a party going, or making an acquaintance. *To break the ice, Ted spoke of his interest in mountain climbing, and they soon had a conversation going.* (Mountain climbing proved to be an interest of both, and soon they were talking eagerly.) *Some people use an unusual thing, such as an unusual piece of jewelry, to break the ice.* (Sometimes an unusual piece of jewelry makes it easier to get a conversation going.) **2** To be the first person or team to score in a game. *The Wolves broke the ice with a touchdown.* (The Wolves were the first team to score, making a touchdown.)

break through   *v.*   (Stress on *through*) To be successful after overcoming a difficulty or bar to success. *Dr. Salk failed many times but he finally broke through to find a successful polio vaccine.* (He had a hard time, but he finally found it.) *Jim studied very hard this semester in college, and he finally broke through onto the dean's list for the first time.* (Jim's name was on the dean's list of best students at last.)

break-through   *n.*   (stress on *break*) An innovative invention. *The major break-through in artificial intelligence was the arrival of the micro-chip computers.* (Micro-chip computers revolutionized the industry.)

break up   *v.* (stress on *up*)   **1** To break into pieces. *River ice breaks up in the spring.* (The ice in rivers that have been frozen over melts in the spring and separates into pieces that float away.) **2** *informal* To lose or destroy spirit or self-control.—Usually used in the passive. *Mrs. Lawrence was all broken up after her daughter's death, and did not go out of the house for two months.* (Mrs. Lawrence lost her wish to live; she could not control her sadness.) **3** To come or to put to an end, especially by separation; separate. *Some men kept interrupting the speakers, and finally broke up the meeting.* (People kept booing the speakers until it was impossible to go on with the meeting.) *The party broke up at midnight.* (The party ended at midnight.)—Often used in the informal phrase *break it up*. *The boys were fighting, and a passing policeman ordered them to break it up.* (The policeman ordered them to stop fighting.) **4** *informal* To stop being friends. *Mary and June were good friends and did everything together, but then they had a quarrel and broke up.* (Mary and June quarreled and stopped being friends.)

break-up *n.* (stress on *break*) A separation, a divorce, an end to a relationship. *The final break-up between Sue and John happened when she found out that he was a gambler.* (She left him when she found out.)

break with *v.* To separate oneself from; end membership in; stop friendly association with. *He broke with the Democratic party on the question of civil rights.* (He left the Democratic party.) *He had broken with some friends who had changed in their ideas.* (Because some of his friends had changed their ideas, he ended his friendship with them.)

breathe down one's neck *v. phr., informal* To follow closely; threaten from behind; watch every action. *Too many creditors were breathing down his neck.* (He owed money to many people and they were asking him to pay them.) *The carpenter didn't like to work for Mr. Jones, who was always breathing down his neck.* (Mr. Jones followed him around and watched his work.)

breath easily *or* **breathe freely** *v.* To have relief from difficulty or worry; relax; feel that trouble is gone; stop worrying. *Now that the big bills were paid, he breathed more easily.* (When he had paid the big bills, he was less worried.) *His mother didn't breathe easily until he got home that night.* (She was uneasy until he returned.)

breathe one's last *v. phr.* To die.—A cliché. *The wounded soldier fell back on the ground and breathed his last.* (The wounded soldier fell back and died.)

breeze in *v. phr., slang, informal* To walk into a place casually (like a soft blowing wind). *Betsie breezed in and sat down at the bar.* (She sauntered in casually and sat down at the bar.)

bright and early *adj. phr.* Prompt and alert; on time and ready; cheerful and on time or before time.—A trite phrase. *He came down bright and early to breakfast.* (He came to breakfast in good spirits and on time.) *She arrived bright and early for the appointment.* (She got to the appointment cheerful and a little before the hour.)

bring about *v.* To cause; produce; lead to. *The war had brought about great changes in living.* (The war had made great changes in the way people behaved to each other.) *Drink brought about his downfall.* (Drink caused his failure in life.)

bring around *or* **bring round** *v.* **1** *informal* To restore to health or consciousness; cure. *He was quite ill, but good nursing brought him around.* (Good nursing helped to make him well.) **2** To cause a change in thinking; persuade; convince; make willing. *After a good deal of discussion he brought her round to his way of thinking.* (He got her to agree with him.)

bringdown *n., slang, informal* (stress on *bring*) **1** (from *bring down*, past *brought down*). A critical or cutting remark said sarcastically in order to deflate a braggard's ego. *John always utters the right bringdown when he encounters a braggart.* (He knows how to deflate a braggart's ego.) **2** A person who depresses and saddens others by being a chronic complainer. *John is a regular bringdown.* (He is a person in whose company one gets depressed.)

bring down *v. phr., slang, informal* (stress on *down*) **1** To deflate (someone's ego). *John brought Ted down very cleverly with his remarks.* (He deflated his ego cleverly.) **2** To depress (someone). *The funeral brought me down completely.* (It depressed me very much.)

bring down the house *v. phr., informal* To start an audience laughing or clapping enthusiastically. *The principal's story was funny in itself and also touched their loyalties, so it brought down the house.* (The story made them all laugh.) *The President made a fine speech that brought down the house.* (His speech made them all clap their hands long and hard.)

bring home *v.* To show clearly; emphasize; make (someone) realize; demonstrate. *The accident caused a death in his family, and it brought home to him the evil of drinking while driving.* (The accident showed him that it is dangerous to drink and drive.) *A parent or teacher should bring home to children the value and pleasure of reading.* (Parents or teachers should make children realize the value of reading.)

bring home the bacon *v. phr., informal* **1** To support one's family; earn the family living.—A cliché. *He was a steady fellow, who always brought home the bacon.* (He was a dependable person, and always took good care of his family.) **2** To win a game or prize. *The football team brought home the bacon.* (The team won the game.)

bring in *v. In baseball:* To enable men on base to score; score. *Dick's hit brought in both base runners.* (Dick's hit helped both men on base to score.) *A walk and a triple brought in a run in the third inning.* (A walk and a triple scored a run in the third inning.)

bring off *v.* To do (something difficult); perform successfully (an act of skill); accomplish (something requiring unusual ability). *By skillful discussion, Mr. White had brought off an agreement that had seemed impossible to get.* (He had got the groups to agree when it didn't seem possible.) *He tried several times to break the high jump record, and finally he brought it off.* (He finally succeeded in breaking the record.)

bring on *v.* To result in; cause; produce. *The murder of an Austrian nobleman in the summer of 1914 brought on the First World War.* (The murder of an Austrian nobleman started the First World War.) *Spinal meningitis brought on John's deafness when he was six years old.* (Spinal meningitis at the age of six caused John's deafness.) *Reading in a poor light may bring on a headache.* (Reading in a poor light may result in a headache.)

bring out *v.* **1** To cause to appear; make clear. *His report brought out the foolishness of the plan.* (His report made the foolishness of the plan clear.) *Brushing will bring out the beauty of your hair.* (Brushing your hair will make its beauty appear.) **2** To help (an ability or skill) grow or develop. *The teacher's coaching brought out a wonderful singing voice of great power and warmth.* (He developed the singer's fine voice.) **3** To offer to the public by producing, publishing, or selling. *He brought out a new play.* (He produced a new play.) *The company brought out a line of light personal airplanes.* (The company began to make small private airplanes for sale.)

bring to *v.* (stress on *to*) **1** To restore to consciousness; wake from sleep, anesthesia, hypnosis, or fainting. *Smelling salts will often bring a fainting person to.* (A special salt with a strong smell will often wake up a person who has fainted.) **2** To bring a ship or boat to a stop. *Reaching the pier, he brought the boat smartly to.* (He stopped the boat expertly at the pier.)

bring to light *v. phr.* To discover (something hidden); find out about; expose. *Many things left by the ancient Egyptians in tombs have been brought to light by scientists and explorers.* (Many things have been found in the tombs.) *His enemies brought to*

light some foolish things he had done while young, but he was elected anyway, because people trusted him.* (His enemies revealed some foolish things he had done.)

bring to pass *v. phr., formal* To make (something) happen; succeed in causing. *The change in the law was slow in coming, and it took a disaster to bring it to pass.* (The change was slow in coming, and required a terrible event to get people to accept it.)

bring to terms *v. phr.* To make (someone) agree or do; make surrender. *The father brought the two brothers to terms for riding the bicycle.* (Their father made them agree about using the same bicycle.) *The war won't end until we bring the enemy to terms.* (We must make the enemy surrender.)

bring up *v.* **1** To take care of (a child); raise; train; educate. *He gave much attention and thought to bringing up his children.* (He tried to raise them well.) *Joe was born in Texas but brought up in Oklahoma.* (He was born in Texas but raised in Oklahoma.) **2** *informal* To stop; halt.—Usually used with *short*. *He brought the car up short when the light changed to red.* (He stopped the car suddenly.) *Bill started to complain; I brought him up short.* (I quickly told him to stop complaining.) **3** To begin a discussion of; speak of; mention. *At the class meeting Bob brought up the idea of a picnic.* (He started talking about a future picnic.)

bring up the rear *v. phr.* **1** To come last in a march, parade, or procession; end a line. *The fire truck with Santa on it brought up the rear of the Christmas parade.* (Santa on the fire truck was at the end of the parade.) **2** *informal* To do least well; do the most poorly of a group; be last. *In the race, John brought up the rear.* (John came in last.)

brown bagger *n., slang, informal* A person who does not go to the cafeteria or to a restaurant for lunch at work, but brings homemade lunch. *John became a brown-bagger not because he can't afford the restaurant, but because he is too busy to go there.* (He just wants to get lunch finished quickly so he can return to work.)

brown nose *v., slang, vulgar, avoidable* To curry favor in a subservient way, as by obviously exaggerated flattery. *Al brown noses his teachers; that's why he gets all A's in his courses.* (He flatters the teachers and gets A grades.)

brush off *or* **give the brush-off** *v. phr.* **1** To refuse to hear or believe, quickly and impatiently; not take seriously or think important. *John brushed off Bill's warning that he might fall from the tree.* (John paid no attention.) *I said that it might rain and to take the bus, but Joe gave my idea the brush-off.* (He didn't believe it would rain.) *Father cut his finger but he brushed it off as not important and kept working.* (He didn't think the cut was serious.) **2** *informal* To be unfriendly to; not talk or pay attention to (someone); get ₃rid of. *Mary brushed off Bill at the dance.* (She wouldn't pay attention to Bill or dance with him.) *I said hello to Mr. Smith, but he gave me the brush-off.* (He didn't talk to me.)

brush up *or* **brush up on** *v.* To refresh one's memory of or skill at by practice or review; improve; make perfect. *She spent the summer brushing up on her American history, as she was to teach that in the fall.* (She gave the summer to reviewing American history as she was to teach that in the fall.) *He brushed up his target shooting.* (He practiced target shooting.)

buckle down *or* **knuckle down** *v.* To give complete attention (to an effort or job); attend. *They chatted idly for a few moments; then each buckled down to work.* (They talked for a little while, and then started to work.) *Jim was fooling around instead of studying; so his father told him to buckle down.* (His father told him to get serious and study.)

bug-eyed *adj., slang* Wide-eyed with surprise. *He stood there bug-eyed when told that he had won the award.* (He was wide-eyed with surprise when told of the prize.)

bug in one's ear *n. phr., informal* A hint; secret information given to someone to make him act; idea. *I saw Mary at the jeweler's admiring the diamond pin; I'll put a bug in Henry's ear.* (I know Mary likes the pin, so I'll tell Henry secretly so he can buy it as a present for Mary.)

build a fire under *v. phr.* To urge or force (a slow or unwilling person) to action; get (someone) moving; arouse. *The health department built a fire under the restaurant owner and got him to clean the place up by threatening to cancel his license.* (The health department got action by saying they would take away his license.)

build castles in the air *or* **build castles in Spain** *v. phr.* To make impossible or impractical plans; dream about future successes that are unlikely. *He liked to build castles in the air, but never succeeded in anything.* (He liked to dream about the future, but never was a success.) *To build castles in Spain is natural for young people, and they may work hard enough to get part of their wishes.* (Young people dream and plan great things, some of which may come true.)

build up *v.* **1** To make out of separate pieces or layers; construct from parts. *Johnny built up a fort out of large balls of snow.* (Johnny made a snow fort.) *Lois built up a cake of three layers.* (Lois made a cake three layers high.) **2** To cover over or fill up with buildings. *The fields where Tom's father played as a boy are all built up now.* (The town has spread out and now the fields are covered with streets and houses.) *A driver should slow down when he comes to an area that is built up.* (A driver should slow down where there are many houses.) **3a** To increase slowly or by small amounts; grow. *John built up a bank account by saving regularly.* (John gradually made his bank account larger.) *The noise built up until Mary couldn't stand it any longer.* (The noise grew louder and louder until Mary couldn't stand it.) **3b** To make stronger or better or more effective. *Fred exercised to build up his muscles.* (Fred exercised to make his muscles big and strong.) *Joanne was studying to build up her algebra skills.* (Joanne was studying so that she could solve algebra problems more easily.) **3c** *informal* To advertise quickly and publicize so as to make famous. *The press agent built up the young actress.* (The news writer succeeded in making the young actress famous.) *The movie company spent a lot of money building up its new picture.* (The movie company spent a lot of money advertising its new picture.)

bull in a china shop *n. phr.* A person who clumsily says or does something to anger others or upset plans; a tactless person.—A cliché. *We were talking politely and carefully with the teacher about a class party, but John came in like a bull in a china shop and his rough talk made the teacher say no.* (John's lack of tact spoiled the plans.)

bull session *n., slang* A long informal talk about something by a group of persons. *After the game the boys in the dormitory had a bull session until the lights went out.* (After the game the boys had a long talk until the lights went out.)

bullshit[1] *v., slang, vulgar, but gaining in social acceptance* To exaggerate or talk insincerely in an effort to make oneself seem impressive. *Stop bullshitting me, John; I can't believe a word you're saying.* (Stop this exaggerated and unbelievable talk.)

bullshit[2] *n.* Exaggerated or insincere talk meant to impress others. *John, this is a lot of bullshit.* (This is a lot of exaggerated, insincere talk.)

bullshit artist *n., slang, vulgar, but gaining in social acceptance* A person who habitually makes exaggerated or insincerely flattering speeches designed to impress others. *Al is a regular bullshit artist; small wonder he keeps getting promoted ahead of everyone else.* (His success is due to his exaggerated and insincerely flattering speeches.)

bump off *v., slang* To kill in a violent way; murder in gangster fashion. *Hoodlums in a speeding car bumped him off with tommy guns.* (Gangsters speeding by in a car shot him to death with machine guns.)

burn a hole in one's pocket *v. phr.* To make one want to buy something; be likely to be quickly spent. *Money burns a hole in Linda's pocket.* (Linda can't save money; she spends it almost as soon as she gets it.) *The dollar that Don got for his birthday was burning a hole in his pocket, and Don hurried to a store.* (Don was impatient to spend the money he had gotten.)

burn one's bridges *also* **burn one's boats** *v. phr.* To make a decision that one cannot change; remove or destroy all the ways one can return from a position; leave no way to escape from a position. *The coach burned his bridges in the ninth inning by putting in a pinch hitter for his best pitcher.* (The coach could not put the pitcher back in the game if he needed him again.) *When Dorothy became a nun, she burned her bridges behind her.* (After she promised to be a member of a religious order, she could not later decide to do something else instead.)

burn one's fingers *v. phr., informal* To get into trouble doing something and fear to do it again; learn caution through an unpleasant experience. *He had burned his fingers in the stock market once, and didn't want to try again.* (He had lost money in stocks once, and didn't want to try trading again.) *Some people can't be told; they have to burn their fingers to learn.* (Some people can't accept advice; they have to learn from unhappy experience.)

burn out *v.* **1** To destroy by fire or by overheating. *Mr. Jones burned out the clutch on his car.* (Mr. Jones let the clutch get too hot and it had to be fixed.) **2** To destroy someone's house or business by fire so that they have to move out. *The Christmas tree caught fire, and the family was burned out.* (The family had to leave their home because it caught fire and was badly damaged.) **3a** To make or become no good because of long use or overheating. *The light bulb in the bathroom burned out, and Father put in a new one.* (The bathroom light bulb stopped making light, and Father put in a new bulb.) *The electric motor was too powerful, and it burned out a fuse.* (The motor needed more electric current than the wires could safely carry. A special small wire in the fuse got hot very quickly and broke.) **3b** To break, tire, or wear out by using up all the power, energy, or strength of. *Bill burned himself out in the first part of the race and could not finish.* (Bill tired himself out by running too fast in the early part of the race.) *The farmer burned out his field by planting the same crop every year for many years.* (The field was no longer good for raising crops because all of the plant foods in the soil were used up.)

burn the candle at both ends *v. phr.* To work or play too hard without enough rest; get too tired. *He worked hard every day as a lawyer and went to parties and dances every night; he was burning the candle at both ends.* (He worked all day and was up late at parties, not getting enough rest.)

burn the midnight oil *v. phr.* To study late at night.—A cliché. *Exam time was near, and more and more pupils were burning the midnight oil.* (Examinations were getting close, and pupils were studying late.)

burn up *v.* **1** To burn completely; destroy or be destroyed by fire. *Mr. Scott was burning up old letters.* (He was burning them to ashes.) *The house burned up before the firemen got there.* (When the firemen got there, the house was destroyed.) **2** *informal* To irritate; anger; annoy. *The boy's laziness and rudeness burned his teacher up.* (His laziness and rudeness made the teacher angry.) *The breakdown of his new car burned Mr. Jones up.* (It made Mr. Jones cross.)

burn up the road *v. phr., informal* To drive a car very fast. *In his eagerness to see Alice again, he burned up the road on his way to see her.* (He drove at high speeds because he was impatient.) *Speed demons burning up the road often cause accidents.* (Motorists driving too fast often cause accidents.)

burst at the seams *v. phr., informal* To be too full or too crowded. *John ate so much he was bursting at the seams.* (John ate too much, and felt uncomfortably full.) *Mary's album was so full of pictures, it was bursting at the seams.* (Mary's album was too full, and pictures were falling out of it.)

bury the hatchet *v. phr., informal* To settle a quarrel or end a war; make peace. *The two men had been enemies a long time, but after the flood they buried the hatchet.* (They ended a long bitterness after the flood showed them their need of each other.)

busy work *n.* Work that is done not to do or finish anything important, but just to keep busy. *When the teacher finished all she had to say, it was still a half hour before school was over. So she gave the class a test for busy work.* (She wasn't really testing the children. She was just keeping them busy.)

butterflies in one's stomach *n. phr.* A queer feeling in the stomach caused by nervous fear or uncertainty; a feeling of fear or anxiety in the stomach. *When Bob walked into the factory office to ask for a job, he had butterflies in his stomach.* (He was excited and nervous.)

butter up *v., informal* To try to get the favor or friendship of (a person) by flattery or pleasantness. *He began to butter up the boss in hope of a better job.* (He tried to gain the boss's favor by saying and doing nice things for him.)

butt in *v., slang* To join what other people are doing without asking or being asked; interfere in other people's business; meddle. *Mary was explaining to Jane how to write the tax return, when Barbara butted in.* (Barbara started to explain to Jane without being asked.) Often used with *on*. *John butted in on Bill and Tom's fight, and got hurt.* (John tried to help, but they didn't want any help. So both of them started fighting John.)

button one's lip *also* **zip one's lip** *v. phr., slang* To stop talking; keep a secret; shut one's mouth; be quiet. *The man was getting loud and insulting and the cop told him to button his lip.* (The man was shouting offensive language, and the cop ordered him to shut up.) *John wanted to talk, but Dan told him to keep his lip buttoned.* (Dan told him not to say anything.)

buy off *v.* To divert from duty or purpose by a gift. *When the police threatened to stop the gambling business, the owner bought them off.* (The gambler paid the police to let him continue his gambling business.)

buy out *v.* **1** To buy the ownership or a decisive share of; purchase the stock of. *He bought out several small stockholders.* (He bought the stock of several small owners.) **2** To buy all the goods of; purchase the merchandise of. *Mr. Harper bought out a nearby hardware store.* (He bought all the store's goods.)

by a long shot *adv. phr., informal* By a big difference; by far.—Used to add emphasis. *Bert was the best swimmer in the race, by a long shot.* (Bert was certainly the best swimmer.) Often used with a negative. *Tom isn't the kind who would be fresh to a teacher, by a long shot.* (Tom would never be fresh.) *Our team didn't win—not by a long shot.* (Our team didn't come near winning; they were badly beaten.)

by and large *adv. phr.* As it most often happens; more often than not; usually; mostly. *There were bad days, but it was a pleasant summer, by and large.* (There were unpleasant happenings, but in general it was a good summer.) *By and large, women can bear pain better than men.* (Usually women can bear pain better.)

by chance *adv. phr.* Without any cause or reason; by accident; accidentally. *Tom met Bill by chance.* (Tom met Bill without planning to meet him and not knowing Bill was near.) *The ap-*

ple fell by chance on Bobby's head. (Bobby happened to be passing underneath when the apple dropped and hit him.)

by dint of *prep.* By the exertion of; by the use of; through. *By dint of sheer toughness and real courage, he lived through the jungle difficulties and dangers.* (By firmness and courage, he came through alive.) *His success in college was largely by dint of hard study.* (He succeeded because he studied.)

by fits and starts *adv. phr.* With many stops and starts; a little now and a little more later; not all the time; irregularly. *He had worked on the invention by fits and starts for several years.* (He had worked irregularly on his invention for years.) *You will never get anywhere if you study just by fits and starts.* (If you keep studying and stopping you will not learn much.)

by heart *adv. phr.* By exact memorizing; so well that one remembers it; by memory. *The pupils learned many poems by heart.* (The pupils memorized many poems.) *He knew the records of the major league teams by heart.* (He knew perfectly the records of the major league teams.)

by hook or by crook *adv. phr.* By honest ways or dishonest; in any way necessary. *The wolf tried to get the little pigs by hook or by crook.* (He tried any way he could.) *The team was determined to win that last game by hook or by crook, and three players were put out of the game for fouling.* (The players wanted to win very badly, and they used both fair and unfair ways.)

by leaps and bounds *adv. phr.* With long steps; very rapidly. *Production in the factory was in-*

creasing by leaps and bounds. (Production was rising very rapidly.) *The school enrollment was going up by leaps and bounds.* (The school enrollment was increasing very fast.)

B.Y.O.B. Bring Your Own Bottle. Frequently written on invitations for the kind of party where people bring their own liquor.

by the dozen *or* **by the hundred** *or* **by the thousand** *adv. phr.* Very many at one time; in great numbers. *Tommy ate cookies by the dozen.* (Tommy ate a great many cookies.) Often used in the plural, meaning even larger numbers. *The ants arrived at the picnic by the hundreds.* (Very many ants came to the picnic.) *The enemy attacked the fort by the thousands.* (The enemy attacked the fort with thousands of soldiers.)

by the skin of one's teeth *adv. phr.* By a narrow margin; with no room to spare; barely. *The drowning man struggled, and I got him to land by the skin of my teeth.* (The drowning man fought me and I was just about able to bring him to land.) *She passed English by the skin of her teeth.* (She barely passed English.)

by the sweat of one's brow *adv. phr.* By hard work; by tiring effort; laboriously.—A cliché. *Even with modern labor-saving machinery, the farmer makes his living by the sweat of his brow.* (In spite of modern machinery, farming is still hard work.)

by virtue of *also* **in virtue of** *prep.* On the strength of; because of; by reason of. *By virtue of his high rank and position, the President takes social leadership over almost everyone else.* (Because of his high office, the President outranks nearly everyone else at dinners and parties.) *Plastic bags are useful for holding many kinds of food, by virtue of their transparency, toughness, and low cost.* (Plastic bags are good packages for foods, because they are clear, tough, and cheap.)

by way of *prep.* **1** For the sake or purpose of; as. *By way of example, he described his own experience.* (As an example, he described his own experience.) **2** Through; by a route including; via. *He went from New York to San Francisco by way of Chicago.* (He went from New York to San Francisco by a route that passed through Chicago.)

by word of mouth *adv. phr.* From person to person by the spoken word; orally. *The news got around by word of mouth.* (The news was passed from person to person orally.) *The message reached him quietly by word of mouth.* (Someone came up and told him the message quietly.)

C

calculated risk *n.* An action that may fail but is judged more likely to succeed. *The sending of troops to the rebellious island was a calculated risk.* (The sending of troops to the island might have started a war, but the country that sent them thought the troops would end the rebellion without a war starting.)

call a halt *v. phr.* To give a command to stop. *The scouts were tired during the hike, and the scoutmaster called a halt.* (The scouts were tired, and the scoutmaster let them rest from their hike.) *When the children's play got too noisy, their mother called a halt.* (When the children got too noisy, their mother made them quiet down.)

call a spade a spade *v. phr.* To call a person or thing a name that is true but not polite; speak bluntly; use the plainest language.—A cliché. *A boy took some money from Dick's desk and said her borrowed it, but I told him he stole it; I believe in calling a spade a spade.* (I believe in calling things by their true names, and taking money without permission is stealing.)

call down *also* **dress down** *v., informal* To scold. *Jim was called down by his teacher for being late to class.* (The teacher scolded Jim for coming to class late.) *Mother called Bob down for walking into the kitchen with muddy boots.* (Mother told Bob he did something bad.)

call girl *n., slang* A prostitute, especially one who is contacted by telephone for an appointment. *Rush Street is full of call girls.* (There are many prostitutes on Rush Street.)

calling down *also* **dressing down** *n. phr., informal* A scolding; reprimand. *The landowner gave the hunter a calling down for trespassing on posted property.* (The owner reprimanded the trespassing hunter.)

call in question *or* **call into question** *or* **call in doubt** *v. phr.* To say (something) may be a mistake; express doubt about; question. *Bill called in question Ed's remark that basketball is safer than football.* (Ed said "Basketball is safer than football," and Bill said, "I don't believe that. Can you prove it?")

call it a day *v. phr., informal* To stop for the day; quit. *Bob studied hard till 10 P.M.. and then decided to call it a day and went to bed.* (He decided he had done enough work for one day and quit.) *Mr. Johnson painted his house all morning; then he called it a day and went to the ball game.* (After lunch Mr. Johnson quit work for the day.) *The four golfers played nine holes and then called it a day.* (They quit and went home.)

call it quits *v. phr., informal* **1** To decide to stop what one is doing; quit. *When Tom had painted half the garage, he called it quits.* (Tom decided to stop painting when he was half-finished.) **2** To agree that each side in a fight is satisfied; stop fighting because a wrong has been paid back; say things are even. *Pete called Tom a bad name, and they fought till Tom gave Pete a bloody nose; then they called it quits.* (They agreed that Tom had paid Pete back for calling him a bad name; they said they were even again.)

call names *v. phr..* To use ugly or unkind words when speaking to someone or about someone. *Bill* *got so mad he started calling Frank names.* (Bill spoke to Frank in ugly, nasty, and unkind words.)

call off *v.* To stop (something planned); quit; cancel. *When the ice became soft, we had to call off the ice-skating party.* (We had to stop skating because of the danger of soft, weak ice.) *The baseball game was called off because of rain.* (It was cancelled.)

call on *or* **call upon** *v.* **1** To make a call upon; visit. *Mr. Brown called on an old friend while he was in the city.* (He went to visit an old friend while he was in the city.) **2** To ask for help. *He called on a friend to give him money for the bus fare to his home.* (He asked his friend to help him when he didn't have enough money.)

call one's bluff *v. phr., informal* To ask someone to prove what he says he can or will do. *Tom said he could jump twenty feet and so Dick called his bluff and said "Let's see you do it!"* (Dick knew Tom was bragging and could not jump that far, so he asked him to prove it.)

call one's shot *v. phr.* **1** To tell before firing where a bullet will hit. *An expert rifleman can call his shot regularly.* (An expert is able to say where on the target his shots will hit.) *The wind was strong and John couldn't call his shots.* (A strong wind was pushing the bullet to the side so John couldn't be sure where it would land.) **2** *or* **call the turn** To tell in advance the result of something before you do it. *Mary won three games in a row, just as she said she would. She called her shots well.* (Mary predicted well when she said she would win three games in a row.) *Nothing ever happens as Tom says it will. He is very poor at calling his shots.*

(Tom is very poor at predicting what will happen.)

call on the carpet *v. phr., informal* To call (a person) before an authority (as a boss or teacher) for a scolding or reprimand. *The worker was called on the carpet by the boss for sleeping on the job.* (The worker was asked to come into the boss's office and was scolded for sleeping on the job.) *The principal called Tom on the carpet and warned him to stop coming to school late.* (The principal called Tom into his office and warned him against coming to school late.)

call the shots *v. phr., informal* To give orders; be in charge; direct; control. *Bob is a first-rate leader who knows how to call the shots.* (Bob knows how to give orders and control people.) *The quarterback called the shots well, and the team gained twenty yards in five plays.* (The quarterback gave good directions, and the team made quick gains.)

call up *v.* **1** To make someone think of; bring to mind; remind. *The picture of the Capitol called up memories of our class trip.* (The picture brought memories of our class trip; it made us think of things that happened on the trip.) **2** To tell to come (as before a court). *The district attorney called up three witnesses.* (He told them to come to court and tell what they saw.) **3** To bring together for a purpose; bring into action. *Jim called up all his strength, pushed past the players blocking him, and ran for a touchdown.* (Jim collected all his strength so that he had enough to make a touchdown.) *The army called up its reserves when the war seemed near.* (The army called all the men on its lists to active service.) **4** To call on the telephone. *She called up a friend just for a chat.* (She called a friend on the telephone just to talk.)

cancel out *v.* To destroy the effect of; balance or make useless. *The boy got an "A" in history to cancel the "C" he got in arithmetic.* (The boy got an "A" in history to balance the "C" he got in arithmetic.) *Our track team won the mile relay to cancel out the other team's advantage in winning the half-mile relay.* (Our track team won the mile relay to make the score even after the other team won the half-mile relay.) *Tom's hot temper cancels out his skill as a player.* (Tom's hot temper makes his skill as a player useless.)

can of worms *n., slang, informal* A complex problem, or complicated situation. *Let's not get into big-city politics—that's a different can of worms.* (Let us avoid the subject of big-city politics—that is a different messy problem.)

can't see the wood for the trees *or* **can't see the woods for the trees** *or* **can't see the forest for the trees** *v. phr.* To be unable to judge or understand the whole because of attention to the parts; criticize small things and not see the value or the aim of the future achievement. *Teachers sometimes notice language errors and do not see the good ideas in a composition; they cannot see the woods for the trees.* (They see small errors and miss big ideas.) *The voters defeated a bond issue for the new school because they couldn't see the forest for the trees; they thought of their taxes rather than of their children's education.* (They paid more attention to the cost of the new school than to the

need for it.) *We should think of children's growth in character and understanding more than of their little faults and misdeeds; some of us can't see the wood for the trees.* (We do not understand what is most important.)

card up one's sleeve *n. phr., informal* Another help, plan, or argument kept back and produced if needed; another way to do something. *John knew his mother would lend him money if necessary, but he kept that card up his sleeve.* (He didn't borrow it, but waited until it was necessary.) *Bill always has a card up his sleeve, so when his first plan failed he tried another.* (He was smart enough to have thought of another plan.)

car pool *n.* A group of people who own cars and take turns driving each other to work or on some other regular trip. *It was John's father's week to drive his own car in the car pool.* (It was John's father's turn to drive his friends to work in his car.)

carrot and stick *n. phr.* The promise of reward and threat of punishment, both at the same time. *John's father used the carrot and stick when he talked about his low grades.* (John's father promised to reward him if he would get better grades and to punish him if he didn't.)

carry a torch *or* **carry the torch** *v. phr.* **1** To show great and unchanging loyalty to a cause or a person. *Although the others gave up fighting for their rights, John continued to carry the torch.* (Although the others gave up fighting for their rights, John continued to be faithful to the cause by fighting on.) **2** *informal* To be in love, usually without success or return. *He is carrying a torch for Anna,* *even though she is in love with someone else.* (He loves Anna, even though she loves someone else.)

carry away *v.* To cause very strong feeling; excite or delight to the loss of cool judgment. *The music carried her away.* (The music pleased her so much that she couldn't do anything but listen.) *He let his anger carry him away.* (He was so angry that he lost all judgment.)—Often used in the passive. *She was carried away by the man's charm.* (She was very much attracted by him and saw nothing against him.) *He was carried away by the sight of the flag.* (Seeing the flag greatly impressed him.)

carry coals to Newcastle *v. phr.* To do something unnecessary; bring or furnish something of which there is plenty. *The man who waters his grass after a good rain is carrying coals to Newcastle.* (The watering is not needed; the grass is soaked.) *Joe was carrying coals to Newcastle when he told the doctor how to cure a cold.* (The doctor knew more about it than Joe.) [Newcastle is an English city near many coal mines, and coal is sent out from there to other places.]

carry off *v.* 1 To cause death of; kill. *Years ago smallpox carried off hundreds of Indians of the Sioux tribe.* (Many Sioux Indians died of smallpox.) 2 To succeed in winning. *Bob carried off honors in science.* (Bob led in science.) *Jim carried off two gold medals in the track meet.* (Jim won two gold medals.) 3 To succeed somewhat unexpectedly in. *The spy planned to deceive the enemy soldiers and carried it off very well.* (He succeeded in doing what he had planned.) *In the class play,*

Lloyd carried off his part surprisingly well. (He performed his part in the play very well.)

carry on *v.* 1 To work at; be busy with; manage. *Bill and his father carried on a hardware business.* (They managed and worked in a hardware store.) *Mr. Jones and Mr. Smith carried on a long correspondence with each other.* (They wrote many letters to each other.) 2 To keep doing as before; continue. *After his father died, Bill carried on with the business.* (He kept on running the store.) *The colonel told the soldiers to carry on while he was gone.* (He told them to keep on doing their duties.) *Though tired and hungry, the scouts carried on until they reached camp.* (They kept on walking to the camp.) 3a *informal* To behave in a noisy, foolish, and troublesome manner. *The boys carried on in the swimming pool until the lifeguard ordered them out.* (The boys were so rough and disorderly that the lifeguard got them out.) 3b *informal* To make too great a show of feeling, such as anger, grief, and pain. *John carried on for ten minutes after he hit his thumb with the hammer.* (He yelled and cried for ten minutes.) 4 *informal* To act in an immoral or scandalous way; act disgracefully. *The townspeople said that he was carrying on with a neighbor girl.* (The community were scandalized by his sexual behavior.)

carry one's cross or (*literary*) **bear one's cross** *v. phr.* To live with pain or trouble; keep on even though one is suffering. *Weak ankles are a cross Joe carries while the other boys play basketball.* (Weak ankles are a trouble Joe has to live with while the other boys play basketball.) *We didn't know the cheerful woman was bearing her cross, a son in prison.* (We didn't know the cheerful woman was keeping on, even though she had trouble, a son in prison.)

carry out *v.* To put into action; follow; execute. *The generals were determined to carry out their plans to defeat the enemy.* (The generals wanted to fulfill their plans to defeat the enemy.) *John listened carefully and carried out the teacher's instructions.* (John followed the teacher's instructions.)

carry over *v.* 1 To save for another time. *The store had some bathing suits it had carried over from last year.* (The store had bathing suits kept from last year.) *What you learn in school should carry over into adult life.* (You should remember the things you learn in school and use them in adult life.) 2 To transfer (as a figure) from one column, page, or book to another. *When he added up the figures, he carried over the total into the next year's account book.* (He transferred the total from one account book to the next year's book.) 3 To continue in another place. *The story was carried over to the next page.* (The story was continued on the next page.)

carry the ball *v. phr., informal* To take the most important or difficult part in an action or business. *When the going is rough, Fred can always be depended on to carry the ball.* (When things are difficult, you can be sure that Fred will lead in fixing the trouble.)

carry the day *v. phr.* Win completely. *Joan's ideas carried the day.* (Joan's ideas won over all the others.) *The defense law-yer's summary to the jury helped her carry the day.* (Her summary helped her to win the case.)

carry through *v.* 1a To put into action. *Mr. Green was not able to carry through his plans for a hike because he broke his leg.* (He could not put his plans into action; he could not go on the hike.) 1b To do something one has planned; put a plan into action. *Jean makes good plans but she cannot carry through with any of them.* (Jean cannot finish what she starts to do.) 2 To keep (someone) from failing; bring through; help. *When the tire blew out, the rules Jim had learned in driving class carried him through safely.* (What Jim learned in driving class helped him stop the car safely.)

cart before the horse *n. phr., informal* Things in wrong order; something backwards or mixed up. Usually used with *put* but sometimes with *get* or *have*. *When the salesman wanted money for goods he hadn't delivered, I told him he was putting the cart before the horse.* (When he wanted to be paid first, and deliver the things later, I told him he was going at things the wrong way around.) *To get married first and then get a job is getting the cart before the horse.* (One should get a job first before thinking of marriage.)

case in point *n. phr.* An example that proves something or helps to make something clearer. *An American can rise from the humblest beginnings to become President. Abraham Lincoln is a case in point.* (His life shows that a man from the humblest beginnings can become President.)

cash-and-carry[1] *adj.* Selling things for cash only and letting the customer carry them home, not having the store deliver them;

also sold in this way. *This is a cash-and-carry store only.* (This store sells only for cash, and does not deliver.) *You can save money at a cash-and-carry sale.* (You can save money at a sale of things to be bought for cash and carried away.)

cash-and-carry² *adv.* With no credit, no time payments, and no deliveries. *Some stores sell cash-and-carry only.* (They do not allow time payments and do not deliver.) *It is cheaper to buy cash-and-carry.* (It is cheaper to pay cash and to carry home your purchases.)

cash in *v.* **1** To exchange (as poker chips or bonds) for the value in money. *He paid the bill by cashing in some bonds.* (He paid the bill by first selling some bonds.) *When the card game ended, the players cashed in their chips and went home.* (They traded their chips for real money.) **2** *or* **cash in one's chips** *slang* To die. *When the outlaw cashed in his chips, he was buried with his boots on.* (When he died, he was buried with his boots on.) *He was shot through the body and knew he was going to cash in.* (He knew he was going to die.)

cash in on *v., informal* To see (a chance) and profit by it; take advantage of (an opportunity or happening). *Mr. Brown cashed in on people's great interest in camping and sold three hundred tents.* (He noticed people were interested in camping and sold many tents.)

cash on the barrelhead *n. phr., informal* Money paid at once; money paid when something is bought. *Father paid cash on the barrelhead for a new car.* (He paid cash on delivery [C.O.D.] for a new car.) *Some lawyers want*

cash on the barrelhead. (Some lawyers want to be paid at once.)

cast off *v.* **1a** *or* **cast loose** To unfasten; untie; let loose (as a rope holding a boat). *The captain of the boat cast off the line and we were soon out in open water.* (The captain untied the rope holding the boat and we were soon out in open water.) **1b** To untie a rope holding a boat or something suggesting a boat. *We cast off and set sail at 6 A.M.* (We untied the boat and set sail at 6 A.M.) **2** To knit the last row of stitches. *When she had knitted the twentieth row of stitches, she cast off.* (When she had finished knitting the twentieth row of stitches she knit one more row, which was the last.) **3** To say that one doesn't know (someone) any more; not accept as a relative or friend. *Mr. Jones cast off his daughter when she married against his wishes.* (He said she could not be his daughter after that.)

cast pearls before swine *or* **cast one's pearls before swine** *n. phr., literary* To waste good acts or valuable things on someone who won't understand or be thankful for them, just as pigs won't appreciate pearls. *I won't waste good advice on John any more because he never listens to it. I won't cast pearls before swine.* (Why should I throw away good advice on John, if he never follows it?)

cast the first stone *v. phr., literary* To be the first to blame someone; lead accusers against a wrongdoer. *Jesus said that a person who was without sin could cast the first stone.* (Jesus said that a person should not criticize unless he was perfect himself.) *Although Ben saw the girl cheating, he did not want to cast the* *first stone*. (He did not want to be the first to accuse her.)

catch-as-catch-can[1] *adv. phr.* In a free manner; in any way possible; in the best way one can. *On moving day everything is packed and we eat meals catch-as-catch-can.* (We eat whatever we can find and sit almost anywhere.)

catch-as-catch-can[2] *adj. phr.* Using any means or method; unplanned; free. *He was an expert at catch-as-catch-can wrestling.* (He was an expert at a kind of free and unlimited wrestling.) *Rip van Winkle seems to have led a catch-as-catch-can life.* (He lived freely without much care for his future.) *Politics is rather a catch-as-catch-can business.* (In politics one has to meet many unexpected emergencies.)

catch cold *v. phr.* **1** *or* **take cold** To get a common respiratory sickness that causes a running nose, sneezing, and sometimes sore throat, fever, or other symptoms. *Don't get your feet wet or you'll catch cold.* (Wear your rubbers in wet, cold, weather or you may become sick.) **2** *informal*—Usually in the passive. To catch unprepared for a question or unexpected happening. *I had not studied my lesson, and the teacher's question caught me cold.* (I was not ready for the question and could not answer it.) *The opposing team were big and sure of winning, and they were caught cold by the fast, hard playing of our smaller players.* (The tall team was surprised and upset by our small, fast players.)

catch fire *v. phr.* **1** To begin to burn. *When he dropped a match in the leaves, they caught fire.* (When he dropped the match in the leaves, they began to burn.) **2** To become excited. *The audi-ence caught fire at the speaker's words and began to cheer.* (The audience became wildly excited at the speaker's words and began to cheer.) *His imagination caught fire as he read.* (His imagination was excited to great activity as he read.)

catch on *v., informal* **1** To understand; learn about.—Often used with *to*. *You'll catch on to the job after you've been here awhile.* (You'll get the idea of how to do the job.) *Don't play any tricks on Joe. When he catches on, he will beat you.* (When Joe sees that you are playing a trick on him, he will beat you.) **2** To become popular; be done or used by many people. *The song caught on and was sung and played everywhere.* (The song was liked by many people.) **3** To be hired; get a job. *The ball player caught on with a big league team last year.* (He was hired to play for the team.)

catch one's breath *v. phr.* **1** To breathe in suddenly with fear or surprise. *The beauty of the scene made him catch his breath.* (The beauty of the scene surprised him and he took a quick breath.) **2a** To rest and get back one's normal breathing, as after running. *After running to the bus stop, we sat down to catch our breath.* (We stopped until our hard breathing had slowed down to normal.) **2b** To relax for awhile after any work. *After the day's work, we sat down over coffee to catch our breath.* (We relaxed over coffee after the day's work.)

catch one's death of *or* **take one's death of** *v. phr., informal* To become very ill with (a cold, pneumonia, flu). *Johnny fell in the icy water and almost took his death of a cold.* (Johnny got wet and caught a very bad cold.)

Sometimes used in the short form "catch your death." *Johnny! Come right in here and put your coat and hat on. You'll catch your death!* (You will get a bad cold.)

catch one's eye *v. phr.* To attract one's attention. *I caught his eye as he moved through the crowd, and waved at him to come over.* (I attracted his attention as he moved through the crowd.) *The dress in the window caught her eye when she passed the store.* (The dress in the window attracted her attention when she passed the store.)

catch sight of *v. phr.* To see suddenly or unexpectedly. *Allan caught sight of a kingbird on a wire fence.* (Allen suddenly saw a kingbird on a wire fence.)

catch some rays *v. phr., slang, informal* To get tanned while sunbathing. *Tomorrow I'll go to the beach and try to catch some rays.* (I'll try to get a suntan on the beach.)

catch some Z's *v. phr., slang, informal* To take a nap, to go to sleep. (Because of the *z* sound resembling snoring.) *I want to hit the sack and catch some Z's.* (I want to go to bed and get some sleep.)

catch-22 *n., informal* —From Joseph Heller's novel *CATCH-22*, set in World War II. **1** A regulation or situation that is self-contradictory or that conflicts with another regulation. In Heller's book catch-22 was the regulation that flight crews must report for duty unless excused for reasons of insanity, but that any one claiming such an excuse must, by definition, be sane. *Government rules require workers to expose wrongdoing in their offices, but the catch-22 prevents their doing so because they are not allowed to disclose any information about their work.* (The rule about secrecy denies the possibility of reporting, so the workers are unable to comply.) **2** A paradoxical situation. *The catch-22 of job-hunting was that the factory wanted to hire only workers who had experience making cigars, but the only way to get the experience was by working at the cigar factory.* (Those conditions seemed to make getting a job impossible.)

catch up *v.* **1** To take or pick up suddenly; grab (something). *She caught up the book from the table and ran out of the room.* (She grabbed the book and ran away.) **2** To capture or trap (someone) in a situation; concern or interest very much.—Usually used in the passive with *in*. *The Smith family was caught up in the war in Europe and we did not see them again till it was over.* (They were in Europe while the war was going on and couldn't leave till it was over.) *We were so caught up in the movie we forgot what time it was.* (We got so interested in the movie we forgot the time.) **3** To go fast enough or do enough so as not to be behind; overtake; come even.—Often used with *to* or *with*. *Johnny ran hard and tried to catch up to his friends.* (He ran so that he could be with them.) *Mary missed two weeks of school; she must work hard to catch up with her class.* (She is behind in her studies.) **4** To find out about or get proof to punish or arrest.—Usually used with *with*. *Billy is always fooling in class but the teacher will catch up with him someday.* (The teacher will find out and punish him.) *A man told the police where the robbers were hiding, so the police finally caught up with them.* (The police finally arrested them.) **5** To result in something bad; bring punishment.—Usually used with *with*. *Smoking will catch up with you.* (Your health will be impaired because you smoke.) **6** To finish; not lose or be behind.—Used with *on* and often in the phrase *get caught up on*. *I have to catch up on my sleep.* (I did not get enough sleep. I must go to bed early to get enough sleep.) *We caught up on all the latest news when we got back to school and saw our friends again.* (We found our what had happened and what our friends had done.)

catch with one's pants down *v. phr., slang* To surprise someone in an embarrassing position or guilty act. *They thought they could succeed in the robbery, but they got caught with their pants down.* (They thought they could succeed in the robbery, but the police caught them when they broke into the store.) *When the weather turned hot in May, the drive-in restaurant was caught with its pants down, and ran out of ice cream before noon.* (The drive-in was caught unprepared for hot weather.)

cat get ones' tongue One is not able or willing to talk because of shyness. Usually said about children or as a question to children. *Tommy's father asked Tommy if the cat got his tongue.* (His father asked if he could not speak.) *The little girl had a poem to recite, but the cat got her tongue.* (She became too shy and nervous to speak her piece.)

cathouse *n., slang* A house of ill repute, a house of prostitution. *Massage parlors are frequently cathouses in disguise.* (Massage parlors are often houses of prostitution.)

caught dead *v. phr., informal* To see or hear (someone) in an embarrassing act or place at any time; ever catch.—Used in the negative, usually in the passive. *Bill wouldn't be caught dead taking his sister to the movies.* (Bill wouldn't take his sister to the movies. If he were made to, he wouldn't let anyone see him. That would be embarrassing.) *John wouldn't be caught dead in the necktie he got for Christmas.* (John wouldn't ever want to be seen wearing it. He is ashamed of it.)

cave in *v.* **1** To fall or collapse inward. *The mine caved in and crushed three miners.* (The roof of the mine fell down and covered the miners.) *Don't climb on that old roof. It might cave in.* (The roof might break and fall in if you walk on it.) **2** *informal* To weaken and be forced to give up. *The children begged their father to take them to the circus until he caved in.* (He weakened and took them.) *After the atomic bomb, Japan caved in and the war ceased.* (Japan gave up fighting.)

chain letter *n.* A letter asking each person receiving it to copy and send it to several others. *Most chain letters die out quickly.* (Most letters that each person is asked to copy and send to several others soon stop because people just throw them away.)

chain-smoke *v.* To smoke cigarettes or cigars one after another without stopping. *Mr. Jones is very nervous. He chain-smokes cigars.* (Mr. Jones smokes cigars one after another.) **—chain-smoker** *n. Mr. Jones is a chain-smoker.* (Mr. Jones smokes cigars one after another.) **chain-smoking** *adj. or n. Chain-smoking is very dangerous to* *health.* (Smoking cigarettes continuously is very unhealthy.)

chalk up   *v., informal*   **1** To write down as part of a score; record. *The scorekeeper chalked up one more point for the home team.* (The scorekeeper added another point to the home team's score.) **2** To make (a score or part of a score); score. *The team chalked up another victory.* (The team won another victory.) *Bob chalked up a home run and two base hits in the game.* (Bob made a home run and two base hits.) *Mary chalked up good grades this term.* (Mary got good grades this term.)

change horses in midstream   *v. phr.*   To make new plans or choose a new leader in the middle of an important activity. *When a new President is to be elected during a war, the people may decide not to change horses in midstream.* (They may decide to keep the same President until the war is over.)

change of heart   *n. phr.*   A change in the way one feels about something. *Edith had a change of heart and decided to be a doctor instead of a nurse.* (Edith decided to go on to medical school.)

change one's tune   *v. phr., informal*   To make a change in one's story, statement, or claim; change one's way of acting. *The man said he was innocent, but when they found the stolen money in his pocket he changed his tune.* (He admitted that he was guilty.) *Bob was rude to his teacher, but she threatened to tell the principal and he changed his tune.* (He apologized and was polite.)

cheapskate   *n., informal*   A selfish or stingy person; a person who will not spend much.—An insulting term. *Mark was too much of* a cheapskate to contribute to the community fund. *(He is too miserly to be charitable.)*

cheat on   *v. phr., informal*   To be unfaithful (to one's wife or husband, or to one's sweetheart or fiancé). *It is rumored that Joe cheats on his wife.* (It is rumored that Joe is having an affair with another woman.)

check in   *v.*   **1** To sign one's name (as at a hotel or convention). *The last guests to reach the hotel checked in at 12 o'clock.* (The last guests at the hotel signed their names in the hotel book at 12 o'clock.) **1b** *informal* To arrive. *The friends we had invited did not check in until Saturday.* (The friends we had invited did not arrive until Saturday.) **2** To receive (something) back and make a record of it. *The coach checked in the football uniforms at the end of the school year.* (The coach took back the uniforms and noted that each one had been returned.) *The students put their books on the library desk, and the librarian checked them in.* (The librarian made a record of their return.)

check off   *v.*   To put a mark beside (the name of a person or thing on a list) to show that it has been counted. *The teacher checked off each pupil as he got on the bus.* (The teacher counted each pupil and put a check beside his name when he got on the bus.) *Bill wrote down the names of all the states he could remember, and then he checked them off against the list in his book.* (Bill compared his list with the list in his book to see which he had forgotten.)

check on *or* **check up on**   *v.*   To try to find out the truth or rightness of; make sure of; examine; inspect; investigate. *We checked* on Dan's age by getting his birth record. (We found out how old he really was.) *Mrs. Brown heard someone downstairs and went down to check up on it.* (She went down to find out.) *You can check on your answers at the back of the book.* (You can find out if you have the right answers.) *The police are checking up on the man to see if he has a police record.* (They are investigating the man's past.) *Grandfather went to have the doctor check on his health.* (The doctor examined Grandfather to see if he was healthy.)

check out *v.*   **1a** To pay one's hotel bill and leave. *The last guests checked out of their rooms in the morning.* (The last guests paid their accounts and moved out of the hotel in the morning.) **1b** *informal*   To go away; leave. *I hoped our guest would stay but he had to check out before Monday.* (I hoped our guest would stay but he had to leave before Monday.) **2a** To give or lend (something) and make a record of it. *The boss checked out the tools to the workmen as they came to work.* (The boss gave the tools to the men and wrote down what he gave them.) **2b** To get (something) after a record has been made of it. *I checked out a book from the library.* (I went and got a book from the library; the librarian wrote down what I took.) **3** *informal* To test (something, like a part of a motor). *The mechanic checked out the car battery.* (He tested the car battery.) **4** *slang* To die. *He seemed too young to check out.* (He seemed to young to die.)

check up *v.* (stress on *up*)   To find out or try to find out the truth or correctness of something; make sure of something; investigate.

Mrs. Brown thought she had heard a burglar in the house, so Mr. Brown checked up, but found nobody. (Mr. Brown went to find out if Mrs. Brown was right.)

check-up *n.* (stress on *check*)   A periodic inspection of a patient by a doctor, or of an engine by a mechanic. *It's time for my annual dental check-up.* (It's time to see the dentist.) *It's time for my 50,000 mile car check-up.* (The car needs servicing.)

cheer up *v.*   **1** To feel happy; stop being sad or discouraged; become hopeful, joyous, or glad. *Jones was sad at losing the business, but he cheered up at the sight of his daughter.* (Jones was sad when he lost the business, but just the sight of his daughter made him feel better.) *Cheer up! The worst is over.* (Be hopeful! The worst is past.) **2** To make cheerful or happy. *The support of the students cheered up the losing team and they played harder and won.* (The students' support made the team feel better.) *We went to the hospital to cheer up a sick friend.* (We went to the hospital to make our sick friend happier.) *Flowers cheer up a room.* (Flowers make a room more cheerful.)

cheesecake *n., slang, informal*   A photographic display of a woman's body, especially her legs, as in certain magazines, known as cheesecake magazines. *Photographer to model: Give us some cheesecake in that pose!* (I am about to take your picture for an advertisement; show more of your legs.)

chew out *v., slang*   To scold roughly. *The boy's father chewed him out for staying up late.* (The boy's father scolded him for staying up late.) *The coach chews out* *lazy players*. (The coach scolds lazy players roughly.)

chew the fat *or* **chew the rag** *v. phr., slang* To talk together in an idle, friendly fashion; chat. *We used to meet after work and chew the fat over coffee and doughnuts.* (We used to talk together over coffee and doughnuts after work.) *The old man would chew the rag for hours with anyone who would join him.* (He would talk about various things with anyone.)

chew the scenery *v. phr., slang* To act over-emotionally in a situation where it is inappropriate; to engage in histrionics. *I don't know if Joe was sincere about our house, but he sure chewed up the scenery!* (He certainly exaggerated.)

chicken feed *n., slang* A very small sum of money. *John and Bill worked very hard, but they were paid only chicken feed.* (John and Bill were paid very little money for the work they did.) *Mr. Jones is so rich he thinks a thousand dollars is chicken feed.* (Mr. Jones is so rich he doesn't think a thousand dollars is very much money.)

chicken-livered *adj., slang, informal* Easily scared, cowardly. *Joe sure is a chicken-livered guy.* (He certainly is a cowardly person.)

chicken out *v. phr., informal* To stop doing something because of fear; to decide not to do something after all, even though previously one had decided to try it. *I used to ride a motorcycle on the highway, but I've chickened out.* (I stopped riding it because I lost my nerve; I got scared.) *I decided to take flying lessons, but just before they started I chickened out.* (I changed my mind in the last minute because of fear.)

chickens come home to roost *informal* Words or acts come back to cause trouble for a person; something bad one said or did boomerangs; one gets the punishment that one deserves. *Fred's chickens finally came home to roost today. He was late so often that the teacher made him go to the principal.* (He had to go to the the principal for a scolding or punishment.)—Often used in a short form. *Mary's selfishness will come home to roost some day.* (She will get what she deserves.)

chicken switch *n., slang, space English* **1** The emergency eject button used by test pilots, by means of which they can parachute to safety if the engine fails; later adopted by astronauts in space capsules. *Don't pull the chicken switch unless absolutely necessary.* (Don't use the eject button unless you are in real danger.) **2** The panic button; a panicky reaction, such as unreasonable or hysterical telephone calls to friends for help. *Joe pulled the chicken switch on his neighbor when the grease starting burning in the kitchen.* (Joe telephoned his neighbor for help when he burned the grease, instead of putting the fire out himself.)

chime in *v.* **1** *informal* To join in. *The whole group chimed in on the chorus.* (The whole group joined in singing the chorus.) *When the argument got hot, John chimed in.* (When the argument got hot, John joined in it.) **2** To agree; go well together.—Usually used with *with*. *Dick was happy, and the holiday music chimed in with his feelings.* (The holiday music was in harmony with his mood.) *When Father suggested going to the shore for vacation, the whole family chimed* *in with the plan.* (When Father suggested a shore vacation, the whole family agreed readily.)

chip in *or* **kick in** *v., informal* To give together with others; contribute. *The pupils chipped in a dime apiece for the teacher's Christmas present.* (They gave a dime apiece toward the teacher's Christmas present.) *All the neighbors kicked in to help after the fire.* (All the neighbors contributed to help the people who had a fire.) *Lee chipped in ten points in the basketball game.* (Lee scored ten of his team's points.) *Joe didn't say much, but chipped in a few words.* (Joe talked a little.)

chip off the old block *n. phr., informal* A person who looks or acts like one of his parents. *From both his looks and his acts, you could see that he was a chip off the old block.* (You could see that he was his father's son.)

choke off *v.* To put a sudden end to; stop abruptly or forcefully. *It was almost time for the meeting to end, and the presiding officer had to move to choke off debate.* (The presiding officer had to act quickly to stop debate completely.) *The war choked off diamond shipments from overseas.* (The war stopped diamond shipments from other countries.)

choke up *v.* **1a** To come near losing calmness or self-control, from strong feeling; be upset by one's feelings. *When one speaker after another praised John, he choked up and couldn't thank them.* (The praise was almost too much, and John's feelings nearly upset him.) **1b** *informal* To be unable to do well because of excitement or nervousness. *Bill was a good batter, but in the championship game he choked up and did poorly.* (He was nervous and

did not bat well.) **2** To fill up; become clogged or blocked; become hard to pass through. *The channel had choked up with sand, so that boats couldn't use it.* (The channel had got so full of sand that boats found it useless.)

clam up *v., slang* To refuse to say anything more; stop talking. *The suspect clammed up, and the police could get no more information out of him.* (The suspect would not give the police any more information.)

clean bill of health *n. phr.* **1** A certificate that a person or animal has no disease. *The government doctor gave Jones a clean bill of health when he entered the country.* (He wrote that Jones had no infectious disease.) **2** *informal* A report that a person is free of guilt or fault. *The stranger was suspected in the bank robbery, but the police gave him a clean bill of health.* (People thought the stranger might have been the bank robber, but the police said he didn't have anything to do with it.)

clean out *v.* **1** *slang* To take everything from; empty; strip. *George's friends cleaned him out when they were playing cards last night.* (George's friends won all his money playing cards.) *The sudden demand for paper plates soon cleaned out the stores.* (Everyone wanted paper plates and soon there were none left in the stores.) **2** *informal* To get rid of; remove; dismiss. *The new mayor promised to clean the crooks out of city government.* (The new mayor promised to get rid of the crooks in city government.)

clean slate *n. phr.* A record of good conduct, without any errors or bad deeds; past acts that are all good. *Mary stayed after school for a week, and after that the* *teacher let her off with a clean slate.* (After Mary finished her punishment, the teacher let her begin again and try for a perfect record.)

clean up *v.* **1** To clean everything; put in order. *She cleaned up the house for her party.* (She cleaned everything in the house for her party.) *After the dirty job he cleaned up for supper.* (He washed himself well and put on clean clothes for supper.) **2** *informal* To finish doing. *John kept at the job until he had cleaned it up.* (John worked until he had finished doing the job.) **3** *slang* To make a lot of money; make a big profit. *Dick cleaned up in the stock market.* (Dick made a lot of money buying and selling stocks.) *The company cleaned up in real estate.* (The company made large profits in land and buildings.) *Jim cleaned up in a crap game.* (Jim won much money in a dice game.)

clear out *v.* **1** To take everything out of; empty. *When Bill was moved to another class he cleared out his desk.* (He took everything out and left the desk empty.) **2** *informal* To leave suddenly; go away; depart. *The cop told the boys to clear out.* (The policeman told the boys to leave at once.) *Bob cleared out without paying his room rent.* (He went away without paying his room rent.) *Clear out of here! You're bothering me.* (Go away! You are disturbing me.)

clear the air *v. phr.* To remove angry feelings, misunderstanding, or confusion. *The President's statement that he would run again for office cleared the air of rumors.* (The President's statement ended rumors and guessing about the situation.) *When Bill was angry at Bob, Bob made a joke, and*

it cleared the air between them. (They laughed and relaxed and didn't feel angry any more.)

clear up *v.* **1** To make plain or clear; explain; solve. *The teacher cleared up the harder parts of the story.* (The teacher made the harder parts of the story understandable.) *Maybe we can clear up your problem.* (Maybe we can solve your problem.) **2** To become clear. *The weather cleared up after the storm.* (The sun came out after the storm.) **3** To cure. *The pills cleared up his stomach trouble.* (The pills cured his stomach trouble.) **4** To put back into a normal, proper, or healthy state. *The doctor can give you something to clear up your skin.* (The doctor can give you something to bring your skin back to its normal healthy condition.) *Susan cleared up the room.* (She put the room back into a neat and orderly condition.) **5** To become cured. *This skin trouble will clear up in a day or two.* (This trouble will go away in a day or two.)

cliffdweller *n., slang, informal* A city person who lives on a very high floor in an apartment building. *Joe and Nancy have become cliffdwellers—they moved up to the 30th floor.* (They moved up very high in a high-rise apartment building.)

cliffhanger *n., informal* A sports event or a movie in which the outcome is uncertain to the very end, keeping the spectators in great suspense and excitement. *Did you see the "Guns of Navarone"? It's a real cliffhanger.* (It is a very exciting and suspenseful movie.)

climb the wall *v. phr., slang, informal* **1** To react to a challenging situation with too great an emotional response, frustration, tension, and anxiety. *By the time I got the letter that I was hired, I was ready to climb the wall.* (I almost went crazy with frustration.) **2** To be so bored as to be most anxious to get away at any cost. *If the chairman doesn't stop talking, I'll climb the wall.* (If he doesn't stop talking, I'll be ready to escape no matter how.)

clip joint *n., slang* A low-class business where people are cheated. *The man got drunk and lost all his money in a clip joint.* (The man got drunk and was cheated of all his money in a low-class night club.) *The angry woman said the store was a clip joint.* (The angry woman said the store was a business where people were cheated.)

clip one's wings *v. phr.* To limit or hold one back; bring one under control; prevent one's success. *When the new president tried to become dictator, the generals soon clipped his wings.* (When the new president tried to become a dictator, his generals kept him from doing it by limiting his power.) *Jim was spending too much time on dates when he needed to study, so his father stopped his allowance; that clipped his wings.* (Stopping Jim's allowance stopped him from spending too much time with girls.)

cloak-and-dagger *adj.* Of or about spies and secret agents. *It was a melodramatic cloak-and-dagger story about some spies who tried to steal atomic secrets.* (It was a story about spies and secret activity.) *The book was written by a retired colonel who used to take part in cloak-and-dagger plots.* (The book was written by a retired colonel who used to work with spies and undercover men in laying traps for enemy agents.)

[From the wearing of cloaks and daggers by people in old adventure stories.]

closed book *n.* A secret; something not known or understood. *The man's early life is a closed book.* (The man's early life is a secret.) *Outerspace is no longer a closed book.* (We are beginning to learn about outer space.)

close down *or* **shut down** *v.* To stop all working, as in a factory; stop work entirely; *also:* to stop operations in. *The factory closed down for Christmas.* (The factory stopped all working until after Christmas.) *The company shut down the factory for Christmas.* (The company stopped work in the factory until after Christmas.)

close in *v.* To come in nearer from all sides. *We wanted the boat to reach shore before the fog closed in.* (We wanted to get to shore before we were surrounded by fog.)—Often used with *on. The troops were closing in on the enemy.* (The troops were coming in towards the enemy from all sides.)

close out *v.* To sell the whole of; end (a business or a business operation) by selling all the goods; *also,* to sell one's stock and stop doing business. *The store closed out its stock of garden supplies.* (The store sold all its garden supplies and stopped selling goods of that kind.) *Mr. Jones closed out his grocery.* (Mr. Jones sold all his grocery stock and went out of business.) *Mr. Randall was losing money in his shoe store, so he decided to close out.* (He decided to sell all the shoes and close shop.)

close ranks *v. phr.* **1** To come close together in a line, especially for fighting. *The soldiers closed ranks and kept the enemy away from the bridge.* (The moved close together in lines and did not let the enemy soldiers come through.) **2** To stop quarreling and work together; unite and fight together. *The Democrats and Republicans closed ranks to win the war.* (The Democrats and Republicans stopped quarreling to work together to win the war.) *The leader asked the people to close ranks and plan a new school.* (The leader asked the people to stop quarreling and work together and plan a new school.)

close the books *v. phr.* To stop taking orders; end a bookkeeping period. *The tickets were all sold, so the manager said to close the books.* (The tickets were all sold, so the manager said to stop taking orders.) *The department store closes its books on the 25th of each month.* (The department store ends its bookkeeping period on the 25th of each month.)

close the door *or* **bar the door** *or* **shut the door** *v. phr.* To prevent any more action or talk about a subject. *The President's veto closed the door on any new attempt to pass the bill.* (The President's refusal to approve the bill stopped any more action on it.) *Joan was hurt by what Mary said, and she closed the door on Mary's attempt to apologize.* (Joan would not listen to Mary's explanation.) *After John makes up his mind, he closes the door on any more arguments.* (When John makes up his mind, he will not listen to any more argument.)

close to home *adv. phr.* Near to someone's personal feelings, wishes, or interests. *When John made fun of Bob's way of walking, he struck close to home.* (John was talking about something very personal to Bob and Bob didn't like it.) *When the preacher spoke about prejudice, people felt he had*

come close to home. (They began to think about their own intolerance.)

close up shop *also* **close shop** *v. phr.* **1** To shut a store at the end of a day's business; *also,* to end a business. *The grocer closes up shop at 5 o'clock.* (The grocer closes his shop for the day at 5 o'clock.) *After 15 years in business at the same spot, the garage closed up shop.* (The garage went out of business after 15 years at the same spot.) **2** *informal* To stop some activity; finish what one is doing. *After camping out for two weeks, the scouts took down their tents and closed up shop.* (The scouts took down their tents and finished their camping trip.) *The committee finished its business and closed up shop.* (The committee finished its business and adjourned.)

coast is clear No danger is in sight; there is no one to see you. *When the teacher had disappeared around the corner, John said, "Come on, the coast is clear."* (When the teacher was out of sight, John said, "Come on, no one will see us now.") *The men knew when the night watchman would pass. When he had gone, and the coast was clear, they robbed the safe.* (When the watchman had passed and no one else was in sight, the men robbed the safe.) *When Dad stopped the car at the stop sign, Mom said, "The coast is clear on this side."* (Mom told Dad that no car was coming from the side on which she was sitting.)

coffee break *n.* A short recess or time out from work in which to rest and drink coffee. *The staff take a coffee break in the middle of the morning and the afternoon.* (The staff are given a short recess from work in the middle of each morning and afternoon to drink coffee and relax.)

cold cash *or* **hard cash** *n.* Money that is paid at the time of purchase; good checks or cash on delivery (C.O.D.); silver and bills. *Mr. Jones bought a new car and paid cold cash for it.* (Mr. Jones bought a new car. He paid for it with a certified bank check.) *Some stores sell things only for cold cash.* (Some stores sell only for immediate payment in money. They do not sell on credit.)

cold feet *n. phr., informal* A loss of courage or nerve; a failure or loss of confidence in oneself. *Ralph was going to ask Mary to dance with him but he got cold feet and didn't.* (He lost his nerve and didn't ask Mary to dance with him.)

cold fish *n., informal* An aloof, unsociable person; a person who is unfriendly or does not mix with others. *No one knows the new doctor; he is a cold fish.* (The new doctor is unfriendly and does not mix with others.) *Nobody invites Eric, because he is a cold fish.* (Nobody invites him because he does not mix with others.)

cold-shoulder *v., informal* To act towards a person with dislike or scorn; be unfriendly to. *Fred cold-shouldered his old friend when they passed on the street.* (Fred pretended not to see his old friend.) *It is impolite and unkind to cold-shoulder people.* (It is impolite and unkind to snub other people.)

cold shoulder *n., informal* Unfriendly treatment of a person; a showing of dislike for a person or looking down on a person.—Used in the expressions *give the cold shoulder* or *turn a cold shoulder to* or *get the cold shoulder.* *When*

Bob asked Mary for a date she gave him the cold shoulder. (When Bob asked Mary for a date she didn't even answer him and turned her back on him.) *The membership committee turned a cold shoulder to Jim's request to join the club.* (The committee wouldn't even think about Jim's request to join the club.)

cold snap *n.* A short time of quick change from warm weather to cold. *The cold snap killed everything in the garden.* (It was cold enough to kill the vegetables and flowers.)

cold turkey *adv., slang, informal* **1** Abruptly and without medical aid; said of withdrawal from the use of an addictive drug or from a serious drinking problem. *Joe is a very brave guy; he kicked the habit cold turkey.* (He gave up his addictive habit on his own and without medical help.) **2** *n.* An instance of withdrawal from drugs, alcohol, or cigarette smoking. *Joe did a cold turkey.* (Joe withdrew from his addictive habit without help.)

cold war *n.* A struggle that is carried on without military action; a war without shooting or bombing. *After World War II, a cold war began between Russia and the United States.* (Russia and the United States engaged in an arms race and psychological and economic conflict, but they did not fight with guns and bombs.)

come about *v.* To take place; develop; occur. *Sometimes it is hard to tell how a quarrel comes about.* (You can't always be sure what causes a quarrel.) *When John woke up he was in the hospital, but he didn't know how that had come about.* (John wasn't sure what had happened to put him in the hospital.)

come a cropper **1** To fall off one's horse. *John's horse stumbled, and John came a cropper.* (John's horse stumbled and John fell off.) **2** To fail. *Mr. Brown did not have enough money to put into his business and it soon came a cropper.* (It soon failed.)

come across *v.* **1** *or* **run across** To find or meet by chance. *He came across a dollar bill in the suit he was sending to the cleaner.* (He found a dollar bill that he had forgotten in a suit that he was sending to the cleaner.) *The other day I ran across a book that you might like.* (I happened to find a book that you might like.) *I came across George at a party last week; it was the first time I had seen him in months.* (I happened to meet George.) **2** To give or do what is asked. *The robber told the woman to come across with her purse.* (He told the woman to give him her purse.) *For hours the police questioned the man suspected of kidnapping the child, and finally he came across with the story.* (Finally the man told the police about his stealing the child.)

come again *v.*, *informal* Please repeat; please say that again.—Usually used as a command. *"Harry has just come into a fortune,"* my wife said. *"Come again?"* I asked her, not believing it.* (I asked her to repeat, because I didn't believe her at first.) *"Come again,"* said the hard-of-hearing man.* (He asked his friend to say it again; he had not heard it.)

come alive *or* **come to life** *v.* **1** *informal* To become alert or attentive; wake up and look alive; become active. *When Mr. Simmons mentioned money, the boys came alive.* (When Mr. Simmons mentioned money, the boys showed interest.) *Bob pushed the starter button, and the engine came alive with a roar.* (The engine started.) **2** To look real; take on a bright, natural look. *Under skillful lighting, the scene came alive.* (The scene looked real when the lighting had been arranged.) *The President came alive in the picture as the artist worked.* (The painting made it seem as if the President was right there.)

come along *v.* To make progress; improve; succeed. *He was coming along well after the operation.* (He was doing well after the operation.) *Rose is coming right along on the piano.* (Rose is getting better at playing the piano.)

come a long way *v. phr.* To show much improvement; make great progress. *The school has come a long way since its beginnings.* (It has made great progress. It has more buildings, more students, and better teaching.) *Little Jane has come a long way since she broke her leg.* (Jane can almost walk again.)

come apart at the seams *v. phr.*, *slang*, *informal* To become upset to the point where one loses self-control and composure, as if having suffered a sudden nervous breakdown. *After his divorce Joe seemed to be coming apart at the seams.* (His divorce upset him so much that he was no longer in control of himself.)

come at *v.* **1** To approach; come to or against; advance toward. *The young boxer came at the champion cautiously.* (The challenger moved cautiously toward the champion.) **2** To understand (a word or idea) or master (a skill); succeed with. *The sense of an unfamiliar word is hard to come at.* (The meaning of a new word is often hard to understand.)

come back v., informal (stress on *back*) **1** To reply; answer. *The lawyer came back sharply in defense of his client.* (The lawyer answered sharply in defense of the man that he was acting for.) *No matter how the audience heckled him, the comedian always had an answer to come back with.* (No matter how hard people in the audience tried to upset him, the comedian always had a quick, sharp reply.) **2** To get a former place or position back; reach again a place that one has lost. *After a year off to have her baby, the singer came back to even greater fame.* (She returned to the stage and gained even greater honors.) *It is hard for a retired prizefighter to come back and beat a younger man.* (Age and lack of practice make it hard for him to win against a younger man.)

come-back n., (stress on *come*) A successful reappearance after temporary absence from an activity. *The baseball pitcher staged a successful come-back after his six-month suspension.* (He went back to playing baseball.)

come back to earth or **come down to earth** v. phr. To return to the real world; stop imagining or dreaming; think and behave as usual. *After Jane met the movie star it was hard for her to come back to earth.* (Jane was thrilled and excited to meet the movie star and it was hard to return to routine.) *Bill was sitting and daydreaming, so his mother told him to come down to earth and to do his homework.* (Bill's mother wanted him to think about his homework and not be dreaming about something else.)

come between v. To part; divide; separate. *John's mother-in-law came to live in his home, and as time passed she came between him and his wife.* (John's mother-in-law caused trouble between him and his wife that broke up his marriage.) *Bill's hot rod came between him and his studies, and his grades went down.* (Bill spent too much time on his car.)

come by v. To get; obtain; acquire. *A good job like that is hard to come by.* (A good job like that is hard to get.) *Money easily come by is often easily spent.* (Money obtained easily is likely to be easily spent.) *She came by her interest in painting from an artistic family.* (She acquired a desire to paint because her family are artists.)

come clean v. phr., slang To tell all; tell the whole story; confess. *The boy suspected of stealing the watch came clean after long questioning.* (He confessed everything after long questioning.)

come down v. (stress on *down*) **1** To reduce itself; amount to no more than.—Followed by *to*. *The quarrel finally came down to a question of which boy would do the dishes.* (The quarrel finally became no more than a question of which boy had to do the dishes.) **2** To be handed down or passed along; descend from parent to child; pass from older generation to younger ones. *Mary's necklace had come down to her from her grandmother.* (Mary's necklace had been passed along to her by her grandmother.)

come-down n. (stress on *come*) A lowering in status, income, or influence. *It was a big come-down for Joe to be put back on the floor after being division manager for a year.* (They lowered him from manager to salesman.)

come down hard on *v. informal* **1** To scold or punish severely. *The principal came down hard on the boys for breaking the window.* (He scolded them hard.) **2** To oppose strongly. *The minister in his sermon came down hard on drinking.* (He was very much against drinking liquor.)

come down with *v., informal* To become sick with; catch. *We all came down with the mumps.* (We all got the mumps.) *After being out in the rain, George came down with a cold.* (George caught a cold.)

come full circle *v. phr.* **1** To be completely opposite in belief or action from one's starting point. *The conservative businessperson has come full circle from former radical student days.* (That individual's philosophy is totally different from what it was.) **2** To change and develop, only to end up as one started. *From modern permissiveness, ideas of child-raising have come full circle to the practices of our grandparents.* (The newest idea is much the same as the old ones that came before.)

come hell or high water *adv. phr., informal* No matter what happens; whatever may come. *Grandfather said he would go to the fair, come hell or high water.* (Grandfather said that nothing would stop him from going to the fair.)

come in *v.* **1** To finish in a sports contest or other competition. *He came in second in the hundred-yard run.* (He took second place in the hundred-yard run.) **2** To become the fashion; begin to be used. *Swimming trunks for men came in after World War I; before that men used full swimsuits.* (Men

began to use trunks for swimming after World War I.)

come in for *v.* To receive. *He came in for a small fortune when his uncle died.* (He got a lot of money when his uncle died.) *His conduct came in for much criticism.* (Many people found fault with the way he acted.)

come in handy *v. phr., informal* To prove useful. *Robinson Crusoe found tools in the ship, which came in handy when he built a house.* (The tools were useful in building his house.) *The French he learned in high school came in handy when he was in the army in France.* (He found his knowledge of French a useful thing.)

come into *v.* To receive, especially after another's death; get possession of. *He came into a lot of money when his father died.* (He inherited a lot of money when his father died.) *He came into possession of the farm after his uncle died.* (His uncle left the farm to him.)

come into one's own *v. phr.* To receive the wealth or respect that one should have. *John's grandfather died and left him a million dollars; when John is 21, he will come into his own.* (When John is 21, he will receive his money.) *With the success of the Model T Ford, the automobile industry came into its own.* (It received the respect that it deserved. People began to see its worth.)

come off *v.* **1** To take place; happen. *The picnic came off at last, after being twice postponed.* (The picnic was finally held, after being put off twice.) **2** *informal* To do well; succeed. *The attempt to bring the quarreling couple together again came off, to people's astonishment.* (The effort to settle the quarrel of the two succeeded, although people had not expected it would.)

come off it *also* **get off it** *v. phr., slang* Stop pretending; stop bragging, or kidding; stop being silly.—Used as a command. *"So I said to the duchess . . ." Jimmy began. "Oh, come off it," the other boys sneered.* (Jimmy pretended to have known a duchess personally, but the other boys told him to quit boasting.) *Fritz said he had a car of his own. "Oh, come off it," said John. "You can't even drive."* (Fritz said he owned his own car, but John told him to stop trying to fool him.)

come on *v.* (stress on *on*) **1** To begin; appear. *Rain came on toward morning.* (Rain began just before morning.) *He felt a cold coming on.* (He felt he was catching a cold.) **2** To grow or do well; thrive. *The wheat was coming on.* (The wheat was growing well.) *His business came on splendidly.* (His business succeeded.) **3** *or* **come upon** To meet accidentally; encounter; find. *He came on an old friend that day when he visited his club.* (He met an old friend that day when he called at his club.) *He came upon an interesting idea in reading about the French Revolution.* (He found an interesting idea in reading about the French Revolution.) **4** *informal* Lets get started; let's get going; don't delay; don't wait.—Used as a command. *"Come on, or we'll be late," said Joe,* but *Lou still waited.* ("Let's get started, or we'll be late," said Joe.) **5** *informal* Please do it!—Used in begging someone to do something. *Sing us just one song, Jane, come on!* (Please sing us just one song.) *Come on, Laura, you can

tell me. I won't tell anybody.* (Please tell me the secret.)

come-on *n., slang* (stress on *come)* An attractive offer made to a naive person under false pretenses in order to gain monetary or other advantage. *Joe uses a highly successful come-on when he sells vacant lots on Grand Bahama Island.* (He uses promises that cannot be kept when he sells the lots.)

come on strong *v. phr., slang* To overwhelm with excessively strong language, personality, or mannerisms: to insist extremely strongly and claim something with unusual vigor. *Joe came on very strong last night about the war in Indochina; most of us felt embarrassed.* (He made his points so vigorously that it was embarrassing.)

come out *v.* **1** *Of a girl:* To be formally introduced to society at about age eighteen, usually at a party. *In society, girls come out when they reach the age of about eighteen, and usually it is at a big party in their honor.* (Girls are formally introduced to society at a big party in their honor when they are about eighteen.) *Mary came out with her cousin at a joint party.* (Mary went to her first big party, which was in honor of both her cousin and herself.) **2** To be published. *The book came out two weeks ago.* (The book was published two weeks ago.) **3** To become publicly known. *The truth finally came out at his trial.* (The truth at last became known at his trial.) **4** To end; result; finish. *How did the story come out?* (How did the story end?) *The game came out as we had hoped.* (The game ended in victory for our team.) *The snapshots came out well.* (The pictures were good.) **5** To announce support or opposition; declare oneself (for or against a person or thing). *The party leaders came out for an acceptable candidate.* (They gave their support to a candidate they thought everyone would vote for.) *Many congressmen came out against the bill.* (Many congressmen announced they were against the proposed law.) **6**—*of the closet:* To reveal one's homosexuality. *After deciding not to marry, he came out of the closet publicly.* (After deciding not to marry, he announced that he was homosexual.)

come out with   *v. phr.* **1** To make a public announcement of; make known. *He came out with a clear declaration of his principles.* (He made known his ideas and beliefs.) **2** To say. *He comes out with the funniest remarks you can imagine.* (He says the funniest things you can imagine.)

come over   *v.*   To take control of; cause sudden strong feeling in; happen to. *A sudden fit of anger came over him.* (A sudden feeling of anger seized him.) *A great tenderness came over her.* (A great tenderness affected her.) *What has come over him?* (What is causing him to act this way?)

come round *or* **come around**   *v.* **1** To happen or appear again and again in regular order. *And so Saturday night came around again.* (It was Saturday night again in the passing of the week.) *I will tell him when he comes round again.* (I well tell him when he appears again.) **2** *informal* To get back health or knowledge of things; get well from sickness or a faint. *Someone brought out smelling salts and Mary soon came round.* (Mary woke from her faint when someone let her smell a

strong chemical.) *Jim has come around after having had stomach ulcers.* (Jim has recovered his health after trouble with ulcers.) **3** To change direction. *The wind has come round to the south.* (The wind has changed to the south.) **4** *informal*   To change one's opinion or purpose to agree with another's. *Tom came round when Dick told him the whole story.* (Tom changed his idea and agreed with the others instead of opposing them.)

come through   *v., informal* To be equal to a demand; successfully meet trouble or a sudden need; satisfy a need. *When the baseball team needed a hit, Willie came through with a double.* (When the baseball team needed a hit badly, Willie was able to do it and hit a double.) *John needed money for college and his father came through.* (John needed help and his father got the money for college.)

come to   (stress on *to*) *v.* **1** To wake up after losing consciousness; get the use of one's senses back again after fainting or being knocked out. *She fainted in the store and found herself in the first-aid room when she came to.* (She was in the first-aid room when she woke up from her faint.)

come to blows   *v. phr.*   To begin to fight. *The two quarreling boys came to blows after school.* (The boys' quarrel led to a fight between them after school.) *The two countries came to blows because one wanted to be independent from the other.* (The countries went to war.)

come to grief   *v. phr.*   To have a bad accident or disappointment; meet trouble or ruin. *Nick's hopes for a new house came to grief* *when the house he was building burned down.* (Nick's hopes for a new house were ruined when the one he was building burned down.)

come to grips with *v. phr.* **1** To get hold of (another wrestler) in close fighting. *After circling around for a minute, the two wrestlers came to grips with each other.* (They began to fight seriously.) **2** To struggle seriously with (an idea or problem). *Mr. Blake's teaching helps students come to grips with the important ideas in the history lesson.* (He helps boys and girls think seriously about the big ideas.) *Harry cannot be a leader, because he never quite comes to grips with a problem.* (Harry never completely understands and solves a problem.)

come to light *v. phr.* To be discovered; become known. *John's thefts came to light when the police made an inspection.* (John's thefts were discovered by the police.)

come to nothing *also formal* **come to naught** *v. phr.* To end in failure; fail; be in vain. *The dog's attempts to climb the tree after the cat came to nothing.* (The dog could only jump up. He could not climb the tree like a cat.)

come to one's senses *v. phr.* To think clearly; behave as usual or as one should; act sensibly. *A boy threw a snowball at me and before I could come to my senses he ran away.* (I was surprised and before I could think what to do the boy ran away.) *Don't act so foolishly. Come to your senses!* (Behave yourself properly.)

come to pass *v. phr., literary* To happen; occur. *Strange things come to pass in troubled times.* (Strange things happen in times of trouble.)

come to terms *v. phr.* **1** To reach an agreement. *Management and the labor union came to terms about a new wage agreement and a strike was averted.* (They negotiated the agreement so a strike could be avoided.)

come to the point *or* **get to the point** *v. phr.* To talk about the important thing; reach the important facts of the matter; reach the central question or fact. *Henry was giving a lot of history and explanation, but his father asked him to come to the point.* (Henry was telling about everything that led to his trouble, but his father asked him just to tell what the matter was.) *A good newspaper story must come right to the point and save the details for later.* (A good newspaper story must begin with the essential facts and give the rest of the details later.)

come to think of it *v. phr., informal* As I think again; indeed; really. *Come to think of it, he has already been given what he needs.* (He really has already been given what he needs.) *Come to think of it, I should write my daughter today.* (I had forgotten, but really I should write her.)

come true *v.* To really happen; change from a dream or a plan into a fact. *It took years of planning and saving, but the dream of their seagoing vacation came true at last.* (After years of saving, their sea trip became a reality.) *It was a dream come true when he met the President.* (Meeting the President made his dream become true.) *His hope of living to 100 did not come true.* (He died before he was 100.)

come up v. **1** To become a subject for discussion or decision. *"He was a good salesman, and price never came up until the very last,"* Mary said. (Mary said they did not talk about price until the very last.) *The question of wage increases came up at the board meeting.* (Pay raises were among the things the board members talked about.) *Mayor Jones comes up for reelection this fall.* (Mayor Jones will run for reelection this fall.) **2** To be equal; match in value.—Used with *to*. *The new model car comes up to last year's.* (The new car is fully as good as last year's model.) **3** To approach; come close. *We saw a big black bear coming up on us from the woods.* (The bear was getting near us.) *Christmas is coming up soon.* (It will soon be here.) *The team was out practicing for the big game coming up.* (The team was practicing for the game they would soon play.) **4** To provide; supply; furnish.—Used with *with*. *For years Jones kept coming up with new and good ideas.* (He gave us many new ideas that proved good.) *The teacher asked a difficult question, but finally Ted came up with a good answer.* (Ted gave a good answer.)

comings and goings n. pl., informal Activities; doings; business. *Mary knows all the comings and goings in the neighborhood.* (She knows everything that is happening.)

common ground n. Shared beliefs, interests, or ways of understanding; ways in which people are alike. *Bob and Frank don't like eacy other because they have no common ground.* (Bob and Frank don't like or believe the same things.) *The only common ground between us is that we went to the same school.* (The only thing we know about each other and talk about is the school we both went to.)

common touch n. The ability to be a friend of the people; friendly manner with everyone. *Voters like a candidate who has the common touch.* (People like a candidate who is a friend of the people.)

compare notes v. phr., informal To exchange thoughts or ideas about something. *Mother and Mrs. Barker like to compare notes about cooking.* (They talk about the ways they cook and how they are the same or different.)

conk out v. phr., slang, informal To fall asleep quickly with great fatigue or after having drunk too much. *We conked out right after the guests had left.* (We fell asleep immediately after they left.)

conversation piece n. Something that interests people and makes them talk about it; something that looks unusual, comical, or strange. *Fred keeps a glass monkey on top of his piano as a conversation piece.* (Fred keeps the glass monkey where people can see it and will laugh and talk about it.)

cook one's goose v. phr., slang To ruin someone hopelessly; destroy one's future expectations or good name. *The bank treasurer cooked his own goose when he stole the bank's funds.* (He ruined himself for life when he stole the bank's money.) *She cooked John's goose by reporting what she knew to the police.* (She ruined John completely by telling the police what she knew.) *The dishonest official knew his goose was cooked when the newspapers printed the story about him.* (He knew that he was discovered when the newspapers printed the story.)

cook up v., *informal* To plan and put together; make up; invent. *The boys cooked up an excuse to explain their absence from school.* (The boys made up an excuse to explain why they were absent from school.)

cool as a cucumber adj. phr., *informal* Very calm and brave; not nervous, worried, or anxious; not excited; composed. *Bill is a good football quarterback, always cool as a cucumber.* (He never gets nervous or excited.)

cool down or **cool off** v. **1** To lose or cause to lose the heat of any deep feeling (as love, enthusiasm, or anger); make or become calm, cool, or indifferent; lose interest. *A heated argument can be settled better if both sides cool down first.* (If two angry people let their feelings quiet down, they can usually settle their quarrel better.)

cool one's heels v. phr., *slang* To be kept waiting by another's pride or rudeness; be forced to wait by someone in power or authority; wait. *He cooled his heels for an hour in another room before the manager would see him.* (He had to wait for an hour for the manager, who seemed to want to show his importance and power.) *I was left to cool my heels outside while the others went into the office.* (I had to wait outside while the others went into the office.)

cop a plea v. phr., slang, *informal* To plead guilty during a trial in the hope of getting a lighter sentence as a result. *The murderer of Dr. Martin Luther King, Jr. copped a plea of guilty, and got away with a life sentence in-*stead of the death penalty. (He pleaded guilty to the murder and as a result he drew the lighter sentence of a life term instead of the electric chair.)

cop out v., slang, *informal* To avoid committing oneself in a situation where doing so would result in difficulties. *Nixon copped out on the American people with Watergate.* (In order to avoid the consequences, Nixon didn't commit himself to revealing the truth about Watergate to the American people.)

cop-out n. An act of copping out. i.e., of not committing oneself. *Joe's answer to the question of forced busing in Boston was a regular cop-out.* (He gave a noncommittal answer in order to avoid unpleasantness.)

copycat n. Someone who copies another person's work or manner.—Usually used by children or when speaking to children. *He called me a copycat just because my new shoes look like his.* (He said I was copying him because my shoes look like his.)

corn ball n., slang, informal **1** A trivially sentimental movie or theatrical performance. *That movie last night was a corn ball.* (It was boringly sentimental.) **2** A person who behaves in a superficial sentimental manner or likes performances portraying such behavior. *Suzie can't stand Joe; she thinks he's a corn ball.* (She thinks of him as a sappy, sentimental fellow.)

couch case n., slang, informal A person judged emotionally so disturbed that people think he ought to see a psychiatrist (who, habitually, makes patients lie down on a couch). *Joe's divorce messed him up so badly that he* *became a couch case.* (He became so disturbed that he had to see a psychiatrist.)

couch doctor *n., slang, informal* A psychoanalyst or psychiatrist who puts his patients on a couch following the practice established by Sigmund Freud. *I didn't know your husband was a couch doctor; I thought he was a gynecologist!* (I didn't know he was a psychiatrist.)

cough up *v., slang* **1** To give (money) unwillingly; pay with an effort. *Bob coughed up the money for the party with a good deal of grumbling.* (He paid for the party unwillingly.) **2** To tell what was secret; make known. *He coughed up the whole story for the police.* (He told the whole story to the police.)

couldn't care less *v. phr.* To be indifferent; not care at all. *The students couldn't care less about the band; they talk all through the concert.* (The students are not interested in listening to the band.) Also heard increasingly as *could care less (substandard).*

countdown *n., space English, informal* **1** A step-by-step process that leads to the launching of a rocket. *Countdown starts at 23:00 hours tomorrow night and continues for 24 hours.* **2** Process of counting inversely during the acts leading to a launch; liftoff occurs at zero. **3** The time immediately preceding an important undertaking, borrowed from space English. *We're leaving for Hawaii tomorrow afternoon; this is countdown time for us.* (We are feverishly preparing for our imminent departure.)

count on *v.* To depend on; rely on; trust. *The team was counting on Joe to win the race.* (The team

expected Joe to win the race.) *I'll do it; you know you can count on me.* (I'll do it; you know you can depend on me.)

count one's chickens before they're hatched *v. phr., informal* To depend on getting a profit or gain before one has it. *When Jim said that he would be made captain of the team, John told him not to count his chickens before they were hatched.* (John told Jim not to be so sure that he would be made captain.)

count out *v.* **1** To leave (someone) out of a plan; not expect (someone) to share in an activity; exclude. *"Will this party cost anything? If it does, count me out, because I'm broke."* (If the party will cost something, leave me out, because I have no money.) **2** To count out loud to ten to show that (a boxer who has been knocked down in a fight) is beaten or knocked out if he does not get up before ten is counted. *The champion was counted out in the third round.* (The referee counted to ten while the champion was knocked down and the champion was beaten.) **3** To add up; count again to be sure of the amount. *Mary counted out the number of pennies she had.* (She counted them to find out the number.)

count to ten *v. phr., informal* To count from one to ten so one will have to time to calm down or get control of oneself; put off action when angry or excited so as not to do anything wrong. *Dad always told us to count to ten before doing anything when we got angry.* (Dad meant for us to wait a little while and calm down so we would not do anything foolish.)

covered-dish supper *or* **potluck supper** A meal to which each guest brings a share of the food. *Dolly made a chicken casserole for the covered-dish supper.* (She made a chicken casserole as her contribution to the party.)

cover girl *n.* A pretty woman whose picture is put on the cover of a magazine. *Ann is not a cover girl, but she is pretty enough to be.* (Even though Ann's picture is not on magazine covers, she is very pretty.)

cover ground *or* **cover the ground** *v. phr.* **1** To go a distance; travel. *Mr. Rogers likes to travel in planes, because they cover a lot of ground so quickly.* (Mr. Rogers likes air travel, because he can quickly go a distance.) **2** *informal* To move over an area at a speed that is pleasing; move quickly over a lot of ground. *The new infielder really covers the ground at second base.* (The team's new player can go quickly a long way to catch batted balls.) *Herby's new car really covers ground!* (Herby's new car goes very fast.) **3** To give or receive the important facts and details about a subject. *The class spent two days studying the Revolutionary War, because they couldn't cover that much ground in one day.* (They couldn't learn the important facts about the Revolutionary War in one day.)

cover one's tracks *or* **cover up one's tracks** *v. phr.* **1** To hide and not leave anything, especially foot marks, to show where one has been. *The deer covered his tracks by running in a stream.* (The deer knew that the hunter was following him and ran in the water so there would be no marks to follow.) **2** *informal* To hide or not say where one has been or what one has done. *The boys covered their tracks when they went swimming by saying that they were going for a walk.* (The boys did not tell where they were really going.)

cover the waterfront *v. phr.* To talk or write all about something; talk about something all possible ways. *The principal pretty well covered the waterfront on student behavior.* (The principal talked all about what students should do and should not do. He didn't forget anything.)

cover up *v., informal* **1** To hide something wrong or bad. *The spy covered up his picture-taking by pretending to be just a tourist.* (The spy took pictures of secret places and things while pretending to be taking tourist pictures.) **2** To protect someone else from blame or punishment. *The teacher wanted to know who broke the window and told the boys not to try to cover up for anyone.* (The teacher told the boys not to try to protect the one who did it.)

cover-up *n., slang* **1** A plan or excuse to escape blame or punishment; lie, alibi. *When the men robbed the bank, their cover-up was to dress like policemen.* (The robbers dressed like policemen so that no one would think they were robbers.) *Joe's cover-up to his mother after he had been fighting was that he fell down.* (Joe used the excuse to his mother that he fell down.) **2** A mask. *His bragging is a cover-up for his insecurity.* (He masks his insecurity by being boastful.)

cowboy *n., slang, informal* A person who drives his car carelessly and at too great a speed in order to show off. *Joe's going to* *be arrested some day—he is a cowboy on the highway.* (He drives much faster than the speed limit.)

cow college *n., slang* **1** An agricultural college; a school where farming is studied. *A new, bigger kind of apple is being grown at the cow college.* (The apple is being studied at the college and they are trying to grow big apples.) **2** A new or rural college not thought to be as good as older or city colleges. *John wanted to go to a big college in New York City, not to a cow college.* (John didn't want to go to a small school in a farm area.)

cozy up *v., slang* To try to be close or friendly; try to be liked. —Usually used with to. *John is cozying up to Henry so he can join the club.* (John is trying to become friends with Henry so he can join the club too.)

crack a book *v. phr., slang* To open a book in order to study.—Usually used with a negative. *John did not crack a book until the night before the exam.* (John did not study until the night before the exam.)

crack a joke *v. phr., informal* To make a joke; tell a joke. *The men sat around the stove, smoking and cracking jokes.* (The men sat around the stove, smoking and telling jokes.)

crack a smile *v. phr., informal* To let a smile show on one's face. *Bob told the whole silly story without even cracking a smile.* (Bob told the silly story and didn't smile once.)

crack down *v. phr., informal* To enforce laws or rules strictly. *After a speeding driver hit a child, the police cracked down.* (They got strict about speeding.)

crackpot *n., informal* An eccentric person with ideas that don't make sense to most other people. *Don't believe what Uncle Noam tells you—he is a crackpot.* (His ideas are weird or absurd; pay no attention to him.)

crackpot *attrib. adj., informal* *That's a crackpot idea.* (That is a stupid, unrealistic idea.)

crack the whip *v. phr., informal* To get obedience or cooperation by threats of punishment. *If the children won't behave when I reason with them, I have to crack the whip.* (When the children won't behave even when they know they should, I have to threaten to punish them.)

crack up *v.* **1** To wreck or be wrecked; smash up. *The airplane cracked up in landing.* (The airplane was wrecked in landing.) *He cracked up his car.* (He wrecked his car.) **2** *informal* To become mentally ill under physical or mental overwork or worry. *He had kept too busy for years, and when failures came, he cracked up.* (He broke down when his business got into difficulties.) *It seemed to be family problems that made him crack up.* (He broke down under the worry of problems at home.) **3** To burst into laughter, *or* cause to burst into laughter. *That comedian cracks me up.* (That comedian makes me burst out laughing.)

cramp one's style *v. phr., informal* To limit one's natural freedom; prevent one's usual behavior; limit one's actions or talk. *It cramped his style a good deal when he lost his money.* (Being poor kept him from doing many things he used to do.) *Army rules cramped George's style.* (Army rules kept George from living as he was accustomed.)

crash dive *n.* A sudden dive made by a submarine to escape an enemy; a dive made to get deep under water as quickly as possible. *The captain of the submarine told his crew to prepare for a crash dive when he saw the enemy battleship approaching.* (The captain wanted the submarine to go deep in the water suddenly so it could not be seen or reached by enemy bombs.)

crash-dive *v.* **1** To dive deep underwater in a submarine as quickly as possible. *We shall crash-dive if we see enemy planes coming.* (We shall dive our submarine quickly underwater if we see enemy planes.) **2** To dive into (something) in an airplane. *When the plane's motor was hit by the guns of the enemy battleship, the pilot aimed the plane at the ship and crash-dived into it.* (The pilot crashed his plane into the battleship.)

crash the gate *v. phr., slang* To enter without a ticket or without paying; attend without an invitation or permission. *Bob got into the circus without paying. He crashed the gate.* (Bob sneaked into the circus without paying.) *Three boys tried to crash the gate at our party but we didn't let them in.* (Three boys who weren't invited tried to get in.)

cream of the crop *n. phr.* The best of a group; the top choice. *May Queen candidates were lovely, but Betsy and Nancy were the cream of the crop.* (They were the top choice. It was hard to decide which one was prettier.) *The students had drawn many good pictures and the teacher chose the cream of the crop to hang up when* *the parents came to visit.* (The teacher chose the best pictures to hang up.)

creep up on *v.* **1** To crawl quietly towards. *The mouse did not see the snake creeping up on it over the rocks.* (The snake crawled quietly so that the mouse didn't see it.) **2** *or* **sneak up on** To come little by little; arrive slowly and unnoticed. *The woman's hair was turning gray as age crept up on her.* (Her hair turned gray gradually as she became older.)

crew cut *or* **crew haircut** *n.* A boy's or man's hairstyle, cut so that the hair stands up in short, stiff bristle. *Some boys get crew cuts during the summer to keep cooler.* (Some boys get their hair cut short during summer because it keeps them cooler.)

crocodile tears *n.* Pretended grief; a show of sorrow that is not really felt. *When his rich uncle died, leaving him his money, John shed crocodile tears.* (John pretended to be sorry when his uncle died, but he was really glad to have his money.) [From the legend that crocodiles make weeping sounds to attract victims and then shed tears while eating them.]

crop out *v.* To appear at the surface; come through or show through from concealment. *Rocks often crop out in New England pasture land.* (Rocks often push through the soil in New England pastures.) *A hidden hatred cropped out in his words.* (His words showed hatred that he had hidden before.)

crop up *v.* To come without warning; appear or happen unexpectedly. *Problems cropped up almost every day when Mr. Reed was building his TV station.* (He kept meeting difficulties when he was building his TV station.) *Serious trouble cropped up just when Martin thought the problem of his college education was solved.* (A big difficulty appeared just when he thought his college education was sure.)

cross a bridge before one comes to it *v. phr.* To worry about future events or trouble before they happen—Usually used in negative sentences. *"Can I be a soldier when I grow up, Mother?" asked Johnny. "Don't cross that bridge until you come to it," said his mother.* (It is time enough to worry about being a soldier when you grow up.)

cross one's fingers *v. phr.* **1a** To cross two fingers of one hand for good luck. *Mary crossed her fingers during the race so that Tom would win.* (Mary crossed her two fingers to bring Tom good luck.) **1b** *or* **keep one's fingers crossed** *informal* To wish for good luck. *Keep your fingers crossed while I take the test.* (Hope that I am lucky and that I pass the test.) **2** To cross two fingers of one hand to excuse an untruth that one is telling. *Johnny crossed his fingers when he told his mother the lie.* (Johnny put one finger over the other because he believed it was all right to lie if he did that.)

cross one's heart *or* **cross one's heart and hope to die** *v. phr.*, *informal* To say that what one has said is surely true; promise that it is true.—Often used by children in the longer form. Children often make a sign of a cross over the heart as they say it, for emphasis. *"Cross my heart, I didn't hide your bicycle," Harry told Tom.* (Harry told him that it was surely true that he had not hidden his bicycle.) *"I didn't tell the teacher what you said. Cross my heart and hope to die," Mary said to Lucy.* (Mary promised Lucy solemnly that she did not tell the teacher.)

cross one's mind *or* **pass through one's mind** *v. phr.* To be a sudden or passing thought; be thought of by someone; come to one's mind; occur to one. *At first Bob was puzzled by Virginia's waving, but then it crossed his mind that she was trying to tell him something.* (The idea came to him that Virginia was trying to tell him something.) *When Jane did not come home by midnight, many terrible fears passed through Mother's mind.* (Mother thought of many things that might have happened to Jane.)

cross swords *v. phr.*, *literary* To have an argument with; fight.—Often used with *with*. *Don't argue with the teacher; you're not old enough to cross swords with her.* (You don't know enough to beat the teacher in an argument.)

cross the wire *v. phr.* To finish a race. *The Russian crossed the wire just behind the American.* (The Russian runner finished the race just behind the American.)

cry for *or* **cry out for** *v.*, *informal* To need badly; be lacking in. *It has not rained for two weeks and the garden is crying for it.* (The garden is very dry and needs rain.) *The school is crying out for good teachers.* (The school needs good teachers.)

cry out *v.* **1** To call out loudly; shout; scream. *The woman in the water cried out "Help!"* (The woman shouted for help.) **2** To complain loudly; protest strongly.—Used with *against*. *Many people are crying out against the new rule.* (Many people don't like the new rule and are complaining about it.)

cry over spilled milk *or* **cry over spilt milk** *v. phr., informal* To cry or complain about something that has already happened; be unhappy about something that cannot be helped. *After the baby tore up Sue's picture book, Sue's mother told her there was no use crying over spilled milk.* (Sue's mother told her not to cry, because the book was already torn up.) *You have lost the game, but don't cry over spilt milk.* (Don't feel sorry about the game. It is already lost.)

crystal ball *n.* **1** A ball, usually made out of quartz crystal (glass) that is used by fortune-tellers. *The fortune-teller at the fair looked into her crystal ball and told me that I would take a long trip next year.* (The fortune-teller told me what might happen next year by looking into her big glass ball.) **2** Any means of predicting the future. *My crystal ball tells me you'll make the honor roll.* (I have a feeling you'll make the honor roll.)

cry wolf *v. phr.* To give a false alarm; warn of a danger that one knows is not there. *The general said that the candidate was just crying wolf when he said that the army was too weak to fight for the country.* (The general said that the candidate's warnings of the army's weakness were false and made up to frighten people so they would vote for him.) [From an old story about a shepherd boy who falsely claimed a wolf was killing his sheep, just to start some excitement.]

cue in *v. phr., informal* To add new information to that which is already known. *Let's not forget to cue in Joe on what has been happening.* (Let us not forget to tell him what has been happening.)

culture vulture *n., slang, informal* A person who is an avid cultural sightseer, one who ostentatiously seeks out cultural opportunities such as going to the opera or seeing every museum in a town, and brags about it. *My Aunt Mathilda is a regular culture vulture; she spends every summer in a different European capital going to museums and operas.* (She is a culturally snobbish tourist.)

cup of tea *also* **dish of tea** *n. phr., informal* **1** Something one enjoys or does well; a special interest, or favorite occupation. Used with a possessive. *You could always get him to go for a walk; hiking was just his cup of tea.* (Hiking was his favorite occupation.) **2** Something to think about; thing; matter. *That's another cup of tea.* (That's a different matter entirely.)

curiosity killed the cat *informal* Getting too nosy may lead a person into trouble. *"Curiosity killed the cat,"* Fred's father said, when he found Fred hunting around in closets just before Christmas. (Fred's father warned him about being nosy.)

curl one's hair *v. phr., slang* To shock; frighten; horrify; amaze. *Wait till you read what it says about you—this'll curl your hair.* (You'll be shocked by what it says about you.) *The movie about monsters from another planet curled his hair.* (The movie about monsters frightened him.)

curry favor *v.* To flatter or serve someone to get his help or friendship. *Joe tried to curry favor with the new teacher by doing little services that she didn't really want.* (Joe hoped to improve his marks by doing things for the teacher; he was seeking profit, not *trying to be kind.*) *Jim tried to curry favor with the new girl by telling her she was the prettiest girl in the class.* (He tried to make her like him.)

cut across *v.* **1** To cross or go through instead of going around; go a short way. *John didn't want to walk to the corner and turn, so he cut across the yard to the next street.* (John walked across the yard instead of going around the corner.) **2** To go beyond to include; stretch over to act on; affect. *The love for reading cuts across all classes of people, rich and poor.* (Love of reading is experienced by people of all classes, rich and poor alike.)

cut-and-dried *adj. phr.* Decided or expected beforehand; following the same old line; doing the usual thing. *The decision of the judge was cut-and-dried.* (His decision was what everyone expected.) *The ways of the king's court were cut-and-dried.* (The court always followed the old customs.) *People at the convention heard many cut-and-dried speeches.* (They heard many dull and boring speeches.)

cut back *v.* **1** To change direction suddenly while going at full speed. *The halfback started to his left, cut back to his right, and ran for a touchdown.* (The halfback turned suddenly and ran to his right after starting to his left, and made a touchdown.) **2** To use fewer or use less. *After the big job was finished, the builder cut back the number of men working for him.* (The builder fired many of his workers.) *The school employed forty teachers until a lower budget forced it to cut back.* (After the school received less money, it had to let some teachers go.)

cut both ways *or* **cut two ways** *v. phr.* To have two effects; cause injury to both sides. *People who gossip find it cuts both ways.* (They find that gossip may cause people to think less of the person they talk about, but it also causes people to think less of the gossiper.)

cut corners *v. phr.* **1** To take a short way; not go to each corner. *He cut corners going home in a hurry.* (He went the shortest way, across lots and through fields.) **2** To save cost or effort; manage in a thrifty way; be saving. *John's father asked him to cut corners all he could in college.* (John's father asked him to be as saving as he could in college.) **3** To do less than a very good job; do only what one must do on a job. *He had cut corners in building his house, and it didn't stand up well.* (He had done a poor job in building his house, and the house soon showed the poor materials and workmanship.)

cut down *v.* To lessen; reduce; limit. *Tom had to cut down expenses.* (Tom had to lessen his spending.) *The doctor told Mr. Jones to cut down on smoking.* (The doctor told Mr. Jones to do less smoking.)

cut down to size *v. phr., informal* To prove that someone is not as good as he thinks. *The big boy told John he could beat him, but John was a good boxer and soon cut him down to size.* (John beat the big boy, proving that he was not as good as he said.)

cut ice *v. phr., informal* To make a difference; make an impression; be accepted as important.—Usually used in negative, interrogative, or conditional sentences. *When Frank had found a movie he liked, what others said* *cut no ice with him.* (He did not care what they said.) *Jones is democratic; a man's money or importance never cuts any ice with him.* (Rich or poor, it was all the same to him.) *I don't know if beauty in a woman cuts any ice with him.* (I don't know if he thinks beauty important.)

cut in *v.* **1** To force one's way into a place between others in a line of cars, people, etc.; push in. *After passing several cars, Fred cut in too soon and nearly caused an accident.* (Fred got back in line too close to the car behind.) **2** To stop a talk or program for a time; interrupt. *While Mary and Jim were talking, Mary's little brother cut in on them and began to tell about his fishing trip.* (Her little brother began to speak while they were talking to each other and they had to stop.) **3** *informal* To tap a dancer on the shoulder and claim the partner. *Mary was a good dancer and a boy could seldom finish a dance with her; someone always cut in.* (When Mary was dancing, another boy was always there to take her away from her partner.) **4** To connect to an electrical circuit or to a machine. *Harry threw the switch and cut in the motor.* (Harry turned on the electric power and set the motor going.) *The airplane pilot cut in a spare gas tank.* (The pilot connected a spare gas tank to his motors.) **5** *informal* To take in; include. *When John's friends got a big contract, they cut John in.* (When they got a big contract, John's friends gave him part of the business and profits.)

cut into *v.* **1** To make less; reduce. *The union made the company pay higher wages, which cut into the profits.* (The higher wages to the workers made the profits for the owners smaller.) **2** To get into by cutting in. *She heard the other women talking and cut into the conversation.* (She joined in the conversation.) *While Bill was passing another car, a truck came around a curve heading for him, and Bill cut back into line quickly.* (Bill quickly turned back into line.)

cut off *v.* **1** To separate or block. *The flood cut the townspeople off from the rest of the world.* (The flood separated the townspeople from the rest of the world.) *The woods cut off the view.* (The woods block the view.) *His rudeness cuts him off from friends he might have.* (His rudeness shuts him off from making friends he might have.) **2** To interrupt or stop. *The television show was cut off by a special news report.* (The television show was interrupted by a special news report.) *We were told to pay the bill or the water would be cut off.* (We had to pay the bill or the water coming to the house would be stopped.)

cut off one's nose to spite one's face *v. phr.* To make things worse for oneself because one is angry, usually at someone else. *When Ted's father wouldn't let him go to the ball game, Ted cut off his nose to spite his face. He wouldn't eat his frankfurters for dinner, even though he liked them very much.* (Ted hurt himself, not anybody else, by not eating.)

cut one's throat *v. phr., informal* To spoil one's chances; ruin a person. *He cut his own throat by his carelessness.* (He lost his chances by seeming not to care about his job.) *The younger personnel in the company were cutting each other's throats in their eagerness to win success.* (Each was spoiling the others' chances in the effort to advance.)

cut out[1] *v., slang* **1** To stop; quit. *All right, now—le: s cut out the talking.* (Please stop the talking.) *He was teasing the dog and Joe told him to cut it out.* (Joe told him to stop teasing the dog.) **2** To displace in favor. *Tony cut Ed out with Mary.* (Tony got Mary to like him better.) *John cut out two or three other workers in trying for a better job.* (John was promoted over two or three other workers.)

cut out[2] *adj.* **1** Made ready; given for action; facing. *Mary agreed to stay with her teacher's children all day; she did not know what was cut out for her.* (Mary did not know all the work and problems of the job.)—Often used in the phrase *have one's work cut out for one.* *If Mr. Perkins wants to become a senator, he has his work cut out for him.* (Perkins has a big job ahead of him to get elected to the Senate.) **2** Suited to; fitted for. *Sybil seemed to be cut out for the law.* (She seemed to be naturally suited to be a lawyer.) *It was clear very early that Fred was cut out to be a doctor.* (Fred early showed his fitness to be a doctor.)

cut-rate *adj.* Sold for a price lower than usual; selling cheap things. *If you buy cut-rate things, be sure they are good quality first.* (Be sure you aren't buying things that are not very good for a low price.) *John's brother bought a cut-rate bicycle at the second-hand store.* (He bought the bicycle at a low price.) *There is a cut-rate drugstore on the corner.* (The drugstore sells its goods cheap.)

cut short *v.* To stop or interrupt suddenly; end suddenly or too soon. *Rain cut short the ball game.* (Rain stopped the ball game in the middle.) *An auto accident cut short the man's life.* (An auto accident killed the man.) *When Dick began to tell about his summer vacation, the teacher cut him short, saying "Tell us about that another time."* (The teacher stopped Dick and did not let him finish his story.)

cut the mustard *v. phr., slang* To do well enough what needs to be done; succeed. *Kind teachers helped him through high school, but he couldn't cut the mustard in college.* (He was not able to pass college courses.)

cut to the quick *v. phr.* To hurt someone's feelings deeply. *The children's teasing cut Mary to the quick.* (The children were unkind and made Mary feel very unhappy.)

cut up *v.* **1** *informal* To hurt the feelings of; wound.—Usually used in the passive. *John was badly cut up when Suzie gave him back his ring.* (John's feelings were hurt.) **2** *slang* To act funny or rough; clown. *Joe would always cut up if there were any girls watching.* (Joe would always act the clown if he had an audience of girls.) *At the party Jim and Ron were cutting up and broke a chair.* (They were playing in a rough way and broke a chair.)

D

dance to another tune *v. phr.*
To talk or act differently, usually
better, because things have
changed; be more polite or obedient because one is forced to do
it. *Johnny refused to do his homework but punishment made him
dance to another tune.* (The
teacher punished him, and he did
what she wanted.)

dare say *v. phr.* To think probable; suppose; believe.—Used in
first person. *Mary is unhappy now
but I dare say she will be laughing
about this tomorrow.* (I think that
Mary will be happy again tomorrow.) *There is no more ice cream
on the table, but I dare say we
can find some in the kitchen.* (I
think there is ice cream in the
kitchen.)

dark horse *n., informal* A candidate little known to the general
voting public; a candidate who
was not expected to run. *Every
once in a while a dark-horse candidate gets elected President.*
(Every once in a while a candidate is elected who is relatively
unknown.)

dash off *v.* To make, do, or finish quickly; especially, to draw,
paint, or write hurriedly. *Ann took
out her drawing pad and pencil
and dashed off a sketch of the
Indians.* (Ann drew a picture of
the Indians quickly.) *Joan can
dash off several letters while Mary
writes only one.* (Joan can write
two or three letters while Mary is
writing one.) *Charles had forgotten to write his English report and
dashed it off just before class.*
(Charles wrote it hurriedly in a
few minutes.)

dawn on *v.* To become clear
to. *It dawned on Fred that he*
*would fail the course if he did not
study harder.* (Fred began to understand that he must study
harder.)

day and night *or* **night and day**
adv. **1** For days without stopping; continually. *Some filling
stations on highways are open day
and night 365 days a year.* (Some
filling stations never close.) *The
three men took turns driving the
truck, and they drove night and
day for three days.* (They drove
for three days without stopping to
sleep.) **2** Every day and every
evening. *The girl knitted day and
night to finish the sweater before
her mother's birthday.* (The girl
worked every day and every evening.)

day in and day out *or* **day in, day
out** *adv. phr.* Regularly; consistently; all the time; always. *He
plays good tennis day in and day
out.* (He always plays good tennis.)—Also used with several
other time words in place of *day:
week, month, year. Every summer, year in, year out, the ice-
cream man comes back to the park.*
(The ice-cream man comes back
every summer to sell ice cream.)

day in court *n. phr.* Chance to
be heard; a fair hearing; chance to
explain. *The letters from readers
of the newspaper gave Mr. Jones
his day in court.* (People wrote to
the newspaper and told Mr. Jones's
side of the story.)

dead ahead *adv., informal* Exactly in front; before. *The school
is dead ahead about two miles
from here.* (The school is straight
on from here, in the direction you
are going.) *Father was driving in
a fog, and suddenly he saw another car dead ahead of him.* (He
saw another car very close in front
of him.)

deadbeat *n., slang* A person who never pays his debts and who has a way of getting free things that others have to pay for. *You'll never collect from Joe—he's a deadbeat.* (Joe will never pay you; that's the way he is.)

dead center *n.* The exact middle. *The treasure was buried in the dead center of the island.* (The treasure was buried exactly in the middle of the island.) Often used like an adverb. *The arrow hit the circle dead center.* (The arrow hit the exact middle of the circle.)

dead duck *n., slang* A person or thing in a hopeless situation or condition; one to whom something bad is sure to happen. *When the pianist broke her arm, she was a dead duck.* (She couldn't play her recital.)

deadpan *adj., adv., slang* With an expressionless or emotionless face; without betraying any hint of emotion. *She received the news of her husband's death deadpan.* (She betrayed no emotion when she received the news of his death.)

dead tired *adj. phr., informal* Very tired; exhausted; worn out. *She was dead tired at the end of the day's work.* (She had no energy left at the end of the day's work.)

dead to the world *adj. phr., informal* **1** Fast asleep. *Tim went to bed very late and was still dead to the world at 10 o'clock this morning.* (Tim was still fast asleep.) **2** As if dead; unconscious. *Tom was hit on the head by a baseball and was dead to the world for two hours.* (Tom was knocked unconscious by the baseball.)

death knell *n., formal* **1** The ringing of a bell at a death or funeral. *The people mourned at the death knell of their friend.* (They were sad when they heard the bell ringing to honor him when he died.) **2** *literary* Something that forewarns of future defeat. *Bill's poor grade on his final examination sounded the death knell of his hope to be a doctor.* (His failure in examinations meant he could not become a doctor.) *His sudden deafness was the death knell of his hope to become President.* (When he lost his hearing, he knew he could never be President.)

decked out *adj. phr.* Dressed in fancy clothes; specially decorated. *The band was decked out in bright red uniforms with brass buttons.* (They wore fancy uniforms.) *Main Street was decked with flags for the Fourth of July.* (Main Street was adorned with American flags.)

deep-six *v., slang* (stress on *deep*) To throw away; dispose of. *As the police boat came near, the drug smugglers deep-sixed their cargo.* (They threw the illegal drugs out of their boat.) (An expression originally used by sailors, suggesting throwing something into water six fathoms deep.)

deep water *n.* Serious trouble or difficulty. *When Dad tried to take Mom's place for a day, he found himself in deep water.* (He found the housework and children too much for him to manage.)

deliver the goods *v. phr.* **1** To carry things and give them to the person who wants them. *Lee delivered the goods to the right house.* (He carried them to the right person.) **2** *slang* To succeed in doing well what is expected. *The new pitcher delivered the goods by striking out 20 men in his first game.* (He pitched very well and won his game.) *This power saw surely delivers the goods.* (It works very satisfactorily.)

devil-may-care *adj.* Not caring what happens; unworried. *Johnny has a devil-may-care feeling about his school work.* (Johnny doesn't care about how well he does in school.) *Alfred was a devil-may-care youth but became more serious as he grew older.* (Alfred was foolish and careless but learned to be wise and careful.)

die away *or* **die down** *v.* To come slowly to an end; grow slowly less or weaker. *The wind died down.* (The wind stopped blowing.) *The music died away.* (The sound of the music grew weaker.) *He waited until the excitement had died down.* (He waited until they were no longer excited.) *His mother's anger died away.* (Her anger lessened and was gone.)

die off *v.* To die one after another until the number remaining is small. *The flowers are dying off because there has been no rain.* (When no rain falls to bring water, flowers and plants die one after the other.)

die on the vine *or* **wither on the vine** *v. phr.* To fail or collapse in the planning stages. *The program for rebuilding the city died on the vine.* (The program was partly planned but never carried out.)

die out *v.* To die or disappear slowly until all gone. *This kind of bird is dying out.* (The birds of this kind are dying, and someday all will be dead; there will be none of this kind.) *If you pour salt water on grass, it dies out.* (Salt water slowly kills grass.) *The American colonists started colleges so that learning would not die out.* (The colonists knew that the young people must be educated or someday there would be no educated people left.)

die with one's boots on *or* **die in one's boots** *v. phr., informal* **1** To be killed or hanged rather than die in bed. *The badmen of the Old West usually died in their boots.* (They were often killed by other outlaws or by law officers.) **2** To die while still active in one's work. *Roger chose not to retire from his business; he preferred to die with his boots on.* (He chose to work until the end of his life.)

dig *v., slang* **1** To like something, to be attracted to it; also said of persons. *Do you dig this kind of work?* (Do you enjoy/like your work?) *You dig, man?* (Do you like what you see?) *I sure don't dig this kind o' jive, man!* (I don't appreciate this kind of talk.) **2** To understand. *This guy is so far out, I don't dig it.* (He is so outlandish that it is incomprehensible.) **3** To have sex with. *When you really dig a chick, man, you don't just split!* (A serious involvement means that one doesn't just leave suddenly.) *n.* **1** An archeological site or discovery. *The explorers set up their tents near the dig.* (They camped beside the place where the digging went on.) **2** An act of sexual intercourse or the subject of such an act (female). *The guys said in the locker room that Sue was an easy dig.* (They said that Sue was easy to go to bed with.)

dig in *v., informal* **1** To dig ditches for protecton against an enemy attack. *The soldiers dug in and waited for the enemy to come.* (The soldiers dug ditches and hid in them for protection.) **2a** To go seriously to work; work hard. *John* *dug in and finished his homework very quickly.* (John began to work hard.) **2b** To begin eating. *Mother set the food on the table and told the children to dig in.* (She told them to start eating.)

dig out *v.* **1** To find by searching; bring out (something) that was put away. *Jack dug his sled out of the cellar.* (He brought the sled from where it was stored away.) *The newspaper printed an old story dug out of their records.* (The reporters searched their records for the story.) **2** *informal* To escape.—Usually used with *of.* Often used in the phrase *dig oneself out of a hole. The pitcher dug himself out of a hole by striking the batter out.* (He got out of difficulty.)

dig up *v., informal* To find or get (something) with some effort. *Sue dug up some useful material for her English composition.* (Sue found this information in books and magazine articles.) *Jim asked each boy to dig up a dollar to pay for the hot dogs and soda.* (Jim asked each boy to get a dollar somehow.)

dime a dozen *adj. phr., informal* Easy to get and so of little value; being an everyday thing because there are many of them; common. *Mr. Jones gives A's to only one or two students, but in Mr. Smith's class, A's are a dime a dozen.* (Mr. Jones gives few A's and they are a special honor; but Mr. Smith gives many A's, so they signify less.)

dirty look *n., informal* A look that shows dislike. *Miss Parker sent Joe to the principal's office for giving her a dirty look.* (Joe's face showed anger because of something that Miss Parker had done or said.)

dirty one's hands *or* **soil one's hands** *v. phr.* To hurt one's character or good name; do a bad or shameful thing. *The teacher warned the children not to dirty their hands by cheating in the examination.* (The teacher told the children not to cheat in the examination, because it would give them a bad name.) *I would not soil my hands by going with bad people and doing bad things.* (I would not hurt my good name by being bad.)

discretion is the better part of valor *literary* When one is in danger or trouble, good sense helps more than foolish risks; it is better to be careful than to be foolishly brave. *When you are riding a bicycle, discretion is the better part of valor.* (It is better for you to be careful than to take foolish chances on your bicycle.)

dish out *v.* **1** To serve (food) from a large bowl or plate. *Ann's mother asked her to dish out the beans.* (Mother asked Ann to take beans from the serving bowl and put some on each person's plate.) **2** *informal* To give in large quantities. *That teacher dished out so much homework that her pupils complained to their parents.* (The teacher gave the students much homework.) **3** *slang* To scold; treat or criticize roughly. *Jim likes to dish it out, but he hates to take it.* (Jim likes to scold or criticize other people, but he does not like to have other people scold him.)

dish the dirt *v. phr., slang* To gossip; to spread rumors about others. *Stop dishing the dirt, Sally, it's not like you!* (Stop gossiping, the role doesn't fit you.)

do a double take *v. phr., informal* To look again in surprise; suddenly understand what is seen or said. *John did a double take when he saw Bill*. (He didn't expect to see Bill there, so he was surprised.) *When Evvie said she was quitting school, I did a double take*. (I did not understand at first but suddenly I caught her meaning.)

do a job on *v. phr., slang* To damage badly; do harm to; make ugly or useless. *The baby did a job on Mary's book*. (The baby tore the pages and chewed on the cover of Mary's book.) *Jane cut her hair and really did a job on herself*. (Jane cut her own hair and didn't do it well.)

do away with *v.* **1** To put an end to; stop. *The teachers want to do away with cheating in their school*. (The teachers want the cheating to stop.) *The city has decided to do away with overhead wires*. (The city has decided to put all the wires underground; there will be no overhead wires.) **2** To kill; murder. *The robbers did away with their victims*. (The robbers killed their victims.)

dog-eat-dog *adj.* Ready or willing to fight and hurt others to get what one wants. *During the California gold rush, men had a dog-eat-dog life*. (They had a life in which every man tried to get what he wanted for himself without thinking of other people.)

do in *v., slang* **1** To ruin; destroy. *Mr. Smith's business was done in by a fire that burned down his store*. (Mr. Smith had to go out of business because of the fire.) **2a** To kill; murder. *The poor man was done in by two gangsters who ran away after the crime*. (The man was killed by two gangsters.) **2b** To make tired; exhaust. *The boys were done in after their long hike*. (The long hike made the boys very tired.) **3** To cheat;

swindle. *Mr. Jones was done in by two men who claimed to be collecting money for orphans and widows*. (Mr. Jones gave money to two swindlers who were not what they claimed to be. The men fooled him and took his money.)

doll up *v., slang* **1** To dress in fine or fancy clothes. *The girls dolled up for the big school dance of the year*. (They put on their best clothes for the dance.) **2** To make prettier or more attractive. *The students dolled up the classrooms with Christmas decorations*. (The students decorated the classrooms.)

done for *v., informal* Ruined, defeated, dying. *The poor fellow is done for and will die before morning*. (He has had such a serious accident that he must die soon.) *If Jim fails that test, he is done for*. (If Jim fails that test, he cannot pass his grade.)

do one's thing *or* **do one's own thing** *v. phr., informal* To do what one does well and enjoys. *Two thousand fans paid $10 each to hear the rock group do their thing*. (They wanted to hear the musicians sing and play with skill and pleasure.)

do-or-die *adj.* Strongly decided; very eager and determined. *With a real do-or-die spirit, the team scored two touchdowns in the last five minutes of the game*. (The team tried very hard to win the game.) *The other army was larger, but our men showed a do-or-die determination and won the battle*. (Our soldiers fought stubbornly and did not give up before they had won.)

do out of *v., informal* To cause to lose by trickery or cheating.— .A nonstandard phrase. *The clerk in the store did me out of $2.00 by overcharging me*. (The clerk cheated me out of $2.00 by charging me more than the article really cost.)

dope out *v., slang* To think of something that explains. *The detectives tried to dope out why the man was murdered.* (By putting the facts together in their minds, the detectives tried to discover why the man had been killed.)

dose of one's own medicine or **taste of one's own medicine** *n. phr.* Being treated in the same way one treats others; something bad done to one as one has done bad to other people. *Jim was always playing tricks on other boys. Finally they decided to give him a dose of his own medicine.* (They decided to play a trick on Jim.)

do the honors *v. phr.* To act as host or hostess (as in introducing guests, carving, or paying other attentions to guests.) *The president of the club will do the honors at the banquet.* (The club president will be the host at the dinner; he will introduce speakers and be sure the guests enjoy themselves.)

do the trick *v. phr., informal* To bring success in doing something; have a desired result. *Jim was not passing in English, but he studied harder and that did the trick.* (Jim studied harder and succeeded in improving.) *The car wheels slipped on the ice, so Tom put sand under them, which did the trick.* (The sand kept the wheels from slipping and the car went on.)

double back *v.* To turn back on one's way or course. *The escaped prisoner doubled back on his tracks.* (He went back the same way that he came.)

double-cross *v.* To promise one thing and do another; deceive. *The lawyer double-crossed the inventor by manufacturing the gadget instead of fulfilling the promise to arrange a patent on the inventor's behalf.* (The lawyer betrayed the client's trust.)

double-talk *n.* **1** Something said that is worded, either on purpose or by accident, so that it may be understood in two or more different ways. *The politician avoided the question with double-talk.* (He escaped giving a real answer by saying something that could be understood two different ways.) **2** Something said that does not make sense; mixed-up talk or writing; nonsense. *The man's explanation of the new tax bill was just a lot of double-talk.* (It was mixed up; it meant nothing.)

double up *v.* **1** To bend far over forward. *Jim was hit by the baseball and doubled up with pain.* (He fell down holding his stomach, with his knees up to his chest.) **2** To share a room, bed, or home with another. *When relatives came for a visit, Ann had to double up with her sister.* (Ann had to give up her room and share her sister's room.)

do up *v.* **1a** To clean and prepare for use or wear; launder. *Ann asked her mother to do up her dress.* (Ann asked her mother to clean and iron the dress.) **1b** To put in order; straighten up; clean. *At camp the girls have to do up their own cabins.* (The girls clean their own cabins.) **2** To tie up or wrap. *Joan asked the clerk to do up her purchases.* (Joan asked the clerk to wrap the things she had bought.) **3a** To set and fasten (hair) in place. *Grace helped her sister to do up her hair.* (Grace helped her sister make her hair look pretty.) **3b** *informal* To dress or clothe. *Suzie was done up in her* *fine new skirt and blouse.* (Suzie was prettily dressed.)

do with *v.* **1** To find enough for one's needs; manage.—Usually follows *can. Some children can do with very little spending money.* (Some children can buy what they need for only a little money.) **2** To make use of; find useful or helpful. *Follows* can *or* could. *After a hard day's work, a person can do with a good, hot meal.* (A person needs or wants a good hot meal.) *After cleaning out the basement, the boy could do with a bath.* (He needs a bath.)

do without *or* **go without** *v.* **1** To live or work without (something one wants); manage without. *Ann said that she likes candy, but can do without it.* (Ann likes candy, but it does not make her unhappy to be without it.) *We had to go without hot food because the stove was broken.* (We lived without having hot food.) **2** To live or work without something one wants; manage. *If George cannot earn money for a bicycle, he will have to do without.* (George must live without a bicycle.)

down in the dumps *adj. phr., informal* Sad or discouraged; gloomy; dejected. *The boys and girls were certainly down in the dumps when they heard that their team had lost.* (They felt very unhappy because their team had lost the game.)

down on *adj. phr., informal* Having a grudge against; angry at. *John is down on his teacher because she gave him a low grade.* (John is angry at his teacher.)

down one's alley *or* **up one's alley** *adj. phr., slang* Suited to one's tastes and abilities; what one likes or likes to do. *Baseball is right down Jim's alley.* (Jim likes

to play baseball and does well at it.)

down the drain *adj. or adv. phr., informal* Wasted; lost. *It is money down the drain if you spend it all on candy.* (The money is wasted because it is all eaten up.) *Our plans to go swimming went down the drain when it rained.* (The rain spoiled our plans.)

down the line *adv. phr., informal* **1** Down the road or street; straight ahead. *The church is down the line a few blocks.* (The church is along the street several blocks.) **2** All the way; completely; thoroughly. *Bob always follows the teacher's directions right down the line.* (Bob follows the directions completely.)

down-to-earth *adj.* Showing common sense; practical. *The committee's first plan for the party was too fancy, but the second was more down-to-earth.* (The second plan could be used.) *Mr. Jenkins never seems to know what is happening around him, but his wife is friendly and down-to-earth.* (Mrs. Jenkins sees and likes the people and things around her.)

down to the wire *adj., slang* **1** Running out of time, nearing a deadline. *Bob is down to the wire on his project.* (He is nearing the deadline for completion of his project.) **2** Being financially almost broke; being very low on cash or other funds. *We can't afford going to a restaurant tonight—we're really down to the wire!* (We cannot afford to go out; we are so low on funds.)

drag in *v.* To insist on bringing (another subject) into a discussion; begin talking about (something different). *No matter what we talk about, Jim drags in politics.* (No matter what we talk about, Jim brings politics into the discussion.) *Whenever anyone mentions travel, Grace has to drag in the trip to Mexico she took ten years ago.* (Whenever anyone speaks abut travel, Grace insists on talking about her trip to Mexico.)

drag on *or* **drag out** *v.* **1** To pass very slowly. *The cold winter months dragged on until we thought spring would never come.* (The cold winter months passed so slowly that we thought spring would never come.) **2** To prolong; make longer. *The meeting would have been over quickly if the members had not dragged out the argument about dues.* (The meeting would have been shorter if the members had not made the argument about higher dues.)

drag one's feet *or* **drag one's heels** *v. phr.* To act slowly or reluctantly. *The children wanted to watch television, and dragged their feet when their mother told them to go to bed.* (The children wanted to watch television, and dawdled when their mother told them to go to bed.) *The city employees said the mayor had promised to raise their pay, but was now dragging his feet.* (They said he was too slow about keeping his promises.)

drag race *n., slang* An automobile race in which the drivers try to cover a certain distance (usually one quarter mile) in the shortest possible time. *Drag races are often held on airport landing strips.* (Races in which the drivers try to cover some distance in the shortest possible time are often held on airport landing strips.)

draw a blank *v. phr., informal* **1** To obtain nothing in return for an effort made, or to get a negative result. *I looked up all the Joneses in the telephone book but I drew a blank every time I asked for Archibald Jones.* (I was unable to locate Archibald Jones.) **2** To fail to remember something. *I am trying to think of the name but I keep drawing a blank.* (The name just won't come to me.) **3** To be consistently unsuccessful at doing something. *I keep trying to pass that math exam, but each time I try it I draw a blank.* (Each time I try it, I fail it.)

draw a line *or* **draw the line** *v. phr.* **1** To think of as different. *The law in this country draws a line between murder and manslaughter.* (The law in this country distinguishes between murder and manslaughter.) **2** To set a limit to what will be done; say something cannot be done. *We would like to invite everybody to our party, but we have to draw a line somewhere.* (We would like to invite everybody, but we must set a limit somewhere.)

draw blood *v. phr., informal* To make someone feel hurt or angry. *If you want to draw blood, ask Jim about his last money-making scheme.* (If you want to hurt Jim's feelings, ask him about his last plan to make money.) *Her sarcastic comments drew blood.* (Her mean talk caused hurt and angry feelings.)

draw fire *v. phr.* **1** To attract or provoke shooting; be a target. *The general's white horse drew the enemy's fire.* (The white horse was a good target for the enemy.) **2** To bring criticism or argument; make people say bad things about one. *Having the newest car in your group is sure to draw fire.* (Having the newest car may cause some remarks about whether you need it or can pay for it.)

draw out *v. phr.* To make (a person) talk or tell something. *Jimmy was bashful but Mrs. Wilson drew him out by asking him about baseball.* (Mrs. Wilson made Jimmy talk because he liked to talk about baseball.)

draw up *v.* To write (something) in its correct form; put in writing. *The man had his lawyers draw up his will so that each of his children would receive part of his estate when he died.* (The lawyers wrote the man's will in the proper way.)

dress up *v.* **1a** To put on best or special clothes. *Billy hated being dressed up and took off his best suit as soon as he got home from church.* (Billy didn't like to wear his best clothes.) **1b** To put on a costume for fun or for a part in a play. *Mary was dressed up to play Cinderella in her school play.* (Mary wore a costume to look like Cinderella.) **2** To make (something) look different; make (something) seem better or more important. *A fresh coat of paint will dress up the old bicycle.* (The paint will make the old bicycle look newer and better.) *Tommy dressed up the story of what he did on vacation and made it seem twice as interesting as it was.* (The stories Tommy told about his vacation were not exactly true, but they were interesting.)

drive a bargain *v. phr.* **1** To buy or sell at a good price; succeed in a trade or deal. *Tom's collie is a champion; it should be easy for Tom to drive a bargain when he sells her puppies.* (It should be easy for Tom to get a good price for the puppies.) *Father drove a hard bargain with the real estate agent when we bought our new house.* (Father bought the

house for a very low price.) **2** To make an agreement that is better for oneself than for the other person; make an agreement to one's advantage. *The French drove a hard bargain in demanding that Germany pay fully for World War I damages.* (The French said firmly that Germany must pay for all the damage it did to France.)

drive at *v.* To try or want to say; mean.—Used in the present participle. *John did not understand what the coach was driving at.* (John did not understand what the coach was trying to tell him.) *He had been talking for half an hour before anyone realized what he was driving at.* (No one understood what he meant until he had been explaining for half an hour.)

drop a line *v. phr., informal* To write and mail a note or letter. *Judy's friend asked her to drop her a line while she was away on vacation.* (Her friend wanted Judy to write to her.) *Please drop a line to me when you get to Quebec.* (Please write to me when you arrive.)

drop back *v.* To move or step backwards; retreat. *The soldiers dropped back before the enemy's attack.* (The soldiers retreated when the enemy attacked.) *The quarterback dropped back to pass the football.* (The quarterback stepped backwards to pass.)

drop by *or* **stop by** *v.* **1** *or* **drop around** To make a short or unplanned visit; go on a call or errand; stop at someone's home. *Drop by any time you're in town.* (Pay a visit any time you come.) *My sister dropped around last night.* (My sister came on a short visit.) *Don't forget to stop by at the gas station.* (Don't forget to go to the gas station to get what is needed.) **2** or **drop into** To stop (somewhere) for a short visit or a short time. *We dropped by the club to see if Bill was there, but he wasn't.* (We stopped for a short time at the club to see if Bill was there.) *I dropped into the drugstore for some toothpaste and a magazine.* (I stopped at the drugstore to get some toothpaste and a magazine.)

drop dead *v., slang, rude* To go away or be quiet; stop bothering someone.—Usually used as a command. *"Drop dead!" Bill told his little sister when she kept begging to help him build his model airplane.* (Bill didn't want his little sister's help, and when she kept asking he told her to go away.)

drop in *v.* To make a short or unplanned visit; pay a call.—Often used with *on*. *We were just sitting down to dinner when Uncle Willie dropped in.* (Uncle Willie paid a visit at dinner time.) *The Smiths dropped in on some old friends on their vacation trip to New York.* (The Smiths visited their friends in New York, but their friends were not expecting them.)

drop off *v.* **1** To take (someone or something) part of the way one is going. *Joe asked Mrs. Jones to drop him off at the library on her way downtown.* (Joe asked Mrs. Jones to give him a ride to the library on her way downtown.) **2** To go to sleep. *Jimmy was thinking of his birthday party as he dropped off to sleep.* (He was thinking of his party as he went to sleep.) **3** To die. *The patient dropped off in his sleep.* (The patient died in his sleep.) **4** or **fall off** To become less. *Business picked up in the stores during December, but dropped off again after Christmas.* (Business became less after Christmas.)

drop out *v.* (stress on *out*) To stop attending; quit; stop; leave. *In the middle of the race, Joe got a blister on his foot and had to drop out.* (He got a blister on his foot and had to leave the race.) *Teenagers who drop out of high school have trouble finding jobs.* (Teenagers who leave high school before graduation have trouble finding jobs.)

drop-out *n.* (stress on *drop*) A person who stops in mid-training whether in school, college, or on a job. *John was a high school drop-out, yet he became a millionaire.* (Although he never finished high school, he is successful.)

drown out *v.* To make so much noise that it is impossible to hear (some other sound). *The children's shouts drowned out the music.* (The children made so much noise shouting that no one could hear the music.)

drum up *v.* **1** To achieve by trying or asking again and again; attract or encourage by continued effort. *The car dealer tried to drum up business by advertising low prices.* (The car dealer tried to get customers by advertising low prices.) **2** To invent. *I will drum up an excuse for coming to see you next week.* (I will make up an excuse for coming to see you next week.)

duck soup *n., slang* **1** A task easily accomplished or one that does not require much effort. *That history test was duck soup.* (That history test was very easy to pass.) **2** A person who offers no resistance; a pushover. *How's the new history teacher?—He's duck soup.* (He is easy to handle; he offers no serious challenge.)

dumb bunny *n., slang, informal*
A person who is gullible and stupid. *Jack is a regular dumb bunny.*
(He is a naive person lacking in brains and common sense.)

dutch treat *n., informal* A meal in a restaurant or an outing at the movies, orchestra, or theater, where each party pays his/her own way. *"I am willing to accept your invitation,"* Mary said, *"but it will have to be Dutch treat."* (She is accepting the invitation on the condition that she will pay her own way.)

E

each and every *adj. phr.* Every.—Used for emphasis. *The captain wants each and every man to be here at eight o'clock.* (The captain wants every man to be here at eight o'clock.) *The teacher must learn the name of each and every pupil.* (The teacher must learn every pupil's name.)

eager beaver *n. phr., slang* A person who is always eager to work or do anything extra, perhaps to win the favor of his leader or boss. *Jack likes his teacher and works hard for her, but his classmates call him an eager beaver.* (The other pupils think he tries to please the teacher.) *The man who was promoted to be manager was an eager beaver who got to work early and left late and was always offering to do extra work.* (He worked harder than other employees.)

early bird catches the worm *or* **early bird gets the worm** A person who gets up early in the morning has the best chance of succeeding; if one arrives early or is quicker, one gets ahead of others. *When Billy's father woke him up for school he said, "The early bird catches the worm."* (Children who get to school early will be more successful than pupils who are late.)

ear to the ground *n. phr., informal* Attention directed to the way things are going, or seem likely to go, or to the way people feel and think. *The city manager kept an ear to the ground for a while before deciding to raise the city employees' pay.* (The city manager found out how people felt before he raised the pay of city employees.)

ease off *or* **ease up** *v.* To make or become less nervous; relax; work easier. *When the boss realized that John had been overworking, he eased off his load.* (The boss gave John less work.) *With success and prosperity, Mr. Smith was able to ease off.* (When success came, Mr. Smith did not work so hard.)

easy come, easy go *adv. phr., informal* Something one gets quickly and easily may be lost or spent just as easily. *Grandpa thought Billy should have to work for the money Dad gave him, saying "Easy come, easy go."* (Grandpa thought that if Billy got the money too easily, he would spend it quickly and foolishly.)

easy does it *informal* Let's do it carefully, without sudden movements and without forcing too hard or too fast; let's try just hard enough but not too hard. *"Easy does it," said the boss, as they moved the piano through the narrow doorway.* ("Let's do it slowly and carefully," the boss said.)

eat away *v.* To rot, erode, or destroy. *Rust was eating away the pipe.* (Rust was destroying the pipe.) *Cancer ate away the healthy flesh.* (Cancer turned healthy flesh into diseased and unhealthy tissue.)

eat crow *v. phr.* To admit one is mistaken or defeated; take back a mistaken statement. *John had boasted that he would play on the first team, but when the coach did not choose him, he had to eat crow.* (He had to admit that he was not good enough.)

eat dirt *v. phr., informal* To act humble; accept another's insult or bad treatment. *Mr. Johnson was so much afraid of losing his job that he would eat dirt* *whenever the boss got mean.* (He would let the boss treat him badly.)

eat humble pie *v. phr.* To be humbled; to accept insult or shame; admit one's error and apologize. *Tom told a lie about George, and when he was found out, he had to eat humble pie.* (Tom had to confess that he had lied and to ask George's pardon.)

eat like a bird *v. phr.* To eat very little; have little appetite. *Mrs. Benson is on a diet and she eats like a bird.* (She eats very little.)

eat like a horse *v. phr.* To eat a lot; eat hungrily. *The harvesters worked into the evening and then came in and ate like horses.* (The harvesters put in a long day, and then came in and ate a great deal, as they were very hungry.)

eat one's cake and have it too *v. phr.* To use or spend something and still keep it. *Roger can't make up his mind whether to go to college or get a job. You can't eat your cake and have it too.* (Roger can't do both; he must choose one.)

eat one's heart out *v. phr.* To grieve long and hopelessly; to become thin and weak from sorrow. *We sometimes hear of a dog eating its heart out for a lost owner.* (The dog is so unhappy that it will not eat.)

eat one's words *also* **swallow one's words** *v. phr.* To take back something one has said; admit something is not true. *John had called Harry a coward, but the boys made him eat his words after Harry bravely fought a big bully.* (The boys made John admit that Harry was no coward.)

eat out *v.* **1** To eat in a restaurant; eat away from home. *Fred ate out often, even when he wasn't out of town.* (Fred ate in restaurants often, even when he wasn't

traveling.) **2** To rust, rot, or in time be destroyed. *Rust had eaten out the gun barrel.* (Rust had ruined the inside of the gun barrel and made it useless.) **3** *vulgar, avoidable* To engage in oral sexual intercourse. *"Eat me out if you can't get it up,"* Hermione groaned lasciviously. (Use your tongue if you can't get an erection.)

eat up *v., slang* To accept eagerly; welcome. *The girls told John he was a hero because he made the winning touchdown, and he ate up their praise.* (John received their praise greedily.) *Jim told Martha that she was as smart as she was beautiful and Martha ate it up.* (Martha liked very much to hear his praise.)

egg on *v.* To urge on; excite; lead to action. *Gail's brother egged her on to find a professional voice teacher.* (He encouraged Gail to pursue her musical gifts.)

eke out *v.* **1** To fill out or add a little to; increase a little. *Mr. Jones eked out a country teacher's small salary by hunting and trapping in the winter.* (Mr. Jones added a little to his small salary by hunting and trapping in the winter.) **2** To get (little) by hard work; to earn with difficulty. *Fred eked out a bare living by farming on a rocky hillside.* (With hard work he managed to earn a poor living trying to grow food on a rocky hillside.)

end in itself *n. phr.* Something wanted for its own sake; a purpose, aim, or goal one wants for itself alone, and not as a way to something else. *The miser never spent his gold, because for him it was an end in itself.* (The miser didn't want the gold so he could buy things with it; he wanted to keep the gold.)

end of one's rope *or* **end of one's tether** *n. phr., informal* The end of one's endurance; the last of one's ability, or ideas of how to do more. *Frank was out of work and broke, and he was at the end of his rope.* (Frank couldn't think what to do next.)

end up *v.* **1** To come to an end; be ended or finished; stop. *How does the story end up?* (Tell the end of the story.) **2** To finally reach or arrive; land. *I hope you don't end up in jail.* (I hope the things you do won't get you arrested.) **3** *informal* To die, be killed. *The gangster ended up in the electric chair.* (He was put to death.) **4** *or* **finish up.** To put an end to; finish; stop. *The politician finally ended up his speech.* (He finally finished his speech.)

end zone *n.* Either of the marked areas behind the goal line. *He caught a pass in the end zone for a touchdown.* (He caught the pass back of the goal line and inside the marked area, and it counted for a touchdown.)

every cloud has a silver lining Every trouble has something hopeful that one can see in it, like the bright edge around a dark cloud. *The doctor told Tommy to cheer up when he had measles. "Every cloud has a silver lining," he said.* (The doctor told Tommy that he would soon be better again.)

every dog has his day *also* **his day will come** *or* **he will get his comeuppance** Everyone will have his chance or turn; often negatively—everyone gets what he deserves (his just deserts). *Finally, Norris will be heavily fined for dumping his factory's wastes into the river. Every dog has his day.* (He broke the law, and the law will catch up with him.)

eye for an eye and a tooth for a tooth A blow or injury should be given back as hard as each one that is received; every crime or injury should be punished or paid back. *In ancient times if a man's eye was put out by his enemy, he might get revenge by putting his enemy's eye out. This was the rule of an eye for an eye and a tooth for a tooth.* (In old times it was common to punish crimes and enemies severely.)

eyes are bigger than one's stomach *informal* One wants more food than one can eat. *Annie took a second big helping of pudding, but her eyes were bigger than her stomach.* (Annie took a second big helping of pudding, but she couldn't eat it all.)

eyes in the back of one's head *n. phr., informal* Ability to know what happens when one's back is turned. *Mother must have eyes in the back of her head, because she always knows when I do something wrong.* (Even though Mother is not looking, she knows I've done something wrong.)

eyes pop out *informal* One is very much surprised.—Used with a possessive noun or pronoun. *Mary's eyes popped out when her mother entered her classroom.* (Mary was very surprised to see her mother come into the classroom.) *When Joan found a clock radio under the Christmas tree, her eyes popped out.* (She was very surprised.)

F

face down v. To confront boldly and win; defy. *The President faced down the heckler who interrupted his speech.* (The President opposed the man boldly until the man stopped interrupting him.)

face the music v. phr., informal To go through trouble or danger, especially because of something one did; accept one's punishment. *The boy was caught cheating in an examination and had to face the music.* (He could not escape being punished.)

face up to v. To accept (something hard or unpleasant). *The boy knew he should tell his neighbor that he broke the window, but he couldn't face up to it.* (He couldn't make himself do it.) *We must face up to our responsibilities and not try to get out of them.* (We must accept our responsibilities.)

face value n. **1** The worth or price printed on a stamp, bond, note, piece of paper money, etc. *The treasury bond had a face value of $10,000.* (The bond would be worth $10,000 at maturity.) **2** The seeming worth or truth of something. *She took his stories at face value and did not know he was joking.* (She believed his stories, but they were not true, only jokes.)

facts of life n. phr. **1** what one should know about sex, marriage, and birth. *His father told him the facts of life in answer to his questions.* (His father answered his questions about sex and marriage.) **2** The truths one learns about people and their good and bad habits of life, work, or play. *As a cub reporter he would learn the facts of life in the newspaper world.* (Beginning a job as a newspaper writer, he would learn how people work on a newspaper.)

fair game n. phr. A likely object of aggressive interest. *Politicians are fair game for the cartoonists.* (Politicians must expect to be the subjects of satire in cartoons.)

fair-haired boy n., informal A person that gets special favors; favorite; pet. *If he wins the election by a large majority, he will become his party's fair-haired boy.* (He will be the most favored member of his party if he wins the election by a large majority.)

fair play n. Equal and right action (to another person); justice. *The visiting team did not get fair play in the game.* (The home team were unsportsmanlike.) *The judges decided against Bob, but he said that he had gotten fair play.* (The judges decided against him, but he said they were honest and impartial.) *Sally's sense of fair play made her a favorite with her classmates.* (Sally's classmates liked her because she treated them fairly.)

fair sex n., informal Women, the female sex. *"Better not use that word in front of a member of the fair sex,"* Joe said. (He warns against using the word in front of women.)

fair shake n., informal Honest treatment. *Joe has always given me a fair shake.* (He has never cheated me; he has always treated me honestly.)

fair-weather friend n. A person who is a friend only when one is successful. *Everyone knows that John's only a fair-weather friend.* (Everyone knows that John is friendly only with people who are successful. He does not stay friendly if a person has bad luck.)

91

fall back v. To move back; go back.—Usually used with a group as subject. *The army fell back before their stubborn enemies.* (The army stopped fighting and went back.) *The crowd around the hurt boy fell back when someone shouted "Give him air!"* (The crowd moved back away from the boy.)

fall back on *or* **fall back upon** v. **1** To retreat to. *The enemy made a strong attack, and the soldiers fell back on the fort.* (The soldiers retreated to the fort.) **2** To go for help; turn to in time of need. *When the big bills for Mother's hospital care came, Father was glad he had money in the bank to fall back on.* (Father was glad he had money saved to use in a time of special need.)

fall behind v. To go slower than others and be far behind them. *When the campers took a hike in the woods, two boys fell behind and got lost.* (Two boys walked slowly and let the others get very far ahead of them; then they could not find the group.)

fall by the wayside *also* **drop by the wayside** v. phr. To give up or fail before the finish. *The boys tried to make a 50-mile hike, but most of them fell by the wayside.* (The boys tried to walk 50 miles, but most of them gave up before the finish.)

fall flat v., *informal* To be a failure; fail. *The party fell flat because of the rain.* (The party was a failure because of the rain.) *His joke fell flat because no one understood it.* (His joke failed because no one understood it.)

fall for v., *slang* (stress on *fall*) **1** To begin to like very much. *Dick fell for baseball when he was a little boy.* (He began to play baseball and liked it from the first.)

2 To begin to love (a boy or a girl). *Helen was a very pretty girl and people were not surprised that Bill fell for her.* (People were not surprised that he loved her.) **3** To believe (something told to fool you). *Nell did not fall for Joe's story about being a jet pilot.* (Nell did not believe he was a jet pilot.)

fall from grace v. phr. To go back to a bad way of behaving; to lose approval. *The boys behaved well during dinner until they fell from grace by eating their dessert with their fingers instead of their forks.* (The boys behaved well until they went back to their old bad manners by eating dessert with their fingers instead of their forks.) *The boy fell from grace when he lied.* (The boy lost approval when he lied.)

fall in v. (stress on *in*) To go and stand properly in a row like soldiers. *The captain told his men to fall in.* (He told them to stand right in line.)

falling-out n. Argument: disagreement; quarrel. *Mary and Jane had a falling-out about who owned the book.* (Mary and Jane had an argument about who owned the book.) *The boys had a falling-out when each said that the other had broken the rules.* (They disagreed about the rules, became angry with each other, and were not friends after that.)

fall in with v. **1** To meet by accident. *Mary fell in with some of her friends downtown.* (Mary met some of her friends by accident downtown.) **2** To agree to help with; support. *I fell in with Jack's plan to play a trick on his father.* (I agreed to help Jack with his plan.) **3** To become associated with a group detrimental to the newcomer. *John fell in with a wild bunch; small wonder he flunked* *all of his courses.* (He became associated with a harmful group.)

fall off the wagon *v. phr., slang, alcohol and drug culture* To return to the consumption of an addictive, such as alcohol or drugs, after a period of abstinence. *Poor Joe has fallen off the wagon again; he is completely incoherent today.* (Joe returned to drinking and is drunk again.)

fall on *or* **fall upon** *v.* **1** To go and fight with; attack. *The robbers fell on him from behind trees.* (The robbers hid and attacked him.) **2** *formal* To meet (troubles). *The famous poet fell upon unhappy days.* (The poet was famous at first but became poor and unhappy.)

fall out *v.* (stress on *out*) **1** To happen. *As it fell out, the Harpers were able to sell their old car.* (They did not know if they could sell the car, but at last they did sell it.) **2** To quarrel; fight; fuss; disagree. *The thieves fell out over the division of the loot.* (The thieves quarreled about dividing the stolen goods.) **3** To leave a military formation. *You men are dismissed. Fall out!* (You men may leave now.) **4** To leave a building to go and line up. *The soldiers fell out of the barracks for inspection.* (The men came out of the barracks to stand in line for inspection.)

fallout *n.* (stress on *fall*) **1** Result of nuclear explosion; harmful radioactive particles drifting with the winds. *Some experts consider fallout as dangerous as the bomb itself.* **2** Undesirable aftereffects in general. *As a fallout of Watergate, many people lost their faith in the government.* (They lost their faith as a result of Watergate.) *Well, there may be some positive fallout of the firings as well.* (Not

all the consequences are necessarily bad.) **3** *adj.* Something that could protect from fallout. *Many people think the way to survive World War III is to build a fallout shelter.* (They plan to construct a shelter that can keep out nuclear radiation.)

fall over backwards *or* **fall over oneself** *v. phr.* To do everything one can to please someone; try very hard to satisfy someone. *The hotel manager fell over backwards to give the movie star everything she wanted.* (The manager gave the movie star many services that ordinary people at the hotel would not get.) *The boys fell over themselves trying to get the new girl's attention.* (The boys tried very hard to make the new girl notice them.)

fall short *v.* To fail to reach (some aim); not succeed. *His jump fell three inches short of the world record.* (His jump was three inches less than the best in the world.) *The movie fell short of expectations.* (The movie was not as good as we thought it would be.)

fall through *v., informal* To fail; be ruined; not happen or be done. *Jim's plans to go to college fell through at the last moment.* (His plans did not succeed.) *Mr. Jones' deal to sell his house fell through.* (The deal was not completed.)

fall to *v.* (stress on *to*) **1** To begin to work. *The boys fell to and quickly cut the grass.* (They began to work and quickly cut the grass.) **2** To begin to fight. *They took out their swords and fell to.* (They took out their swords and began to fight.) **3** To begin to eat. *The hungry boys fell to before everyone sat down.* (The boys began to eat before everyone sat down.) **4** Begin; start. *The old* *friends met and fell to talking about their school days.* (They began to talk about things they did in school.)

far and wide *adv. phr.* Everywhere, in all directions. *The wind blew the papers far and wide.* (The wind blew the papers away in all directions.) *My old school friends are scattered far and wide now.* (My friends have moved far away from each other.) *The movie company looked far and wide for a boy to act the hero in the new movie.* (The movie people looked everywhere for a boy who could act the important part in the new movie.)

far cry *n.* Something very different. *His last statement was a far cry from his first story.* (He changed his first story and said something different.) *The first automobile could run, but it was a far cry from a modern car.* (It could run but it did not look like our cars now.)

farm out *v.* **1** To have another person do (something) for one; send away to be done. *Our teacher had too many test papers to read, so she farmed out half of them to a friend.* (The teacher gave half of the papers to a friend to read for her.) **2** To send away to be taken care of. *While Mother was sick, the children were farmed out to relatives.* (Father sent the children to relatives to be taken care of.) **3** To send a player to a league where the quality of play is lower. *The player was farmed out to Rochester to gain experience.* (The player was sent to Rochester to gain experience in a league where the competition is not so keen.)

far-out *adj., informal* Very different from others; eccentric; odd, unusual. *He enjoyed being with beatniks and other far-out people.* (He liked to be with unconventional people.) *Susan did not like some of the paintings at the art show, because they were too far-out for her.* (Susan did not like some of the pictures at the show because they were odd and did not look like anything real.)

fast buck *or* **quick buck** *slang* Money earned quickly and easily and sometimes dishonestly. *You can make a fast buck at the golf course by fishing balls out of the water trap.* (You can easily earn money at the golf course by finding golf balls in the pond.) *He isn't interested in a career; he's just looking for a quick buck.* (He is just looking for a way to get money without working hard.)

fast talker *n., slang, informal* A con artist or a swindler; one who is particularly apt to get away with illegitimate transactions because of the clever way he talks. *I wouldn't trust uncle Noam if I were you; he is a fast talker.* (I wouldn't trust him, because he is a swindler.)

fat chance *n. phr., slang* Little or no possibility; almost no chance. *A high school team would have a fat chance of beating a strong college team.* (I do not think the high school team would win.) *Jane is pretty and popular; you will have a fat chance of getting a date with her.* (She has many friends; I don't think she would go with you.)

fat of the land *n. phr.* The best and richest food, clothes, everything. *When I'm rich, I'll retire and live off the fat of the land.* (When I become rich, I'll stop working and have the best of everything.)

favorite son *n*. A candidate supported by his home state for President. *At a national convention, states often vote for their favorite sons first.* (They vote first for candidates from their own states to honor them.)

feather in one's cap *n. phr.* Something to be proud of; an honor. *It was a feather in his cap to win first prize.* (It was an honor for him to win first prize.) [From the medieval practice of placing a feather in the helmet of one who won honors in battle.]

feather one's nest *v. phr., informal* **1** To look after one's own interest, especially while holding public office or a job in which one is trusted to help other people. *The district attorney was supposed to return the money to the robbery victims, but instead feathered his nest with it.* (The district attorney kept the money for his own use.)

fed up *(informal)* ALSO *(slang)* **fed to the gills** *or* **fed to the teeth** *adj. phr.* Having had too much of something; at the end of one's patience; disgusted; bored; tired. *People get fed up with anyone who brags all the time.* (People become bored and disgusted with anyone who is always talking about how wonderful he is.)

feel out *v*. To talk or act carefully with someone and find what he thinks or can do. *The pupils felt out the principal about a party after the game.* (They talked with him to see if he would agree about a party.)

feel up *v. phr.; vulgar, avoidable* To arouse sexually by manual contact. *You mean to tell me that you have been going out with the guy for six months and he hasn't even felt you up?* (Are you

telling me that he didn't even try to arouse you with his hands?)

feel up to *v. phr., informal* To feel equipped to handle a certain task. *Do you feel up to jogging a mile a day?* (Do you think you're strong enough to do it?)

feet of clay *n. phr.* A hidden fault or weakness in an esteemed person. *The famous general showed he had feet of clay when he began to drink liquor.* (People thought the general was a fine man, but he began to drink liquor.) *The banker seemed to be honest, but he had feet of clay and was arrested for stealing.* (People found he was dishonest.)

feet on the ground *n. phr.* An understanding of what can be done; sensible ideas.—Used with a possessive. *John has his feet on the ground; he knows he cannot learn everything at once.* (He understands that it will take time to get an education.)

few and far between *adj. phr.* Not many; few and scattered; not often met or found; rare.—Used in the predicate. *People who will work as hard as Thomas A. Edison are few and far between.* (Not many people will work as hard as Thomas A. Edison.) *Places where you can get water are few and far between in the desert.* (There are very few places to find water in the desert.)

fifty-fifty[1] *adv., informal* Equally; evenly. *The two boys divided the marbles they won fifty-fifty.* (Each boy gave the other boy half the marbles he won.) *When Dick and Sam bought an old car, they divided the cost fifty-fifty.* (Each paid half the cost.)

fifty-fifty[2] *adj., informal* **1** Divided or shared equally. *It will be a fifty-fifty arrangement; half the*

money for me and half for you.
(The agreement is to divide the
money equally.) **2** Half for and
half against; half good and half
bad. *There is only a fifty-fifty
chance that we will win the game.*
(The chances of winning or losing
are the same.)

figure on *v.* **1** To expect and
think about while making plans.
*We did not figure on having so
many people at the picnic.* (We
did not think so many people
would come.) *He figured on going
to town the next day.* (He planned
to go to town the next day.) **2** To
depend on; be sure about. *You
can figure on him to be on time.*
(You can be sure he will be on
time.)

figure out *v.* **1** To find an answer by thinking about (some
problem or difficulty); solve. *Tom
couldn't figure out the last problem on the arithmetic test.* (Tom
could not find the answer; he did
not know how to work the problem.) *Sam couldn't figure out how
to print a program until the teacher
showed him how.* (Sam tried to
think of the things the teacher
would do to print a program, but
he could not.)

fill in *v.* **1** To write words
needed in blanks; put in; fill. *You
should fill in all the blanks on an
application for a job.* (You should
write your name, age, and other
things asked.) **2** *informal* To tell
what one should know. *The new
boy didn't know the rules, so Bob
filled him in.* (Bob told the new
boy what the rules were.)

fill one's shoes *v. phr.* To take
the place of another and do as
well; to substitute satisfactorily for.
*When Jack got hurt, the coach
had nobody to fill his shoes.* (Jack
was a fine player and nobody could

do as well.) *Joe hopes to fill his
father's shoes.* (Joe hopes to have
his father's job when he grows up
and to do the work as well.)

fill out *v.* **1** To put in what is
missing; to write down facts that
are asked for in (a report or application). *After Tom passed his
driving test, he filled out an application for his driver's license.* (He
wrote his name and other facts on
a form to get his driver's license.)
2 To become heavier and fatter;
gain weight. *The girl was pale
and thin after her sickness, but in
a few months she filled out.* (After
getting well and resting a few
months, she gained back her lost
weight.)

fill the bill *v. phr., informal* To
be just what is needed; be good
enough for something; be just
right. *The boss was worried about
hiring a deaf boy, but after he
tried Tom out for a few weeks, he
said that Tom filled the bill.* (He
found that Tom did good work.) *I
thought I would need a special
tool, but this wrench fills the bill.*
(This wrench seems to work in
place of a special tool.)

find out *v.* **1** To learn or discover (something one did not know
before). *One morning the baby
found out for the first time that
she could walk.* (She discovered
by trying that she could walk.) **2**
To get facts; to get facts about.
*He wrote to find out about a job
in Alaska.* (He wrote for information on a job in Alaska.) *She
found out how much the house
would cost.* (She got the facts on
how much the house would cost.)
3 To discover (someone) doing
wrong; catch. *Some children mis-
behave when no one is watching
them, but they are usually found
out.* (Some children behave badly

when no one is watching them, but their parents usually catch them or learn about it later.)

fine-tooth comb *n. phr.* Great care; careful attention so as not to miss anything. *The police searched the scene of the crime with a fine-tooth comb for clues.* (The police searched very carefully for clues.) *My room is so clean you couldn't find dirt if you went over it with a fine-tooth comb.* (You won't find any dirt in my room no matter how hard you look.)

finger in the pie *n. phr., informal* Something to do with what happens; part interest or responsibility. *When the girls got up a Christmas party, I felt sure Alice had a finger in the pie.* (I was sure Alice was one of the girls who planned the party.)

first come, first served *informal* If one arrives first, one will be served first; people will be waited on in the order they come; the person who comes first will have his turn first. *Get in line for your ice cream, boys. First come, first served.* (You will get ice cream in your turn in the line.)

first-run *adj. phr.* Shown for the first time; new. *The local theater showed only first-run movies.* (The local theater showed only new movies that had not been seen there before.)

fish for *v., informal* To try to get or to find out (something); by hinting or by a roundabout way to try to lead someone else to give or tell you what you want. *Jerry was always fishing for an invitation to Bob's house.* (He was always saying something to show he would like to be invited to Bob's house.) *Near examination time, some of the students fish for infor-*

mation. (They try to make the teacher give them a hint about what will be in the examination.)

fish out of water *n. phr.* A person who is out of his proper place in life; someone who does not fit in. *Because Ed could not swim, he felt like a fish out of water at the beach.* (Ed did not know how to swim and felt uncomfortable at the beach where everyone else was swimming.) *She was the only girl at the party not in a formal dress and she felt like a fish out of water.* (All the other girls were in formal dresses and she was embarrassed.)

fit as a fiddle *adj. phr.* In very good health. *The man was almost 90 years old but fit as a fiddle.* (He was almost 90 but in very good health.) *Mary rested at home for a few weeks after her operation; then she felt fit as a fiddle.* (She felt very well after her rest.)

fit like a glove *v. phr.* To fit perfectly. *Her new dress fits her like a glove.* (Her new dress fits perfectly.)

fit to be tied *adj. phr., informal* Very angry or upset. *She was fit to be tied when she saw the broken glass.* (She was very angry and upset at seeing the glass broken.)

fix someone's wagon *or* **fix someone's little red wagon** *v. phr., informal* **1** (Said to a child as a threat) to administer a spanking. *Stop that right away or I'll fix your (little red) wagon!* (Stop that or I'll spank you.) **2** (Said of an adult) to thwart or frustrate another, to engineer his failure. *If he sues me for slander, I will counter-sue him for malicious prosecution. That will fix his wagon!* (I will counter his moves to engineer his downfall.)

fix up someone with *v. phr., informal* To help another get a date with a woman or man by arranging a meeting for the two. *Say Joe, can you possibly fix me up with someone this weekend? I am so terribly lonesome!* (Can you possibly get me a date with a girl; I have no one to go out with.)

fizzle out *v., informal* **1** To stop burning; die out. *The fuse fizzled out before exploding the firecracker.* (The fuse didn't stay lit long enough to blow up the firecracker.) **2** To fail after a good start; end in failure. *The power mower worked fine for a while but then it fizzled out.* (The mower ran fine for a short time but then sputtered and stopped.) *The party fizzled out when everyone went home early.* (The party ended in failure when the people went home early.)

flare up *v.* (stress on *up*) **1** To burn brightly for a short time, especially after having died down. *The fire flared up again and then died.* (The fire burned brightly for a short time and then died.) **2** To become suddenly angry. *The mayor flared up at the reporter's remark.* (The mayor suddenly got angry at what the reporter said.) **3** To begin again suddenly. *Mr. Gray's arthritis flared up sometimes.* (He sometimes had attacks of arthritis.) *Even after they had conquered the country, revolts sometimes flared up.* (New fighting sometimes started suddenly.)

flare-up *n.* (stress on *flare*) A sudden worsening of a health condition or a war. *Mother's ulcers had a flare-up; she's back in the hospital.* (Her stomach condition suddenly worsened again.) *There was a flare-up of hostilities between Iran and Iraq.* (They started fighting again.)

flat-out *adv. phr., informal* Without hiding anything; plainly; openly. *The student told his teacher flat-out that he was not listening to her.* (The student told his teacher honestly that he was not listening to her.)

flea in one's ear *n. phr., informal* An idea or answer that is not welcome; an annoying or surprisingly sharp reply or hint. *I'll put a flea in his ear if he bothers me once more.* (I'll give him a sharp hint not to bother me if he comes to see me again.)

flea market *n. phr.* A place where antiques, secondhand things, and cheap articles are sold, especially in the open air. *The local antique dealers held a flea market and fair on the high-school athletic field.* (The local antique dealers set up an open-air market on the high-school field for the sale of antiques and other items.) *There are many outdoor flea markets in Europe.* (There are many places in Europe where cheap and used things are sold outdoors.)

flesh and blood *n.* **1** A close relative (as a father, daughter, brother); close relatives.—Used in the phrase *one's own flesh and blood. Such an answer from her—and she's my own flesh and blood, too!* (I am shocked at such an answer from a near relation.) **2** The appearance of being real or alive. *The author doesn't give his characters any flesh and blood.* (The characters in his book do not seem real.) **3** The human body. *Before child labor laws, small children often had to work 50 or 60 hours a week in factories. It was more than flesh and blood could bear.* (It was too hard for children, and many became sick or had their health ruined for life.)

flip one's lid *also* **flip one's wig** *slang* **1** To lose one's temper. *When that pushy salesman came back, Mom really flipped her lid.* (Mother grew very angry when the stubborn salesman came back.) **2** To lose one's mind; become insane. *When he offered me three times the pay I was getting, I thought he had flipped his lid.* (I thought he must be crazy when he offered me three times as much money.) **3** To become unreasonably enthusiastic. *She flipped her lid over a hat she saw in the store window.* (She just had to have that new hat.)

flip out *v. phr., slang, informal* To go insane; to go out of one's mind. *It is impossible to talk to Joe today—he must have flipped out.* (It is impossible to talk to him—he must have gone mad.)

flush it *v. phr., slang* **1** To fail (something). *I really flushed it in my math course.* (I failed my math course.) **2** *Interj., used imperatively* Expression registering refusal to believe something considered stupid or false. *You expect me to buy that story? Flush it!* (You expect me to believe that? Nonsense!)

fly by the seat of one's pants *v. phr., slang* **1** To fly an airplane by feel and instinct rather than with the help of the instruments. *Many pilots in World War I had to fly by the seat of their pants.* (Many pilots in World War I flew with few or no instruments, by touch or feeling.) **2** To do a job instinctively rather than by concrete information. *The architect was flying by the seat of his pants when he designed that house.* (The architect designed the house without reference to formal rules.)

flying high *adj., slang* Very happy; joyful. *Jack was flying high after his team won the game.* (He was very happy when his team won.)

fly in the ointment *n. phr., informal* An unpleasant part of a pleasant thing: something small that spoils one's fun. *We had a lot of fun at the beach; the only fly in the ointment was George's cutting his foot on a piece of glass.* (The only thing that spoiled our fun was the cut on George's foot.) *Your new job sounds too good to be true—interesting work, high pay, short hours. Isn't there any fly in the ointment?* (Isn't there something about the job that you don't like?)

fly off the handle *v. phr., informal* To become very angry. *John flew off the handle whenever Mary made a mistake.* (Every time Mary made a mistake, John became very angry.)

foam at the mouth *v. phr., slang* To be very angry, like a mad dog. *By the time Uncle Henry had the third flat tire, he was really foaming at the mouth.* (He was as angry as he could be when he had the third flat tire.)

follow in one's footsteps *also* **follow in one's tracks** *v. phr.* To follow someone's example; follow someone exactly. *He followed in his father's footsteps and became a doctor.* (He followed his father's example and became a doctor.)

follow suit *v. phr.* **1** To play a card of the same color and kind that another player has put down. *When diamonds were led, I had to follow suit.* (When a diamond card was put down, I had to play another diamond.) **2** To do as someone else has done; follow someone's example. *When the others went swimming, I followed suit.* (When the others went swimming, I went too.)

follow through *v. phr.* **1** To finish a movement that one has started; continue an action to its natural ending. *A football passer should follow through after he throws the ball.* (He shouldn't stop the motion of his arm after the ball has left his hand.) **2** To finish an action that one has started. *Bob drew plans for a table for his mother, but he did not follow through by making it.* (Bob made good plans but did not finish the job; he did not make the table.)

follow up (stress on *up*) *v. phr., informal* **1** Make (one action) more successful by doing something more. *After Mary sent a letter to apply for a job; she followed it up by going to talk to the personnel manager.* (She showed she was interested in the job by going to see the man who hired new workers for the company.) *The doctor followed up Billy's operation with x-rays and special exercises to make his foot stronger.* (The doctor kept caring for his foot until it was all right again.) **2a** To hunt for (more news about something that has already been in the newspapers, radio or TV news); find more about. *The day after news of the fire at Brown's store, the newspaper sent a reporter to follow up Mr. Brown's future plans.* (The newspaper sent a reporter to ask for more news.) **2b** To print or broadcast (more news about some happening that has been in the news before). *The fire story was printed Monday, and Tuesday's paper followed it*

up *by saying that Mr. Brown planned to build a bigger and better store at the same place.* (The newspaper told more about the fire story on Tuesday.)

follow-up (stress on *follow*) *n.* Additional work or research by means of which an earlier undertaking's chances of success will increase. *I hope you're willing to do a bit of follow-up.* (I hope you will continue to evaluate the success of your previous work.)

food for thought *n. phr.* Something to think about or worth thinking about; something that makes one think. *There is much food for thought in this book.* (The book is interesting and makes you think.)

fool around *or* **mess around** *or* **play around** *or* **monkey around** *v., informal* **1** To spend time playing, fooling, or joking instead of being serious or working; waste time. *If you go to college, you must work, not fool around.* (You must study seriously, not waste your time.) *The boys fooled around all afternoon in the park.* (They played lazily.) **2** To treat or handle carelessly. *Bob cut himself by fooling around with a sharp knife.* (Bob didn't handle the dangerous knife carefully.) *Mother says she wishes John would quit playing around with the girls and get married.* (She says he should be serious about one girl and marry her.) **3** *or* **fiddle around** To work or do something in an irregular or unplanned way; tinker. *Jimmy likes to monkey around with automobile engines.* (He likes to tinker and try out the engines and learn about them.) *Alice is fooling around with the piano in her spare time.* (She plays the piano sometimes, but not too seriously.)

foot in the door *n. phr., informal* The first step toward getting or doing something; a start toward success; opening. *Don't let Jane get her foot in the door by joining the club or soon she'll want to be president.* (If you give Jane a chance she'll want to run the club.)

for all *adv. phr.* **1** In spite of; even with.—Used for contrast. *For all his city ways, he is a country boy at heart.* (He has city ways, but he is still a country boy.) *There may be mistakes occasionally, but for all that, it is the best book on the subject.* (It is the best book on the subject, even though it has a few mistakes; it is best, anyhow.) *For all his money, he was very unhappy.* (He was sad, even though he was rich.)

for all one is worth *adv. phr.* With all one's strength; as hard as one can. *Roger ran for all he was worth to catch the bus.* (He ran as fast as he could to catch the bus.)

for all the world *adv. phr.* **1** For anything; for any price.— Used with a negative. *I would not change places with him for all the world.* (I wouldn't change places with him for anything.) **2** Just exactly. *When he came through that door he looked for all the world like his father when he was a boy.* (When he came through the door he looked exactly like his father when his father was a boy.)

for a song *adv. phr., informal* At a low price; for a bargain price; cheaply. *He sold the invention for a song and its buyers were the ones who got rich.* (He sold his invention for very little money and the people who bought it got rich.) *They bought the house for a song and sold it a few years later at a good profit.* (They bought the

house cheaply and sold it for a good profit.)

for better or worse *or* **for better or for worse** *adv. phr.* **1** With good or bad effect, depending on how one looks at the matter. *The historian did justice, for better or worse, to the careers of several famous men.* (He wrote the truth about the men, telling what they really were—good or bad.) **2** *adv. phr.* Under all conditions, in all eventualities. *(archaic) With this ring I thee wed, for richer or poorer, for better or for worse, till death do us part.* (I marry you with this ring no matter what may happen in the future.)

force one's hand *v. phr.* To make one do something or tell what one will do sooner than planned. *Ben did not want to tell where he was going, but his friend forced his hand.* (He did not want to tell where he was going, but his friend made him tell.) *Mr. Smith planned to keep his land until prices went up, but he had so many doctor bills that it forced his hand.* (He had to sell his land before he was ready, because he needed money.)

for crying out loud *interj., informal* —Used as an exclamation to show that one feels surprised or cross. *For crying out loud, look who's here!* (Well! I am surprised to see you.) *For crying out loud! That's the third time you've done it wrong.* (I am getting quite cross; that's the third time you've done it wrong.)

for dear life *adv. phr.* As though afraid of losing one's life. *He was running for dear life toward town.* (He was running toward town as if he thought his life was in danger.) *When the horse began to run, she held on for dear* *life.* (When the horse began to run, she held on as tightly as she could.)

forever and a day *adv. phr., informal* For a seemingly endless time; forever; always. *We waited forever and a day to find out who won the contest.* (We waited for what seemed like a very long time to find out who won.) *They promised to remain friends forever and a day.* (They promised to be friends always.)

for keeps *adv. phr.* **1** For the winner to keep. *They played marbles for keeps.* (The winner could keep the marbles.) **2** *informal* For always; forever. *He left town for keeps.* (He went away from town and stayed away.) **3** Seriously, not just for fun. *This is not a joke; it's for keeps.* (It is meant seriously, not as a joke.)—Often used in the phrase *play for keeps. The policeman knew that the robber was trying to shoot him. He was playing for keeps.* (The robber wasn't trying to scare him; he was trying to shoot him.)

fork over *or* **fork out** *also* **fork up** *v.* To pay; pay out. *He had to fork over fifty dollars to have the car repaired.* (He had to pay fifty dollars to have the car fixed.)

for love or money *adv. phr.* For anything; for any price.—Used in negative sentences. *I wouldn't give him my dog for love or money.* (I wouldn't give him my dog no matter what he offered.)

for sure *or* **for certain** *adv. phr.* **1** Without doubt; certainly; surely. *He couldn't tell for sure from a distance whether it was George or Tom.* (He was too far away to be sure if the person he saw was George or Tom.) *He didn't know for certain which bus to take.* (He was not sure which bus he should

get on.) *I know for certain that he has a car.* (Without doubt he has a car.) **2** *slang* Certain. *"That car is smashed so badly it's no good any more." "That's for sure!"* (It's certain that the smashed car will never be fixed again.)

for that matter *adv. phr.* With regard to that; about that. *I don't know, and for that matter, I don't care.* (I don't care about that either.) *Alice didn't come, and for that matter, she didn't even telephone.* (Alice didn't even telephone about not coming.)

for the asking *adv. phr.* By asking; by asking for it; on request. *John said I could borrow his bike any time. It was mine for the asking.* (All I had to do was to ask if I wanted to borrow it.) *Teacher said her advice was free for the asking.* (If the pupils wanted advice, they just had to ask.)

for the birds *adj. phr., slang* Not interesting; dull; silly, foolish; stupid. *I think history is for the birds.* (I think history is dull and boring.) *I saw that movie. It's for the birds.* (I saw the movie and I did not like it.)

for the life of one *adv., informal* No matter how hard one tries.—Used for emphasis with negative statements. *I can't for the life of me remember his name.* (I can't remember his name no matter how hard I try.)

foul up (stress on *up*) *v., informal* **1** To tangle up. *He tried to throw a lasso, but he got the rope all fouled up.* (He tried to throw a cowboy rope, but the rope got all tangled.) **2** To ruin or spoil by stupid mistakes; botch. *He fouled the whole play up by forgetting his part.* (He spoiled the whole play by forgetting his part.) **3** To make a mistake; to blunder. *Blue suit and brown socks! He had fouled up again.* (He had made a mistake in wearing brown socks with his blue suit.) **4** To go wrong. *Why do some people foul up and become criminals?* (Why do some people go wrong and become criminals?)

foul-up (stress on *foul*) *n.* **1** *informal* Mismanagement; confusion; mistake. *The luncheon was handled with only one or two foul-ups.* (There were very few mistakes in plans for the luncheon.) **2** *informal* A breakdown. *There was a foul-up in his car's steering mechanism.* (Something broke in the car's steering mechanism.) **3** *slang* A person who fouls up or mixes things up. *He had gotten a reputation as a foul-up.* (He had become known as a person who mixes things up.)

fraidy-cat *or* **fraid-cat** *or* **scaredy-cat** *or* **scared-cat** *n.*, *informal* A shy person; someone who is easily frightened.—Usually used by or to children. *Tom was a fraidy-cat and wouldn't go into the water.* (Tom was afraid to go into the water.)

freak *n., slang* **1** The opposite of a square; one likely (or known) to be a drug user; a highly individualistic critic or rebel. *Is Joe a square, establishment type?—Oh no, he's a freak.* (Oh no, he is a nonconformist.) **2** An enthusiast; a person who does or cultivates something to excess. *Ellen is a film freak.* (She avidly enjoys seeing films.)

freak-out (stress on *freak*) *n.*, *slang* An act of losing control; a situation that is bizarre or unusual. *The party last night was a regular freak-out.* (It was a bizarre experience.)

freak out (stress on *out*) *v. phr.*, *slang* To lose control over one's conscious self due to the influence of hallucinogenic drugs, or any sort of psychological shock. *Joe freaked out last night.* (He was out of his mind.)

free and easy *adj.* Not strict; relaxed or careless. *The teacher was free and easy with his students.* (The teacher was not strict.) *He had a free and easy way of acting that attracted many friends.* (He attracted many friends by his relaxed pleasant manner.) *They were free and easy with their money and it was soon gone.* (They soon used up all their money by spending it carelessly.)

free hand *n.* **1** Great freedom. *The teacher had a free hand in her classroom.* (The teacher had great freedom to conduct her classes.) **2** Abundance. *Bob put paint on the fence with a free hand.* (He put a large amount of paint on the fence.)

freeload *v.* To accept food and housing at someone else's expense. *When are you guys going to stop freeloading and do some work?* (When will you stop being a parasite and do some work?)

freeze out *v., informal* To force out or keep from a share in something by unfriendly or dishonest treatment. *The other boys froze John out of the club.* (The others were so unfriendly that John left the club.)

from hand to hand *adv. phr.* From one person to another and another. *The box of candy was passed from hand to hand.* (The candy was passed from one person to another.) *Jane brought her engagement ring, and it passed* *from hand to hand until all the girls had admired it.* (Each girl in turn looked at the ring and passed it on to another.)

from scratch   *adv. phr., informal*   With no help from anything done before; from the beginning; from nothing. *Dick built a radio from scratch.* (Dick bought the parts and put them together himself.) *In sewing class, Mary already knew how to sew a little, but Jane had to start from scratch.* (Jane had to learn sewing from the beginning.)

from the bottom of one's heart *or* **with all one's heart**   *adv. phr.*   With great feeling; sincerely. *John thanked his rescuer from the bottom of his heart.* (John very warmly thanked the man who had saved him.) *The people welcomed the returning soldiers from the bottom of their hearts.* (The people were sincerely happy to have the soldiers come back home.)

from the heart   *adv.*   Sincerely; honestly. *John always speaks from the heart.* (John always speaks sincerely.)

from time to time   *adv. phr.*   Not often; not regularly; sometimes; occasionally; at one time and then again at another time. *Even though the Smiths have moved, we still see them from time to time.* (We still see the Smiths sometimes.) *Mother tries new recipes from time to time, but the children never like them.* (The children don't like the new foods their mother occasionally cooks.)

from way back   *adv. or adj. phr., informal*   Since a long time ago; for a long time. *Mr. Jones said he knew my father from way back.* (Mr. Jones knew my father when he was young.)

fuck around   *v. phr., vulgar, avoidable*   **1** To be promiscuous. *John fucks around with the secretaries.* (He engages in sex with them.) **2** To play at something without purpose, to mess around. *He doesn't accomplish anything, because he fucks around so much.* (His purposeless waste of time is his downfall.)

fuck off   *v. phr., vulgar, avoidable*   **1** Go away! *Can't you see you're bothering me? Fuck off!* (Go away, said very rudely.) **2** To be lazy. *John said "I don't feel like working, so I'll fuck off today."* (He said he feels lazy.)

fuck up   *v. phr., vulgar, avoidable*   To make a mess of something or oneself. *Because he was totally unprepared, he fucked up his exam.* (He made a mess of it.) *He is so fucked up he doesn't know whether he is coming or going.* (His confusion is so great he has no idea what he is doing.)

fuddy-duddy   *n.*   A person whose ideas and habits are old-fashioned. *His students think Professor Jones is an old fuddy-duddy.* (His students think him old-fashioned, not modern in his ideas.)

full-fledged   *adj.*   Having everything that is needed to be something; complete. *A person needs three years of training to be a full-fledged nurse.* (The rules say that a person must have three years of training to be a regular nurse.) *The book was a full-fledged study of American history.* (The book was a complete study of American history.)

full of beans   *adj. phr., slang*   **1** Full of pep; feeling good; in high spirits. *The football team was full of beans after winning the tournament.* (After winning the last game, the students were very happy.) *The children were full of beans as they got ready for a picnic.* (The idea of going on a picnic put the children in high spirits.) **2** *also* **full of prunes** Being foolish and talking nonsense. *You are full of prunes; that man's not 120 years old.* (You are being foolish; he is not 120 years old.)

fun and games *n., slang, informal* **1** A party or other entertaining event. *There were fun and games after the office closed.* (The staff had a party after the office closed.) **2** Something trivially easy. *The crossword puzzle was just fun and games.* (It was easy.) **3** Petting, or sexual intercourse. *Those two are having fun and games.* (They are having an affair.) **4** (Ironically) An extraordi-

narily difficult task. *How was your math exam?—(With a dismayed expression):—Yeah, it was all fun and games, man.* (It was extraordinarily difficult.)

fun house *n.* A place in an amusement park where people see many funny things and have tricks played on them to make them laugh. *The boys and girls had a good time looking at themselves in mirrors in the fun house.* (The mirrors made them look thin, fat, or tall.)

funny bone *n.* **1** The place at the back of the elbow that tingles when hit. *He hit his funny bone on the arm of the chair.* (He banged his elbow.) **2** *or informal* **crazy bone** Sense of humor. *Her way of telling the story tickled his funny bone.* (He thought the way she told the story was funny.)

G

gain ground v. phr. 1 To go forward; move ahead. *The soldiers fought hard and began to gain ground.* (The soldiers began to move ahead; they began to seize land from the enemy.) 2 To become stronger; make progress; improve. *The sick man gained ground after being near death.* (The sick man became stronger after almost dying.) *Under Lincoln, the Republican party gained ground.* (The party became stronger by gaining more members and power.)

gang up on or gang up against v., informal To attack in a group; get together to do harm to. *The older boys ganged up on the boy who beat up a younger boy.* (The older boys together beat up the boy who was mean to a weaker boy.) *A group of people ganged up against the man who beat his dog.* (The people got together and stopped the man.)

garbage down v. phr., slang To eat eagerly and at great speed without much regard for manners or social convention. *The children garbaged down their food.* (They devoured their food in great haste.)

gas up v., informal To fill the gasoline tank. *The mechanics gassed up the planes for their long trip.* (The mechanics filled up the gasoline tanks of the planes for their long trip.) *The big truck stopped at the filling station and gassed up.* (The attendant at the filling station filled the tank with gas.)

gee whiz interj., informal Used as an exclamation to show surprise or other strong feeling. Rare in written English. *Gee whiz! I am late again.* (Oh! I am late again.)

generation gap n., informal The difference in social values, philosophies, and manners between children and their parents, teachers, and relatives that causes lack of understanding and confrontations. *My daughter is twenty and I am forty, but we have no generation gap in our family.* (We get along fine with each other.)

get across v. 1 To explain clearly, make (something) clear; to make clear the meaning of. *Mr. Brown is a good coach because he can get across the plays.* (He is a good coach because he makes the plays easy to understand.) 2 To become clear. *The teacher tried to explain the problem, but the explanation did not get across to the class.* (The teacher tried to explain the problem, but the explanation was not clearly understood by the class.)

get a fix or give a fix v. phr., slang, drug culture To provide (someone) with an injection of narcotics. *The neighborhood pusher gave Joe a fix.* (The local dealer in illegal narcotics supplied Joe with a shot of heroin or some other drug.)

get a fix on v. phr., informal Receive a reading of a distant object by electronic means, as by radar or sonar. *Can you get a fix on the submarine?* (Can you locate the submarine electronically?)

get after v., informal 1 To try or try again to make someone do what he is supposed to do. *Ann's mother gets after her to hang up her clothes.* (Ann's mother keeps trying to make her hang up her clothes.) 2 To scold or make an attack on. *Bob's mother got after him for tracking mud into the house.* (Bob's mother scolded him for tracking mud into the house.) *The police are getting after the crooks in the city.* (They are arresting or chasing them out.)

get ahead *v.* **1** *informal* To become successful. *Mr. Brown was a good lawyer and soon began to get ahead.* (Mr. Brown was a good lawyer and soon began to be successful.) *The person with a good education finds it easier to get ahead.* (A good education helps a person to become successful.) **2** To be able to save money; get out of debt. *In a few more years he will be able to get ahead of his debts.* (He will be earning more money than he spends.) *After Father pays all the doctor bills, maybe we can get a little ahead financially and buy a car.* (When we don't owe any more money, maybe we can buy a car.)

get a load of *v. phr., slang* **1** To take a good look at; see (something unusual or interesting.)—Often used to show surprise or admiration. *Get a load of that pretty girl!* (See how pretty that girl is!) *Get a load of Dick's new car!* (Look at that fine new car!) **2** To listen to carefully or with interest, especially exciting news.—Often used as a command. *Get a load of this: Alice got married yesterday!* (Listen to this. Alice got married!)

get along *also* **get on** **1** To go or move away; move on. *The policeman told the boys on the street corner to get along.* (He told them to get away from the corner.) **2** To go forward; make progress; advance. *John is getting along well in school. He is learning more every day.* (John is doing well.) **3** To advance; become old or late. *It is getting along towards sundown.* (It is getting dark.) *Grand-*

mother is 68 and getting along. (She looked quite old.) **4** To get or make what one needs; manage. *It isn't easy to get along in the jungle.* (It isn't easy to get what you need and stay alive.) *We can get along on $100 a week.* (We can live on it.) **5** To live or work together in a friendly way; agree, cooperate; not fight or argue. *We don't get along with the Jones family.* (We disagree with them.) *Jim and Jane get along fine together.* (They are friendly.) *Don't be hard to get along with.* (Don't be disagreeable.)

get a move on *informal or slang* **get a wiggle on** *v. phr.* To hurry up; get going.—Often used as a command. *Get a move on, or you will be late.* (Hurry up, or you will be late.)

get a rise out of *v. phr., slang* To have some fun with (a person) by making (him) angry; tease. *The boys get a rise out of Joe by teasing him about his girlfriend.* (The boys make Joe angry by teasing him about his girlfriend.)

get around *v.* **1a** *or* **get about** To go to different places; move about. *Mary's father really gets around: Monday he was in Washington; Wednesday he was in Chicago; and today he is in New York.* (Mary's father often travels from one place to another.) *Fred broke his leg, but he is able to get about on crutches.* (Fred is able to walk on crutches.) **1b** *or* **get about** To become widely known especially by being talked about. *Bad news gets around quickly.* (Bad news spreads fast.) **2a** *informal* To get by a trick or flattery what you want from (someone). *Mary knows how to get around her father.* (Mary knows how to talk or act to get what she wants from her father.) **2b** *informal* To find a way of not obeying or doing; escape from. *Some people try to get around the tax laws.* (Some people try to find ways of not paying their taxes.) *John did not weigh enough to join the Navy, but he got around that; he drank a lot of water before his physical examination.* (John found a way to get into the Navy, even though the rule said he didn't weigh enough.)

get around to *v.* To do (something) after putting it off; find time for. *Mr. Lee hopes to get around to washing his car next Saturday.* (Mr. Lee hopes to find time to wash his car next Saturday.)

get at *v.* **1** To reach an understanding of; find out the meaning. *This book is very hard to get at.* (It is hard to understand it.) **2** To do harm to. *The cat is on the chair trying to get at the canary.* (The cat is trying to reach him and eat him.) **3** To have a chance to do; attend to. *I hope I have time to get at my homework tonight.* (I hope I have time to take care of it.) **4** To mean; aim at; hint at. *What was Betty getting at when she said she knew our secret?* (What secret did she mean?) *What the teacher was getting at in this lesson was that it is important to speak correctly.* (What he was trying to explain was the importance of talking grammatically.)

get away *v.* **1** To get loose or get free; become free from being held or controlled; succeed in leaving; escape. *As Jim was trying the bat, it got away from him and hit Tom.* (The bat flew out of Jim's hands and hit Tom.) *Someone left the door open, and the puppy got away.* (The puppy escaped from the house.) *Mary tried to catch a butterfly, but it got away from her.*

(The butterfly succeeded in flying away free; it was not caught.) *The bank robbers used a stolen car to get away.* (The bank robbers used a stolen car to escape with the money.) *If Mr. Graham can get away from his store this afternoon, he will take Johnny fishing.* (If he isn't too busy at work, he will go fishing.) **2** To begin; start. *We got away early in the morning on the first day of our vacation.* (We started early.) *The race got away to a fast start.* (The racers started fast.)

get away with *v., informal* To do (something bad or wrong) without being caught or punished. *Some students get away with not doing their homework.* (They leave their work undone without being caught or punished.)

get away with murder *v. phr., informal* To do something very bad without being caught or punished. *John is scolded if he is late with his homework, but Robert gets away with murder.* (Robert is very late with his homework or doesn't do it at all, but he is not caught or punished.) *Mrs. Smith lets her children get away with murder.* (She doesn't punish them even when they are very bad.)

get a word in *or* **get a word in edgewise** *v. phr.* To find a chance to say something when others are talking. *The little boy listened to the older students and finally got in a word.* (The little boy found a chance to say something at last.) *Mary talked so much that Jack couldn't get a word in edgewise.* (He hardly had a chance to talk.)

get back at *v., informal* To do something bad to (someone who has done something bad to oneself); hurt in return. *John played* *a joke on Henry, and next day Henry got back at him.* (John played a joke on Henry, and then Henry did the same thing to John.)

get behind *v.* **1** To go too slowly; be late; do something too slowly. *The post office got behind in delivering Christmas mail.* (They are late because there is so much mail.) **2** *informal* To support; help. *A club is much better if members get behind their leaders.* (If members help their leaders as much as they can, the club is better.) *We got behind Mary to be class president.* (We gave her our support.) **3** *informal* To explain; find out the reason for. *The police are questioning many people to try and get behind the bank robbery.* (They are asking questions to find out who did it.)

get by *v.*, *informal* **1** To be able to go past; pass. *The cars moved to the curb so that the fire engine could get by.* (The cars moved to the side of the street so that the fire engine could pass.) **2** To satisfy the need or demand. *Mary can get by with her old coat this winter.* (She does not need a new coat.) *The janitor does just enough work to get by.* (He does only the work his employer demands and no more.) **3** Not to be caught and scolded or punished. *The soldier thought he could get by with his dirty rifle.* (He thought the officer would not see the dirt on his rifle and punish him.) *The boy got by without answering the teacher's question, because a visitor came in.* (The boy was not scolded for failing to answer the question.)

get cracking *v. phr.*, *slang*, *informal* To hurry up, to start moving fast. (Used mostly as an imperative). *Come on, you guys, let's get cracking!* (Let's hurry up!)

get —— down *v. phr.*, *informal* To make (someone) unhappy; cause low spirits; cause discouragement. *Low grades are getting Helen down.* (Low grades are causing Helen to be unhappy.) *Three straight losses got the team down.* (Three straight losses caused the team to be discouraged.)

get down to *v.*, *informal* To get started on. *Joe wasted a lot of time before he got down to work.* (He wasted a lot of time before he got started on his work.)

get down to brass tacks *also* **get down to cases** *v. phr.*, *informal* To begin the most important work or business; get started on the most important things to talk about or know. *The men talked about little things and then got down to brass tacks.* (They talked about little things and then talked about important business.) *A busy doctor wants his patients to get down to brass tacks.* (He wants his patients to tell him what is wrong with them instead of talking a long time about other things.)

get even *v.*, *informal* **1** *or be* **even** To owe nothing. *Mr. Johnson has a lot of debts, but in a few years he will be even.* (He owes a lot of money now, but in a few years he will be able to pay all he owes.) **2** To do something bad to pay someone back for something bad; get revenge; hurt back. *Jack is waiting to get even with Bill for tearing up his notebook.* (Jack is waiting to pay Bill back by doing something to hurt him.) *Last April first Mr. Harris got fooled by Joe, and this year he will get even.* (This year Mr. Harris will fool Joe.)

get going *v.*, *informal* **1** To excite; stir up and make angry. *The boys' teasing gets John going.*

(The teasing excites him and makes him angry.) **2** *or* **get cracking** To begin to move; get started. *The teacher told Walter to get going on his history lesson.* (The teacher told Walter to get started on the lesson.) *The foreman told the workmen to get cracking.* (He told them to start work.) *Let's get going. It's almost supper time.* (Let's go. Supper will be soon.)

get hold of *v.* **1** To get possession of. *Little children sometimes get hold of sharp knives and cut themselves.* (They find sharp knives and cut themselves.) **2** To find a person so one can speak with him. *Mr. Thompson spent several hours trying to get hold of his lawyer.* (Mr. Thompson spent several hours trying to find his lawyer so that he could talk with him.)

get it all together *v. phr., informal* **1** To be in full possession and control of one's mental faculties: have a clear purpose well pursued. *You've sure got it all together, haven't you?* (You certainly are a cool and levelheaded person who knows what he is doing.) **2** To retain one's self-composure under pressure. *A few minutes after the burglars left, he got it all together and called the police.* (He regained his self-composure and made the call.)

get lost *v. phr., slang* Go away!—Usually used as a command. *Get lost! I want to study.* (Go away; I want to study.) *John told Bert to get lost.* (John told Bert to go away.)

get off *v.* **1** To come down from or out of. *The bus stopped, the door opened, and Father got off.* (Father stepped out of the bus.) **2** To take off. *Joe's mother told him to get his wet clothes off.* (She told him to take off his wet clothes.) **3** To get away; leave. *Mr. Johnson goes fishing whenever he can get off from work.* (He goes fishing whenever he can get away from work.) *William got off early in the morning.* (He left early in the morning.) **4** To go free. *Mr. Andrews got off with a $25 fine when he was caught passing a stop sign.* (He was allowed to go free after paying a $25 fine.) **5** To make (something) go. *The half-back got off a long pass.* (He threw a long pass.) *John got a letter off to his grandmother.* (He sent a letter to his grandmother.) **6** To tell. *The governor got off several jokes at the beginning of his speech.* (He told several jokes first.) **7** To enjoy *slang* *We really get off on Chinese food.* (We really enjoy Chinese food.)

get off easy *v. phr., informal* To have only a little trouble; escape something worse. *The children who missed school to go to the fair got off easy.* (They were not punished much for missing school.) *John got off easy because it was the first time he had taken his father's car without permission.* (He was not punished much because he had never done that before.)

get off one's back *v. phr., slang, informal* To stop criticizing or nagging someone. *Get off my back! Can't you see how busy I am?* (Stop bothering, nagging, and criticizing me; don't you see how busy I am?)

get off one's tail *v. phr., slang* To get busy; to start working. *OK, you guys! Get off your tails and get cracking!* (All right, boys, let's get busy and do the job!)

get off on the wrong foot *v. phr.* To make a bad start; begin with a mistake. *Peggy got off on the* *wrong foot with her new teacher; she chewed gum in class and the teacher didn't like it.* (Peggy made a bad start with the teacher. She made the teacher angry by chewing gum.)

get off the ground *v. phr., informal* To make a successful beginning; get a good start; go ahead; make progress. *Our plans for a party didn't get off the ground, because no one could come.* (We couldn't even begin to make plans for the party, because no one could come.)

get on *or* **get onto** *v., informal* **1** To speak to (someone) roughly about something he did wrong; blame; scold. *Mrs. Thompson got on the girls for not keeping their rooms clean.* (Mrs. Thompson scolded the girls.) *The fans got on the new shortstop after he made several errors.* (The fans began to boo and yell insults at the new shortstop for making errors.) **2** To grow older. *Work seems harder these days; I am getting on, you know!* (I am getting older.)

get one's brains fried *v. phr., slang also informal* **1** To sit in the sun and sunbathe for an excessive length of time. *Newcomers to Hawaii should be warned not to sit in the sun too long—they'll get their brains fried.* (They'll get a sunstroke.) **2** To get high on drugs. *He can't make a coherent sentence anymore—he's got his brains fried.* (He is so high on drugs that he cannot talk coherently.)

get one's dander up *or* **get one's Irish up** *v. phr.* To become or make angry. *The boy got his dander up because he couldn't go to the store.* (He became angry because he couldn't go to the store.) *The children get the teacher's dander up when they make a lot*

of noise. (The children make the teacher angry.)

get one's feet wet *v. phr., informal* To begin; do something for the first time. Often used as a command. *The party was at Bill's house, and when Ruth and I got there, the party had already started. "Jump right in and don't be afraid to get your feet wet," said Bill.* (Join the other boys and girls in the party.) *"It's not hard to dance once you get your feet wet," said the teacher.* (It's not hard to dance after you've begun and stopped being bashful.)

get one's rear in gear *v. phr., slang* To hurry up; to get going. *I'm gonna have to get my rear in gear.* (I will have to hurry up.)

get one's teeth into *or* **sink one's teeth into** *v. phr., informal* To have something real or solid to think about; go to work on seriously; struggle with. *After dinner, John got his teeth into the algebra lesson.* (John went to work in earnest on his algebra.) *Frank chose a subject for his report that he could sink his teeth into.* (It was a hard subject to struggle with; it needed a lot of thought.)

get on one's nerves *v. phr.* To make one nervous. *John's noisy eating habits get on your nerves.* (His noisy eating habits make you nervous.) *Children get on their parents' nerves by being wakeful at night.* (Children make their parents nervous by being wakeful at night.)

get on the stick *v. phr., slang, informal* To get moving; to stop being idle and to start working vigorously. *All right, man, let's get on the stick!* (Let's get going, and do something worthwhile!)

get over *v.* **1** *or* **get over with** To finish. *Tom worked fast to get his lesson over.* (He worked fast to finish his lesson.) **2** To pass over. *It was hard to get over the muddy road.* (It was hard to travel over the muddy road.) **3** To get well from; recover from. *The man returned to work after he got over his illness.* **4** To accept or forget (a sorrow or surprise.) *It is hard to get over the death of a member of one's family.* (It is hard to forget one's sorrow when a member of the family dies.) *We could not get over the speed of Mary's recovery from pneumonia.* (We were surprised for a long time because Mary got well so fast.) **5** To communicate so as to be understood. *The teacher got over the idea of subtraction to the students.* (The teacher made them understand it.)

get set *v. phr.* To get ready to start. *The runners got set.* (They bent down ready to start.) *The seniors are getting set for the commencement.* (They are getting ready to be in the commencement program.)

get the ax *v. phr., slang* **1** To be fired from a job. *Poor Joe got the ax at the office yesterday.* (He was fired from his job.) **2** To be dismissed from school for improper conduct, such as cheating. *Joe got caught cheating on his final exam and he got the ax.* (He was dismissed from school.) **3** To have a quarrel that terminates a relationship. *Joe got the ax from Betsie—they won't see each other again.* (She told him that she doesn't want to see him anymore.)

get the ball rolling *or* **set the ball rolling** *or* **start the ball rolling** *informal* To start an activity or action; make a beginning; begin. *George started the ball rolling at the party by telling a new joke.* (George began the fun by telling a joke.)

get the better of *or* **get the best of** *v. phr.* To win over, beat; defeat. *Our team got the best of the visitors in the last quarter.* (Our team won in the last quarter.) *George got the better of Robert in a game of checkers.* (George beat Robert.) *When the opposing player fouled John, John let his anger get the better of his good sense and hit the boy back.* (John let his anger win out over his good sense.) *Dave wanted to study till midnight, but sleepiness got the best of him.* (Dave fell asleep.)

get the eye *v. phr., informal* **1** To be looked at, especially with interest and liking. *The pretty girl got the eye as she walked past the boys on the street corner.* (The boys looked at her because she was pretty.) **2** To be looked at or stared at, especially in a cold, unfriendly way. *When Mary asked if she could take home the coat and pay later, she got the eye from the clerk.* (The clerk did not know Mary, and gave her an unfriendly look when she asked to take the coat without paying.)

get the feel of *v. phr.* To become used to or learn about, especially by feeling or handling; get used to the experience or feeling of; get skill in. *John had never driven a big car, and it took a while for him to get the feel of it.* (It took him time to get used to driving and handling the big car.) *You'll get the feel of the job after you've been there a few weeks.* (You'll become experienced and more skillful after a few weeks.)

get the goods on *or* **have the goods on** *v. phr., slang* To find out true and, often, bad information about; discover what is wrong with; be able to prove the guilt of. *The police had the goods on the burglar before he came to* *trial.* (They could prove he was guilty before his trial.)

get the message *or* **get the word** *v. phr., slang* To understand clearly what is meant. *The principal talked to the students about being on time, and most of them got the message.* (Most of the students understood.) *Mary hinted to her boyfriend that she wanted to break up, but he didn't get the message.* (He didn't understand that Mary wanted to break up their romance.)

get the sack *v. phr., slang* **1** To be fired or dismissed from work. *John got the sack at the factory last week.* (He was dismissed from his job.) **2** To be told by one's lover that the relationship is over. *Joanna gave Sam the sack.* (She told him that she doesn't want to see him anymore.)

get the show on the road *v. phr., informal* To start a program; get work started. *It was several years before the rocket scientists got the show on the road.* (It was several years before they got the rocket program started.)

get the worst of *also* **have the worst of** *v. phr.* To lose; be defeated or beaten; suffer most. *Joe got the worst of the argument with Molly.* (Joe lost the argument.)—Often used in the phrase *the worst of it.* *If you start a fight with Jim, you may get the worst of it.* (You may be beaten.) *Bill had the worst of it in his race with Al.* (Bill lost the race.)

get through one's head *v. phr.* **1** To understand or believe. *Jack couldn't get it through his head that his father wouldn't let him go to camp if his grades didn't improve.* (Jack couldn't believe that his father wouldn't let him go if his grades weren't better.) *At last Mary got it through her head that*

she had failed to pass the test. (At last she understood that she had failed.) **2** To make someone understand or believe. *I'll get it through his head if it takes all night.* (I'll make him understand it.)

get through to *v.* To be understood by; make (someone) understand. *Deaf people sometimes find it hard to get through to strangers.* (Deaf people sometimes find it hard to make themselves understood by strangers.) *When the rich boy's father lost his money it took a long time for the idea to get through to the boy that he'd have to work and support himself.* (He couldn't understand or believe that he'd have to go to work.)

get to *v. phr., informal* **1** To begin by chance; begin to.—Used with a verbal noun or an infinitive. *George meant to save his half-dollar, but he got to thinking how good an ice-cream cone would taste, and he spent the money.* (George began to think about ice cream, and spent his half-dollar.) *On a rainy day, Sally got to looking around in the attic and found some old pictures of Father.* (Sally happened to look around in the attic and found some old pictures.) *I got to know Mary at the party.* (I began to know Mary.) *I was just getting to know John when he moved away.* (I was beginning to know John well.) **2** To have a chance to; be able to. *The Taylors wanted to go to the beach Saturday, but it rained and they didn't get to go.* (The Taylors could not go to the beach because it rained.) *Did you get to see the king?* (Did you succeed in seeing him?)

get to first base *or* **reach first base** *v. phr.* To make a good start; really begin; succeed.—

Usually in negative, interrogative, or conditional sentences. *Joe had a long paper to write for history class, but when the teacher asked for it, Joe hadn't got to first base yet.* (Joe had not begun writing the report.) *Suppose Sam falls in love with Betty. Can he even get to first base with her?* (Would Betty even give Sam a date?) *George wants to go to college and become a teacher, but I'll be surprised if he even reaches first base.* (I'll be surprised if he even gets into college.) *If you don't dress neatly, you won't get to first base when you look for a job.* (If you don't dress neatly, you won't even be considered.)

get together *v.* To come to an agreement; agree. *Mother says I should finish my arithmetic lesson, and Father says I should mow the lawn. Why don't you two get together?* (Why don't you agree on one thing you want me to do?)

get to the bottom of *v. phr.* To find out the real cause of. *The superintendent talked with several students to get to the bottom of the trouble.* (The superintendent talked with several students to find out the real cause of the trouble.) *The doctor made several tests to get to the bottom of the man's headaches.* (The doctor made several tests to find out the real cause of the man's headaches.)

get to the heart of *v. phr.* To find the most important facts about or the central meaning of; understand the most important thing about. *You can often get to the heart of someone's unhappiness by letting him talk.* (You can often learn the main thing making a person unhappy by letting him talk.) *"If you can find a topic sentence, often it will help you get to the heart of the paragraph,"* said the teacher. (The teacher said that the topic sentence will often give one the most important facts of the paragraph.)

get under one's skin *v. phr.* To bother; upset. *The students get under Mary's skin by talking about her freckles.* (They bother Mary by talking about her freckles.) *Children who talk too much in class get under the teacher's skin.* (Children who talk too much upset the teacher.)

get up *v.* 1 To get out of bed. *John's mother told him that it was time to get up.* (She told him that it was time to get out of bed.) 2 To stand up; get to one's feet. *Everyone got up for the salute to the flag.* (Everyone stood for the pledge of allegiance.) 3 To prepare; get ready. *Mary got up a picnic for her visitor.* (Mary planned a picnic for her visitor.) *The students got up a special number of the newspaper to celebrate the school's 50th birthday.* (The students issued a special edition of the newspaper when their school had its 50th birthday.) 4 To dress up. *One of the girls got herself up as a witch for the Halloween party.* (One of the girls dressed as a witch for the Halloween party.) 5 To go ahead. *The wagon driver shouted, "Get up!" to his horses.* (He told them to go ahead.)

getup (stress on *get*) *n.* Fancy dress or costume. *Some getup you're wearing!* (That's an unusual outfit you have on.)

get-up-and-go *n. phr., informal* Energetic enthusiasm; ambitious determination; pep; drive; push. *Joe has a lot of get-up-and-go and is working his way through school.* (Joe has a lot of ambition and works to pay his own way through school.)

get up on the wrong side of the bed v. phr., informal To awake with a bad temper. Henry got up on the wrong side of the bed and wouldn't eat breakfast. (He woke up in a bad mood and wouldn't eat breakfast.)

get up the nerve v. phr. To build up one's courage until one is brave enough; become brave enough. Jack got up the nerve to ask Ruth to dance with him. (He became brave enough to ask her to dance with him.) The hungry little boy got up nerve to ask for another piece of cake. (He built up enough courage to ask for another piece of cake.)

get what's coming to one or slang **get one's** v. phr. To receive the good or bad that one deserves; get what is due to one; get one's share. At the end of the movie the villain got what was coming to him and was put in jail. (He was put in jail as he deserved.) John didn't think he was getting what was coming to him, so he quit the job. (John didn't think he was being paid enough or treated right.) Mother told Mary that she'd get hers if she kept on being naughty. (Mary would be punished.)

get wind of v. phr. To get news of; hear rumors about; find out about. The police got wind of the plans to rob the bank. (The police in some way found out about the plans to rob the bank.) The captain didn't want the sailors to get wind of where the ship was going. (He didn't want the sailors to find out about where the ship was going.)

get wise v. phr., slang To learn about something kept secret from one; become alert. One girl pre-

tended to be sick on days when she had athletics, until the teacher got wise and made her go to gym anyway. (The teacher finally saw the girls' trick.) Often used with to. If you don't get wise to yourself and start studying, you will fail the course. (If you don't become alert to your laziness, you will fail.)

get with it v. phr., slang To pay attention; be alive or alert; get busy. The students get with it just before examinations. (The students become busy just before examinations.) The coach told the team to get with it. (The coach told the team to pay attention to him.)

ghost of a Least trace of; slightest resemblance to; even the smallest bit of; a very little.— Usually used with chance or idea in negative sentences, or with smile. There wasn't a ghost of a chance that Jack would win. (There was no chance he would win.) We didn't have the ghost of an idea where to look for John. (We had no idea where to look for John.) The teacher scolded Harold for drawing a funny picture on the chalkboard, but she had a ghost of a smile. (She couldn't help smiling a little.)

girl friend n., informal 1 A female friend or companion. Jane is spending the night at her girl friend's house. (Jane is staying at her friend's house.) 2 A boy's steady girl; the girl or woman partner in a love affair; sweetheart. John is taking his girl friend to the dance. (John is taking his steady girl to the dance.)

give a hard time v. phr., informal 1 To give trouble by what one does or says; complain. Jane gave her mother a hard time on the bus by fighting with her sister *and screaming.* (Jane was very troublesome for her mother.) *Don't give me a hard time, George. I'm doing my best on this job.* (Don't scold or criticize too much.) **2** To get in the way by teasing or playing; kid. *Don't give me a hard time, boys. I'm trying to study.* (Don't tease me or play while I'm studying.) *Bob is giving me a hard time because I beat him at checkers.* (Bob is kidding me because I won the checker game.)

give-and-take *n. phr.* **1** A sharing; giving and receiving back and forth between people; a giving up of part of what each one wants so both can agree. *Jimmy is too selfish. He has no notion of give-and-take with the other children but wants everything for himself.* (Jimmy won't give anything to others. He wants to keep everything.) *There has to be give-and-take between two countries before they can be friends.* (Each must be willing to give up something to the other.) **2** Friendly talking or argument back and forth. Friendly sharing of ideas that may not agree; also: an exchange of teasing remarks. *After the meeting there was a lot of give-and-take about plans for the dance.* (Some of us argued for one idea and some for another, but we all learned something from the others and no one became angry.) *Before the game there was a lot of give-and-take between supporters of the opposing teams.* (Supporters of the opposing teams shouted teasing and funny remarks at each other.) *Tom and Jerry were always arguing, but it was all in the friendly spirit of give-and-take.* (Tom and Jerry had

fun arguing with and kidding one another.)

give an ear to *or* **lend an ear to** *v. phr., literary* To listen to. *Children should give an ear to their parents' advice.* (Children should listen to their parents' advice.) *The king lent an ear to the complaints of his people.* (The king listened to his people.)

give ——— a piece of one's mind *v. phr., informal* To scold angrily; say what one really thinks to (someone). *Mr. Allen gave the other driver a piece of his mind.* (Mr. Allen spoke angrily to the other driver.) *The sergeant gave the soldier a piece of his mind for not cleaning his boots.* (The officer angrily scolded the soldier whose boots were dirty.)

giveaway (stress on *give*) *n.* **1** An open secret. *It was a dead giveaway who would be the new boss.* (It wasn't a real secret.) **2** A sale at which items are sold at prices much below their value. *The Smiths' garage sale was a big giveaway.* (They sold everything for a fraction of real worth.)

give away *v.* **1** To give as a present. *Mrs. Jones has several kittens to give away.* (She has several kittens to give away as presents.) **2** To hand over (a bride) to her husband at the wedding. *The custom of the father giving away the bride is changing.* (At some weddings it is not practiced.) **3** To let (a secret) become known; tell the secret of. *The little boy gave away his hiding place when he coughed.* (He let others know where he was hiding when he coughed.) *Mary said she didn't care anything about John, but her blushing face gave her away.* (Her blushing face showed she was not telling the truth; it showed her real feelings.)

give a wide berth *v. phr.* To keep away from; keep a safe distance from. *Mary gave the barking dog a wide berth.* (She kept a safe distance from the dog.) *Jack gave a wide berth to the fallen electric wires.* (He kept a safe distance from the fallen electric wires.) *After Tom got Bob into trouble, Bob gave Tom a wide berth.* (Bob stayed away from Tom.)

give chase *v. phr.* To chase or run after someone or something. *The dog saw a rabbit and gave chase.* (The dog ran after the rabbit.) *The policeman gave chase to the man who robbed the bank.* (The policeman ran after the man who robbed the bank.)

give ground *v. phr.* To go backward under attack; move back; retreat. *After fighting for a while the troops slowly began to give ground.* (The troops began to move backward.) *Although they were outnumbered by the enemy, the men refused to give ground.* (The men held their position firmly.)

give in *v.* To stop fighting or arguing and do as the other person wants; give someone his own way; stop opposing someone. *Mother kept inviting Mrs. Smith to stay for lunch, and finally she gave in.* (Finally Mrs. Smith agreed to stay for lunch.) *After Billy proved that he could ride a bicycle safely, his father gave in to him and bought him one.* (Billy's father did not want him to have a bicycle, but he let him have one after he showed that he was a good rider.)

give it to *v. phr., informal* **1** To give punishment to; beat. *The crowd yelled for the wrestler to*

give it to his opponent. (The crowd yelled for the wrestler to beat his opponent.) **2** To scold. *Jerry's mother gave it to him for coming home late.* (Jerry's mother scolded him for coming home late.)

give off *v.* To send out; let out; put forth. *Rotten eggs give off a bad smell.* (Rotten eggs send out a bad smell.) *Burning leaves give off thick smoke.* (Burning leaves let out thick smoke.)

give one an inch, and he will take a mile If one gives some people a little or yields anything, they will want more and more; some people are never satisfied. *I gave Billy a bite of candy and he wanted more and more. If you give him an inch, he'll take a mile.* (Billy is never satisfied. He always wants more.) *The counselor said to Jack, "No, I can't let you get a haircut until Saturday. It's against the rules, and if I give an inch, someone will take a mile."* (If the counselor made one rule weaker by breaking it, Jack and other boys might think the other rules could be broken.)

give one enough rope and he will hang himself *informal* Give a bad person enough time and freedom to do as he pleases, and he may make a bad mistake or get into trouble and be caught. *Johnny is always stealing and hasn't been caught. But give him enough rope and he'll hang himself.* (If he keeps on stealing he will be caught someday.)

give one's due *v. phr.* To be fair to (a person); give credit that (a person) deserves. *The boxer who lost gave the new champion his due.* (The boxer who lost was fair and gave credit to the man who beat him.) *We should give a* *good worker his due*. (We should be fair and praise a good worker.)

give oneself away *v. phr*. To show guilt; show one has done wrong. *The thief gave himself away by spending so much money*. (The thief showed he had done wrong by spending so much money.) *Carl played a joke on Bob and gave himself away by laughing*. (Carl played a joke on Bob and showed his guilt by laughing.)

give oneself up *v*. To stop hiding or running away; surrender. *The thief gave himself up to the police*. (He went to the police and surrendered.) *Mr. Thompson hit another car, and his wife told him to give himself up*. (Mr. Thompson's wife told him to go to the police and confess.)

give oneself up to *v. phr*. Not to hold oneself back from; let oneself enjoy. *Uncle Willie gave himself up to a life of wandering*. (He spent his life traveling.) *John came inside from the cold and gave himself up to the pleasure of being in a warm room*. (He enjoyed the warm room very much.)

give one's right arm *v. phr*. To give something of great value. *Mr. Thomas would give his right arm to be able to travel in Europe*. (He would give a great deal to be able to go to Europe.) *After it is too late, some people would give their right arm for a better education*. (After it is too late, some people would give a lot for a better education.)

give or take *v. phr*. To add or subtract.—Used with a round number or date to show it is approximate. *The house was built in 1900, give or take five years*. (The house was built around 1900, possibly five years earlier or later.)

give out *v*. **1** To make known; let it be known; publish. *Mary gave out that she and Bob were going to be married*. (She told people.) **2** To let escape; give. *The cowboy gave out a yell*. (He gave a shout.) **3** To give to people; distribute. *The barber gives out free lollipops to all the children*. (He gives away candy.) **4** To fail; collapse. *Tom's legs gave out and he couldn't run any farther*. (His legs were too tired to run anymore.) *The chair gave out under the fat man*. (The chair broke.) **5** To be finished or gone. *When the food at the party gave out, they bought more*. (After the food was all eaten they bought more.) **6** *slang* Not to hold back; act freely; let oneself go.—Often used in the imperative. *You're not working hard, Charley. Give out!* (Don't hold back or be lazy.) **7** *informal* To show how one feels. *When Jane saw the mouse, she gave out with a scream*. (She let people know that she was scared.) *Give out with a little smile*. (Give us a smile.)

give pause *v. phr*. To cause one to stop and think; make one doubt or worry. *The heavy monthly payments gave Mr. Smith pause in his plans to buy a new car*. (The heavy monthly payments caused Mr. Smith to stop and think about his plans to buy a new car.) *The bad weather gave Miss Carter pause about driving to New York City*. (The bad weather caused Miss Carter to stop and think about driving to New York City.)

give rein to *or* **give free rein to** *v. phr*. To allow to move or to do with freedom. *Some parents give rein to their children*. (Some parents let their children do what they want to do.) *The principal gives free rein to the students who* *are honor students.* (The principal lets honor students do things with more freedom than the others.) *Sitting alone in the house at night, Mary gave free rein to her imagination, and was soon badly frightened by every noise and shadow.* (Mary let her imagination work freely; she thought the house was full of things that would hurt her.)

give rise to *v. phr.* To be the reason for; cause. *A branch floating in the water gave rise to Columbus' hopes that land was near.* (A branch floating in the water made Columbus hope that land was near.) *John's black eye gave rise to rumors that he had been in a fight.* (John's black eye made people think he had been in a fight.)

give someone his rights or **read someone his rights** *v. phr., informal* **1** The act of advising arrested criminals that they have the right to remain silent and that everything they say can be held against them in a court of law; that they have the right to the presence of an attorney during questioning and that if they can't afford one and request it, an attorney will be appointed for them by the state. *The cops gave Smith his rights immediately after the arrest.* (The police advised Smith of his legal defenses.) **2** To sever a relationship by telling someone that he or she can go and see a divorce lawyer or the like. *Sue gave Mike his rights before she slammed the door in his face.* (Sue told Mike he could go to a lawyer if he wished to do so.)

give the ax *v. phr., informal* **1** Abruptly to finish a relationship. *She gave me the ax last night.* (Our romantic engagement came to an abrupt end.) **2** To fire an

employee in a curt manner. *His boss gave John the ax last Friday.* (He fired him curtly.)

give the benefit of the doubt *v. phr.* To believe (a person) is innocent rather than guilty when one is not sure. *The money was stolen and John was the only boy who had known where it was, but the teacher gave him the benefit of the doubt.* (The teacher believed John was innocent rather than guilty of stealing the money because it was not certain that he did.) *George's grade was higher than usual and he might have cheated, but his teacher gave him the benefit of the doubt.* (George's teacher had no proof he had cheated, so he did not doubt his grade.)

give the devil his due *v. phr.* To be fair, even to someone who is bad; tell the truth about a person even though one doesn't like him. *I don't like Mr. Jones, but to give the devil his due, I must admit that he is a good teacher.* (To be fair to Mr. Jones, he is a good teacher.)

give —— the eye *v. phr., slang* **1** To look at, especially with interest and liking. *A pretty girl went by and all the boys gave her the eye.* (They all looked, because she was pretty.) **2** To look or stare at, especially in a cold or unfriendly way. *Mrs. Jones didn't like Mary and didn't speak. She just gave her the eye when they met on the street.* (She stared at Mary in an unfriendly way.)

give the glad eye *v. phr., slang* To give (someone) a welcoming look, as if saying, "Come over here, I want to talk to you." *I was surprised when Joe gave me the glad eye.* (I was surprised by his looking at me so cordially.)

give the slip *v.* To escape from (someone); run away from unexpectedly; sneak away from. *An Indian was following, but Boone gave him the slip by running down a hill.* (Boone escaped the Indian by unexpectedly running down a hill.) *Some boys were waiting outside the school to beat up Jack, but he gave them the slip.* (Jack got out of the school and away, and the boys did not see him.)

give to understand *v. phr., informal* **1** To make a person think that something is true but not tell him; suggest; hint. *Mr. Johnson gave Billy to understand that he would pay him if he helped him clean the yard.* (Mr. Johnson did not say so, but Billy thought he meant it.) **2** To make a person understand by telling him very plainly or boldly. *Frank was given to understand in a short note from the boss that he was fired.* (He was told very clearly.)

give up *v.* **1a** To stop trying to keep; surrender; yield. *The dog had the ball in his mouth and wouldn't give it up.* (He wouldn't drop the ball from his mouth.) *Jimmy is giving up his job as a newsboy when he goes back to school.* (He won't keep the job when he goes back to school.) **1b** To allow; permit. *Ford gave up two walks in the first inning.* (Ford allowed two men to walk in the first inning.) **2** To stop doing or having; abandon; quit. *The doctor told Mr. Harris to give up smoking.* (He told him to stop smoking.) *Jane hated to give up her friends when she moved away.* (She didn't want to stop having them for friends.) **3** To stop hoping for, waiting for, or trying to do. *Johnny was given up by the doctors after the accident, but he lived just the same.* (He was hurt so badly that the doctors stopped believing he could live.) *When Mary didn't come by nine o'clock, we gave her up.* (We stopped waiting.) *I couldn't do the puzzle, so I gave it up.* (I quit trying.) **4** To stop trying; quit, surrender. *The war will be over when one of the countries gives up.* (When one country stops fighting the war will be finished.)

give up the ghost *v. phr.* To die; stop going. *After a long illness, the old woman gave up the ghost.* (After a long illness, the old woman died.) *The motor turned over a few times and gave up the ghost.* (The motor turned over a few times and stopped.)

give up the ship *v. phr.* To stop fighting and surrender; stop trying or hoping to do something.—Usually used in negative sentences. *"Don't give up the ship, John"* said his father when John failed a test.* (He told him not to quit trying because he failed one test.)

give voice *v. phr., formal* To tell what one feels or thinks, especially when one wants to object.—Used with *to. The students gave voice to their pleasure over the new building.* (The students spoke up about their pleasure over the new building.) *Little Willie gave voice to his pain by crying loudly when the dog bit him.* (He cried because he was hurt.)

give way *v.* **1** To go back; retreat. *The enemy army is giving way before the cannon fire.* (They are going back.) **2** To make room; get out of the way. *The children gave way and let their mother through the door.* (They stepped aside to make room for their mother to get through the door.) **3** To lose control of oneself; lose one's courage or hope; yield. *Mrs.*

Jones didn't give way during the flood, but she was very frightened. (She didn't become too upset.) **4** To collapse; fail. *The river was so high that the dam gave way.* (There was so much water that it broke the dam.) *Mary's legs gave way and she fainted.* (Her legs would not hold her up.) **5** To let oneself be persuaded; give permission. *Billy kept asking his mother if he could go to the movies, and she finally gave way.* (His mother finally let him go to the movies.)

glad hand *n., informal* A friendly handshake; a warm greeting. *Father went to the front door to give Uncle Fred the glad hand when he arrived.* (Father welcomed him by shaking hands and saying hello.) *The politician went down the street on election day giving everyone the glad hand.* (He shook hands with everyone, hoping people would vote for him.)

gloss over *v.* To try to make what is wrong or bad seem right or not important; try to make a thing look easy; pretend about; hide. *Billy broke a window and Mother tried to gloss it over by saying it wouldn't cost much to have it fixed, but Father spanked Billy anyway.* (Mother tried to make the broken window seem unimportant so that Father wouldn't spank Billy.) *John glossed over his mistake by saying that everybody did the same thing.* (He tried to make it seem not as bad as it was.)

go about *v.* **1** To be busy with; keep busy at or working on; start working on; do. *Bobby is going about his homework very seriously tonight.* (He is working hard at his homework.) *Just go about your business and don't keep*

looking out of the window. (Just keep on doing your work.) *How will you go about building the bird house?* (How will you start it?) **2a** To move from one place or person to another. *Some people go about telling untrue stories.* (They tell stories to one person after another wherever they are.) **2b** To go together.—Usually used with *with*. *Mother doesn't want me to go about with Jane and her friends anymore.* (She doesn't want me to go with them.)

go after *v.* To try to get. *"First find out what job you want and then go after it," said Jim's father.* (Try to get the job that you want.)

go ahead *v.* To begin to do something; not wait. *The teacher told the students not to write on the paper yet, but John went ahead and wrote his name.* (John did not wait until the teacher told him to write his name.) *"May I ask you a question?" "Go ahead."* (Ask the question.)

go along *v.* **1** To move along; continue. *Uncle Bill made up the story as he went along.* (He made up the story while he was telling it.) **2** To go together or as company; go for fun.—Often used with *with*. *Mary went along with us to Jane's house.* (Mary kept us company.) *John just went along for the ride to the ball game. He didn't want to play.* (He just went for fun or company.) *When one filling station cuts gasoline prices, the others usually go along.* (When one filling station cuts gasoline prices, the others usually follow.) **3** To agree; cooperate.—Often used with *with*. *"Jane is a nice girl." "I'll go along with that," said Bill.* (I agree that she is a nice girl.) *Just because the other boys do something bad, you don't* *have to go along with it.* (You don't have to do it too.)

go ape *v. phr., slang* To become highly excited or behave in a crazy way. *Amy went ape over the hotel and beautiful beaches.* (Amy was very excited and enthusiastic about the hotel and beaches.) *The electric door opener malfunctioned and caused the garage door to go ape.* (Something went wrong in the electric door opener, and the garage door went up and down crazily.)

go around *v.* **1a** To go from one place or person to another. *Mr. Smith is going around looking for work.* (He is going to different places looking for a job.) *Don't go around telling lies like that.* (Don't go to different people and tell such lies.) *Chicken pox is going around the neighborhood.* (Chicken pox is passing from one person to another.) *A rumor is going around school that we will get the afternoon off.* (Everyone says there will be no school this afternoon.) **1b** To go together; keep company.—Usually used with *with. Bill goes around with boys older than he is because he is big for his age.* (He has big boys for friends and is often with them.) **2** To be enough to give to everyone; be enough for all. *There are not enough desks to go around in the classroom.* (There are more children than there are desks.)

go at *v.* **1** To start to fight with; attack. *The dog and the cat are going at each other again.* (They are fighting.) **2** To make a beginning; approach; tackle. *How are you going to go at the job of fixing the roof?* (How are you going to begin to do it?)

go at it hammer and tongs *v. phr., informal* **1** To attack or fight with great strength or en-

ergy; have a bad argument. *Bill slapped George's face and now they're going at it hammer and tongs in back of the house.* (They are fighting as hard as they can.) *Helen and Mary have been arguing all day, and now they are going at it hammer and tongs again.* (They are having another argument.) **2** To start or do something with much strength, energy, or enthusiasm. *The farmer had to chop down a tree and he went at it hammer and tongs.* (He began to chop it down with a lot of energy.) *Charles had a lot of homework to do and he went at it hammer and tongs till bedtime.* (He studied hard and seriously.)

go back on *v. phr.* **1** To turn against; not be faithful or loyal to. *Many of the man's friends went back on him when he was sent to prison.* (Many of the man's friends turned against him when he was sent to prison.) *The boy's father told him not to go back on his promise.* (The boy's father told him not to break his promise or be unfaithful.) **2** To fail to do necessary work; not work. *Grandfather's eyes are going back on him.* (His eyes are getting poor.)

go broke *v. phr., slang* To lose all one's money; especially by taking a chance; owe more than one can pay. *The inventor went broke because nobody would buy his machine.* (The inventor owed more than he could pay because nobody would buy his machine.) *Dan had a quarter but he went broke matching pennies with Fred.* (He lost the money he had.)

go by the board *also* **pass by the board** *v. phr.* To go away or disappear forever; be forgotten or not used. *Tom had several chances to go to college, but he let them go by the board.* (Tom let the chances go by; he did not take them.) *Grandfather said he was too old to go to the beach. "Those days have passed by the board," he said.* (The days when he was young enough to go to the beach were over.)

go Dutch *v. phr., informal* To go out for fun together but have each person pay for himself. *Sometimes boys and girls go Dutch on dates.* (Sometimes boys and girls each pay their own expenses on dates.) *The girl knew her boyfriend had little money, so she offered to go Dutch.* (The girl knew her boyfriend had little money, so she offered to pay her way while he paid his.)

go for *v. phr., informal* **1** To try to get; aim for; try for. *Our team is going for the championship in the game tonight.* (They will try to win the championship.) *The dog went for Bob's leg.* (He aimed at Bob's leg to bite it.) **2** To favor; support; like. *Little Susie really goes for ice cream.* (Little Susie likes ice cream very much.)

go for broke *v. phr., slang* To risk everything on one big effort; use all one's energy and skill; try as hard as possible. *The racing car driver decided to go for broke in the biggest race of the year.* (The driver decided he would have to go as hard and as fast as he could with no thought for later if he wanted to win the big race.)

go-getter *n.* A person who works hard to become successful; an active, ambitious person who usually gets what he wants. *The governor of the stae has always been a go-getter.* (The governor of the state has always been a person who works hard and fast to become successful.) *The best salesmen are the go-getters.* (The

best salesmen are the persons who work hard.)

go-go *adj., slang, informal* **1** vigorous, youthful, unusually acitve. *Joe is a go-go kind of guy.* (He is extremely vigorous, and unusually active.) **2** Of a discotheque or the music or dances performed there

go haywire *v. phr., informal* Become inoperative, be damaged. Go out of order. *My electric typewriter has gone all haywire; I have to call the repair man.* (Something went wrong with the machine and it won't work properly.)

go in for *v. phr., informal* To try to do; take part in; take pleasure in. *Most girls do not go in for rough games.* (Most girls do not take part in rough games.) *Mrs. Henry goes in for simple meals.* (Mrs. Henry tries to cook simple meals.)

going through changes *v. phr., slang, informal* To be in trouble, to have difficulties; to be trapped in unfavorable circumstances. *What's the matter with Joe?—He's going through changes.* (He is caught up in unfavorable circumstances and has a hard time extricating himself from them.)

going for one *adj. phr.* Working to help; in one's favor. *The young woman will surely get the job; she has everything going for her.* (Everything is working to help her get the job.)

go into orbit *v. phr., slang* **1** To become very happy or successful. *Our team has gone into orbit.* (Our team has become successful.) **2** To lose one's temper or control completely; become very angry. *John was afraid his father would go into orbit when he found out about the car acci-*

dent. (John was afraid his father would go into a rage.)

go jump in the lake *v. phr., informal* To go away and quit being a bother. *George was tired of Tom's advice and told him to go jump in the lake.* (George was tired of Tom's advice and told him to go away and quit bothering him.)

goldfish bowl *n., slang, informal* **1** A situation in which it is not possible to keep things secret for any length of time. *Washington Society is a goldfish bowl.* (It is not possible to keep secrets in Washington Society.) **2** A place that provides no privacy for its occupant, e.g., an office that has too many windows. *Joe's office is a goldfish bowl, that's why we didn't kiss there.* (We didn't kiss there because anybody can see in from the street.)

gone with the wind *adj. phr.* Gone forever; past; vanished. *All the Indians who used to live here are gone with the wind.* (They are gone and won't come back.) *Joe knew that his chance to get an "A" was gone with the wind when he saw how hard the test was.* (He knew that he had no chance.)

good deal *or* **great deal** *n., informal* A large amount; much.—Used with *a. Mrs. Walker's long illness cost her a good deal.* (Mrs. Walker's long sickness cost her much money.) *George spends a great deal of his time watching television.* (George spends much of his time watching television.)—Often used like an adverb. *Cleaning up after the party took a great deal more work than the girls expected.* (Cleaning up took much more work than the girls thought it would take.)

good grief *interj., informal* Wow!, indication of surprise, good or bad. *"Good grief!" Joe*

cried out loud, *"Is this all I am getting for my work?"* (He exclaims in disbelief over how little he is getting.)

good riddance *n.* A loss that one is glad about. Often used as an exclamation, and in the sentence *good riddance to bad rubbish.* To show that one is glad that something or somebody has been taken or sent away. *The boys thought it was good riddance when the troublemaker was sent home.* (The boys were glad when the troublemaker was sent home.)

go off *v.* **1** To leave; to depart. *Helen's mother told her not to go off without telling her.* (Helen's mother told her not to leave without telling her.) **2a** To be ignited; exploded. *The firecracker went off and scared Jack's dog.* (The firecracker was exploded and scared Jack's dog.) **2b** To begin to ring or buzz. *The alarm clock went off at six o'clock and woke Father.* (The alarm clock began to buzz at six o'clock.) **3** To happen. *The party went off without any trouble.* (The party took place without any trouble.) *The parade went off without rain.* (The parade was held without rain.)

go off half-cocked *also* **go off at half cock** *v. phr., informal* To act or speak before getting ready; to do something too soon. *Bill often goes off half-cocked.* (Bill often acts or speaks before getting ready.) *Mr. Jones was thinking about quitting his job, but his wife told him not to go at half cock.* (Mr. Jones was thinking about quitting his job, but his wife told him not to quit before he had thought carefully about it and was ready.)

go off the deep end *or* **go overboard** *v. phr., informal* To act excitedly and without careful thinking. *John has gone off the deep end about owning a motorcycle.* (John has become excited about motorcycles and decided to buy one without first thinking about it carefully.) *Louise went overboard and bought an expensive home computer.* (She made a big investment without being sure of its usefulness.)

goof off *v., slang* To loaf or be lazy; not want to work or be serious; fool around. *Tom didn't get promoted because he goofed off all the time and never did his homework.* (Tom didn't want to work or be serious.)

go on *v.* **1a** To continue; not stop. *After he was hit by the ball, Billy quit pitching and went home, but the game went on.* (The game did not stop when Billy quit.) *The TV picture began to jump, and it went on like that until Father turned a knob.* (The picture did not stop jumping till Father turned a knob.) *I asked Jane a question but she went on reading and didn't answer.* (She didn't stop reading.) **2** To happen. *Mr. Scott heard the noise and went to see what was going on in the hall.* (Mr. Scott heard the noise and went to see what was happening in the hall.) **3** To talk for too long, often angrily. *We thought Jane would never finish going on about the amount of homework she had.* (We thought Jane would never stop complaining about her homework.) **4** To fit on; be able to be worn. *My little brother's coat wouldn't go on me. It was too small.* (I couldn't wear his coat.)

go ——— one better *v. phr., informal* To do something better than (someone else); do more or better than; beat. *Bill's mother gave the boys in Bill's club hot dogs for refreshments, so Tom's* mother *said that she would go her one better next time by giving them hot dogs and ice cream.* (Tom's mother said that she would do more than Bill's mother did.) *John made a good dive into the water, but Bob went him one better by diving in backwards.* John did well, but Bob beat him by doing something harder.)

go one's way *v. phr.* **1** To start again or continue to where one is going. *The postman left the mail and went his way.* (He left and continued his mail route.) **2** To go or act the way one wants to or usually does. *Joe just wants to go his way and mind his own business.* (He just does what he wants and doesn't want trouble.) *Don't tell me how to do my job. You go your way and I'll go mine.* (You do your job the way you want and I'll do my job the way I want.) *George was not a good sport; when the game did not go his way he became angry and quit.* (When the game did not go the way George wanted, George got angry and quit playing.)

go out of one's way *v. phr.* To make an extra effort; do more than usual. *Jane went out of her way to be nice to the new girl.* (Jane tried especially to be friendly to the new girl.)

go out the window *v. phr.* To go out of effect; be abandoned. *During the war, the school dress code went out the window.* (Conditions caused the rules about what students could wear to be forgotten or disregarded.)

go over *v.* **1** To examine; think about or look at carefully. *The teacher went over the list and picked John's name.* (He looked at the list in order to decide which name to pick.) *The police went over the gun for fingerprints.*

(They examined the gun closely to find fingerprints.) **2** To repeat; do again. *Don't make me go all over it again.* (Don't make me say it all again.) *We painted the house once, then we went over it again.* (We painted the house again.) **3** To read again; study. *After you finish the test, go over it again to look for mistakes.* (Read it again carefully.) *They went over their lessons together at night.* (They studied and read their lessons together at night.) **4** To cross; go to stop or visit; travel. *We went over to the other side of the street.* (We crossed the street.) *I'm going over to Mary's house.* (I'm going to visit Mary.) *We went over to the next town to the game.* (We traveled to the next town.) **5** To chage what one believes. *Father is a Democrat, but he says that he is going over to the Republicans in the next election.* (He will change from one political party to the other.) *Many of the natives on the island went over to Christianity after the white men came.* (They changed their religion.) **6** To be liked; succeed.—Often used in the informal phrase *go over big. Bill's joke went over big with the other boys and girls.* (They liked Bill's joke.) *Your idea went over well with the boss.* (The boss liked the idea.)

go over like a lead balloon *v. phr., informal* To fail to generate a positive response or enthusiasm; to meet with boredom or disapproval. *The president's suggested budget cuts went over like a lead balloon.* (His budget cut proposal was received with great displeasure.)

go steady *v. phr.* To go on dates with the same person all the time; date just one person. *At first Tom and Martha were not serious about each other, but now they are going steady.* (Now they go to all the dances and parties together; Tom does not date other girls and Martha does not date other boys.)

go straight *v. phr., slang* To become an honest person; lead an honest life. *After the man got out of prison, he went straight.* (After the man got out of prison, he led an honest life.) *Mr. Wright promised to go straight if the judge would let him go free.* (Mr. Wright promised to lead an honest life if the judge would let him go free.)

got a thing going *v. phr., slang, informal* To be engaged in a pleasurable or profitable activity with someone else as a partner either in romance or in mutually profitable business. *You two seem to've got a thing going, haven't you?* (You two are having an affair, aren't you?) *You've got a good thing going with your travel bureau; why quit now?* (You are successful with your travel bureau; don't give it up.)

go the whole hog *or* **go whole hog** *v. phr., informal* To do something completely or thoroughly; to give all one's strength or attention to something. *When Bob became interested in model airplanes, he went the whole hog.* (When Bob became interested in model airplanes, he gave them all his time.) *The family went whole hog at the fair, and spent a lot of money.* (The family saw and did everything at the fair.)

go through *v.* **1** To examine or think about carefully; search. *I went through the papers looking for Jane's letter.* (I looked at each paper to see if it was the letter.) *Mother went through the drawer looking for the sweater.* (She searched in the drawer.) **2** To experience; suffer; live through. *Frank went through many dangers during the war.* (He was in danger many times.) **3** To do what one is supposed to do; do what one promised. *I went through my part of the bargain, but you didn't go through your part.* (I did my part of the bargain.) **4** To go or continue to the end of; do or use all of. *Jack went through the magazine quickly.* (He read it quickly.) *We went through all our money at the circus.* (We used all of our money.) **5** To be allowed; pass; be agreed on. *I hope the new law we want goes through Congress.* (I hope that Congress passes the law.) *The sale of the store went through quickly.* (The sale was quickly agreed on.)

go through with *v. phr.* To finish; do as planned or agreed; not stop or fail to do. *Mr. Trent hopes the city won't go through with its plans to widen the street.* (Mr. Trent hopes the city won't widen the street.)

go to one's head *v. phr.* **1** To make one dizzy. *Beer and wine go to a person's head.* (Beer and wine make a person dizzy.) *Looking out the high window went to the woman's head.* (Looking out the high window made the woman dizzy.) **2** To make someone too proud; make a person think he is too important. *Being the star player went to John's head.* (Being the star player made John bigheaded.) *The girl's fame as a movie actress went to her head.* (The girl's fame as a movie actress made her big-headed.)

go to pieces *v. phr.* To become very nervous or sick from nervousness; become wild. *Mrs. Vance went to pieces when she heard her daughter was in the hospital.* (Mrs. Vance became very nervous when she heard her daughter was in the hospital.) *The man went to pieces when the judge said he would have to go to prison for life.* (The man became wild when the judge said he would have to go to prison for life.) *Mary goes to pieces when she can't have her own way.* (Mary becomes wild when she can't have her own way.)

go to pot *v. phr. informal* To be ruined; become bad; be destroyed. *Mr. Jones' health has gone to pot.* (Mr. Jones' health has become weak.) *The motel business went to pot when the new highway was built.* (The motel business began to lose money when the new highway was built.)

go to town *v. phr., slang* **1** To do something quickly or with great force or energy; work fast or hard. *The boys went to town on the old garage, and had it torn down before Father came home from work.* (The boys quickly tore down the old garage.) *While Sally was slowly washing the dishes, she remembered she had a date with Pete that evening; then she really went to town.* (Then Sally finished the dishes very quickly.) **2** *or* **go places.** To do a good job; succeed. *Our team is going to town this year. We have won all five games that we played.* (Our team is doing very well this year.) *Dan was a good student and a good athlete; we expect him to go places in business.* (We expect Dan to succeed in business.)

go up in smoke *or* **go up in flames** *v. phr.* To burn; be destroyed by fire. **1** *The house went up in flames.* (The house burned.) *The barn full of hay went up in smoke.* (The barn full of hay was destroyed by fire.) **2** Disappear; fail; not come true. *Jane's hopes of going to college went up in smoke when her father lost his job.* (Jane lost any chance to go to college.) *The team's chances to win went up in smoke when their captain was hurt.* (They lost their chance to win.)

go without saying *v. phr.* To be too plain to need talking about; not be necessary to say or mention. *It goes without saying that children should not be given knives to play with.* (It is clear that children should not be given knives to play with.) *A person with weak eyes should wear glasses. That goes without saying.* (It is not necessary to say that a person with weak eyes should wear glasses.)

grasp at straws *or* **clutch at straws** *v. phr.* To depend on something that is useless or unable to help in a time of trouble or danger; try something with little hope of succeeding. *To depend on one's memory without studying for a test is to grasp at straws.* (You can't depend on your memory alone; you must study.) *The robber clutched at straws to make excuses. He said he wasn't in the country when the robbery happened.* (He tried to lie and excuse himself even though everyone knew he was lying.)

grass is always greener on the other side of the fence *or* **grass is always greener on the other side of the hill** We are often not satisfied and want to be somewhere else; a place that is far away or different seems better than where we are. *John is always changing his job because the grass always looks greener to him on the other side of the fence.* (Other jobs always seem better to him than the one he has.)

gravy train *n., slang, informal* The kind of job that brings in a much higher income than the services rendered would warrant. *Jack's job at the Athletic Club as Social Director is a regular gravy train.* (He gets a high salary at the Athletic Club as Social Director and works little for it.)

grease one's palm *or* **grease the palm** *slang* **1** To pay a person for something done or given, especially dishonestly; bribe. *Some politicians will help you if you grease their palms.* (They will do what you ask if you bribe them.) **2** To give a tip; pay for a special favor or extra help. *We had to grease the palm of the waiter to get a table in the crowded restaurant.* (We had to pay him to find a table for us.)

greasy spoon *n., informal* Any small, inexpensive restaurant not noted for its excellence of cuisine or its decor. *I won't have time to eat lunch at the club today; I'll just grab a sandwich at the local greasy spoon.* (I'll just go to the little neighborhood restaurant around the corner where service is fast and cheap.)

great guns *adv. phr., informal* **1** Very fast or very hard.—Usually used in the phrase *go great guns. The wind was blowing great guns, and big waves beat the shore.* (The wind was blowing very hard.) *The men were going great guns to finish the job.* (The men were working very hard.) **2** Very well; successfully. *Smith's new store opened last week and it's going great guns.* (The new store has many customers.)

green thumb *n., informal* A talent for gardening; ability to make things grow. *Mr. Wilson's neighbors say his flowers grow because he has a green thumb.*

(The neighbors say flowers grow better for Mr. Wilson because he has a talent for gardening.)

green with envy *adj. phr.* Very jealous; full of envy. *Alice's girl friends were green with envy when they saw her new dress.* (Alice's classmates were very jealous when they saw her new dress.) *The other boys were green with envy when Joe bought a secondhand car.* (The other boys were full of envy when Joe bought a secondhand car.)

grind to a halt *v. phr., informal* To slow down and stop like a machine does when turned off. *The old car ground to a halt in front of the house.* (The old car slowed down and stopped in front of the house.) *The Cardinals' offense ground to a halt before the stubborn Steeler defense.* (The Cardinals' attack was unsuccessful against the Steeler defense.)

ground floor *n., informal* The first or best chance, especially in a business. *That man got rich because he got in on the ground floor of the television business.* (That man got rich because he was one of the first in the television business.)

gum up *v., slang* To cause not to work or ruin; spoil; make something go wrong.—Often used in the phrase *gum up the works*. *Jimmy has gummed up the typewriter.* (He has made the typewriter stop working or work wrong.) *Don't gum up the works by telling Mother what we are going to do.* (Don't spoil the plans.)

gun for *v., informal* **1** To hunt for with a gun; look hard for a chance to harm or defeat. *The cowboy is gunning for the man who stole his horse.* (The cowboy wanted to punish the man.) *Bob is gunning for me because I got a higher mark than he did.* (He is jealous and wants to hurt me.) **2** To try very hard to get. *The man is gunning for first prize in the golf tournament.* (The man is trying to get the first prize in the golf tournament.)

gung-ho *adj., informal* Enthusiastic, full of eagerness in an uncritical or unsophisticated manner. *Suzie is all gung-ho on equal rights for women.* (She is uncritically enthusiastic on equal rights for women.)

H

had better *or* **had best** *informal*
Should, must. *I had better leave now, or I'll be late.* (I must leave now, or I'll be late.) *If you want to stay out of trouble, you had best not make any mistakes.* (You must not make any mistakes.) *Jim decided he had better do his homework instead of playing ball.* (Jim decided that his homework was the best thing to do instead of other things.)

hair stand on end *informal*
The hair of one's head rises stiffly upwards as a sign or result of great fright or horror. *When he heard the strange cry, his hair stood on end.* (He was very much frightened.) *The sight of the dead man made his hair stand on end.* (Seeing the dead man horrified him and his hair rose.)

hale and hearty *adj. phr.* In very good health; well and strong. *Grandfather will be 80 years old tomorrow, but he is hale and hearty.* (Grandfather is in good health though he is quite old.) *That little boy looks hale and hearty, as if he is never sick.* (The little boy is strong and well.)

half-baked *adj., informal* Not thought out or studied thoroughly; not worth considering or accepting. *We wish Tom would not take our time at meetings to offer his half-baked ideas.* (His ideas are not good; he does not study them well.) *We cannot afford to put the government in the hands of people with half-baked plans.* (We should vote for leaders with reasonable ideas.)

half the battle *n. phr.* A large part of the work. *When you write an essay for class, making the outline is half the battle.* (When you finish the outline for your essay, you have done much of the work.) *To see your faults and decide to change is half the battle of self-improvement.* (Understanding and decision are a good beginning.)

hammer out *v.* **1** To write or produce by hard work. *The President sat at his desk till midnight hammering out his speech for the next day.* (He worked hard writing his speech.) **2** To remove, change, or work out by discussion and debate; debate and agree on (something). *Mrs. Brown and Mrs. Green have hammered out their difference of opinion.* (They have discussed the matter and have come to an agreement.) *The club members have hammered out an agreement between the two groups.* (They have discussed their differences and have come to an agreement.)

hand down *v.* To arrange to give or leave after death. *Joe will have his father's gold watch because it is handed down in the family.* (The watch passes to someone in the family and is never sold.) *In old times, property was usually handed down to the oldest son at his father's death.* (The oldest son was given all or almost all of the property.)

hand it to *v. phr., informal* To admit the excellence of; give credit or praise to. *You have to hand it to Jim; he is very careful and hardworking in all he does.* (Everyone must admit that Jim always does his work well.) *The teacher said, "I hand it to Jane for the way she managed the Music Club."* (Jane deserves praise for the fine way in which she led the Music Club.)

handle with gloves *or* **handle with kid gloves** *v. phr., informal* To treat very gently and

130

carefully. *Sally is such a baby that she cries if the teacher does not handle her with gloves.* (Sally cries if the teacher is not very gentle and careful with her.) *An atomic bomb is handled with kid gloves.* (It is handled very carefully.)

hand-me-down *n., informal* Something given away after another person has no more use for it; especially clothing. *Alice had four older sisters, so all her clothes were hand-me-downs.* (Alice's sisters gave her the clothes that they had outgrown.)

hand out *v., informal* (stress on *out*) To give (things of the same kind) to several people. *The teacher handed out the examination papers.* (The teacher gave each pupil an examination paper.) *At the Christmas party Santa Claus handed out the presents under the tree.* (Santa Claus gave each person one of the presents.) *Handing out free advice to all your friends will not make them like you.* (Your friends do not want you always telling them what to do.)

hand-out *n.* (stress on *hand*) **1** a gift, usually from the government. *The Smiths are so poor, they depend on government handouts.* (They must survive on gifts from the government.) **2** A sheet or more of paper containing the outline of a paper presented at a conference. *"Please look at Figure 5 on the hand-out"* Professor Higgins said. (He asks the audience to look at the drawing he gave them.)

hand over *v.* To give control or possession of; give (something) to another person. *When the teacher saw Johnny reading a comic book in the study period, she made him hand over the book.* (Johnny had to give the teacher the comic book.) *When Mr. Jones gets old, he will hand over his business to his son.* (It will be the son's turn to run the business so Mr. Jones will give it to him.)

hand over fist *adv. phr., informal* Fast and in large amounts. *Fred may get a pony for Christmas because his father is making money hand over fist.* (Fred's father is making a lot of money very fast.) *Business is so bad that the store on the corner is losing money hand over fist.* (The store is losing a lot of money fast.)

hands-down *adj., informal* **1** Easy. *The Rangers won a hands-down victory in the tournament.* (It was easy for the Rangers to win the tournament.) **2** Unopposed; first; clear. *Johnny was the hands-down favorite for president of the class.* (Everybody wanted Johnny for president of the class.)

hands down[2] *adv. informal* **1** Without working hard; easily. *The Rangers won the game hands down.* (They won easily.) **2** Without question or doubt; without any opposition; plainly. *Johnny was hands down the best player on the team.* (Johnny was clearly the best player.)

hands off[1] *informal* Keep hands off or do not interfere; leave that alone.—Used as a command. *I was going to touch the machine, but the man cried, "Hands off!" and I let it alone.* (The man warned me not to touch the machine, and I did not.)

hands-off[2] *adj., informal* Leaving alone, not interfering; inactive. *The United States told the European governments to follow a hands-off policy toward Latin America.* (The United States told European governments not to terfere in Latin America.) *I did not approve of his actions, but I have a hands-off rule in personal matters, so I said nothing.* (I do not believe in personal criticism, so I did not say anything.)

hand——to——on a silver platter *v. phr.* To give a person a reward that has not been earned. *The lazy student expected his diploma to be handed him on a silver platter.* (He thought he should get it without having to study.)

handwriting on the wall *n. phr.* A sign that something bad will happen.—Usually used with *see* or *read. When Bill's team lost four games in a row, he saw the handwriting on the wall.* (Bill could see that his team would have a very bad season.) *John's employer had less and less work for him; John could read the handwriting on the wall and looked for another job.* (John knew that he would soon be fired.)

hang around *v., informal* **1** To pass time or stay near without any real purpose or aim; loaf near or in. *The principal warned the students not to hang around the corner drugstore after school.* (He told them not to gather in or near the drugstore after school.) **2** To spend time or associate. *Jim hangs around with some boys who live in his neighborhood.* (Jim spends much of his time with some boys who live near him.)

hang back *or* **hang off** *or* **hang behind** **1** To stay some distance behind or away; be unwilling to move forward. *Mary offered the little girl candy, but she was shy and hung back.* (The little girl did not come forward and take the candy.) **2** To hesitate or be unwilling to do something. *Lou wanted Fred to join the club, but*

Fred hung off. (Fred hesitated to join the club.)

hang by a thread *or* **hang by a hair** *v. phr.* To depend on a very small thing; be in doubt. *For three days Tom was so sick that his life hung by a thread.* (It was hard to tell if he would live or die.) *As Joe got ready to kick a field goal, the result of the game hung by a hair.* (The field goal would win the game.)

hang in the balance *v. phr.* To have two equally possible results; to be in doubt; be uncertain. *Until Jim scored the winning touchdown, the outcome of the game hung in the balance.* (Either team might win.) *She was very sick and her life hung in the balance for several days.* (The doctor did not know if she would live or die.)

hang in (there) *v. phr., slang, informal* To persevere; not give up; to stick a project and not lose faith or courage. *Hang in there, old buddy; the worst is yet to come.* (Don't give up, old friend; harder times are yet ahead.)

hang it *interj., informal* An exclamation used to express annoyance or disappointment. *Oh, hang it! I forgot to bring the book I wanted to show you.* (I am annoyed because I forgot the book!) *Hang it all, why don't you watch where you're going?* (I am displeased by your carelessness in bumping into me.)

hang on *v.* **1** To hold on to something, usually tightly. *Jack almost fell off the cliff, but managed to hang on until help came.* (Jack held tightly to the cliff until help came.) **2a** To continue doing something; persist. *The grocer was losing money every day, but he hung on, hoping that business would improve.* (He continued to do business although things were very difficult.) **3** To continue to give trouble or cause suffering. *Lou's cold hung on from January to April.* (Lou's cold continued from January to April.) **4** To continue listening on the telephone. *Jerry asked John, who had called on the phone, to hang on while Jerry ran for a pencil and a sheet of paper.* (Jerry asked John to stay on the phone.)

hang one on *v. phr., slang* **1** To give a heavy blow to; hit hard. *The champion hung one on his challenger in the second round and knocked him out of the ring.* (The champion hit the other man very hard and knocked him out of the ring.) **2** To get very drunk. *After Smith lost his job, he went to a bar and hung one on.* (Smith went to an eating place where liquor is sold and got very drunk.)

hang on to *v.* To hold tightly; keep firmly. *The child hung on to its mother's apron, and would not let go.* (The child held its mother's apron firmly.) *John did not like his job, but decided to hang on to it until he found a better one.* (He decided to keep his job until he found a better one.)

hang out *v.* **1** *slang* To spend one's time idly or lounging about. *The teacher complained that Joe was hanging out in poolrooms instead of doing his homework.* (Joe was spending time idling in poolrooms.) **2** *slang* To live; reside. *Two policemen stopped the stranger and asked him where he hung out.* (They wanted to know where the stranger lived.) **3** To reach out farther than the part below. *The branches of the trees hung out over the road.* (The trunks of the trees were beside the road, but the branches went out over the road.) *The upper floor of that house hangs out above the*

first. (The second floor is wider than the first; its floor and wall go out farther than the wall of the first floor.)

hang out one's shingle *v. phr., informal* To give public notice of the opening of an office, especially a doctor's or lawyer's office, by putting up a small signboard. *The young doctor hung out his shingle and soon had a large practice.* (He put up a small sign to tell people he was a doctor.)

hang up *v.* (stress on *up*) **1** To place on a hook, peg, or hanger. *When the children come to school, they hang up their coats in the cloakroom.* (They put their coats on hooks in the cloakroom.) **2a** To place a telephone receiver back on its cradle and break the connection. *Carol's mother told her she had talked long enough on the phone and made her hang up.* (Her mother made her stop talking and put the receiver back in place.) **2b** To put a phone receiver back in place while the other person is still talking.—Used with *on*. *I said something that made Joe angry, and he hung up on me.* (Joe put the receiver back so I could not talk to him anymore.) **3** *informal* To set (a record.) *Bob hung up a school record for long distance swimming.* (Bob did better in long distance swimming than anyone else in that school had done.)

hang-up *n., informal* (stress on *hang*) **1** A delay in some process. *The mail had been late for several days; there must be some hang-up with the trucks somewhere.* (There has to be some trouble and/or some delay with the mail trucks.) **2** A neurotic reaction to some life situation, probably stemming from a traumatic shock that has gone unconscious. *Doc-*

tor Simpson believes that his patient's phobia is due to some hang-up about snakes. (He thinks the fear is due to a traumatic shock settled in the patient's unconscious.)

happy hour *n., informal* A time in bars or restaurants when cocktails are served at a reduced rate, usually one hour before they start serving dinner. *Happy hour is between 6 and 7 PM at Celestial Gardens.* (They serve cocktails at reduced rates between 6 and 7 PM.)

hard-and-fast *adj.* Not to be broken or changed; fixed; strict. *The teacher said that there was a hard-and-fast rule against smoking in the school.* (The rule could not be broken for any reason.)

hard as nails *adj. phr., informal* **1** Not flabby or soft; physically very fit; tough and strong. *After a summer of work in the country, Jack was hard as nails, without a pound of extra weight.* (Jack was strong and tough.) **2** Not gentle or mild; rough, stern. *Johnny works for a boss who is hard as nails and scolds Johnny roughly whenever he does something wrong.* (His boss is very rough and strict.)

hard feeling *n.* Angry or bitter feeling; enmity.—Usually used in the plural. *Jim asked Andy to shake hands with him, just to show that there were no hard feelings.* (Jim wanted Andy to show that he was not angry at Jim.) *Bob and George once quarreled over a girl, and there are still hard feelings between them.* (The boys are still not friendly to each other.)

hard-nosed *adj., slang* Tough or rugged; very strict; not weak or soft; stubborn, especially in a fight or contest. *Joe's father was a hard-nosed army officer who had seen service in two wars.* (Joe's father

was strict and tough.) *Pete is a good boy; he plays hard-nosed football.* (He is a rough and tough player.)

hard nut to crack *also* **tough nut to crack** *n. phr., informal* Something difficult to understand or to do. *Tom's algebra lesson was a hard nut to crack.* (Tom had trouble understanding his algebra lesson.)

hard-on *n. vulgar, avoidable.* (stress on *hard*) Erection of the male organ. *"Why are you in such a hurry to get me into bed?"* Sue cried. *"You don't even have a hard-on."* (She wonders why he is in such a rush when he doesn't even have an erection.)

hard put *or* **hard put to it** *adj* In a difficult position; faced with difficulty; barely able. *John was hard put to find a good excuse for his lateness in coming to school.* (John had trouble in thinking up a good excuse for coming late.) *The scouts found themselves hard put to it to find the way home.* (They had trouble finding the way home.)

hard sell *n., informal* A kind of salesmanship characterized by great vigor, aggressive persuasion, and great eagerness on the part of the person selling something; opposed to "soft sell." *Your hard sell turns off a lot of people; try the soft sell for a change, won't you?* (A lot of people resent your energetic persuasions and will not buy from you; if you try less hard, you might do better.)

hard up *adj., informal* Without enough money or some other needed thing. *Dick was hard up and asked Lou to lend him a dollar.* (Dick had no money or almost no money.) *The campers were hard up for water because their well had run dry.* (They had very little water or had to get it from a distance.)

harp on v. To mention again and again. *In his campaign speeches, Jones harps on his rival's great wealth and powerful friends.* (He continually draws attention to those things.)

hatchet man n., informal **1** A politician or newspaper columnist whose job is to write and say unfavorable things about the opposition. *Bill Lerner is the hatchet man for the Mayor's party; he smears all the other candidates regularly.* (It is Lerner's job to write derogatory pieces on members of the opposition.) **2** An executive officer in a firm whose job it is to fire superfluous personnel, cut back on the budget, etc., in short, to do the necessary but unpleasant things. *The firm hired Cranhart to be the hatchet man; his title is that of Executive Vice-President.* (Cranhart has to do the unpopular but necessary things for the firm.)

hate one's guts v. phr., slang To feel a very strong dislike for someone. *Dick said that he hated Fred's guts because Fred had been very mean to him.* (Dick said he hated Fred.)

have a ball v. phr., slang Enjoy oneself very much; have a wonderful time. *Johnny had a ball at camp.* (Johnny enjoyed himself at camp.) *Mary and Tom had a ball exploring the town.* (Mary and Tom had a wonderful time.)

have a fit or **have fits** or **throw a fit** v. phr. **1** To have sudden illness with stiffness or jerking of the body. *Our dog had a fit yesterday.* (He was suddenly sick and his body jerked about.) **2** informal To become angry or upset. *Father will throw a fit when he sees the dent in the car.* (Father

will be angry at us for damaging his car.) *Howard will have a fit when he learns that he lost the election.* (He will be upset.) *When John decided to drop out of college, his parents had fits.* (John's parents were very angry.)

have a go at v. phr., informal To try, especially after others have tried. *Bob asked Dick to let him have a go at shooting at the target with Dick's rifle.* (Bob asked Dick to let him try the gun.) *She had a go at archery, but did not do very well.* (She tried archery, at which she was not expert.)

have a hand in v. phr. To have a part in or influence over; to be partly responsible for. *Sue's schoolmates respect her and she has a hand in every important decision made by the student council.* (She has a leading part in decisions.) *Ben had a hand in getting ready the senior play.* (He did some of the work on it.)

have all one's buttons or **have all one's marbles** v. phr., slang To have all one's understanding; be reasonable.—Usually used in the negative or conditionally. *Mike acts sometimes as if he didn't have all his buttons.* (Mike acts at times in a strange or senseless way.) *He would not go to town barefooted if he had all his marbles.* (He acts queerly; he would not do so if his mind were clear.)

have an edge on v. phr., informal **1** To have an advantage (over someone). *I can't beat you at tennis, but I have an edge on you at ping-pong.* (When it comes to ping-pong, I am slightly better than you are.) **2** To be mildly intoxicated; to have had a few drinks. *Joe sure had an edge on when I saw him last night.* (He was slightly drunk when I saw him.)

have an eye for v. phr. To be able to judge correctly; have good taste in. *She has an eye for color and style in clothes.* (She can choose colors and styles correctly.) *He has an eye for good English usage.* (He can tell good English.)

have an eye on or **have one's eye on** v. phr., informal To look at or think about (something wanted); have a wish for; have as an aim. *I bought ice cream, but Jimmy had his eye on some candy.* (Jimmy wanted to buy candy.) *John has his eye on a scholarship so he can go to college.* (John would like to get a scholarship.)

have a screw loose v. phr., slang To act in a strange way; to be foolish. *Now I know he has a screw loose—he stole a police car this time.* (Now I know he is crazy; he stole a police car.) *He was a smart man but had a screw loose and people thought him odd.* (He was not crazy but somewhat peculiar.)

have a time v. phr., informal 1 To have trouble; have a hard time. *Poor Susan had a time trying to get the children to go to bed.* (Susan had trouble putting the children to bed.) *John had a time passing his math course.* (John had a hard time with math.) 2 To have a good time; to have fun.—Used with a reflexive pronoun. *Bob had himself a time going to every nightclub in town.* (John had a good time.)

have a way with v. phr. To be able to lead, persuade, or influence. *Dave has such a way with the campers that they do everything he tells them to do.* (Dave knows how to make the campers like and agree with him.) *Ted will be a good veterinarian, because*

he has a way with animals. (He is able to manage them and make friends with them.)

have been around v. phr., informal Have been to many places and done many things; know people; have experience and be able to take care of oneself. *Uncle Willie is an old sailor and has really been around.* (He knows the world and people.) *Betty likes to go out with Jerry, because he has been around.* (Jerry has a lot of experience and knows places to go and things to do that are fun.)

have dibs on or **put dibs on** v. phr., slang To demand a share of something or to be in line for the use of an object usable by more than one person. *Don't throw your magazine away! I put (my) dibs on it, remember?* (Don't put the magazine away; it is my turn to read it after you have finished with it.)

have eyes only for. v. phr. To see or want nothing else but; give all one's attention to; be interested only in. *Of all the horses in the show, John had eyes only for the big white one.* (The only horse that John cared about was the white one.) *All the girls liked Fred, but he had eyes only for Helen.* (Helen was the only girl Fred was interested in.)

have had it v. phr., slang To have experienced or suffered all one can; to have come to the end of one's patience or life. *"I've had it," said Lou, "I'm resigning from the job of chairman right now."* (Lou has been patient with the job as long as he can, and that is why he is resigning.) *When the doctor examined the man who had been shot, he said, "He's had it."* (The doctor thought the man would die.)

have it *v. phr.* **1** To hear or get news; understand. *I have it on the best authority that we will be paid for our work next week.* (I have the news from someone that I believe.) **2** To do something in a certain way. *Make up your mind because you can't have it both ways. You must either stay home or come with us.* (You can't do both things.) *Bobby must have it his way and play the game by his rules.* (He wants to play the way he understands the game, not the way anyone else does.) **3** To claim; say. *Rumor has it that the school burned down.* (There is a story that the school burned down.) *The man is very smart the way his family has it, but I think he's silly.* (His family says he's smart.) **4** To allow it—Usually used with *will* or *would* in negative sentences. *Mary wanted to give the party at her house, but her mother wouldn't have it.* (She wouldn't let Mary.) **5** To win. *When the senators vote, the ayes will have it.* (The senators who vote "Aye" or "Yes" will win.) **6** To get or find the answer; think of how to do something. *"I have it!" said John to Mary. "We can buy Mother a nice comb for her birthday."* (I have thought of the right present to buy for Mother.)

have it coming *v. phr.* To deserve the good or bad things that happen to one. *I feel sorry about Jack's failing that course, but he had it coming to him.* (Jack deserved to fail, because he did not study hard enough.) *Everybody said that Eve had it coming when she won the scholarship.* (They knew she had worked hard and deserved to win.)

have it in for *v. phr., informal* To wish or mean to harm; have a bitter feeling against. *George has it in for Bob because Bob told the teacher that George cheated in the examination.* (George hates Bob and wants to hurt him.) *After John beat Ted in a fight, Ted always had it in for John.* (After John beat Ted, Ted wanted to get even.)

have it made *v. phr., slang* To be sure of success; have everything one needs. *With her fine grades Alice has it made and can enter any college in the country.* (Alice is a very successful student and can get into the college of her choice.) *The other seniors think Joe has it made because his father owns a big factory.* (They think Joe's father will give him a good job.)

have it out *v. phr.* To settle a difference by a free discussion or by a fight. *Joe called Bob a bad name, so they went in back of the school and had it out. Joe got a bloody nose and Bob got a black eye.* (Joe insulted Bob, and they had a fight.) *The former friends finally decided to have it out in a free argument and they became friends again.* (They discussed their trouble and finished with it.)

have on *v.* **1** To be dressed in; wear. *Mary had on her new dress.* (Mary was wearing her new dress.) **2** To have (something) planned; have an appointment; plan to do. *Harry has a big weekend on.* (Harry has plans for a big weekend.) *I'm sorry I can't attend your party, but I have a meeting on for that night.* (I have a meeting to attend on that night.)

have one's ass in a sling *v. phr., slang, vulgar, avoidable* To be in an uncomfortable predicament; to be in the doghouse; to be at a disadvantage. *Al sure had his ass in a sling when the boss found out about his juggling the account.*

(He was in serious trouble when he was found to be an embezzler.)

have one's ears on v. phr., slang, citizen's band radio jargon To have one's CB radio in receiving condition. *Good buddy in the eighteen-wheeler — got your ears on?* (Hello there in the truck and trailer ; can you hear me?)

have one's hands full v. phr. To have as much work as you can do; be very busy. *He had his hands full and could not take another job for two weeks.* (He had as much work as he could do and so could not take any more jobs.) *With three small children to take care of, Susie's mother has her hands full.* (The care of three small children keeps Susie's mother busy.)

have rocks in one's head v. phr., informal To be stupid; not to have good judgment. *When Mr. James quit his good job with the coal company to begin teaching school, some people thought he had rocks in his head.* (They thought he showed bad judgment in giving up his good job.)

have something going for one v. phr., slang, informal To have talent, ability, or good looks; to have influence in important places, helping one to be successful. *Well now, Pat Jones, that's another story—she's got something going for her.* (Unlike others, Pat Jones has talent, intelligence, good looks, and influence in important places.)

have something on v. phr., informal To have information or proof that someone did something wrong. *Mr. Jones didn't want to run for office because he knew the opponents had something on him.* (Mr. Jones knew that his opponents could prove that he had done something wrong.) *Mr. Smith keeps paying black-mail to a man who has something on him.* (Mr. Smith pays a man not to tell what he knows about him.) *Although Miss Brown is not a good worker, her boss does not fire her because she has something on him.* (Miss Brown knows something about her boss which she might tell if he fires her.)

have something on the ball v. phr., slang, informal To be smart, clever; to be skilled and have the necessary know-how. *You can trust Syd; he's got a lot on the ball* or *he's got something on the ball.* (You can trust Syd because he knows what he's doing.)

have the last laugh or **get the last laugh** v. phr. To make someone seem foolish for having laughed at one. *Other schools laughed at us when our little team entered the state championship, but we had the last laugh when we won it.* (We got to laugh at them for being wrong about us.)

have to or **have got to** v., informal To be obliged or forced to; need to; must. *Do you have to go now?* (Is it really necessary for you to go now?) *He had to come.* (His parents made him.) (His parents forced him to come.) *I have got to go to the doctor.* (I need to go. It is necessary for me to go.) *I have to go to church.* (It is my duty to go.)

have to do with v. phr. **1** to be about; be on the subject of or connected with. *The book has to do with airplanes.* (The book is about airplanes.) **2** To know or be a friend of; work or have business with. —Usually used in negative sentence. *Tom said he didn't want to have anything to do with the new boy.* (Tom didn't want to know the boy or be his friend.) *I had nothing to do with the party; I was home last night.* (I wasn't at the party and wasn't connected with it in any way.)

have two strikes against one *or* **have two strikes on one** *v. phr., informal* To have things working against one; be hindered in several ways; be in a difficult situation; be unlikely to succeed. *Children from the poorest parts of the city often have two strikes against them before they enter school.* (Children from the poor neighborhoods often are not prepared for school work and do poorly.) *George has two strikes against him already. Everybody is against what he wants to do.* (He will have a hard time doing what he wants to do because everybody is against it.) [In baseball, three strikes are out. If the umpire calls two strikes against the batter, he has only one strike left and will be out if he gets one more strike.]

head above water *n. phr.* out of difficulty; clear of trouble. *How are your marks at school? Are you keeping your head above water?* (Are you getting passing grades?) *Business at the store is bad. They can't keep their heads above water.* (The store does not make enough money. They can't make a living from it.)

head-hunting *n., slang, informal* **1** A search for qualified individuals to fill certain positions. *The president sent a committee to the colleges and universities to do some head-hunting; we hope he finds some young talent.* (A committee was sent to recruit some young people for special jobs.) **2** Systematic destruction of opponents, especially in politics. *Billings was hired by the party to do some head-hunting among members of the opposition.* (He

was hired to destroy some prominent members of the opposition.)

head off *v.* **1** To get in front of and stop, turn back, or turn aside. *The sheriff said to head the cattle thieves off at the pass.* (The sheriff said to take the shortest way to the pass and catch the theives there.) **2** To block; stop; prevent. *He will get into trouble if someone doesn't head him off.* (If someone doesn't stop him before he does what he wants to do, he will be in trouble.)

head-on *adj. or adv. phr.* **1** With the head or front pointing at; with the front facing; front end to front end. *Our car skidded into a head-on crash with the truck.* (The front of the car hit the front of the truck.) *There is a head-on view of the parade from our house.* (Our house faces the front of the parade.) **2** In a way that is exactly opposite; against or opposed to in argument. *If you think a rule should be changed, a head-on attack against it is best.* (It is best to attack the rule by arguing the exact opposite.) *Tom did not want to argue head-on what the teacher said, so he said nothing.* (He didn't want to say the opposite of what the teacher said.)

head out *v.* **1** To go or point away. *The ship left port and headed out to sea.* (The ship sailed out towards the sea.) *The car was parked beside the house. It was headed out towards the street.* (The car faced towards the street.) **2** *informal* Leave, start out. *I have a long way to go before dark. I'm going to head out.* (I have a long way to go. I'm going to start now.)

head over heels *also* **heels over head** **1** In a somersault; upside down; head first. *It was so dark, Bob fell head over heels into a big* *hole in the ground.* (Bob fell head first into the hole.) **2** *informal* Completely; deeply. *He was head over heels in debt.* (He was very much in debt.) *She was head over heels in love.* (She was deeply in love.)

head shrinker *n., slang, informal* A psychiatrist; also called a *shrink. Forrester is falling apart; his family physician sent him to a head shrinker (to a shrink.)* (He was sent to a psychiatrist for treatment.)

head start *n.* **1** A beginning before someone; lead or advantage at the beginning. *The other racers knew they couldn't catch Don if he got too big a head start.* (They knew they couldn't catch him if they let him get too far ahead.) *Joe has a head start. He began to study earlier than we did.* (Joe is ahead of us. He has an advantage because he started to study earlier than we did.) **2** A good beginning. *Let's get a head start in painting the house by getting up early.* (If we get up early, we will be able to start sooner and get more done.) *The teacher gave the class a head start on the exercise by telling them the answers to the first two problems.* (The teacher gave them answers that put them ahead and helped them.)

head up *v., informal* **1** To be at the head or front of. *The elephants headed up the whole parade.* (The elephants walked in front of everyone else.) **2** To be the leader or boss of. *Mr. Jones will head up the new business.* (Mr. Jones will be in charge of the new business.) *The class planned a candy sale, and they elected Mary to head it up.* (They elected Mary to be chairman of the committee working on the candy sale.)

heap coals of fire on someone's head *v. phr., literary* To be kind or helpful to someone who has done wrong to you, so that he is ashamed. *Alice heaped coals of fire on Mary's head by inviting her to a party after Mary had gossiped about her.* (Mary gossiped about Alice, but Alice invited her to a party and made her ashamed.) *Jean Valjean stole the bishop's silver, but the bishop heaped coals of fire on Valjean's head by giving the silver to him.* (The bishop returned good for bad and shamed Jean.)

heart goes out to One feels very sorry for; one feels sympathy for.—Used with a possesive. *Frank's heart went out to the poor children playing in the slum street.* (He felt pity for them.) *Our hearts went out to the young mother whose child had died.* (We were sorry for her.)

heart is in the right place *or* **have one's heart in the right place** To be kindhearted, sympathetic, or well-meaning; have good intentions. *All the tramps and stray dogs in the neighborhood knew that Mrs. Brown's heart was in the right place.* (They knew that she was kind and friendly and would give them food.) *Tom looks very rough but his heart is in the right place.* (Tom means well and is good, even though he doesn't look it.)

heart of gold *n. phr.* A kind, generous, or forgiving nature. *John has a heart of gold. I never saw him angry at anyone.* (John is very kind to people. He never gets angry at them.) *Mrs. Brown is a rich woman with a heart of gold.* (She is rich, but she is not stingy. She is very generous with her money.)

heart of stone *n. phr.* A nature without pity. *Mr. Smith has a heart of stone. He whipped his horse until it fell down.* (Mr. Smith has no mercy or pity. He beat the horse so badly that it fell down.)

heart skip a beat *or* **heart miss a beat** 1 The heart leaves out or seems to leave out a beat; the heart beats hard or leaps from excitement or strong feeling. *When Paul saw the bear standing in front of him, his heart skipped a beat.* (When he saw the bear, his heart seemed to stop for a moment from fright.) 2 To be startled or excited from surprise, joy, or fright. *When Linda was told that she had won, her heart missed a beat.* (She was very surprised and happy that she had won.)

heart stand still *v. phr.* To be very frightened or worried. *Johnny's heart stood still when he saw his dog run into the street in front of a car.* (Johnny was very frightened.) *Everybody's heart stood still when the President announced that war was declared.* (Everybody was worried.)

heart-to-heart *adj.* Speaking freely and seriously about something private. *The father decided to have a heart-to-heart talk with his son about smoking.* (He decided to have an honest talk with him and ask him if it was true that he smoked.) *She waited until they were alone so she could have a heart-to-heart talk with him.* (She wanted to talk to him in private about something serious.)

heavy heart *n. phr.* A feeling of being weighed down with sorrow; unhappiness. *They had very heavy hearts as they went to the funeral.* (The felt very sad and unhappy as they went to the funeral.)

hedge about *or* **hedge in** *v. phr.* 1 To surround with a hedge or barrier; protect or separate by closing in. *The house is hedged about with bushes and trees.* (The house has bushes and trees all around it.) *The little garden is hedged in to keep the chickens out.* (The garden has bushes around it to keep out the chickens.) 2 To keep from getting out or moving freely; keep from acting freely; block in. *The boys are hedged in today. They can only play in the backyard.* (They are kept from going outside the backyard.) *The king said he could not make new laws if he was so hedged in by old ones.* (The king could not make new laws because old laws kept him from doing so. He was not free to make new laws.)

he laughs best who laughs last A person should go ahead with what he is doing and not worry when others laugh at him. When he succeeds he will enjoy laughing at them for being wrong more than they enjoyed laughing at him. *Everyone laughed at Mary when she was learning to ski. She kept falling down. Now she is the state champion. He laughs best who laughs last.* (Mary looked silly falling down all the time, but now she can enjoy being a champion skier when the people who laughed at her can't ski at all.)

hell and high water *n. phr.* Troubles or difficulties of any kind. *After John's father died he went through hell and high water, but he managed to keep the family together.* (John had lots of difficulties.)

hell-on-wheels *n., slang* A short-tempered, nagging, or crabby person, especially one who makes another unhappy by constantly criticizing him even when he has done nothing wrong. *Finnegan complains that his wife is hell on wheels; he is considering getting a divorce.* (He complains that she is unduly nagging and critical and he wants to divorce her.)

helter-skelter *adv.* **1** At a fast speed, but in confusion. *The batted ball broke Mr. Jones's window, and the boys ran away helter-skelter.* (The boys ran away in every direction.) *When the bell rang, the pupils ran helter-skelter out of the door.* (Each of the pupils tried to get out of the room first, and they all got in each other's way.) **2** In a confusing group; in disorder. *The movers piled the furniture helter-skelter in the living room of the new house.* (The movers piled the furniture all together in one mixed pile.)

he-man *n., informal* A man who is very strong, brave, and healthy. *Larry was a real he-man when he returned from service with the Marines.* (Larry was strong, brave, and healthy when he came home from the service.)

hem and haw *v. phr.* **1** To pause or hesitate while speaking, often with little throat noises. *The man was a poor lecturer because he hemmed and hawed too much.* (He paused and made little noises.) **2** To avoid giving a clear answer; be evasive in speech. *The principal asked Bob why he was late to school, and Bob only hemmed and hawed.* (Bob didn't have a good reason and he said only a few words, avoiding a clear answer.)

here goes *interj., informal* I am ready to begin; I am now ready and willing to take the chance; I am hoping for the best.—Said especially before beginning something that takes skill, luck, or courage. *"Here goes!" said* Charley, *as he jumped of the high diving board.* (I am jumping and I hope nothing goes wrong.) *"Here goes!" said Mary as she started the test.* (I hope I'm lucky and know the answers.)

here goes nothing *interj., informal* I am ready to begin, but this will be a waste of time; this will not be anything great; this will probably fail.—Used especially before beginning something that takes skill, luck or courage. *"Here goes nothing," said Bill at the beginning of the race.* (I don't think I'll win but wish me luck anyway.)

hide one's head in the sand *or* **bury one's head in the sand** *or* **have one's head in the sand** To keep from seeing, knowing, or understanding something dangerous or unpleasant; to refuse to see or face something. *If there is a war, you cannot just bury your head in the sand.* (If there is war, you can't act as if there were not, as if nothing had happened.) [Some people think that the ostrich buries its head in the sand when danger comes, believing that it will not be seen and harmed.]

hide one's light under a bushel *v. phr.* To be very shy and modest and not show one's abilities or talents; be too modest in letting others see what one can do. *When Joan is with her close friends she has a wonderful sense of humor, but usually she hides her light under a bushel.* (When Joan is with people that she doesn't know, she is too shy to show her sense of humor.) *Mr. Smith is an expert in many fields, but most people think he is not very smart, because he hides his light under a bushel.* (Mr. Smith is too modest to show how much he knows.)

high and dry *adv. or adj. phr.*
1 Up above the water; beyond the
reach of splashing or waves. *Mary
was afraid she had left her towel
where the tide would reach it, but
she found it high and dry.* (Mary
found her towel higher up the
beach than the tide reached.) *When
the tide went out the boat was
high and dry.* (The boat was left
out of the water and lying on the
beach.) **2** Without anyone to help;
alone and with no help. *When the
time came to put up the decorations, Mary was left high and dry.*
(Mary was left to do the work all
by herself.) *At first the other boys
helped, but when the work got
hard, Bob found himself high and
dry.* (The other boys left, and Bob
had to do the hard work without
any help.)

high-and-mighty *adj., informal*
Feeling more important or superior to someone else; too proud of
oneself. *John wasn't invited to
the party, because he acted too
high-and-mighty.* (John wasn't
invited because the other children
did not like his snobbery.) *Mary
became high-and-mighty when she
won the prize, and Joan would
not go around with her any more.*
(Mary's new pride lost her Joan's
friendship.)

high gear *n. phr., informal* Top
speed; full activity. *Production
went into high gear after the vacation.* (The factory began to work
at full speed after the vacation.)
*An advertising campaign for the
new toothpaste promptly moved
into high gear.* (Advertising for
the new toothpaste showed up in
all the media.)

high-handed *adj.* Depending
on force rather than right; bossy;
dictatorial. *With high-handed
daring, John helped himself to the
best food on the table.* (John took

the best there was simply because
he was big and strong and no one
dared stop him.) *Mr. Smith was a
high-handed tyrant in his office.*
(Mr. Smith managed his office as
he pleased without considering the
feelings or wishes of others.)

high seas *n. phr.* The open
ocean, not the waters near the
coast. *It was a big powerful liner
built to sail on the high seas.* (It
was a ship built to sail the open
ocean.) *The ships of every country have the right to sail on the
high seas.* (All ships have the right
to sail freely on the ocean far from
shore.)

high time *n.* A time before
which something should already
have been done.—Usually used
after *it is. Now that November has
arrived, it's high time we put the
snow tires on the car.* (We could
already be caught unprepared in a
snowstorm.)

highway robbery *n. phr.* **1** A
holdup or theft committed on an
open road usually by an armed
person. *Highway robbery was
common in England in Shakespeare's day.* (People were often
robbed on the roads of England in
Shakespeare's day.) **2** An extremely high price or charge; a
profiteer's excessive charge. *To
someone from a small town, the
prices of meals and theater tickets
in New York often seem to be
highway robbery.* (The prices
seem very high.)

hire out *v., informal* **1** To accept a job; take employment.
*Frank hired out as a saxophonist
with a dance band.* (Frank got a
job as a saxophonist with a dance
band.) **2** To rent (as owner). *John
used to hire out his tractor sometimes when he didn't need it himself.* (John used to rent his tractor

to people sometimes when he didn't need it.)

hit-and-run *adj.* **1** Of or about an accident after which the responsible motorist drives away without giving his name and offering help. *Judges are stern with hit-and-run drivers.* (Judges are stern with drivers who leave the scene of an accident without giving their names.) **2** Striking suddenly and leaving quickly. *The Indians often made hit-and-run attacks on wagon trains.* (They attacked wagon trains and then quickly rode away.)

hit and run *n.* A play in baseball in which a runner on base starts to run as the ball is pitched and the batter must try to hit the ball. *As the pitcher started to pitch to the batter, Jack ran toward second base as if he were going to steal the base, but the batter hit the ball, so Jack scored from first base on the hit and run.* (Jack began to run sooner than he usually would, so he could run farther if the ball was hit.)

hit between the eyes *v. phr., informal* To make a strong impression on; surprise greatly. *Helen hit Joe right between the eyes the moment he saw her.* (Helen greatly impressed Joe at first sight.) *It was a wonderfully lifelike picture, and it hit Sol right between the eyes.* (It made a strong impression on Sol.) *To learn that his parents had endured poverty for his sake hit John between the eyes.* (When he learned of his parents' sacrifice for him, John was greatly surprised and grateful.)

hit bottom *or* **touch bottom** *v. phr., informal* **1** To be at the very lowest. *In August there was a big supply of corn and the price hit bottom.* (In August the price of corn was lower than it had ever

been.) *When Johnny failed the exam, his spirits hit bottom.* (Johnny felt worse than he had ever felt before.) **2** To live through the worst; not to be able to go any lower. *After all their troubles, they thought they had hit bottom and then something else happened.* (They thought nothing worse could happen to them, but it did.)

hitch one's wagon to a star *v. phr.* To aim high; follow a great ambition or purpose. *In trying to be a famous pianist, Mary had hitched her wagon to a star.* (She had aimed high; it would have taken less effort just to sing in the church choir.) *John hitched his wagon to a star and decided to try to become President.* (He was very ambitious and aimed for the presidency.)

hither and thither *or* **hither and yon** *adv. phr., literary* In one direction and then in another. *Bob wandered hither and thither looking for a playmate.* (Bob wandered around looking for a playmate.)

hit it off *v. phr., informal* To enjoy one another's company; be happy and comfortable in each other's presence. *Tom and Fred hit it off well with each other.* (Tom and Fred get along well together.) *Mary and Jane hit it off from the first.* (Mary and Jane liked each other from the time they first met.)

hit on *or* **hit upon** *v.* To happen to meet, find, or reach; to choose or think by chance. *John hit on a business that was just starting to grow rapidly.* (John happened to choose a business that was soon to grow fast.) *There seemed to be several explanations of the crime, but the detectives hit on the right one the first* *time*. (The detectives thought of the right explanation the first time.)

hit-or-miss *also* **hit-and-miss** *adj.* Unplanned; uncontrolled; aimless; careless. *John did a lot of hit-or-miss reading, some of it about taxes.* (He didn't pick out just the things that had to do with taxes; he read a lot, and once in a while some of it would be about taxes.) *Mary packed her bag in hurried, hit-or-miss fashion.* (She threw things in without selecting what she knew she would need; she packed things she would have no use for, and forgot some that she would want.)

hit or miss *also* **hit and miss** *adv.* In an unplanned or uncontrolled way; aimlessly; carelessly. *George didn't know which house on the street was Jane's, so he began ringing doorbells hit or miss.* (George rang the doorbell of one house and then another in no order, just any way.)

hit parade *n.* **1** A list of songs or tunes arranged in order of popularity. *Tom was overjoyed when his new song was named on the hit parade on the local radio station.* (It was chosen as one of the best-liked new songs.) **2** *slang* A list of favorites in order of popularity. *Jack is no longer number one on Elsie's hit parade.* (Jack is not her best boyfriend now.)

hit the books *v. phr., informal* To study one's school assignments; prepare for classes. *Jack broke away from his friends, saying, "I've got to hit the books."* (Jack told his friends he had to study.)

hit the bull's-eye *v. phr., informal* To go to the important part of the matter; reach the main question. *John hit the bull's-eye when he said the big question was one of simple honesty.* (John

named the important question as that of simple honesty. John was exactly right.)

hit the ceiling *or* **hit the roof** *v. phr., slang* To become violently angry; go into a rage. *When Elaine came home at three in the morning, her father hit the ceiling.* (Her father became very angry.) *Bob hit the roof when Joe teased him.* (Bob became very angry.)

hit the deck *v. phr.* To get up from bed; to start working. (From sailor's language as in "All hands on deck!") *OK boys, it's time to hit the deck!* (It is time to get up and start working.)

hit the dirt *v. phr., slang, military* To take cover under gunfire by falling on the ground. *We hit the dirt the moment we heard the machine-gun fire.* (The moment we heard the machine guns, we threw ourselves down on the ground to avoid being hit.)

hit the hay *or* **hit the sack** *v. phr., slang* To go to bed. *The men hit the hay early, in order to be out hunting at dawn.* (The men went to bed early.) *Louis was so tired that he hit the sack soon after supper.* (He went to bed soon after supper.)

hit the high spots *v. phr.* To consider, mention, or see only the more important parts of something. *In his lecture, the speaker hit the high spots of his subject.* (He mentioned the more important parts.)

hit the jackpot *v. phr., slang* To be very lucky or successful. *Mr. Brown invented a new gadget that hit the jackpot.* (Mr. Brown's gadget was very successful.)

hit the nail on the head *v. phr.* To get something exactly right; speak or act in the most fitting or effective way. *The mayor's talk* *on race relations hit the nail on the head.* (He said the right thing; exactly what should be said.)

hit the road *v. phr., slang* **1** To become a wanderer; to live an idle life; become a tramp or hobo. *When Jack's wife left him, he felt a desire to travel, so he hit the road.* (He became a tramp and wandered about the country.) **2** To leave, especially in a car. *It is getting late, so I guess we will hit the road for home.* (We will start off in the car.)

hit the sauce *v. phr., slang* To drink alcoholic beverages—especially heavily and habitually. *When Sue left him, Joe began to hit the sauce.* (She left him and he became a habitual drinker.)

hit the spot *v. phr., informal* To refresh fully or satisfy one; bring back one's spirits or strength—used especially of food or drink. *A cup of tea always hits the spot when you are tired.* (A cup of tea is very refreshing when you are tired. *Mother's apple pie always hits the spot with the boys.* (The boys think Mother's pies are delicious.)

hoist with one's own petard *adj. phr., slightly archaic* Caught in one's own trap or trick. *Jack carried office gossip to the boss until he was hoisted with his own petard.* (The boss became disgusted with Jack for gossiping about others and fired him.) [From Shakespeare; literally blown up with one's own bomb.]

hold a candle to *also* **hold a stick to** *v. phr.* To be fit to be compared with; be in the same class with. Used in negative, interrogative, and conditional sentences. *Henry thought that no modern ball club could hold a candle to those of 50 years ago.* (Henry thought

that no modern ball club was as good as those of 50 years ago.)

hold all the trumps *v. phr.* To have the best chance of winning; have all the advantages; have full control. *Most of the team want John for captain and he is the best player. He will be elected captain because he holds all the trumps.* (Everything is in John's favor.) *Freddy has a quarter and I have no money, so he holds all the trumps and can buy whatever he wants with it.* (He has charge of the money and he can decide what to buy.)

hold back *v.* **1** To stay back or away; show unwillingness. *The visitor tried to get the child to come to her, but he held back.* (The child stayed away from the visitor.) *John held back from social activity because he felt embarrassed with people.* (John did not take part in social activities because he was shy.) **2** To keep someone in place; prevent from acting. *The police held back the crowd.* (The police prevented the crowd from acting.)

hold court *v. phr.* **1** To hold a formal meeting of a royal court or a court of law. *Judge Stephens allowed no foolishness when he held court.* (Judge Stephens enforced strict order at meetings of his court.) **2** *informal* To act like a king or queen among subjects. *Even at sixteen, Judy was holding court for numbers of charmed boys.* (She was acting like a queen over boys who admired her.)

hold down *v.* **1** To keep in obedience; keep control of; continue authority or rule over. *Kings used to know very well how to hold down the people.* (Kings understood how to make the people obey.) **2** *informal* To work satisfactorily at. *John had held down* *a tough job for a long time.* (He had worked satisfactorily at the job.)

hold forth *v.* **1** To offer; propose. *As a candidate, Jones held forth the promise of a bright future.* (He offered the promise of a bright future.) **2** To speak in public; preach. —Usually used with little respect. *Senator Smith was holding forth on free trade.* (He was giving a speech on free trade.)

hold good *v.* **1** To continue to be good; last. *The coupon on the cereal box offered a free toy, but the offer held good only till the end of the year.* (After the end of the year you could not send in the coupon and get the toy; the offer was not good after that.) *Attendance at the basketball games held good all winter.* (Crowds of people kept coming to the games all winter.) **2** To continue; endure; last. *The demand for new houses held good all that year.* (The need for new houses continued all year.) *The agreement between the schools held good for three years.* (The agreement lasted three years.)

hold off *v.* **1a** To refuse to let (someone) become friendly. *The president's high rank and chilly manner held people off.* (His rank and manner kept people from being friendly.) **1b** To be rather shy or unfriendly. *Perkins was a scholarly man who held off from people.* (He kept away from people; he wasn't very friendly.) **2** To keep away by fighting; oppose by force. *The man locked himself in the house and held off the police for an hour.* (He fought back the police and was not captured for an hour.) **3** To wait before (doing something); postpone; delay. *Jack held off paying for the television set until the dealer fixed it.* (He postponed

paying for it until it was satisfactory.) *Mr. Smith held off from building while interest rates were high.* (He chose not to build until interest rates were lower.)

hold on *v.* **1** To keep holding tightly; continue to hold strongly. *As Ted was pulling on the rope, it began to slip and Earl cried, "Hold on, Ted!"* (Earl told Ted to hold tightly.) **2** To wait and not hang up a telephone; keep a phone call open. *Mr. Jones asked me to hold on while he spoke to his secretary.* (Mr. Jones asked me to wait on the phone while he spoke to his secretary.) **3** To keep on with a business or job in spite of difficulties. *It was hard to keep the store going during the depression, but Max held on and at last met with success.* (He did not give up; he worked hard and kept the business going.) **4** *informal* To wait a minute; stop.—Usually used as a command. *"Hold on!" John's father said, "I want the car tonight."* (John's father told him to stop, not to take the car.)

hold one's breath *v. phr.* **1** To stop breathing for a moment when one is excited or nervous. *The race was so close that everyone was holding his breath at the finish.* (At the end people were not breathing normally, they were so excited.) **2** To endure great nervousness, anxiety, or excitement. *John held his breath for days before he got word that the college he chose had accepted him.* (He was nervous and worried until he knew that he had been accepted.)

hold one's fire *or* **hold fire** *v. phr.* To keep back arguments or facts; keep from telling something. *Tom could have hurt Fred by telling what he knew, but he held his fire.* (Tom didn't tell the bad thing he knew about Fred.) *Mary held fire until she had enough information to convince the other club members.* (Mary waited until she could explain all the facts at once.)

hold one's horses *v. phr., informal* To stop; wait; be patient.— Usually used as a command. May be considered rude. *"Hold your horses!" Mr. Jones said to David when David wanted to call the police.* (Mr. Jones told David to wait when David wanted to call the police.)

hold one's own *v. phr.* To keep one's position; avoid losing ground; keep one's advantage, wealth, or condition without loss. *Mr. Smith could not build up his business, but he held his own.* (He kept his business from getting smaller, although he could not expand it.) *The team held its own after the first quarter.* (The team did as well as the opponents after the first quarter, even if they couldn't win.) *Mary had a hard time after the operation, but soon she was holding her own.* (After the first difficult days, Mary did not get worse, although she didn't begin to get better.)

hold one's peace *v. phr. formal* To be silent and not speak against something; be still; keep quiet. *I did not agree with the teacher but held my peace, as he was rather angry.* (I did not say anything aginst the teacher's idea.)

hold one's tongue *v. phr.* To be silent; keep still; not talk.— May be considreed rude. *The teacher told Fred to hold his tongue.* (The teacher told Fred to keep still.) *If people would hold their tongues from unkind speech, fewer people would be hurt.* (If people would keep still rather than

say unkind things, fewer people would be hurt.)

hold on to *v. phr.* **1a** *or* **hold to** To continue to hold or keep; hold tightly. *The teacher said that if we believed something was true and good, we should hold on to it.* (We should continue to believe it.) *The old man held on to his job stubbornly and would not retire.* (He continued to work and would not retire.) **1b** To stay in control of. *Ann was so frightened that she had to hold on to herself not to scream.* (She had to try hard and control her feelings so she would not scream.) **2** To continue to sing or sound. *The singer held on to the last note of the song for a long time.* (She continued singing the last note a long time.)

hold out *v.* (stress on *out*) **1** To put forward; reach out; extend; offer. *Mr. Ryan held out his hand in welcome.* (He offered his hand in greeting; he offered to shake hands.) *The clerk held out a dress for Martha to try on.* (The clerk offered a dress to Martha to try on.) **2** To keep resisting; not yield; refuse to give up. *The city held out for six months under siege.* (The city did not surrender while surrounded for six months.) **3** To refuse to agree or settle until one's wishes have been agreed to. *The strikers held out for a raise of one dollar an hour.* (The strikers would not return to work until they got a raise of one dollar an hour.) **4** *slang* To keep something from; refuse information or belongings to which someone has a right. *Mr. Porter's partner held out on him when the big payment came in.* (He didn't tell Mr. Porter about the payment or share it fairly with him.)

hold-out   *n., informal* (stress on *hold*)   A maverick, a non-conformist, someone who sticks to the old ways. *Everyone on the North Shore sold waterfront property to the highest developers; Mr. Smith is the last hold-out.* (He is still resisting.)

hold over   *v.*   **1** To remain or keep in office past the end of the term. *The city treasurer held over for six months when the new treasurer died suddenly.* (The old treasurer kept the job for six months when the newly elected treasurer died.) *The new President held the members of the Cabinet over for some time before appointing new members.* (He kept the old Cabinet members in office for a while.) **2** To extend the engagement of; keep longer. *The theater held over the feature film for another two weeks.* (The theater showed the film for two weeks more.) **3** To delay action on; to postpone; to defer. *The directors held over their decision until they could get more information.* (They waited to make their decision until they had more information.)

hold the fort   *v. phr.*   **1** To defend a fort successfully; fight off attackers. *The little group held the fort for days until help came.* (The group fought off the enemy until more troops came to help them.) **2** *informal* To keep a position against opposing forces. *Friends of civil liberties held the fort during a long debate.* (Congressmen supporting civil liberties did not weaken even during a long debate.) **3** *informal* To keep service or operations going. *It was Christmas Eve, and a few workers held the fort in the office.* (Just a few people were keeping the office open.) *Mother and Father*

went out and told the children to hold the fort. (The children were to take care of the house while their parents were gone.)

hold up   *v.* (stress on *up*)   **1** To raise; lift. *John held up his hand.* (John raised his hand.) **2** To support; bear; carry. *The chair was too weak to hold up Mrs. Smith.* (The chair was not strong enough to support Mrs. Smith's weight.) **3** To show; call attention to; exhibit. *The teacher held up excellent models of composition for her class to imitate.* (The teacher showed her class examples of good writing.) **4** To check; stop; delay. *The wreck held up traffic on the railroad's main line tracks.* (The wreck blocked traffic on the main line.) **5** *informal* To rob at gunpoint. *Masked men held up the bank.* (Masked men robbed the bank with guns.) **6** To keep one's courage or spirits up; remain calm; keep control of oneself. *The grieving mother held up for her children's sake.* (The grieving mother kept control of herself so that her children might not be worried.) **7** To remain good; not get worse. *Sales held up well.* (Selling continued at a steady rate.) *Our team's luck held up, and they won the game.* (The team continued lucky.) *The weather held up and the game was played.* (The weather stayed fair and the game was played.) **8** To prove true. *The police were doubtful at first, but Tony's story held up.* (His story proved true.) **9** To delay action; defer; postpone. Often used with *on*. *The college held up on plans for the building until more money came in.* (The college put off plans for the building.) *The President held up on the news until he was sure of it.* (The President did not announce the news until he was sure of it.)

hold-up *n.*, (stress on *hold*) A robbery. *"Put your wallets on the table,"* the criminal cried, *"This is a hold-up!"* (He ordered the victims to give their possessions as this was a robbery.)

hole in the wall *n. phr.* **1** A small place to live, stay in, or work in; a small, hidden, or inferior place. *The jewelry store occupied a tiny hole in the wall.* (The jewelry store occupied a tiny, narrow store.) *When Mr. and Mrs. Green were first married, they lived in a little hole in the wall, in a cheap apartment building.* (They had a very small, cheap apartment.) **2** *slang, citizen's band radio jargon* A tunnel. *Let's get through this hole in the wall—then we'll change seats.* (We'll change seats after passing the tunnel.)

holier-than-thou *adj.*, *archaic* Acting as if one is better than others in goodness, character, or reverence for God; acting as if morally better than other people. *Most people find holier-than-thou actions in others hard to accept.* (A show of superior goodness annoys most people.) *After Mr. Howard stopped smoking, he had a holier-than-thou attitude toward his friends who still smoked.* (Mr. Howard seemed to think he was a better person than his friends who still smoked.)

holy cats *or* **holy cow** *or* **holy mackerel** *or* **holy Moses** *interj.*, *informal* —Used to express strong feeling (as astonishment, pleasure, or anger); used in speech or when writing conversation. *"Holy cats! That's good pie!"* said Dick. (The pie pleased Dick very much.) *"Holy cow! They can't do that!"* Mary said

when she saw the boys hurting a much smaller boy. (Mary was astonished and angry to see the little boy being hurt.)

holy terror *n.*, *informal* A very disobedient or unruly child; brat. *All the children are afraid of Johnny because he's a holy terror.* (Johnny always causes trouble.)

honeymoon is over The first happy period of friendship and cooperation between two persons or groups is over. *A few months after a new President is elected, the honeymoon is over and Congress and the President begin to criticize each other.* (At first they are friendly and cooperative, but after a while they begin to blame each other.) *The honeymoon was soon over for the new foreman and the men under him.* (At first they got along well, but soon they began to criticize each other.)

honky-tonk *n.* A cheap nightclub or dance hall. *There were a number of honky-tonks near the army camp.* (Many cheap dance halls and taverns were near the camp.)

hook, line, and sinker *adv. phr.*, *informal* Without question or doubt; completely. *Johnny was so easily fooled that he fell for Joe's story hook, line, and sinker.* (Johnny accepted Joe's story without question). *Mary was such a romantic girl that she swallowed the story Alice told her about her date, hook, line, and sinker.* (Mary believed Alice's story completely.)

hook up *v.* (stress on *up*) To connect or fit together. *The company sent a man to hook up the telephone.* (The company sent a man to connect the telephone.) *They could not use the gas stove because it had not been hooked* up. (The company had not connected the stove to the gas pipe.)

hook-up *n.*, (stress on *hook*) A connection. *Americans can call Europe via satellite hook-up.* (We have satellite telephone connections.)

hope against hope *v. phr.* To try to hope when things look black; hold to hope in bad trouble. *The mother continued to hope against hope although the plane was hours late.* (The mother clung to hope for hours after the plane should have arrived.) *Jane hoped against hope that Joe would call her.* (She thought he would not, but anyway she hoped.)

hop to it *v. phr.*, *slang* To get started; start a job; get going. *"There's a lot to do today, so let's hop to it,"* the boss said. ("Let's get started," the boss said.)

hopped up *adj.*, *slang* **1** Doped with a narcotic drug. *Police found Jones hiding in a shooting gallery among other men all hopped up with the drugs.* (Police found him in a drug user's resort where everyone else was under the influence of drugs.) **2** Full of eagerness; excited. *Fred was all hopped up about going over the ocean.* (Fred was excited by the expectation of a trip on a ship.)

horn in *v.*, *slang* To come in without invitation or welcome; interfere. Often used with *on*. *Jack would often horn in on conversations discussing things he knew nothing about.* (Jack often was stubbron about getting into talk, even when he was ignorant of the subject being discussed.) *Lee horned in on Ray and Annie and wanted to dance with Annie.* (Lee went in where he was not wanted.)

horse around *v.*, *slang* (stress on *around*) To join in rough teasing; play around. *They were a bunch of sailors on shore leave, horsing around where there were girls and drinks.* (The sailors were playing a bit rough; they were being noisy and teasing.) *John horsed around with the dog for a while when he· came in from school.* (He played with the dog.)

horse of a different color *or* **horse of another color** *n. phr.*, *informal* Something altogether separate and different. *Anyone can be broke, but to steal is a horse of a different color.* (To be broke is one thing, but to steal is different.) *Do you mean that the boy with that pretty girl is her brother? I though he was her boyfriend. Well, that's a horse of another color.* (That is something different from what I thought.)

horse sense *n.*, *informal* (stress on *horse*) A good understanding about what to do in life; good judgment; wisdom in making decisions. *Bill had never been to college, but he had plenty of horse sense.* (He had common sense.) *Some people are well educated and read many books, but still do not have much horse sense.* (They have poor judgement and make mistakes.)

horse trade *n.* (stress on *horse*) *informal* A business agreement or bargain arrived at after hard and skillful discussion. *Party leaders went around for months making horse trades to get support for their candidate.* (Thet made bargains and promises in return for support.)

hot air *n.*, *informal* (stress on *air*) Nonsense, exaggerated talk, wasted words characterized by emotion rather than intellectual content. *What Joe said was just a lot of hot air.* (What he said was just exaggerated nonsense.)

hot and bothered *adj., informal* Excited and worried, displeased, or puzzled. *Fritz got all hot and bothered when he failed in the test.* (He was excited and disappointed.)

hot dog[1] *n. phr., informal* (stress on *dog*) A frankfurter or wiener in a roll. *The boys stopped on the way home for hot dogs and coffee.* (They had frankfurters on rolls with coffee.)

hot dog[2] *interj., informal* (stress on *hot*) Hurrah!–A cry used to show pleasure or enthusiasm. *"Hot dog!" Frank exclaimed when he unwrapped a birthday gift of a small record player.* ("Hurrah! Isn't that something!" he exclaimed.)

hot potato *n., informal* (stress on *potato*) A question that causes strong argument and is difficult to settle. *Many school boards found segregation a hot potato in the early '60s.* (They found it a question that was hard to handle without stirring up strong feelings.)

hot rod *n., informal* (stress on *hot*) An automobile changed so that it can gain speed quickly and go very fast. *Hot rods are used especially in drag racing.* (Cars with speed and pickup are used especially in races in which quick increase in speed is important.)

hot water *n., informal* (stress on *water*) Trouble—Used with in, into, out of. *John's thoughtless remark about religion got him into a lot of hot water.* (His remark got him into a lot of trouble.) *It was the kind of trouble where it takes a friend to get you out of hot water.* (It was the kind of jam in which a friend is the best means of getting out of trouble.)

house of cards *n. phr.* Something badly put together and easily knocked down; a poorly founded plan, hope, or action. *John's business fell apart like a house of cards.* (John's business failed like a house built of playing cards.) *Their plan for a trip to Europe proved to be just a house of cards.* (The trip to Europe proved to have no chance, and it never came true.)

how about *or* **what about** *interrog.* —Used to ask for a decision, action, opinion, or explanation. **1** Will you have or agree on? *How about another piece of pie?* (Will you have another piece of pie?) *What about a game of tennis?* (Would you like to play tennis?) **2** Will you lend or give me? *How about five dollars until Friday?* (Will you lend me five dollars?) *What about a little help with these dishes?* (Will you help me wash these dishes?) **3** What is to be done about? *What about the windows? Shall we close them before we go?* (What is to be done about the windows before we go?) **4** How do you feel about? What do you think about? What is to be thought or said? *What about a woman for President?* (What do you think about a woman for President?)

how come *interrog., informal also nonstandard* **how's come** *interrog.* How does it happen that? Why? *How come you are late?* (Why are you late?) *You're wearing your best clothes today. How come?* (You are wearing your best clothes. Why?)

how do you do *formal* How are you?—Usually as a reply to an introduction; it is in the form of a question but no answer is expected. *"Mary, I want you to meet my friend Fred. Fred, this is my wife, Mary." "How do you do, Mary?" "How do you do, Fred?"*

how's that *interrog., informal* What did you say? Will you please repeat that? *"I've just been up in a balloon for a day and a half." "How's that?"* ("What did you say?") *"The courthouse is on fire." "How's that again?"* ("Please say that again. I didn't hear you or can't believe it.")

hue and cry *n.* **1** An alarm and chase after a supposed wrong-doer; a pursuit usually by shouting people: *"Stop, thief,"* cried John as he ran. *Others joined him, and soon there was a hue and cry.* (Soon many people were chasing the thief and shouting.) **2** An excited mass protest, alarm, or out-cry. *The explosion was so terrible that people at a distance raised a great hue and cry about an earthquake.* (They spread the alarm that there had been an earthquake.)

hush-hush *adj. informal* Kept secret or hidden; kept from public knowledge; hushed up; con-cealed. *The company had a new automobile engine that it was developing, but kept it a hush-hush project until they knew it was successful.* (They let no news of it leak out until they had succeeded in making the engine successfully.)

hush up *v.* **1** To keep news of (something) from getting out; prevent people from knowing about. *It isn't always easy to hush up a scandal.* (You can't always keep word of a disgraceful story from spreading.) **2** *informal* To be or make quiet; stop talking, crying, or making some other noise.—Often used as a command. *"Hush up,"* Mother said, *when we began to repeat ugly gossip.* (Mother told us to be quiet when we began to repeat gossip.) *The little girl was noisy in church but her mother hushed her up.* (Her mother made her stop talking.)

idiot box *n., slang* A television set. *Phil has been staring at the idiot box all afternoon.* (He has been watching television all afternoon.)

if the mountain won't come to Mahomet, Mahomet will go to the mountain. If one person will not go to the other, then the other must go to him. *Grandfather won't come to visit us, so we must go and visit him. If the mountain won't come to Mahomet, then Mahomet will go to the mountain.* (Because Grandfather won't come to us, we must go to him.)

if the shoe fits, wear it! If what is said describes you, you are meant. *I won't say who, but some children are always late. If the shoe fits, wear it.* (If you are always late, you are one that I mean.)

if worst comes to worst If the worst thing happens that can be imagined; if the worst possible thing happens; if troubles grow worse. *If worst comes to worst and Mr. Jones loses the house, he will send his family to his mother's farm.* (If the worst thing we can think of happens to Mr. Jones, which is to lose his house, he will send his family to his mother.)

ill at ease *adj. phr.* Not feeling at ease or comfortable, anxious, worried; unhappy. *Donald had never been to a big party before and he was ill at ease.* (He was embarrassed and nervous at the party.)

I'll bet you my bottom dollar *interj., informal* An exaggerated assertion of assurance. *I bet you my bottom dollar that the Cubs will win this year.* (I am willing to bet any amount that they will win, I am very sure.)

in a bind *or* **in a box** *adv. phr., informal* Likely to have trouble whether one does one thing or another. *Sam is in a bind because if he carries home his aunt's groceries, his teacher will be angry because he is late, and if he doesn't, his aunt will complain.* (Sam is likely to have trouble whether he does something to please his aunt or something to please his teacher.)

in a circle *or* **in circles** *adv. phr.* Without any progress; without getting anywhere; uselessly. *The committee debated for two hours, just talking in cricles.* (They talked uselessly, solving nothing.)

in a family way *or* **in the family way** *adj. phr., informal* Going to have a baby.—Used as an euphemism. *Sue and Liz are happy because their mother is in the family way.* (Their mother is going to have a baby.) *The Ferguson children are promising kittens to everyone because their cat is in a family way.* (The Ferguson cat is going to have kittens.)

in a fog *or* **in a haze** *adv. phr.* Mentally confused; not sure what is happening. *I didn't vote for Alice because she always seems to be in a fog.* (Alice seems to be confused about things.)

in a hole *or* **in a spot** *adj. phr., informal* In an embarrassing or difficult position; in some trouble. *When the restaurant cook left at the beginning of the busy season, it put the restaurant owner in a hole.* (It made trouble for the owner of the restaurant.)

in and out *adv. phr.* **1** Coming in and going out often. *He was very busy Saturday and was in and out all day.* (He had to go out on business many times and come back to the office.)

in a nutshell *adv. phr., informal* In a few words; briefly, without telling all about it. *We are in a hurry, so I'll give you the story in a nutshell.* (I'll tell you quickly the main facts of the story without all details.) *In a nutshell, the car is no bargain.* (In a few words, the car is not worth the money.)

in any case *also* **in any event** *adv. phr.* **1** No matter what happens; surely; without fail; certainly; anyhow; anyway. *It may rain tomorrow, but we are going home in any case.* (We are going home tomorrow no matter whether it rains or not.) *I may not go to Europe, but in any event, I will visit you during the summer.* (I shall certainly visit you during the summer.)

in a pig's eye *adv., slang, informal* Hardly, unlikely, not so. *Would I marry him? In a pig's eye.* (Not very likely, hardly.)

in arms *adv. phr.* Having guns and being ready to fight; armed. *When our country is at war, we have many men in arms.* (In times of war we have men in the services.)

in a way *adv. phr.* **1** *also informal* **in a kind of way** *or informal* **in a sort of way** To a certain extent; a little; somewhat. *I like Jane in a way, but she is very proud.* (I like Jane partly, even though she is proud.) **2** In one respect. *In a way, this book is easier; it is much shorter.* (This book is shorter. In this respect it is easier.)

in a world of one's own *or* **in a world by oneself** **1** In the place where one belongs; in one's own personal surroundings; apart from other people. *They are in a little world of their own in their house on the mountain.* (Their house is alone and not near other people.) **2a** In deep thought or concentration. *Mary is in a world of her own when she is playing the piano.* (Mary pays no attention to anything else when she plays the piano.) **2b** Not caring about or connected with other people in thoughts or actions. — Usually used sarcastically. *That boy is in a world all by himself. He never knows what is happening around him.* (He doesn't see or care about what is happening.)

in case *adv. phr., informal* In order to be prepared; as a precaution; if there is need. — Usually used in the phrase *just in case. The bus is usually on time, but start early, just in case.* (The bus is usually on time, but you should start early so that you will be there if it leaves early.)

in character *adv. or adj. phr.* **1** In agreement with a person's character or personality; in the way that a person usually behaves or is supposed to behave; as usual; charactreristic; typical; suitable. *John was very rude at the party, and that was not in character, because he is usually very polite.* (John did not behave politely as he usually does.) **2** Suitable for the part or the kind of part being acted; natural to the way a character in a book or play is supposed to act. *The fat actor in the movie was in character because the character he played was supposed to be fat and jolly.* (The fat actor was just right for the part he played in the movie.)

in charge *adv. or adj. phr.* **1** In authority or control; in a position to care for or supervise; responsible. *If you have any questions, ask the boss. He's in charge.* (The boss decides everything and will answer your questions.)

in the charge of Under the care or supervision of. *Mother puts the baby in the charge of the baby-sitter while she is out.* (Mother put the baby under the baby-sitter's care.) *The money was given in charge of Mr. Jackson for safe-keeping.* (The money was given to Mr. Jackson and he will be responsible for it.)

in check *adv. phr.* In a position where movement or action is not allowed or is stopped; under control; kept quiet or back. *The boy was too small to keep the big dog in check, and the dog broke away from his leash.* (The boy was too small to hold the dog by his leash and the dog ran away.)

in clover *adv. or adj. phr., informal* In rich comfort; rich or successful; having a pleasant or easy life. *They live in clover because their father is rich.* (They are wealthy and have everything they need.) *When we finish the hard part we'll be in clover.* (When we finish the hard and pleasant part, we can do the easy and pleasant part.)

in cold blood *adv. phr.* Without feeling or pity; in a purposely cruel way; coolly and deliberately. *The bank robbers planned to shoot in cold blood anyone who got in their way.* (They planned to shoot without pity anyone who got in their way.)

in common *adv. phr.* Shared together or equally; in use or ownership by all. *Mr. and Mrs. Smith own the store in common.* (Mr. and Mrs. Smith own the store together.) *The four boys grew up together and have a lot in common.* (The boys shared many experiences together.)

in deep *adj. phr.* Seriously mixed up in something, especially trouble. *George began borrowing small sums of money to*

bet on horses, and before he knew it he was in deep.* (George was in serious trouble; he lost the money and could not pay it back.)

in fact *also in point of fact* *adv. phr.* Really; truthfully.—Often used for emphasis. *No one believed it but, in fact, Mary did get an A on her book report.* (Mary really got an A on her book report.) *It was a very hot day; in fact, it was 100 degrees.* (It was 100 degrees—a very hot day.)

in for *prep., informal* Unable to avoid; sure to get. *The naughty puppy was in for a spanking.* (The bad little puppy was sure to get spanked.) *On Christmas morning we are in for some surprises.* (We will certainly have some surprises on Christmas morning.)

in good time *or* **in good season** *adv. phr.* **1** A little early; sooner than necessary. *The school bus arrived in good time.* (The bus came into the yard before the bell rang.) *The students finished their schoolwork in good time.* (They finished it before the time when the teacher said they must stop.) **2** *or* **in due course** *or* **in due season** *or* **in due time** In the usual amount of time; at the right time; in the end. *Spring and summer will arrive in due season.* (The seasons will come when the right amount of time has passed.)

in hand *adv. or adj. phr.* **1** Under control. *The principal was happy to find that the new teacher had her class in hand.* (The teacher had her class under control.) **2** In one's possession; with one.—Often used in the phrase *cash in hand. Tom figured that his cash in hand with his weekly pay would be enough to buy a car.* (Tom thought that the money he already had added to the pay he would get was enough for a car.)

in keeping *adj. phr.* Going well together; agreeing; similar. *Mary's hairstyle was in keeping with the latest fashion.* (Mary's hairstyle was chic.) *Having an assembly on Friday morning was in keeping with the school program.* (The Friday assembly was the usual procedure of the school.)

in kind *adv. phr.* In a similar way; with the same kind of thing. *My neighbor pays me in kind for walking her dog.* (My neighbor often walks my dog to repay me for walking hers.) *Lois returned Mary's insult in kind.* (Because Mary insulted Lois, Lois insulted Mary.)

in league with *or informal* **in cahoots with** *prep.* In secret agreement or partnership with (someone); working together secretly with, especially for harm. *People once believed that some women were witches in league with the devil.* (Long ago people believed that some women secretly helped the devil do harm.) *The mayor's enemies spread a rumor that he was in cahoots with gangsters.* (The mayor's enemies told people that the mayor secretly worked with gangsters.)

in light of *also* **in the light of** *adj. phr.* **1** As a result of new information; by means of new ideas. *The teacher changed John's grade in the light of the extra work in the workbook.* (When the teacher saw the extra work that John had done, he changed the grade.) **2** Because of. *In light of the muddy field, the football team wore their old uniforms.* (The field was muddy, so the team decided to wear old uniforms.)

in line *adj. phr.* Obeying or agreeing with what is right or usual; doing or being what people expect or accept; within ordinary or proper limits. *The coach kept the excited team in line.* (The coach made the team do what was right; he kept them under control.)

in love *adj. phr.* Liking very much; loving. *John is in love with Helen.* (John likes Helen very much.) *Tom and Ellen are in love.* (Tom and Ellen love each other.) *Mary is in love with her new wristwatch.* (Mary likes her new wristwatch very much.)

in luck *adj. phr.* Being lucky; having good luck; finding something good by chance. *Bill was in luck when he found the money on the street.* (Bill found some money that he did not expect to find.)

in memory of *prep.* As something that makes people remember (a person or thing); as a reminder of; as a memorial to. *The building was named Ford Hall in memory of a man named James Ford.* (The people gave the building the name of a man that they wanted to remember.)

in no time *or* **in nothing flat** *adv. phr., informal* In a very little time; soon; quickly. *When the entire class worked together they finished the project in no time.* (Working together, the class finished the project quickly.) *The bus filled with students in nothing flat.* (The bus was quickly filled with students.)

in on *prep.* **1** Joining together for. *The children collected money from their classmates and went in on a present for their teacher.* (The children shared their money and bought a present for their teacher.) **2** Told about; having knowledge of. *Bob was in on the secret.* (Bob knew the secret.) *The other girls wouldn't let Mary in on what they knew.* (The other girls wouldn't tell Mary what they knew.)

in one's element *adv. phr.* **1** In one's natural surroundings. *The deep-sea fish is in his element in deep ocean water.* (The deep-sea fish can live only in the deep ocean.) **2** Where one can do one's best. *John is in his element working on the farm.* (John likes the farm and does his best work there.)

in one's face *adv. phr.* Abruptly, unexpectedly. *The robbers' plan to rob the bank blew up in their faces when a policeman stopped them.* (Their plan went wrong unexpectedly.)

in one's good graces *or* **in one's good books** *adv. phr.* Approved of by someone; liked by someone. *Ruth is in her mother's good graces because she ate all her supper.* (Her mother likes her to eat all her supper.) *Bill is back in the good graces of his neighbor.* (Bill replaced the hammer he had borrowed and lost.)

in one's hair *adj. phr.*, *informal* Bothering one again and again; always annoying. *By running and shouting, Johnny got in Father's hair when he was trying to read the paper.* (Johnny kept disturbing Father while he was reading.)

in one's mind's eye *adv. phr.* In the memory; in the imagination. *In his mind's eye he saw again the house he had lived in when he was a child.* (In his memory, he was able to see the house he had lived in when he was a child.) *In his mind's eye, he could see just what the vacation was going to be like.* (In his imagination he pictured the things he would do on his vacation.)

in one's shell *or* **into one's shell** *adv. or adj. phr.*, *informal* Withdrawn; into silence; not sociable; unfriendly. *After Mary's mother scolded her, she went into her shell.* (Mary became very quiet after the scolding.)

in one's shoes *also* **in one's boots** *adv. phr.* In or into one's place or position. *How would you like to be in a lion tamer's boots?* (How would you like to be a lion tamer?)

in one's tracks *adv. phr.*, *informal* Just where one is at the moment; abruptly; immediately. *The hunter's rifle cracked and the rabbit dropped in his tracks.* (At the sound of the rifle, the rabbit fell down right where he was.) *Mary stopped dead in her tracks, turned around, and ran back home.* (Mary stopped suddenly where she was and turned around.)

in order to *or* **so as to** *conj.* For the purpose of; to.—Used with an infinitive. *In order to follow the buffalo, the Indians often had to move their camps.* (The reason that the Indians moved camp often was to follow the buffalo.) *We picked apples so as to make a pie.* (We picked apples for the purpose of making a pie.)

in part *adv. phr.* To some extent; partly; not wholly.—Often used with *large* or *small*. *We planted the garden in part with flowers. But in large part we planted vegetables.* (We planted a part of the garden with flowers, but we planted mostly vegetables.) *Tom was only in small part responsible.* (Tom was responsible but only a little bit.)

ins and outs *n. phr.* The special ways of going somewhere or doing something; the different parts. *The janitor knows all the ins and outs of the big school building.* (The janitor knows every part of the building.) *Jerry's father is a good life insurance salesman; he knows all the ins and outs of the business.* (Jerry's father knows all about life insurance.)

in short supply *adj. phr.* Not enough; in too small a quantity or amount; in less than the amount or number needed. *The cookies are in short supply, so don't eat them all up.* (There are not enough cookies.) *We have five people and only four beds, so the beds are in short supply.* (We have fewer than the number of beds we need.)

inside out *adv.* **1** So that the inside is turned outside. *Mother turns the stockings inside out when she washes them.* (Mother pulls the inside of the stockings to the outside.) **2** *or* **inside and out** *also* **in and out** In every part; throughout; completely. *David knows the parts of his bicycle inside out.* (David knows all the parts of the bicycle and how they work.) *We searched the house inside and out for the kitten.* (We hunted in every part of the house.)

inside track *n. phr.* **1** The inside, shortest distance around a curved racetrack; the place that is closest to the inside fence. *A big white horse had the inside track at the start of the race.* (A big white horse had the inside place and the other horses were following him in outside places.) **2** *informal* A favored place; an advantage. *John has the inside track for the job because he had the best marks.* (John will probably get the job because he had the best marks in school.)

in spite of *prep. phr.* Against the influence or effect of; in opposition to; defying the effect of; despite. *In spite of the bad storm, John delivered his papers on time.* (John did not let the storm keep him from delivering his papers.) *In spite of all their differences, Joan and Ann remain friends.* (Joan and Ann remain friends even though they are different.)

in stitches *adj. phr., informal* Laughing so hard that the sides ache; in a fit of laughing hard. *The comedian was so funny that he had everyone who was watching him in stitches.* (Everyone laughed at the comedian until it hurt to laugh any more.)

in stock *adj. phr.* Having something ready to sell or use; in present possession or supply; to be sold. *The store had no more red shoes in stock, so Mary chose brown ones instead.* (There were no more red shoes in the store's supply of shoes.)

in store *adv. or adj. phr.* Ready to happen; waiting.—Often used in the phrase *hold* or *have in store*. *What does the future hold in store for the boy who ran away?* (What will happen to the boy?) *There is a surprise in store for Helen when she gets home.* (A surprise is waiting for her.)

in the air *adv. phr.* **1** In everyone's thoughts. *Christmas was in the air for weeks before.* (Everyone was thinking about Christmas and planning for it for weeks before.) *The war filled people's thoughts every day; it was in the air.* (People's minds were kept on the war in many ways.) **2** Meeting the bodily senses; surrounding one so as to be smelled or felt. *Spring is in the air.* (You can smell the smells of spring, and see its signs, and feel it about you.) *Rain is in the air.* (It feels as if it is going to rain.)

in the bag *adj. phr., informal* Sure to be won or gotten; certain. *Jones had the election in the bag after the shameful news about his opponent came out.* (He had the election won.) *We thought we had the game in the bag.* (We thought our team couldn't lose.)

in the black *adv. or adj. phr., informal* In a successful or profitable way; so as to make money. *The big store was running in the black.* (The big store was making a profit; it was in good business condition.) *A business must stay in the black to keep on.* (A business cannot last unless it makes money.)

in the cards *adj. phr., informal* To be expected; likely to happen; foreseeable; predictable. *It was in the cards for the son to succeed his father as head of the business.* (It was in the natural order for the son to take charge.)

in the clear *adj. phr.* **1** Free of anything that makes moving or seeing difficult; with nothing to limit action. *The plane climbed above the clouds and was flying in the clear.* (The plane was flying free of clouds that would make it hard to see where it was going.) **2** *informal* Free of blame or suspicion; not thought to be guilty. *After John told the principal that he broke the window, Martin was in the clear.* (At first the principal thought Martin broke the window, but John said he did, and the principal stopped suspecting Martin.) **3** Free of debt; not owing money to anyone. *Bob borrowed a thousand dollars from his father to start his business, but at the end of the first year he was in the clear.* (He earned enough to repay his father the money and was not in debt any more.)

in the clouds *adj. phr.* Far from real life; in dreams; in fancy; in thought. *Mary is looking out the window, not at the chalkboard; her head is in the clouds again.* (Mary isn't paying attention to the lesson; she is dreaming again.) *A good teacher should have his head*

in the clouds sometimes, but his feet always on the ground. (A good teacher should have imagination, but also be able to really do things.)

in the dark *adj. phr.* In ignorance; without information. *John was in the dark about the job he was being sent to.* (He didn't know what he would find.) *If the government controls the news, it can keep people in the dark on any topic it chooses.* (It can keep them in ignorance.)

in the doghouse *adj. phr., slang* In disgrace or disfavor. *Our neighbor got in the doghouse with his wife by coming home drunk.* (Our neighbor's wife is angry with him for coming home drunk.) *Jerry is in the doghouse because he dropped the ball, and the other team won because of that.* (The other players are angry with Jerry.)

in the groove *adj. phr., slang* Doing something very well; near perfection; at one's best. *The band was right in the grove that night.* (The band was playing its best.) *It was an exciting football game; every player was really in the groove.* (Every player did his part perfectly.)

in the hole *adv. or adj. phr., informal* **1a** Having a score lower than zero in a game, especially a card game; to a score below zero. *John went three points in the hole on the first hand of the card game.* (John lost on the first play and his score was three below zero.) **1b** Behind an opponent; in difficulty in a sport or game. *We had their pitcher in the hole with the bases full and no one out.* (Their pitcher was in danger of losing the game.) **2** In debt; behind financially. *John went in the hole with his hot dog stand.* (He lost money on it.) *It's a lot easier to* *get in the hole than to get out again.* (It's easier to get in debt than to get out of it.)

in the line of duty *adj. phr.* Done or happening as part of a job. *The policeman was shot in the line of duty.* (The policeman was shot while he was working.) *The soldier had to clean his rifle in the line of duty.* (Cleaning his rifle is a part of a soldier's job.)

in the long run *also* **over the long run** *adv. phr.* In the end; in the final result. *John knew that he could make a success of the little weekly paper in the long run.* (John knew that if he had enough time, he could make the paper profitable at last.) *You may make good grades by studying only before examinations, but you will succeed in the long run only by studying hard every day.* (By studying hard every day you will learn what you need to succeed in life.)

in the market for *adj. phr.* Wishing to buy; ready to buy. *Mr. Jones is in the market for a new car.* (Mr. Jones is ready to buy a new car.) *People are always in the market for entertainment.* (People are always ready to pay to be entertained.)

in the red *adv. or adj. phr., informal* In an unprofitable way; so as to lose money. *A large number of American radio stations operate in the red.* (Many American radio stations lose money.) *A rich man who has a farm or ranch often runs it in the red, but makes his money with his factory or business.* (He runs his farm or ranch for pleasure, losing money.) [From the fact that people who in former times kept business records wrote in red ink how much money they lost and in black ink how much money they gained.]

in the saddle *adv. or adj. phr.* In command; in control; in a position to order or boss others. *Mr. Park was in the saddle when he had over half the company's stock.* (He could have his way; he controlled the company.) *Getting appointed chief of police put Stevens in the saddle.* (When he became chief, he could give orders in the police department.)

in the same boat *adv. or adj. phr.* In the same trouble; in the same fix; in the same bad situation. *When the town's one factory closed and hundreds of people lost their jobs, all the storekeepers were in the same boat.* (Nobody had any money to pay any of them.) *Dick was disappointed when Fern refused to marry him, but he knew others were in the same boat.* (He knew she had refused several other men.)

in the soup *adj. phr., slang* In serious trouble; in confusion; in disorder. *The police misunderstood Harry's night errand, and arrested him, which put him in the soup with the boss.* (His boss got the wrong idea, and lost faith in him.)

in the swim *adj. phr.* Doing the same things that other people are doing; following the fashion (as in business or social affairs); busy with what most people are doing. *Jim found some college friends at the lake that summer, and soon was in the swim of things.* (He was soon included in their activities.)

in the wake of *prep., literary* As a result of; right after; following. *Many troubles follow in the wake of war.* (Much trouble follows war.) *There were heavy losses of property in the wake of* *the flood.* (The flood caused much loss of property.)

in the wind *adj. phr.* Seeming probable; being planned; soon to happen. *Changes in top management of the company had been in the wind for weeks.* (It had been rumored for weeks that the directors were going to bring in a new president.) *Tom's close friends knew that marriage was in the wind.* (They knew Tom planned to marry soon.)

in the works *adv. or adj. phr.* In preparation; being planned or worked on; in progress. *John was told that the paving of his street was in the works.* (He was told that paving had been ordered and was being planned.)

in the wrong *adj. phr.* With moral or legal right or truth against one; against justice, truth or fact; wrong. *In attacking a smaller boy, Jack was plainly in the wrong.* (Jack showed himself a bully and a coward.)

in time *adv. or adj. phr.* **1** Soon enough. *We got to Washington in time for the cherry blossoms.* (We visited Washington early enough to see the cherry blossoms.) **2** In the end; after a while; finally. *Fred and Jim did not like each other at first, but in time they became friends.* (After a long time, they became friends.) **3** In the right rhythm; in step. *The marchers kept in time with the band.* (They kept in step with the beat of the music.)

into thin air *adv. phr.* Without anything left; completely. *When Bob returned to the room, he was surprised to find that his books had vanished into thin air.* (Bob's books were not there and he could not understand why.)

in touch *adj. phr.* Talking or writing to each other; giving and getting news. *John kept in touch with his school friends during the summer.* (John and his school friends wrote letters to each other during the summer.)

in tow *adj. phr.* **1** Being pulled. *The tugboat had the large ocean liner in tow as they came into the harbor.* (The tug pulled the liner into the harbor.) **2** Being taken from place to place; along with someone. *Janet took the new girl in tow and showed her where to go.* (Janet told the new girl to follow her.) *Mrs. Hayes went to the supermarket with her four little children in tow.* (Mrs. Hayes took her children along with her to the supermarket.)

in tune *adv. or adj. phr.* Going well together; in agreement; matching, agreeable.—Often used with *with*. *In his new job, John felt in tune with his surroundings and his associates.* (He liked the place where he worked and the people he worked with.)

in turn *adv. phr.* According to a settled order; each following another. *Each man in turn got up and spoke.* (Each man got up and spoke, one after another.)

in two shakes of a lamb's tail *adv. informal* Quickly, in no time at all. *I'll be back in two shakes of a lamb's tail.* (I'll be back right away.)

in vain *adv. phr.* **1** Without effect; without getting the desired result; without success. *The drowning man called in vain for help.* (He called for help without getting it.)

in view of *adv. phr.* After thinking about; because of. *Schools were closed for the day in view of the heavy snowstorm.*

(Schools were closed for the day because of the heavy snow-storm.)

in with *prep.* In friendship, favor, or closeness with. *We assumed Byrd was in with the mayor, not knowing that the mayor no longer liked him.* (We depended on his being a friend of the mayor, but he no longer was.)

iron out *v. informal* To discuss and reach an agreement about (a difference); find a solution for (a problem); remove (a difficulty). *The company and its workers ironed out their differences over hours and pay.* (They talked over their disagreements and reached an agreement.)

irons in the fire *n. phr.* Things one is doing; the projects with which a person is busy. *John had a number of irons in the fire, and he managed to keep all of them hot.* (He was working on several things at the same time, and doing them well.)

itching palm *n., slang* A wish for money; greed. *He was born with an itching palm.* (He always has wanted money.) *The bellboys in that hotel seem always to have itching plams.* (They seem very eager to get tips.)

J

jack of all trades *n., informal* (Often followed by the words 'master of none') A person who is knowledgeable in many areas. (Can be used as praise, or as a derogatory remark depending on the context and the intonation. a) *Peter is a jack of all trades, he can survive anywhere!* (He is being complimented on his versatility.) b) *"How come Joe did such a sloppy job?"* Mary asked. *"He's a jack-of-all-trades,"* Sally answered. (Sally explains his poor performance by blaming it on his overdiversification.)

jack up *v.* **1** To lift with a jack. *The man jacked up his car to fix a flat tire.* (The man used a tool to raise his car off the ground.) **2** *informal* To make (a price) higher; raise. *Just before Christmas, some stores jack up their prices.* (Some stores raise the cost of things just before Christmas because they know that people will buy them.)

jailbait *n., slang* A girl below the legal age of consent for sex; one who tempts another person to intimacy that is possibly punishable by imprisonment. *Stay away from Arabella; she is jailbait.* (Don't become intimate with Arabella, because she is a minor.)

jawbreaker *n.* **1** A large piece of hard candy or bubblegum. *Billy asked his mother for money to buy some jawbreakers and a chocolate bar.* (Billy bought some hard candy and a chocolate bar.) **2** *informal* A word or name that is hard to pronounce. *His name, Nissequogue, is a real jawbreaker.* (His name is very hard to say.)

jazz up *v., slang* To brighten up; add more noise, movement, or color; make more lively or exciting. *The party was very dull until Pete jazzed it up with his drums.* (When Pete played his drums, everyone at the party enjoyed it more.)

John Doe *n.* A name used for an unknown person, especially in police and law business. *The alarm went out for a John Doe who stole the diamonds from the store.* (The police are looking for an unknown person who stole the diamonds.)

John Hancock *or* **John Henry** *n., informal* One's signature; one's name in writing. *The man said, "Put your John Hancock on this paper."* (He asked the person to sign his name on the paper.) *Joe felt proud when he put his John Henry on his very first driver's license.* (Joe was proud to sign his name on his first driver's license.)

Johnny-come lately *n.* Someone new in a place or group; newcomer; *also:* a new person who takes an active part in group affairs before the group has accepted him; upstart. *Everybody was amazed when a Johnny-come-lately beat the old favorite in the race.* (An unknown runner defeated the favorite.)

Johnny-on-the-spot *adj. phr.* At the right place when needed; present and ready to help; very prompt; on time. *The firemen were Johnny-on-the-spot and put out the fire in the house soon after it started.* (The firemen came quickly when they were needed.)

jump at *v.* To take or accept quickly and gladly. *Johnny jumped at the invitation to go swimming with his brother.* (Johnny quickly accepted the invitation to go swimming with his brother.)

jump bail *or* **skip bail** *v. phr., informal* To run away and fail to come to trial, and so to give up a certain amount of money already given to a court of law to hold with the promise that one would come. *The robber paid $2,000 bail so he wouldn't be put in jail before his trial. But he jumped bail and escaped to Mexico.* (When the robber did not come back for his trial, the court kept the bail money.)

jump ball *n.* The starting of play in basketball by tossing the ball into the air between two opposing players, each of whom jumps and tries to hit the ball to a member of his own team. *Two players held onto the ball at the same time and the referee called a jump ball.* (The referee decided to put the ball in play by tossing it up between the two players who were both holding on to it.)

jump down one's throat *v. phr.* To suddenly become very angry at someone; scold severely or angrily. *The teacher jumped down Billy's throat when Billy said he did not do his homework.* (The teacher became very angry and scolded Billy because he did not do his homework.)

jumping-off place *n. phr.* **1** A place so far away that it seems to be the end of the world. *Columbus' sailors were afraid they would arrive at the jumping-off place if they sailed further west.* (They thought they would arrive at the end of the world and fall off.) *So you visited Little America? That sounds like the jumping-off place!* (Little America is so far south that it seems like the end of the world.) **2** The starting place of a long,

hard trip or of something difficult or dangerous. *The jumping-off place for the explorer's trip through the jungle was a little village.* (The village was where the explorer started on his trip.)

jump on *or* **jump all over** *or* **land on** *or* **land all over** *v. phr., informal* To scold; criticize; blame. *Tom's boss jumped all over Tom because he made a careless mistake.* (His boss scolded him crossly for being careless.) *Janice landed on Robert for dressing carelessly for their date.* (Janice complained about the way Robert dressed.) *"I don't know why Bill is always jumping on me; I just don't understand him,"* said Bob. (Bob didn't understand why Bill was always criticizing him.)

jump out of one's skin *v. phr., informal* To be badly frightened; be very much surprised. *The lightning struck so close to Bill that he almost jumped out of his skin.* (Bill was badly frightened when the lightning struck close to him.)

jump pass *n.* A pass (as in football or basketball) made by a player while jumping. *The Bruins scored when the quarterback tossed a jump pass to the left end.* (They scored when the quarterback jumped up and threw a short pass to the left end.)

jump the gun *also* **beat the gun** *v. phr.* **1** To start before the starter's gun in a race. *The runners were called back because one of them jumped the gun.* (One of them began to run before the starter shot off his gun.) **2** *informal* To start before one should; start before anyone else. *The new students were not supposed to come before noon, but one boy jumped the gun and came to school at* *eight in the morning.* (The new students were not supposed to come before noon, but one boy came at eight in the morning.)

jump the track *v. phr., informal* To change from one thought or idea to another without plan. *Bob didn't finish his algebra homework because his mind kept jumping the track to think about the new girl in class.* (Bob couldn't keep his mind on his algebra work because he kept thinking about her.)

jump through a hoop *v. phr., informal* To do whatever one is told to do; obey any order. *Bob would jump through a hoop for Mary.* (Bob would do anything Mary asked him to do.)

jump to a conclusion *v. phr.* To decide too quickly or without thinking or finding the facts. *Jerry saw his dog limping on a bloody leg and jumped to the conclusion that it had been shot.* (When Jerry saw the blood and the lame leg, he decided without really knowing that his dog had been shot.)

junked up *adj., v. phr., slang, drug culture* To be under the influence of drugs, especially heroin. *You can't talk to Billy, he's all junked up.* (You can't talk to him; he is under the influence of drugs.)

just about *adv., informal* Nearly; almost; practically. *Just about everyone in town came to hear the mayor speak.* (Almost everybody came.)

just so *adv. phr.* With great care; very carefully. *In order to raise healthy African violets you must treat them just so.* (In order to raise healthy African violets you must treat them very carefully.)

just what the doctor ordered *n. phr., informal* Exactly what is needed or wanted. *"Ah! Just what the doctor ordered!" exclaimed Joe when Marty brought him a cold soda.* (Joe was so hot he was happy to get the cold soda, which was exactly what he wanted.)

K

kangaroo court *n.* A self-appointed group that decides what to do to someone who is supposed to have done wrong. *The Chicago mob held a kangaroo court and shot the gangster who competed with Al Capone.* (They murdered him after a mock trial.)

keel over *v., informal* **1** To turn upside down; tip over; overturn.—Usually refers to a boat. *The strong wind made the sailboat keel over and the passengers fell into the water.* (The strong wind turned the boat over.) **2** *informal* To fall over in a faint; faint. *When the principal told the girl her father died, she keeled right over.* (The girl fainted when she heard that her father had died.)

keep after *v., informal* To speak to (someone) about something again and again; remind over and over again. *Sue's mother had to keep after Sue to clean her bedroom.* (Sue's mother had to keep reminding Sue to clean her bedroom.)

keep an eye on *or* **keep one's eye on** *v. phr.* **1** *or* **have one's eye on** To watch carefully; continue paying attention to. *Keep an eye on the stove in case the coffee boils.* (Watch the stove.) *You must keep your eye on the ball when you play tennis.* (You have to keep watching the ball.) *The lion tamer keeps a sharp eye on the lions when he is in the cage.* (He doesn't stop watching them carefully.) **2** To watch and do what is needed for; mind. *Mother told Jane to keep an eye on the baby while Mother was in the store.* (Mother told Jane to take care of the baby.)

keep a stiff upper lip *v. phr.* To be brave; face trouble bravely. *He was very much worried about his sick daughter, but he kept a stiff upper lip.* (He didn't become discouraged.)

keep at *v.* To continue to do; go on with. *Mary kept at her homework until she finished it.* (Mary continued doing her homework till she finished it. She did not stop to play or dream.)

keep body and soul together *v. phr.* To keep alive; survive. *John was unemployed most of the year and hardly made enough money to keep body and soul together.* (John hardly earned enough money to keep alive.)

keep books *v. phr.* To keep records of money gained and spent; do the work of a bookkeeper. *Miss Jones keeps the company's books.* (Miss Jones is the company's bookkeeper.)

keep down *v.* Keep from progressing or growing; keep within limits; control. *The children could not keep their voices down.* (The children could not keep their voices from becoming too loud.) *We hoe the garden to keep down the weeds.* (We hoe the garden to stop the weeds from growing.) *You can't keep a good person down.* (You can't stop a good person from progressing.)

keep house *v. phr.* To do the necessary things in a household; do the cooking and cleaning. *Since their mother died, Mary and her brother keep house for their father.* (They do the housework.)

keep on *v.* **1** To go ahead; not stop; continue. *Columbus kept on sailing until he saw land.* (Columbus sailed on; he did not stop.) **2** To allow to continue working for one. *The new owner kept Fred on as gardener.* (Fred continued to work as gardener; the new owner didn't fire him.)

keep one's chin up *v. phr*. To be brave; be determined; face trouble with courage. *He didn't think that he would ever get out of the jungle alive, but he kept his chin up.* (He went on bravely although he was afraid.)

keep one's eye on the ball *v. phr., informal* To be watchful and ready; be wide-awake and ready to win or succeed; be smart. *Tom is just starting on the job but if he keeps his eye on the ball, he will be promoted.* (If he is smart and ready to take the opportunity, he will succeed.)

keep one's head *also* **keep one's wits about one** *v. phr*. To stay calm when there is trouble or danger. *When Tim heard the fire alarm he kept his head and looked for the nearest exit.* (Tim did not get too excited; he thought of the best way to get out.)

keep one's mouth shut *v. phr., informal* To be or stay silent. *Charles began to tell Barry how to kick the ball, and Barry said angrily, "Keep your mouth shut!"* (Barry was angry and impolitely told Charles to be quiet.)

keep one's nose clean *v. phr., slang* To stay out of trouble; do only what one should do. *The boss said Jim could have the job as long as he kept his nose clean and worked hard.* (The boss said Jim could have the job as long as he stayed out of trouble and worked hard.)

keep one's nose to the grindstone *or* **have one's nose to the grindstone** *or* **hold one's nose to the grindstone** *v. phr., informal* To work hard all the time; keep busy with boring or tiresome work. *Sarah keeps her nose to the grindstone and saves as much as possible to start her own business.* (She is willing to work very hard to achieve her ambition.)

keep one's own counsel *v. phr., formal* To keep one's ideas and plans to oneself. *John listened to what everyone had to say in the discussion, but he kept his own counsel.* (John listened to the others, but he did not tell them his thoughts.)

keep one's shirt on *v. phr., slang* To calm down; keep from losing one's temper or getting impatient or excited. *John said to Bob, "Keep your shirt on."* (John said to Bob, "Don't get excited.")

keep pace *v. phr*. To go as fast; go at the same rate; not get behind. *When they go for a walk, Johnny has to take long steps to keep pace with his father.* (Johnny must take long steps or he will not go as fast as his father; his father will get ahead.) *When Billy was moved to a more advanced class, he had to work hard to keep pace.* (Billy had to work hard to do the same work that the other children did.)

keep tab on *or* **keep tabs on** *v. phr., informal* **1** To keep a record of. *The government tries to keep tabs on all the animals in the park.* (The government tries to keep a record of how many animals are in the park, and what kinds.) **2** To keep a watch on; check. *The housemother kept tabs on the girls to be sure they were clean and neat.* (The housemother looked at the girls often.)

keep the ball rolling *v. phr., informal* To keep up an activity or action; not allow something that is happening to slow or stop. *Clyde kept the ball rolling at the party by dancing with a lampshade on his head.* (Clyde kept the people laughing by acting silly.)

keep the home fires burning *v. phr.* To keep things going as usual while someone is away; wait at home to welcome someone back. *While John was in the army, Mary kept the home fires burning.* (Mary took care of things at home until John came back from the army.)

keep time *v. phr.* **1** To show the right time. *My watch has not kept good time since I dropped it.* (My watch has not been running right since I dropped it.) **2** To keep the beat; keep the same rhythm; keep in step. *Many people are surprised at how well deaf people keep time with the music when they dance.* (They keep in step; they dance with the same rhythm as the music.)

keep track *v. phr.* To know about changes; stay informed or up-to-date; keep a count or record. *What day of the week is it? I can't keep track.* (I can't remember the days.)

keep under one's hat *v. phr., informal* To keep secret; not tell. *Mr. Jones knew who had won the contest, but he kept it under his hat until it was announced publicly.* (Mr. Jones did not tell who had won until everyone was told.)—Often used as a command. *Keep it under your hat.* (Don't tell anyone.)

keep up *v.* **1a** To go on; not stop; continue. *The rain kept up for two days and the roads were flooded.* (The rain went on for two days.) **1b** To go on with (something); continue steadily; never stop. *Mrs. Smith told John to keep up the good work.* (Mrs. Smith told John to go on with the good work, not to stop it.) *The teacher asked Dick to stop bothering Mary, but he kept it up.* (Dick did not stop bothering Mary;

he went on doing it.) **2a** To go at the same rate as others. *John had to work hard to keep up.* (John had to work hard to keep from getting behind the others.) **2b** To keep (something) at the same level or rate or in good condition. *The shortage of tomatoes kept the prices up.* (The prices stayed high because there weren't enough tomatoes.) **3** To keep informed.—Usually used with *on* or *with*. *Mary is interested in politics and always keeps up with the news.* (Mary reads the newspapers and always knows what is happening in the world.)

keep up with the Joneses *v. phr.* To follow the latest fashion; compete with one's neighbors. *Mrs. Smith kept buying every new thing that was advertised. Finally Mr. Smith told her to stop trying to keep up with the Joneses and to start thinking for herself.* (Mr. Smith told his wife to stop wanting to have everything the neighbors had.)

kettle of fish *v. phr., informal* Something to be considered; how things are; a happening; business. *This is a fine kettle of fish! I forgot my book.* (This is a bad thing to happen! I forgot my book.)

keyed up *adj.* Excited; nervous. *Mary was all keyed up about the exam.* (She was very nervous.)

kick around *v., informal* **1** To act roughly or badly to; treat badly; bully. *John likes to kick around the little boys.* (He likes to be mean to them.) *Mr. Jones is always kicking his dog around.* (He hurts the dog.) **2** To lie around or in a place; be treated carelessly; be neglected. *This old coat has been kicking around the closet for years.* (The coat has not been used but has been left there carelessly.) *The letter kicked around on my* *desk for days.* (The letter was pushed around on the desk and neglected for days.) **3** *slang* To talk easily or carelessly back and forth about; examine in a careless or easygoing way. *Bob and I kicked around the idea of going swimming, but it was hot and we were too lazy.* (We talked it over carelessly.) **4** To move about often; go from one job or place to another; become experienced. *Harry has kicked around all over the world as a merchant seaman.* (Harry has lived a rough life as a sailor and knows the world.)

kick back *v., slang, informal* (stress on *back*) To pay money illegally for favorable contract arrangements. *I will do it if you kick back a few hundred for my firm.* (I will do it if you bribe me.)

kickback *n., slang, informal* (stress on *kick*) Money paid illegally for favorable treatment. *He was arrested for making kickbacks.* (They arrested him for paying illegal bribes.)

kick down *v. phr., slang* To shift an automobile, jeep, or truck into lower gear by hand-shifting. *Joe kicked the jeep down from third to second; and we slowed down.* (He shifted down from third to second gear).

kick it *v. phr., slang* To end a bad or unwanted habit such as drinking, smoking, or drug addiction. *Farnsworth finally kicked it; he's in good shape.* (He finally stopped his harmful habit, which is good for him.)

kick off *v.* (stress on *off*) **1** To make the kick that begins a football game. *John kicked off and the football game started.* (John started the football game by kicking the ball.) **2** *informal* To begin; launch; start. *The candidate kicked off his campaign with a*

speech on television. (The candidate started his campaign by making a speech on TV.) **3** *slang* To die. *Mr. Jones was almost ninety years old when he kicked off.* (Mr. Jones was almost ninety when he died.)

kick-off *n., informal* (stress on *kick*) A start. *The new university got a tremendous kick-off ceremony from the governor.* (They celebrated the new university's start with a festive occasion.)

kick oneself *v. phr., informal* To be sorry or ashamed; regret. *When John missed the plane, he kicked himself for not having left earlier.* (John felt sorry for not having left early enough to catch the train.) *Mary could have kicked herself for letting the secret out before it was announced officially.* (Mary was sorry that she told the secret before she should have.)

kick out *or* **boot out** *v., informal* To make (someone) go or leave; get rid of; dismiss. *The boys made so much noise at the movie that the manager kicked them out.* (The manager made the boys leave the theater.)

kick over *v.* **1** *Of a motor:* To begin to work. *He had not used his car for two months and when he tried to start it, the motor would not kick over.* (His car would not start after it had been left for so long.) **2** *slang* To pay; contribute. *The gang forced all the storekeepers on the block to kick over $5 a week.* (The storekeepers had to pay the gang every week.) **3** *slang* To die. Mrs. O'Keefe's old cow kicked over this morning. (The cow died.)

kick the bucket *v. phr., slang* To die. *Old Mr. Jones kicked the bucket just two days before his* *ninety-fourth birthday.* (Mr. Jones died.)

kick up a fuss *or* **kick up a row** *or* **raise a row** *also* **kick up the dust** *v. phr., informal* To make trouble; make a disturbance. *When the teacher gave the class five more hours of homework, the class kicked up a fuss.* (The class objected loudly.)

kick up one's heels *v. phr., informal* To have a merry time; celebrate. *When exams were over the students went to town to kick up their heels.* (The students celebrated the end of exams by having a good time.)

kill off *v.* To kill or end completely; destroy. *The factory dumped poisonous wastes into the river and killed off the fish.* (The factory waste materials were poison and killed all the fish in the river.)

kill the goose that laid the golden egg To spoil something that is good or something that one has, by being greedy. *Mrs. Jones gives you an apple from her tree whenever you go by her house, but don't kill the goose that laid the golden egg by bothering her too much.* (Don't be too greedy or Mrs. Jones will stop giving you apples.)

kill two birds with one stone *v. phr.* To succeed in doing two things by only one action. *Mother stopped at the supermarket to buy bread and then went to get Jane at dancing class; she killed two birds with one stone.* (Mother bought bread and brought Jane home with only one trip in the car.)

knock about *or* **knock around** *v.* To travel without a plan; go where one pleases. *After he graduated from college, Joe knocked about for a year seeing the coun-*

try before he went to work in his father's business. (Joe traveled around the country, going where he pleased, before he went to work.)

knocked out *adj., slang* Intoxicated, drugged, out of one's mind. *Kinworthy sounds so incoherent, he must be knocked out.* (He must be drunk or high on drugs; he makes no sense.)

knock it off *v. phr., slang, informal* **1** To stop talking about something considered not appropriate or nonsensical by the listener; used frequently as an imperative. *Come on, Joe, knock it off; you're not making any sense at all!* (Stop talking nonsense; you're not making sense.) **2** To cease doing something, to quit; heavily favored in the imperative. *Come on boys, knock it off; you're breaking the furniture in my room!* (The boys were fighting and breaking the furniture; their father tells them to stop it.)

knock off *v. phr., slang* **1** To burglarize someone. *They knocked off the Manning residence.* (They burglarized the Manning residence.) **2** To murder someone. *The gangsters knocked off Herman.* (They murdered Herman.)

knock off one's feet *v. phr.* To surprise or shock (someone) so much that he does not know what to do. *Her husband's death knocked Mrs. Jones off her feet.* (Mr. Jones's death was such a shock that Mrs. Jones couldn't think of anything else for a while.) *When Charlie was given the prize, it knocked him off his feet for a few minutes.* (Charlie was so surprised he didn't know what to think or say.)

knock one's block off *v. phr., slang* To hit someone very hard; beat someone up. *Stay out of my*

yard or I'll knock your block off.
(Keep out of my yard or I'll beat you up.)

knock oneself out *v. phr., informal* To work very hard; make a great effort. *Mrs. Ross knocked herself out planning her daughter's wedding.* (Mrs. Ross worked very hard planning her daughter's wedding.)

knock on wood *v. phr.* To knock on something made of wood to keep from having bad luck.— Many people superstitiously believe that one will have bad luck if one talks about good luck or brags about something, unless one knocks on wood; often used in a joking way. *Charles said, "I haven't been sick all winter." Grandfather said, "You'd better knock on wood when you say that."* (Grandfather pretended that Charles would get sick if he didn't knock on something made of wood, because he bragged about his good health.)

knockout *n., slang* Strikingly beautiful woman. *Sue is a regular knockout.* (She is a strikingly beautiful woman.)

knock out *v. phr.* To make helpless, unworkable, or unusable. *The champion knocked out the challenger in the third round.* (The champion defeated the challenger by hitting him until he was unconscious.) *The soldier knocked out two enemy tanks with his bazooka.* (The soldier destroyed two enemy tanks.)

knock the living daylights out of *v. phr., slang, informal* To render (someone) unconscious (said in exaggeration.) *The news almost knocked the living daylights out of me.* (I almost fainted when I heard the news.)

know-it-all *n.* A person who acts as if he knows all about everything; someone who thinks no one can tell him anything new. *After George was elected as class president, he wouldn't take suggestions from anyone; he became a know-it-all.* (George became a person who thinks he knows all about a subject and won't let anyone tell him anything.)—Also used like an adjective. *The other students didn't like George's know-it-all attitude.* (The other students did not like the way George acted as though he knew more than anyone else.)

know which side one's bread is buttered on *v. phr.* To know who can help one and try to please him; know what is for one's own gain. *Dick was always polite to the boss; he knew which side his bread was buttered on.* (Dick knew that he would lose his job if he made the boss angry at him.)

knuckle under *v. phr.* To do something because one is forced to do it. *Bobby refused to knuckle under to the bully.* (Bobby refused to do what the bully told him to do.)

L

labor of love *n. phr.* Something done for personal pleasure and not pay or profit. *Building the model railroad was a labor of love for the retired engineer.* (He built the model railroad because he enjoyed doing it, not for money.)

lady friend *n.* **1** A woman friend. *His aunt stays with a lady friend in Florida during the winter.* (His aunt stays with a woman friend in Florida during the winter.) **2** *informal* Used by people trying to appear polite to mean a woman who is a man's mistress. *The lawyer took his lady friend to dinner.* (The lawyer took his mistress to dinner.)

lady killer *n., informal* **1** Any man who has strong sex appeal toward women. *Joe is a regular lady killer.* (He has strong sex appeal toward women.) **2** A man who relentlessly pursues amorous conquests, is successful at it, and then abandons his heartbroken victims. *The legendary Don Juan of Spain is the most famous lady killer of recorded history.* (Don Juan was the most famous conqueror of women whom he subsequently abandoned.)

lady's man *n.* A man or boy who likes to be with women or girls and its popular with them. *Charlie is quite a lady's man now.* (Charlie is with the girls much of his time.)

lame duck *n., informal* An elected public official who has been either defeated in a new election or whose term cannot be renewed, but who has a short period of time left in office during which he can still perform certain duties, though with somewhat diminished powers. *In the last year of their second terms, American presidents are lame ducks.* (They cannot be reelected for a third term.)

lap up *v.* **1** To eat or drink with the tip of the tongue. *The kitten laps up its milk.* (The kitten licks the milk up with its tongue.) **2** *informal* To take in eagerly. *She flatters him all the time and he just laps it up.* (She flatters him and he loves it.)

lash out *v.* **1** To try suddenly to hit. *The woman lashed out at the crowd with her umbrella.* (The woman swung her umbrella at the crowd.) **2** To attack with words. *The senator lashed out at the administration.* (The senator criticized the administration severely.)

last but not least *adv. phr.* In the last place but not the least important. *Billy will bring sandwiches, Alice will bring cake, Susan will bring cookies, John will bring potato chips, and last but not least, Sally will bring the lemonade.* (Sally is mentioned last, but her lemonade is as important to the picnic as the other things.)

last straw *or* **straw that breaks the camel's back** *n. phr.* A small trouble which follows other troubles and makes one lose patience and be unable to bear them. *Bill had a bad day in school yesterday. He lost his knife on the way home, then he fell down, and when he broke a shoelace, that was the last straw and he began to cry.* (He had too many troubles and began to cry.)

last word *n.* **1** The last remark in an argument. *I never win an argument with her. She always has the last word.* (She always has one more thing to say than I do in an argument.) **2** The final say in deciding something. *The superintendent has the last word*

173

in ordering new desks. (He is the one who decides when to order new desks.) **3** *informal* The most modern thing. *Mrs. Green's stove is the last word in stoves.* (Her stove is the most modern stove available.)

laugh off *v.* To dismiss with a laugh as not important or not serious; not take seriously. *You can't laugh off a ticket for speeding.* (You must take a ticket for speeding seriously.)

lay a finger on *v. phr.* To touch or bother, even a little.—Used in negative, interrogative, imperative, and conditional sentences. *Don't you dare lay a finger on the vase!* (Don't you dare touch that vase!) *If you so much as lay a finger on my boy, I'll call the police.* (If you even touch my boy, I will call the police.)

lay an egg *v. phr., slang* To fail to win the interest or favor of an audience. *His joke laid an egg.* (No one laughed at his joke.) *Sometimes he is a successful speaker, but sometimes he lays an egg.* (Sometimes the audience does not like his speech.)

lay away *v.* **1** To save. *She laid a little of her pay away each week.* (She saved a little of her pay each week.) **2** To bury (a person).—Used to avoid the word *bury*, which some people think is unpleasant. *He was laid away in his favorite spot on the hill.* (He was buried in his favorite spot on the hill.)

layaway plan *n.* A plan for buying something that one can't pay cash for; a plan in which one pays some money down and pays a little more when one can, and the store holds the article until one has paid the full price. *She could not afford to pay for the coat all at once, so she used the*

layaway plan. (She paid fifty dollars every month until her coat was paid for; then she could take the coat home.)

lay down the law *v. phr.* **1** To give strict orders. *The teacher lays down the law about homework every afternoon.* (She gives strict orders to the students about their homework.) **2** To speak severely or seriously about a wrongdoing; scold. *The principal called in the students and laid down the law to them about skipping classes.* (The principal called in the students and scolded them for skipping classes.)

lay eyes on *or* **set eyes on** *v. phr.* To see. *She knew he was different as soon as she laid eyes on him.* (She could tell he was different as soon as she saw him.) *I didn't know the man; in fact, I had never set eyes on him.* (I had never seen him before.)

lay hands on *v. phr.* **1** To get hold of; find; catch. *If the police can lay hands on him, they will put him in jail.* (If they can catch him, they will put him in jail.) **2** To do violence to; harm; hurt. *They were afraid that if they left him alone in his disturbed condition he would lay hands on himself.* (They were afraid that he would harm himself if they left him alone because he was so upset.)

lay hold of *v. phr.* **1** To take hold of; grasp; grab. *He laid hold of the rope and pulled the boat ashore.* (He grabbed the rope and pulled the boat ashore.) **2** To get possession of. *He sold every washing machine he could lay hold of.* (He sold every washing machine he could get.)

lay in *v.* To store up a supply of; to get and keep for future use. *Mrs. Mason heard that the price of sugar might go up, so she laid* *in a hundred pounds of it.* (She bought one hundred pounds of sugar.)

lay into *or* **light into** *v., informal* **1** To attack physically; go at vigorously. *The two fighters laid into each other as soon as the bell rang.* (The two fighters began fighting hard as soon as the bout began.) *John loves Italian food and he really laid into the spaghetti.* (John loves Italian food and he really ate a lot of spaghetti.) **2** *slang* To attack with words. *The senator laid into the opponents of his bill.* (The senator spoke strongly against those who were against his idea for a new law.)

lay it on *or* **lay it on thick** *also* **put it on thick** *or* **spread it on thick** *v. phr., informal* To persuade someone by using flattery; flatter. *Bob wanted to go the movies. He laid it on thick to his mother.* (Bob tried to flatter his mother into letting him go to the movies.) *Mary was caught fibbing. She sure spread it on thick.* (Mary tried flattery to get people to forget that she had fibbed.)

lay low *v.* To knock down; to force into a lying position; to put out of action. *Many trees were laid low by the storm.* (Many trees were knocked down by the storm.) *Jane was laid low by the flu.* (Jane had to stay in bed with the flu.) **2** To kill. *The hunters laid low seven pheasants.* (The hunters shot seven pheasants.)

lay off *v.* **1** To mark out the boundaries or limits. *He laid off a baseball diamond on the vacant lot.* (He measured the lines for a baseball diamond.) **2** To pull out of work. *The company lost the contract for making the shoes and laid off half its workers.* (The company had to stop making the

shoes and half the workers lost their jobs.) **3** *slang* To stop bothering; leave alone—Usually used in the imperative. *Lay off me, will you? I have to study for a test.* (Leave me alone; I have to study.) **4** *slang* To stop using or taking. *His doctor told him to lay off cigarettes.* (His doctor told him to stop smoking cigarettes.)

lay one's cards on the table *or* **lay down one's cards** *or* **put one's cards on the table** *v. phr., informal* To let someone know one's position and interest openly; deal honestly; act without trickery or secrets. *In talking about buying the property, Peterson laid his cards on the table about his plans for it.* (In trying to buy the property, he said honestly what he would use it for.)

lay oneself out *v. phr., informal* To make an extra hard effort; try very hard. *Larry wanted to win a medal for his school, so he really laid himself out in the race.* (Larry tried very hard in the race.)

lay one's hands on *or* **get one's hands on** *v. phr.* **1** To seize in order to punish or treat roughly. *If I ever lay my hands on that boy he'll be sorry.* (If I ever get hold of that boy to punish him, he'll be sorry.) **2** To get possession of. *He was unable to lay his hands on a Model T Ford for the school play.* (He couldn't get a Model T Ford for the school play.) **3** *or* **lay one's hand on** *or* **put one's hand on** To find; locate. *He keeps a file of letters so he can lay his hands on one whenever he needs it.* (He keeps a file of letters so he can easily find one when he needs it.)

lay on the line *or* **put on the line** *v. phr., informal* **1** To pay or offer to pay. *The sponsors had to lay nearly a million dollars on the line to keep the show on TV.* (The sponsors had to give nearly a million dollars to keep the show on TV.) **2** To say plainly so that there can be no doubt; tell truthfully. *I'm going to lay it on the line for you, Paul. You must work harder if you want to pass.* (I'm going to make you understand, Paul, by telling you clearly and truthfully.) **3** To take a chance of losing; risk. *The champion is laying his title on the line in the fight tonight.* (The champion is risking the loss of the championship in the fight.) *Frank decided to lay his job on the line and tell the boss that he thought he was wrong.* (He decided to risk making the boss angry and losing his job by saying that the boss was wrong.)

lay out *v.* **1** To prepare (a dead body) for burial. *The corpse was laid out by the undertaker.* (The corpse was readied for burial by the undertaker.) **2** *slang* To knock down flat; to hit unconscious. *A stiff right to the jaw laid the boxer out in the second round.* (A hard right to the jaw knocked him flat in the second round.) **3** To plan. *Come here, Fred, I have a job laid out for you.* (Come here, Fred, I have a job planned for you.) **4** To mark or show where work is to be done. *The foreman laid out the job for the new machinist.* (The foreman marked where he wanted the new machinist to work.) **5** To plan the building or arrangement of; design. *The architect laid out the interior of the building.* (The architect made a drawing showing how the inside of the building was to be built.) *The early colonists laid out towns in the wilderness.* (The early colonists planned and built towns in the wilderness.) **6** *slang* To spend; pay. *How much did you have to lay out for your new car?* (How much did you have to pay for your new car?)

lay over *v.* To arrive in one place and wait some time before continuing the journey. *We had to lay over in St. Louis for two hours, waiting for a plane to Seattle.* (Arriving in St. Louis, we had to wait two hours for the plane to Seattle.)

lay to rest *v. phr. informal* **1** To put a dead person into a grave or tomb; bury. *President Kennedy was laid to rest in Arlington National Cemetery.* (He was buried there.) **2** To get rid of; put away permanently; stop. *The scoutmaster's fears that Tom had drowned were laid to rest when Tom came back and said he had gone for a boat ride.* (The scoutmaster's worries about Tom were stopped when Tom returned.) *The rumor that the principal had accepted another job was laid to rest when he said it wasn't true.* (The rumor was stopped when he said it wasn't true.)

lay up *v.* **1** To collect a supply of; save for future use; store. *Bees lay up honey for the winter.* (They collect a supply of it so that they will have enough to eat until the next spring when they can make more.) **2**—In passive. To be kept in the house or in bed because of sickness or injury; disable. *Jack was laid up with a twisted knee and couldn't play in the final game.* (He was kept in his bed by the injury which stopped him from playing football.) **3** To take out of active service; put in a boat dock or a garage. *Bill had to lay up his boat when school started.* (He had to put it away until summer came again.) *If you lay up a car for the winter, you should take out the battery.* (If you let a car sit unused in a garage, you should remove the battery.)

lay waste *v. phr., literary* To cause wide and great damage to; destroy and leave in ruins, wreck. *Enemy soldiers laid waste the land.* (They caused much damage to it, wrecking buildings and destroying crops as they went on.)

lead a dogs life *v. phr., informal* To live a hard life; work hard and be treated unkindly. *A new college student of long ago led a dog's life.* (He was treated roughly. Any upperclassman could order him to do things.)

lead a merry chase *v. phr.* To delay or escape capture by (someone) skillfully; make (a pursuer) work hard. *Valerie is leading her boyfriend a merry chase.* (She is making him work hard to get her to marry him.)

lead by the nose *v. phr., informal* To have full control of; make or persuade (someone) to do anything whatever. *Don't let anyone lead you by the nose; use your own judgment and do the right thing.* (Don't let anyone tell you what to do unless it is right.)

lead off *v.* To begin, start, open. *Richardson led off the inning with a double.* (Richardson began the inning by hitting a double.)

lead on *v. phr.* To encourage one to believe something untrue or mistaken. *We were led on to think that Jeanne and Jim were engaged to be married.* (We were given reasons to believe that Jeanne and Jim were engaged, when they were not.)

lead the way *v. phr.* To go before and show how to go somewhere; guide. *The boys need someone to lead the way on their hike.* (The boys need someone to go with them and guide them on their hike.)

lean on *v. phr., slang, informal* To pressure (someone) by blackmailing, threats, physical violence, or the withholding of some favor in order to make the person comply with a wish or request. *I would gladly do what you ask if you only stopped leaning on me so hard!* (I would do what you want, if you only stopped pressuring me.)

leave a bad taste in one's mouth *v. phr.* To have a bad impression; make one feel disgusted.— *His rudeness to the teacher left a bad taste in my mouth.* (I got a bad impression of him.)

leave no stone unturned *v. phr.* To try in every way; miss no chance; do everything possible.—*The police will leave no stone unturned in their search for the bank robbers.* (They will try every way they know to find those who robbed the bank.)

leave hanging *or* **leave hanging in the air** *v. phr.* To leave undecided or unsettled. *Because the committee could not decide on a time and place, the matter of the spring dance was left hanging.* (The committee did not make a final decision about the dance.) *Ted's mother didn't know what to do about the broken window, so his punishment was left hanging in the air until his father came home.* (She postponed the matter until his father came.)

leave holding the bag *or* **leave holding the sack** *v. phr., informal* **1** To cause (someone) not to have something needed; leave without anything. *In the rush for seats, Joe was left holding the bag.* (There were not enough seats for everyone, and Joe's slowness left him alone without one.) **2** To force (someone) to take the whole responsibility or blame for something that others should share. *When the ball hit the glass, the team scattered and left George holding the bag.* (They ran away and left Goerge to take all the blame for the broken window.)

leave in the lurch *v. phr.* To desert or leave alone in trouble; refuse to help or support. *The town bully caught Eddie, and Tom left him in the lurch.* (Tom refused to stay and help him. He left Eddie to fight his battle alone.)

leave off *v.* To come or put to an end; stop. *There is a high fence where the school yard leaves off and the woods begin.* (The fence is where the school yard ends.) *Don told the boys to leave off teasing his little brother.* (He told them to stop teasing his little brother.)

left-handed compliment An ambiguous compliment interpretable as offensive. *I didn't know you could look so pretty! Is that a wig you're wearing?* (I find it unusual that you look so good; most often you're not so attractive.)

leg man *n., informal* **1** An errand boy; one who performs messenger services, or the like. *Joe hired a leg man for the office.* (He hired an errand boy to do the running back and forth.) **2** *slang, semi-vulgar, avoidable* A man who is particularly attracted to good-looking female legs and pays less attention to other parts of the female anatomy. *Herb is a leg man.* (He doesn't care what a girl's face looks like as long as she has sexy legs.)

leg to stand on *n. phr.* A firm foundation of facts; facts to support one's claim. *Amos sued for damages, but did not have a leg to stand on.* (Amos had no facts to support his case and lost in court.)

leg work *n., informal* The physical end of a project, such as the typing of research reports; the physical investigating of a criminal affair; the carrying of books to and from libraries, etc. *Joe, my research assistant, does a lot of leg work for me.* (He does the physical part of the work for me.)

let alone *conj. phr.* Even less; certainly not.—Used after a negative clause. *I can't add two and two, let alone do fractions.* (I can't do simple arithmetic, certainly not fractions.) *Jim can't drive a car, let alone a truck.* (He can't drive a car and of course he cannot drive a truck.)

let bygones be bygones *v. phr.* To let the past be forgotten. *After a long, angry quarrel the two boys agreed to let bygones be bygones and made friends again.* (The boys agreed to forget their quarrel and to be friends again.)

let down *v.* **1** To relax, stop trying so hard; take it easy. *The horse let down near the end of the race and lost.* (He ran slower and the other horses beat him.) *The team let down in the fourth quarter because they were far ahead.* (The team had a much bigger score, so they did not play hard in the last quarter.) **2** To fail to do as well as (someone) expected; disappoint. *The team felt they had let the coach down.* (They felt they had disappointed him by not playing as well as he expected them to.)

let down easy *v. phr.* To refuse or say no to (someone) in a pleasant manner; to tell bad news about a refusal or disappointment in a kindly way. *The boss tried to let Jim down easy when he had to tell him he was too young for the job.* (He told him that he was too young but perhaps when he was older he could work there.)

let go v. **1** To weaken and break under pressure. *The old water pipe suddenly let go and water poured out of it.* (The pipe broke and let water out.) **2** To pay no attention to; neglect. *Robert let his teeth go when he was young and now he has to go to the dentist often.* (He did not take care of his teeth and now they are bad.) *After she was married, Jane let herself go and was not pretty anymore.* (She neglected her looks and was not pretty.) **3** To allow something to pass; do nothing about. *When Charles was tardy, the teacher scolded him and let it go at that.* (She did not punish him much, but was satisfied to scold him.) **4** To discharge from a job; fire. *Mr. Wilson got into a quarrel with his boss and was let go.* (His boss fired him because they had an argument.) **5** To make (something) go out quickly; shoot; fire. *The soldiers let go a number of shots.* (The soldiers fired their guns.) **6** *or* **let oneself go** *informal* To be free in one's actions or talk; relax. *Judge Brown let himself go at the reunion of his old class and had a good time.* (Judge Brown enjoyed himself with his old schoolmates and did not have to be polite and dignified.)

let grass grow under one's feet v. phr. To be idle; be lazy; waste time. Used in negative, conditional, and interrogative sentences. *The new boy joined the football team, made the honor roll, and found a girlfriend during the first month of school. He certainly did not let any grass grow under his feet.* (He did not waste any time, but worked hard and made use of every minute.)

let————have it v. phr. **1a** slang To hit hard. *He drew back and let the man have it.* (He hit the man with his fist.) **1b** slang To use a weapon on; shoot; knife. *The guard pulled his gun and let the robber have it in the leg.* (He shot the robber in the leg.)

let it all hang out v. phr., slang, informal Not to disguise anything; to let the truth be known. *Sue can't deceive anyone; she just lets it all hang out.* (She lets the truth be known.)

let it lay v. phr., used imperatively, ungrammatical, slang Forget it; leave it alone; do not be concerned or involved. *Don't get involved with Max again—just let it lay.* (Stay away from him; leave the whole matter alone.)

let it rip v. phr., used imperatively, slang **1** Don't be concerned; pay no attention to what happens. *Why get involved? Forget about it and let it rip.* (Let the situation turn out as it will; be unconcerned.) **2** (Imperatively) Do become involved and make the most of it; get in there and really try to win. *Come on man, give it all you've got and let it rip!* (Try as hard as you can and win!)

let loose v. **1** *or* **set loose** *or* **turn loose.** To set free, loosen or give up one's hold on. *The farmer opened the gate and let the bull loose in the pasture.* (The farmer let the bull go free.) *They turned the balloon loose to let it rise in the air.* (They dropped the rope of the balloon and let it rise in the air.) **2** *informal* To release something held. *Those dark clouds are going to let loose any minute.* (It is going to rain hard.) **3** *informal* To speak or act freely; disregard ordinary limits. *The teacher told Jim that someday she was going to let loose and tell him* *what she thought of him.* (Some day she was going to scold him hard.)

let off *v.* **1** To discharge (a gun); explode; fire. *Willie accidentally let off his father's shotgun and made a hole in the wall.* (Willie touched the trigger of the shotgun accidently and the gun fired.) **2** To permit to go or escape; excuse from a penalty, a duty, or a promise. *Two boys were caught smoking in school but the principal let them off with a warning.* (The principal did not punish the two boys. He only warned them.) **3** *or informal* **let off the hook** To miss a chance to defeat or score against. *The boxer let his opponent off the hook many times.* (The boxer missed many opportunities to knock out his opponent.)

let off steam *or* **blow off steam** *v. phr.* *informal* To get rid of physical energy or strong feeling through activity; talk or be very active physically after forced quiet. *After the long ride on the bus, the children let off steam with a race to the lake.* (They were tired of being quiet in the bus and enjoyed the run.)

let on *v., informal* **1** To tell or admit what one knows. *Frank lost a quarter, but he didn't let on to his mother.* (Frank didn't want his mother to know that he lost the quarter. He didn't tell her.) **2** To try to make people believe; pretend. *The old man likes to let on that he is rich.* (The old man likes to make people believe that he is rich.)

let one's hair down *or* **let down one's hair** *v. phr., informal* Act freely and naturally; be informal; relax. *Kings and queens can seldom let their hair down.* (Their public duties give them very little chance to relax in private.)

let out *v.* **1** To allow to go out or escape. *The guard let the prisoners out of jail to work in the garden.* (The guard let the prisoners go outside of the jail to work in the garden.) **2** To allow to be known; tell. *I'll never tell you another secret if you let this one out.* (If you tell this secret to other people, I'll never tell you a secret again.) **3** To make larger (as clothing) or looser; allow to slip out (as a rope). *Mary's mother had to let out her dress because Mary is growing so tall.* (Mary's mother had to make Mary's dress longer so it would fit.) **4** *informal* To allow to move at higher speed. *The rider let out his horse to try to beat the horse ahead of him.* (The jockey let his horse run faster, or as fast as he could to try to win the race.) **5** *informal* To free from blame, responsibility, or duty— Often used with *of*. *Last time I let you out of it when you were late. I'll have to punish you this time.* (I did not punish you last time you were late. This time you will be punished.) **6** *informal* To discharge from a job; fire. *The shop closed down and all the men were let out.* (All the men who worked at the shop lost their jobs when the shop closed down.) **7** *informal* To dismiss or be dismissed. *The coach let us out from practice at 3 o'clock.* (The coach finished our practice at three o'clock and let us go.) *I'll meet you after school lets out.* (After school is over, I'll meet you.)

let ride *v. phr., informal* To allow to go on without change; accept (a situation or action) for the present. *The committee could not decide what to do about Bob's idea, so they let the matter ride for a month or so.* (They waited another month to see how things would be.)

let sleeping dogs lie   Do not make (someone) angry and cause trouble or danger; do not make trouble if you do not have to. *Don't tell Father that you broke the window. Let sleeping dogs lie.* (You don't have to tell father that you broke the window; he will be angry.)

let the cat out of the bag   *v. phr.*, *informal*   To tell about something that is supposed to be a secret. *We wanted to surprise Mary with a birthday gift, but Allen let the cat out of the bag by asking her what she would like.* (We planned a surprise for Mary, but Allen let her know about it.)

let the chips fall where they may   *v. phr.*   To pay no attention to the displeasure caused others by one's actions. *The senator decided to vote against the bill and let the chips fall where they might.* (He decided to vote as he thought right, no matter who might be angry.)

let up   *v.*, *informal*   **1** To become less or weaker; or quiet; become slower or stop. *It's raining as hard as ever. It's not letting up at all.* (It's still raining as hard as it has been, without changing.) **2** To do less or go slower or stop; relax; stop working or working hard. *Grandfather has been working all his life. When is he going to let up?* (When is he going to stop working so hard?) **3** To become easier, kinder, or less strict.—Usually used with *on*. *Let up on Jane. She is sick.* (Don't be so hard on her.)

let well enough alone   *or*   **leave well enough alone**   *v. phr.*   To be satisfied with what is good enough; not try to improve something because often that might

cause more trouble. *John wanted to make his kite go higher, but his father told him to let well enough alone because it was too windy.* (His father told him to be satisfied; trying to get it higher might damage the kite.)

lie in state   *v. phr.*   *Of a dead person:* To lie in a place of honor, sometimes with an open coffin, and be seen by the public before burial. *When the President died, thousands of people saw his body lying in state.* (The President was seen in his coffin by thousands of people before he was buried.)

lie in wait   *v. phr.*   To watch from hiding in order to attack or surprise someone; hide and wait for someone. *The driver of the stagecoach knew that the thieves were lying in wait somewhere along the road.* (The thieves were hiding somewhere waiting for the stagecoach to come.)

lie low   *v.*, *informal*   **1** To stay quietly out of sight; try not to attract attention; hide. *After holding up the bank, the robbers lay low for a while.* (They lived quietly where not many would see them.) **2** To keep secret one's thoughts or plans. *I think he wants to be elected president, but he is lying low and not saying anything.* (He is keeping his plans secret now.)

life of Riley   *n. phr.*, *informal*   A soft easy life; pleasant or rich way of living. *He's living the life of Riley. He doesn't have to work anymore.* (He has an easy life because he doesn't have to work.)

lift a finger   *or*   **lift a hand**   *also*   **raise a hand**   *v. phr.*   To do something; do one's share; to help.—Usually used in the negative.—*We all worked hard except Joe. He wouldn't lift a finger.* (Joe wouldn't work at all. He did nothing.)

light up v. Suddenly to look pleased and happy. *Martha's face lit up when she saw her old friend.* (Martha suddenly looked pleased and happy when she saw her old friend.)

like father, like son A son is usually like his father in the way he acts. *Frank's father has been on the city council, he is now the mayor, and is running for governor. Frank is on the student council and is likely to be class president. Like father, like son.* (Frank is like his father. His father is in politics, and Frank is in student government.)

like hell adv., slang, vulgar, avoidable **1** With great vigor. *As soon as they saw the cops, they ran like hell.* (As soon as they noticed the police, they started running very fast.) **2** interj. Not so; untrue; indicates the speaker's lack of belief in what he heard. *Like hell you're gonna bring me my dough!* (I don't believe that you will bring me my money.)

like mad or **like crazy** adv., slang, informal With great enthusiasm and vigor; very fast. *We had to drive like mad (OR like crazy) to get there on time.* (We had to drive very fast to get there on time.)

like water off a duck's back adv. phr., informal Without changing one's feelings or opinion; without effect. *Advice and correction roll off him like water off a duck's back.* (He pays no attention to advice, as a duck's back will not absorb water.)

line up v. **1** To take places in line or formation; stand side by side or one behind another; form a line or pattern. *The boys lined up and took turns diving off the springboard.* (They formed a line and dived one after another.) **2** To put in line. *John lined up the pool balls.* (He arranged them in a line.) **3** To adjust correctly. *The garageman lined up the car's wheels.* (He adjusted the wheels so that they would track correctly.) **4a** informal To make ready for action; complete a plan or agreement for; arrange. *Henry's friends lined up so many votes for him that he won the election.* (They persuaded many people to vote for him, and he won.) **4b** informal To become ready for action; come together in preparation or agreement. *The football schedule is lining up well; the coach has arranged all games except one.* (Plans about what other teams our football team will play, and where, are coming well.)

lip service n. Support shown by words only and not by actions; a show of loyalty that is not proven in action.—Usually used with *pay.* *By holding elections, communism pays lip service to democracy, but it offers only one candidate per office.* (Communism pretends to be democratic, but it doesn't give people democratic choices.)

little frog in a big pond or **small frog in a big pond** n. phr. An unimportant person in a large group or organization. *In a large company, even a fairly successful man is likely to feel like a little frog in a big pond.* (He will feel unimportant because the company is so big.)

little pitchers have big ears Little children often overhear things that they are not supposed to hear, or things adults do not expect they would notice. *Be especially careful not to swear in front of little children. Little pitchers have big* *ears*. (Do not swear in front of little children. They will be sure to notice the swear words and start using them.)

live down *v.* To remove (blame, distrust or unfriendly laughter) by good conduct; cause (a mistake or fault) to be forgiven or forgotten by not repeating it. *Frank was rather a bad boy, but he lived it down as he grew up.* (He was at heart a sensible boy and people forgot his early mischief.)

live from hand to mouth *v. phr.* To live on little money and spend it as fast as it comes in; live without saving for the future; have just enough. *Mr. Johnson got very little pay, and the family lived from hand to mouth when he had no job.* (They lived with nothing extra. They were very poor.)

live high off the hog *or* **eat high on the hog** *v. phr., informal* To live in great comfort and plenty; have the best of everything. *The Jones family lived high off the hog after they struck oil.* (The Jones family had everything they wanted after they struck oil.)

live it up *v. phr., informal* To pursue pleasure; enjoy games or night life very much; have fun at places of entertainment. *Joe had had a hard winter in lonesome places; now he was in town living it up.* (He was having fun at the restaurants and shows.)

live up to *v.* To act according to; come up to; agree with; follow. *So far as he could, John had always tried to live up to the example he saw in Lincoln.* (John had tried to act according to Lincoln's example.)

living end *adj. slang* Great, fantastic, the ultimate. *That show we saw last night was the living end.* (It was fantastically good.)

lock the barn door after the horse is stolen To be careful or try to make something safe when it is too late. *After Mary failed the examination, she said she would study hard. She wanted to lock the barn door after the horse was stolen.* (Mary said she would study hard when it was already too late, because she had already failed.)

lock up *v. phr., slang* To be assured of success. *How did your math test go?—I locked it up, I think.* (I think success is assured; I did well at it.)

long face *n.* A sad look; disappointed look. *He told the story with a long face.* (John looked sad when he told the story.)—Often used in the phrase *pull a long face. Don't pull a long face when I tell you to go to bed.* (Don't look so hurt just because you have to go to bed.)

longhair[1] An intellectual who prefers classical music to jazz or acid rock. *Phil is a regular longhair; he never listens to modern jazz.*

longhair[2] *adj., slang* Pertaining to classical art forms; primarily in dancing and music. *Cut out that longhair Mozart symphony and put on a decent pop record.* (Stop the classical music and put on a popular song.)

long haul *or* **long pull** *n., informal* **1** A long distance or trip. *It is a long haul to drive across the country.* (It is a long, hard distance to drive.) **2** A long period of time during which work continues or something is done; a long time of trying. *A boy crippled by polio may learn to walk again, but it may be a long haul.* (It may take a long time.)

long shot *n.* (stress on *long*) **1** A bet or other risk taken though not likely to succeed. *The horse* *was a long shot, but it came in and paid well.* (The horse was figured to have a poor chance, but it won, and people who bet on it made a good profit.)

look a gift horse in the mouth To complain if a gift is not perfect. Usually used with a negative. *John gave Joe a baseball but Joe complained that the ball was old. His father told him not to look a gift horse in the mouth.* (Joe should not complain, because he got the ball for nothing.)

look at the world through rose-colored glasses *or* **see with rose-colored glasses** *v. phr.* To see everything as good and pleasant; not see anything as hard or bad. *When Jean graduated from high school, she looked at the world through rose-colored glasses.* (Jean expected everything in life to be easy and pleasant.)

look down on *also* **look down upon** *v.* To think of (a person or thing) as less good or important; feel that (someone) is not as good as one is, or that (something) is not worth having or doing; consider inferior. *Mary looked down on her classmates because she was better dressed than they were.* (Mary though she was better than her classmates.)

look down one's nose at *v. phr., informal* To think of as worthless; feel scorn for. *Harry has never had to work, and he looks down his nose at people in business.* (He thinks he is much better than people who buy and sell for profit.)

look for *v.* **1** To think likely; expect. *We look for John to arrive any day now.* (We expect that John will arrive any day now.) *The frost killed many oranges, and housewives can look for an increase in their price.* (Housewives can ex-

pect oranges will soon cost more.) **2** To try to find; search for; hunt. *Fred spent all day looking for a job.* (Fred hunted for a job all day.) *Mary and Joe looked for the Smiths at the play.* (They looked all around through the crowd, hoping to find the Smiths.) **3** To do things that cause (one's own trouble); make (trouble) for oneself; provoke. *Joe often gets into fights because he is always looking for trouble.* (Joe says and does things that make other boys angry.)

look forward to *v.* **1** To expect. *At breakfast, John looked forward to a difficult day.* (He expected a tough day.) **2** To expect with hope or pleasure. *Frank was looking forward to that evening's date.* (He expected to enjoy the date.)

look in on *v.* To go to see; make a short visit; make a call on. *On his way downtown, Jim looked in on his aunt.* (Jim made a short call on his aunt.)

look into *v.* To find out the facts about; examine; study; inspect. *The mayor felt he should look into the decrease of income from parking meters.* (The mayor felt he should study the drop in parking meter income, and try to discover it cause.)

look like a million dollars *v. phr., informal* To look well and prosperous; appear healthy and happy and lucky; look pretty and attractive. *John came back from Florida driving a fine new car, tanned, and glowing with health. He looked like a million dollars.* (He gave every evidence of health and prosperity.)

look like the cat that ate the canary *or* **look like the cat that swallowed the canary** *v. phr.* To seem very self-satisfied; look as if one just had a great success. *Peter bet on the poorest horse in the race; when it won, he looked like the cat that ate the canary.* (He looked proud and pleased with himself.)

look out *or* **watch out** *v.* **1** To take care; be careful; be on guard.—Usually used as a command or warning. *"Look out!" John called, as the car came toward me.* (John warned me to be careful not to be hit.) **2** To be alert or watchful; keep watching. *A collector of antique cars asked Frank to look out for a 1906 gas head lamp.* (He asked Frank to keep looking for a 1906 head lamp; he asked him to watch out for one.) **3** *informal* To watch or keep (a person or thing) and do what is needed; provide protection and care.—Used with *for*. *Lillian looked out for her sister's children one afternoon a week.* (Lillian cared for her sister's children one afternoon a week.)

look to *v.* (stress on *look*) **1** To attend to; get ready for; take care of. *Plans had been prepared that looked to every possibility.* (Plans had been arranged to take care of every possibility.) *The president assigned a man to look to our needs.* (The president chose a man to do necessary things for us.) **2** To go for help to; depend on. *The child looks to his mother to cure his hurts.* (He depends on his mother to help when he is hurt.)

look to one's laurels To make sure that one's reputation is not spoiled; protect one's good name; keep one's record from being beaten by others. *Tom won the broad jump, but he had to look to his laurels.* (Tom won the broad jump, but other boys were ready to try again to beat him.)

look up *v.* (stress on *up*) **1** *informal* To improve in future chances; promise more success. *The first year was tough, but business looked up after that.* (Business improved after the first year.) **2** To search for; hunt for information about; find. *It is a good habit to look up new words in a dictionary.* (It is wise to find the meaning of new words in a dictionary.) **3** To seek and find. *While he was in Chicago, Henry looked up a friend from college days.* (He hunted for and found his friend.)

look up to *v.* To think of (someone) as a good example to copy; honor; respect. *Mr. Smith had taught for many years, and all the students looked up to him.* (All the students admired him and wanted to be like him.)

lord it over *v. phr.* To act as the superior and master of; dominate; be bossy over; control. *John learned early to lord it over other children.* (He learned to boss them around.) *The office manager lorded it over the clerks and typists.* (He ruled in a bossy way over his department.)

lose face *v.* To be embarrassed or ashamed by an error or failure; lose dignity, influence, or reputation; lose self-respect or the confidence of others. *The governor lost face with the voters when he failed to keep his commitment to lower taxes.* (He lost his good reputation because he didn't keep his campaign promise.)

lose ground **1** To go backward; retreat. *The soldiers began to lose ground when their leader was killed.* (After their leader was killed, the soldiers wouldn't fight, so they retreated.) **2** To become weaker; get worse, not improve. *The sick man began to lose ground* *when his cough grew worse.* (The sick man became weaker when his cough grew worse.)

lose heart *v. phr.* To feel discouraged because of failure; to lose hope of success. *The team had won no games and it lost heart.* (They were beaten often and felt unable to win.)

lose one's shirt *v. phr., slang* To lose all or most of one's money. *Uncle Joe spent his life savings to buy a store, but it failed and he lost his shirt.* (Uncle Joe lost all his savings.)

lose out *v.* To fail to win; miss first place in a contest; lose to a rival. *John lost out in the rivalry for Mary's hand in marriage.* (Mary married someone else.)

lose touch *v. phr.* To fail to keep in contact or communication.—Usually used with *with*. *After she moved to another town, she lost touch with her childhood friends.* (They did not see each other or write letters.)

lose track *v. phr.* To forget about something; not stay informed; fail to keep a count or record. *What's the score now? I've lost track.* (I haven't been able to follow the score and know what it is.)

loudmouth *or* **bigmouth** *n., slang* A noisy, boastful, or foolish talker. *Fritz is a loudmouth who cannot be trusted with secrets.* (He tells any secrets he finds out.)

louse up *v., slang* To throw into confusion; make a mess of; spoil; ruin. *When the man who was considering John's house heard that the basement was wet, that was enough to louse up the sale.* (He was not willing to buy when he learned that the basement was wet.)

lovers' lane *n.* A hidden road or walk where lovers walk or park in the evening. *A parked car in a lonely lovers' lane is a target for holdup men.* (Holdup men often rob lovers in a lonely place.)

lowdown *n., slang, informal* (stress on *low*) The inside facts of a matter; the total truth. *Nixon has never given the American people the lowdown on Watergate.* (He never divulged the inside facts as he knew them.)

lower the boom *v. phr., informal* To punish strictly; check, or stop fully. *The mayor lowered the boom on outside jobs for city firemen.* (The mayor ordered city firemen not to hold outside jobs.)

luck out *v. phr., slang, informal* **1** Suddenly to get lucky when in fact the odds are against one's succeeding. *I was sure I was going to miss the train, as I was three minutes late; but I lucked out; the train was five minutes late.* (I didn't miss the train because, luckily for me, it was later than I was.) **2** To be extraordinarily fortunate. *Charles really lucked out at Las Vegas last month; he came home with $10,000 in cash.* (He won a great deal of money in gambling casinos in Las Vegas.) **3** (By sarcastic opposition) to be extremely unfortunate; to be killed. *Those poor marines sure lucked out in Saigon, didn't they?* (They were killed in Saigon.)

lucky star *n.* A certain star or planet which, by itself or with others, is seriously or jokingly thought to bring a person good luck and success in life. *John was born under a lucky star.* (He seems always to have good luck and success in life. *Ted was unhurt in the car accident; he thanked his lucky stars.* (He thought he was lucky not to have been hurt.)

M

mad as a hornet *or* **mad as hops** *or* **mad as a wet hen** *adj. phr.,* *informal* In a fighting mood; very angry. *When my father sees the dent in his fender, he'll be mad as a hornet.* (My father told me to be careful when he let me take the car and he's going to very angry when he sees I have dented the fender.) *Bill was mad as hops when the fellows went on without him.* (Bill expected his friends to wait for him and was angry when they didn't.) *Mrs. Harris was mad as a wet hen when the rabbits ate her tulips.* (She was very angry when the rabbits chewed off the tops of the sprouting tulip bulbs and kept them from blooming.)

magic carpet *n.* A rug said to be able to transport a person through the air to any place he wishes; any form of transportation that is comfortable or easy enough to seem magical. *The caliph of Bagdad flew on his magic carpet to Arabia.* (The caliph made his flying carpet carry him to Arabia.) *Mr. Smith's new car drove so smoothly it seemed like a magic carpet.* (Mr. Smith's car seemed to fly through the air just by wishing and not by driving.)

main drag *n., informal* **1** The most important street or thoroughfare in a town. *Lincoln Avenue is the main drag of our town.* (Lincoln Avenue is the most important street in our town.) **2** The Street where the dope pushers and the prostitutes are. *Wells Street is the main drag of Chicago.* (Wells Street, a part of Old Town, is where the pushers and the prostitutes hang out.)

main squeeze *n. slang* **1** The top ranking person in an organization or in a neighborhood; an important person, such as one's boss. *Mr. Bronchard is the main squeeze in this office.* (He is the top man, the boss here.) **2** The top person in charge of an illegal operation, such as drug sales, etc. *Before we can clean up this part of town, we must arrest the main squeeze.* (Before we can get rid of the petty criminals, we must catch their boss.) **3** One's principal romantic or sexual partner. *The singer's main squeeze is a member of the band.* (The singer is dating a band member.)

make a beeline for *v. phr.* To go in a straight line toward. *The runner made a beeline for first base.* (The runner ran straight to first base.)

make a day of it *v. phr., informal* To do something all day. *When they go to the beach they take a picnic lunch and make a day of it.* (When they go to the beach they take a picnic lunch and spend the whole day there.)

make a dent in *v. phr., informal* To make less by a very small amount; reduce slightly. *John shoveled and shoveled, but he didn't seem to make a dent in the pile of sand.* (John shoveled very hard, but the pile didn't seem to get smaller.)

make a difference *or* **make the difference** *v. phr.* To change the nature of something or a situation; be important; matter. *John's good score on the test made the difference between his passing or failing the course.* (By getting a good score on the test, John passed the course instead of failing it.)

make a go of *v. phr. informal* To cause to be a success; produce good results. *He was sure he could make a go of the filling station.* (He felt sure that he could run the

187

gas station so that it would be a success.)

make a hit *v. phr. informal* To be successful; be well-liked; get along well. *Mary's new red dress made a hit at the party.* (Everybody like Mary's new red dress.)

make a mountain out of a molehill To think a small problem is a big one; try to make something unimportant seem important. *You're not hurt badly, Johnny. Stop trying to make a mountain out of a molehill with crying.* (I know you're not hurt badly, even though you are crying.)

make a pass at *v. phr., slang, informal* Make advances toward a member of the opposite sex (usually man to a woman) with the goal of seducing the person. *We've been dating for four weeks but Joe has never even made a pass at me.* (Even though they have been dating for four weeks, Joe has never made sexual advances toward her.)

make a play for *v. phr., slang* To try to get the interest or liking of; flirt with; attract. *Bob made a play for the pretty new girl.* (Bob did his best to attract the new girl.) *John made a play for the other students' votes for class president.* (John tried to get the other students to vote for him for class president.)

make a point *v. phr.* To try hard; make a special effort.—Used with *of* and a verbal noun. *He made a point of remembering to get his glasses fixed.* (He tried hard to remember to take his glasses to be repaired.)

make away with *v. informal* Take; carry away; cause to disappear. *The lumberjack made away with a great stack of pancakes.* (The lumberjack ate a great stack of pancakes.) *Two masked men*

held up the clerk and made away with the payroll. (Masked bandits stole the payroll.)

make believe *v.* To act as if something is true while one knows it is not; pretend. *Let's make believe we have a million dollars.* (Let's pretend we're millionaires.)

make do *v. phr.* To use a poor substitute when one does not have the right thing. *John did not have a hammer, and he had to make do with a heavy rock.* (John had to use the rock for a hammer.)

make ends meet *v. phr.* To have enough money to pay one's bills; earn what it costs to live. *Both husband and wife had to work to make ends meet.* (Living costs were so high that the salaries of husband and wife added together came to just enough money to pay the bills.)

make eyes at *v. phr., informal* To look at a girl or boy in a way that tries to attract; flirt. *The other girls disliked her way of making eyes at their boyfriends instead of finding one of her own.* (The other girls were disgusted at her flirting with their boyfriends.)

make for *v.* To go toward; start in the direction of. *The children took their ice skates and made for the frozen pond.* (The pond was covered with ice. The children took their skates and went toward the pond.) *The bee got his load of pollen and made for the hive.* (The bee got pollen on his hairy legs and started in the direction of the hive.)

make free with *v.* **1** To take or use (things) without asking. *Bob makes free with his roommate's clothes.* (Bob wears his roommate's clothes but does not ask his permission.)

make fun of *or* **poke fun at** *v. phr., informal* To joke about; laugh at; tease; mock. *It is cruel to make fun of another person's disability.* (Joking about someone's physical handicap is not acceptable behavior.)

make good *v. phr.* To do what one promised to do; make something come true. *Mr. Smith borrowed some money. He promised to pay it back on payday. He made good on his promise.* (When he got his money he paid back what he borrowed. He did what he promised to do.)

make hay while the sun shines *v. phr.* To do something at the right time; not wait too long. *Dick had a free hour so he made hay while the sun shone and did his lesson for the next day.* (Dick did not waste time, but used a free hour to do his lesson.)

make head or tail of *v. phr., informal* To find meaning in; understand.—Used in negative, conditional, and interrogative sentences. *She could not make head or tail of the directions on the dress pattern.* (She could not understand the instructions telling how to make her dress.) *Can you make head or tail of the letter?* (Can you understand it?)

make it with *v. phr., slang, informal* **1** To be accepted by a group. *Joe finally made it with the in-crowd in Hollywood.* (He was finally accepted by the in-group in Hollywood.) **2** *vulgar* To have sex with (someone). *I wonder if Joe has made it with Sue.* (I wonder if he has had sex with her.)

make light of *v. phr.* To treat as of little importance; make as small as possible; minimize. *The soldier made light of his wound.* (He talked about it as not important; he said it was only a scratch.)

make love *v. phr.* **1** To be warm, loving and tender toward someone of the opposite sex; try to get him or her to love one too. *There was moonlight on the roses and he made love to her in the porch swing.* (Moonlight on the roses made everything romantic. The boy was warm and loving to the girl as they sat in the porch swing.) **2** To have sexual relations with (someone). *It is rumored that Alfred makes love to his secretary.* (It is rumored that he has sexual relations with his secretary.)

make merry *v. phr., literary* To have fun, laugh, and celebrate. *In Aesop's fable the grasshopper made merry while the ant worked and saved up food.* (The grasshopper had a good time and did not work.)

make no bones *v. phr., informal* **1** To have no doubts; not to worry about right or wrong; not to be against. *Bill makes no bones about telling a lie to escape punishment.* (Bill is not ashamed to lie if it will save him from being punished.) **2** To make no secret; not keep from talking; admit.—Used with *about* or *of the fact. John thinks being poor is no disgrace, and he makes no bones of the fact.* (John does not try to hide the fact that he is poor.)

make off *v.* To go away, run away, leave. *When the deer saw the hunter, it made off at once.* (The deer saw the hunter and ran away.) *A thief stopped John on a dark street and made off with his wallet.* (The thief robbed John and ran away with his money.)

make one's bed and lie in it To be responsible for what one has done and so to have to accept the bad results. *Billy smoked one of his father's cigars and now he is* *sick. He made his bed; now let him lie in it.* (It is Billy's own fault that he is sick. He smoked, and now let him suffer for it.)

make one's blood boil *or* **make the blood boil** *v. phr., informal* To make someone very angry. *When someone calls me a liar it makes my blood boil.* (I get very angry if anyone calls me a liar.)

makes oneself scarce *v. phr., informal* To leave quickly; go away. *The boys made themselves scarce when they saw the principal coming to stop their noise.* (The boys left quickly when the principal came to tell them to be quiet.)

make one's mouth water *v. phr.* **1** To look or smell very good; make one want very much to eat or drink something one sees or smells. *The pies in the store window made Dan's mouth water.* (The pies in the store window looked so good he wanted to eat a piece of the pie.) **2** To be attractive; make one want to have something very much. *Judy collects folk song records, and the records in the store window made her mouth water.* (Judy wanted very much to get the records.)

make out *v.* **1** To write the facts asked for (as in an application blank or a report form); fill out. *The teacher made out the report cards and gave them to the students to take home.* (The teacher wrote the students' grades on the report cards.) **2** To see, hear, or understand what is wanted. *It was dark, and we could not make out who was coming along the road.* (We could not see clearly who was coming.) **3** *informal* To make someone believe; show; prove. *Charles and Bob had a fight, and Charles tried to make out that Bob started it.* (Charles

tried to make people believe that Bob started the fight.) **4** *informal* Do well enough; succeed. *John's father wanted John to do well in school, and asked the teacher how John was making out.* (John's father asked the teacher if John was doing well in school.) **5** To kiss or pet. *What are Jack and Jill up to?—They're making out on the back porch.* (They're kissing and hugging.)

make over *v.* **1** To change by law something from one owner to another owner; change the name on the title (lawful paper) from one owner to another. *Mr. Brown made over the title to the car to Mr. Jones.* (Mr. Brown changed the owner of the car from himself to Mr. Jones by writing a new legal paper saying Mr. Jones was the owner.) **2** To make something look different; change the style of. *He asked the tailor to make over his pants. The tailor cut off the cuffs and put a belt across the back.* (The tailor made the pants look different by making these changes.)

make the grade *v. phr., informal* **1** To make good; succeed. *It was clear that Mr. Baker had made the grade in the insurance business.* (It was clear that he had succeeded in the insurance business.) **2** To meet a standard; qualify. *That whole shipment of cattle made the grade as prime beef.* (All of that shipment of cattle qualified as the best kind of beef.)

make the scene *v. phr., slang* To be present; to arrive at a certain place or event. *I am too tired to make the scene; let's go home.* (I am too tired to be there; let's return home.)

make time *v. phr., slang* **1** To be successful in arriving at a designated place in short or good time.

We're supposed to be there at 6 PM, and it's only 5:30—we're making good time. (We are not going to be late.) **2** To be successful in making sexual advances to someone. *Joe sure is making time with Sue, isn't he?* (He is successful in his advances toward her.)

make up *v.* **1** To make by putting things or parts together. *A car is made up of many different parts.* (It has wheels, tires, seats, and other parts.) **2** To invent; think and say something that is new or not true. *Jean makes up stories to amuse her little brother.* (She invents stories to please him.) **3a** To do or provide (something lacking or needed); do or supply (something not done, lost, or missed); get back; regain; give back; repay. *I have to make up the test I missed last week.* (I have to take the test I missed.) **3b** To do what is lacking or needed; do or give what should be done or given; get or give back what has been lost, missed, or not done; pay back.—Used with *for*. *We made up for lost time by taking an airplane instead of a train.* (We were late but we gained some time by going faster on an airplane.) **4** To put on lipstick, face paint and eye make-up. *Clowns always make up before a circus show.* (They paint their faces and put on funny clothes for the show.) **5** To become friends again after a quarrel. *Mary and Joan quarreled, but made up after a while.* (The two girls quarreled but soon became friends again.) **6** To try to make friends with someone; to win favor. Followed by *to*. *The new boy made up to the teacher by sharpening her pencils.* (The new boy sharpened the teacher's pencils to make her like him.)

makeup *n.* (stress on *make*) **1** Cosmetics *The actors and actresses put on a lot of makeup.* (They used a lot of cosmetics.) **2** *attributively* Auxiliary, or late. *The professor gave a makeup exam for the sick student.* (He gave the student a chance to take another exam for the one missed.)

make up one's mind *v. phr.* To choose what to do; decide. *They made up their minds to sell the house.* (They decided to sell it.) *Tom couldn't make up his mind whether he should tell Mother about the broken window, or let her find it herself.* (Tom could not decide what to do.)

make waves *v. phr., informal* Make one's influence felt; create a disturbance, a sensation. *Joe is the wrong man for the job; he is always trying to make waves.* (He is always overbearing and tries to make his influence felt too strongly.)

make way *v. phr.* To move so someone can go through; stand aside. *The people made way for the king.* (They moved aside so the king could go through.)

man in the street *n. phr.* The man who is like most other men; the average person; the ordinary person. *The newspaper took a poll of the man in the street.* (The newspaper asked a large number of ordinary people what they thought about a problem.)

mark time *v. phr.* **1** To move the feet up and down as in marching, without going forward. *The officer made the soldiers mark time as a punishment.* (He told them to keep lifting their feet up and down.) **2** To be idle; waiting for something to happen. *The teacher marked time until all the children were ready for the test.* (She did nothing, but waited for them.)

3 To seem to be working or doing something, but really not doing it. *It was so hot that the workmen just marked time.* (They moved around and pretended to work.)

matter of course *n. phr.* Something always done; the usual way; habit; rule. *It was a matter of course for John to dress carefully when he was meeting his wife.* (He always wore nice clothes to meet her.)

matter of fact *n. phr.* Something that is really true; something that can be proved. *The town records showed that it was a matter of fact that the two boys were brothers.* (The town books showed that it was true that they were brothers.) For emphasis: **as a matter of fact** *I didn't go yesterday, and as a matter of fact, I didn't go all week.* (I didn't go all week either.)

matter-of-fact *adj.* **1** Simply telling or showing the truth; not explaining or telling more. *The newspaper gave a matter-of-fact account of the murder trial.* (The newspaper told about the court trial in a factual way.) **2** Showing little feeling or excitement or trouble; seeming not to care much. *When Mary's father died she acted in a very matter-of-fact way.* (She did not cry much and seemed not very troubled.) *He was a very matter-of-fact person.* (He never was very excited and never joked much.)

mean business *v. phr., informal* To decide strongly to do what one plans to do; really mean it; be serious. *The boss said he would fire us if we didn't work harder, and he means business.* (The boss said he would fire us if we didn't work harder, and he really will.)

measure up *v.* To be equal; be of high quality; come up. *John didn't measure up to the best catchers, but he was a good one.* (John wasn't equal in ability to the best catchers.)

meet up with *v. phr.* To meet by accident; come upon without planning or expecting to. *When he ran around the tree, Bob suddenly met up with a large bear.* (Bob came upon a large bear by surprise.)

melt in one's mouth *v. phr.* **1** To be so tender as to seem to need no chewing. *The chicken was so tender that it melted in your mouth.* (The chicken was so tender you didn't need to chew it.) **2** To taste very good; be delicious. *Mother's apple pie really melts in your mouth.* (Mother's apple pie tastes very good.)

mend one's fences *v. phr., informal* To do something to make people like or follow one again; strengthen one's friendships or influence. *The senator went home from Washington to mend his fences.* (He went home and talked with everybody to get them to re-elect him.)

mess around *v. phr.* **1** To engage in idle or purposeless activity. *Come on, you guys,—start doing some work; don't just mess around all day!* (Don't just waste your day by doing idle and purposeless things.) **2** *vulgar* To be promiscuous, to indulge in sex with little discrimination as to who the partner is. *Allen needs straightening out; he's been messing around with the women students of his class.* (He has been sexually promiscuous with women classmates.)

mess up *v. phr., slang, informal* **1** To cause trouble, to spoil something. *What did you have to mess* up my accounts for? (Why did you have to cause trouble with the accountants?) **2** To cause someone emotional trauma. *Sue will never get married; she was messed up when she was a teenager.* (She was traumatized emotionally as a teenager.) **3** To beat up someone physically. *When Joe came in after the fight with the boys, he was all messed up.* (He was beaten up badly enough to leave visible marks on him.)

middle of the road *n. phr.* A way of thinking which does not favor one idea or thing too much; being halfway between two different ideas. *The teacher did not support either side in the debate, but stayed in the middle of the road.* (The teacher did not help or favor either side.)

middle-of-the-road *adj.* Favoring action halfway between two opposite movements or ideas; with ideas halfway between two opposite sides; seeing good on both sides. *The men who wrote the Constitution followed a middle-of-the-road plan on whether greater power belonged to the United States government or to the separate states.* (The men divided the power fairly and did not give all of it to either side.)

mind one's p's and q's *v. phr.* To be very careful what one does or says; not make mistakes. *When the principal of the school visited the class, the students all minded their p's and q's.* (When the principal visited the school, the students were very careful to act politely and right.)

mind you *v. phr., informal* I want you to notice and understand. *Mind you, I am not blaming him.* (Understand that I am not blaming him.)

miss out *v., informal* To fail; lose or not take a good chance; miss something good. *Jim's mother told him he missed out on a chance to go fishing with his father because he came home late.* (Jim lost the chance by coming home late.)

miss the boat, also **miss the bus** *v. phr., informal* To fail through slowness; to put something off until too late; do the wrong thing and lose the chance. *Mr. Brown missed the boat when he decided not to buy the house.* (If he had bought it he could sell it for a profit now.)

mix up *v.* (Stress on *up*) To confuse; make a mistake about. *Jimmy doesn't know colors yet; he mixes up purple and blue.* (He thinks that purple is blue, and blue is purple.) *Even the twins' mother mixes them up.* (Even the twins' mother doesn't know which is which.)

mix-up *n., informal* (Stress on *mix*) A confusion, an error. *There was a mix-up about the number of people invited; we are one table setting short.* (They need one more table setting; they counted wrong.)

mixed up *adj. phr.* **1** *informal* Confused; puzzled. *Bob was all mixed up after the accident.* (Bob was confused and didn't remember what had happened.) **2** Disordered; disarranged; not neat. *The papers on his desk were mixed up.* (They were not neatly in order.) **3** *informal* Joined or connected (with someone or something bad.) *Harry was mixed up in a fight after the game.* (He took part in the fight.)

money to burn *n. phr., informal* Very much money, more than is needed. *Dick's uncle died and left him money to burn.* (Now he is so rich he can buy anything.)

monkey business *n. slang, informal* **1** Any unethical, illegitimate, or furtive or deceitful, e.g., undercover sexual advances, cheating, misuse of public funds. *There is a lot of monkey business going on in that firm; you better watch out whom you deal with!* (There is a lot of suspicious activity going on; better be careful.) **2** Comical or silly actions; goofing off. *Come on boys, let's cut out the monkey business and get down to work!* (Stop acting silly and start working!)

more the merrier *n. phr.* The more people who join in the fun, the better it will be. *Come with us on the boat ride; the more the merrier.* (We are glad to have you join us on the boat ride.)

morning after *n. slang* The effects of drinking liquor or staying up late as felt the next morning; a hangover. *One of the drawbacks of drinking too much liquor is the morning after.* (The hangover the next day is very unpleasant.) *Mr. Smith woke up with a big headache and knew it was the morning after.* (Mr. Smith woke up with a big headache and knew it was the result of too much beer the night before.)

move a muscle *v. phr.* To move even a very little. *The deer stood without moving a muscle until the* hunter was gone. (It stood very quietly.)

move heaven and earth *v. phr.* To try every way; do everything one can. *Joe moved heaven and earth to be sent to Washington.* (He tried every possible way to get his boss to send him to work in Washington.)

move in on *v. phr. slang, informal* To take over something that belongs to another. *Frozen foods moved in on the market for fresh poultry.* (Once frozen poultry and home freezers were available, sales of fresh poultry fell.)

musical chairs *n. phr.* The transfer of a number of officers in an organization into different jobs, especially each other's jobs. *The boss regularly played musical chairs with department heads to keep them fresh on the job.* (He moved them from one department to another frequently so they would keep seeing ways to improve the work.) (Originally the name of a children's game.)

music to one's ears *n. phr.* Something one likes to hear. *When the manager phoned to say I got the job, it was music to my ears.* (That was delightful news.)

my God *or* **my goodness** *interj.—* Used to express surprise, shock, dismay, and like feelings. *My God! What happened to the car?* (This is shocking. What caused this damage?)

N

nail down *v. phr., informal* To make certain; make sure; settle. *Joe had a hard time selling his car, but he finally nailed down the sale when he got his friend Sam to give him $300.* (Joe made sure Sam would buy the car by getting $300 from Sam.)

name is mud *informal* One is in trouble; a person is blamed or no longer liked.—Used in the possesive. *If you tell your mother I spilled ink on her rug, my name will be mud.* (If you tell your mother I spilled ink on her rug, I will be in trouble.)

name of the game *n., informal* The crux of the matter; that which actually occurs under the disguise of something else. *Getting medium-income families to support the rest of society—that's the name of the game!* (That's what's really happening.)

neck and neck *adj. or adv., informal* Equal or nearly equal in a race or contest; abreast; tied. *At the end of the race the two horses were neck and neck.* (The two horses were in a tie at the end of the race.)

neck of the woods *n. phr., informal* Part of the country; place; neighborhood; vicinity. *We visited Illinois and Iowa last summer; in that neck of the woods the corn really grows tall.* (In that part of the country the corn really grows tall.) *We were down in your neck of the woods last week.* (Last week we were in the part of the country where you live.)

needle in a haystack *n. phr., informal* Something that will be very hard to find. *"I lost my class ring somewhere in the front yard,"* said June. Jim answered, *"Too bad. That will be like finding a needle in a haystack."* (That will be very hard to find.)

neither fish nor fowl *also* **neither fish, flesh, nor fowl** Something or someone that does not belong to a definite group or known class. *The man is neither fish nor fowl; he votes Democrat or Republican according to which will do him the most good.* (He is not a Democrat or Republican.)

neither here nor there *adj. phr.* Not relevant to the thing being discussed; off the subject; not mattering. *The boys all like the coach, but that's neither here nor there; the question is, "Does he know how to teach football?"* (The important question is, "Can he teach football?" Being liked by the boys does not make him know football; that is another matter.)

nervous Nellie *n., informal* A timid person who lacks determination and courage. *I say we will never win if we don't stop being nervous Nellies!* (I say we will never win unless we stop being cowards.)

never mind *v. phr.* Don't trouble about it; don't worry about it; forget it; skip it.—Usually used in speaking or when writing dialogue. *Never mind preparing a picnic lunch: we'll find a lunchstand when we get to the beach.* (Don't bother making a picnic lunch.) *"What did you say?" "Oh, never mind." ("What did you say?" "Let's just forget it.") "What about money?" "Never mind that: I'll take care of it."* ("What shall we do about money?" "Don't worry about that. I'll take care of it.")

new blood *n.* Something or someone that gives new life or vigor, fresh energy or power. *New blood was brought into the company through appointment of*

195

younger personnel to important positions. (Hiring several young executives gave the company new vigor.)

new broom sweeps clean A new person makes many changes. *The new superintendent has changed many of the school rules. A new broom sweeps clean.* (A new person changes many things.)

new deal *n., informal* **1** A complete change; a fresh start. *People had been on the job too long; a new deal was needed to change the old bad habits.* (There were too many people who had become bored and lazy and it took a complete change to get things moving right again.) **2** Another chance. *The boy asked for a new deal after he had been punished for fighting in school.* (He asked for another chance and promised never to fight again.)

new person *n.* A peson who has become very much better. *Diet and exercise made a new person of him.* (His health and appearance were greatly improved by diet and exercise. He looked like a different person.)

nip and tuck *adj. or adv., informal* Evenly matched; hard fought to the finish. *The game was nip and tuck until the last minute.* (The two teams played equally well and no one knew which team would win till the game ended.) *It was a nip-and-tuck race right to the finish line.* (The race was hard fought right to the end.)

nip in the bud *v. phr.* To check at the outset; prevent at the start; block or destroy in the beginning. *The police nipped the plot in the bud.* (The police stopped the plot before it could get fully organized.)

nobody home *slang* **1** One's attention is somewhere else, not on what is being said or done here; one is absentminded. *The teacher asked him a question three times, but he still looked out the window. She gave up, saying, "Nobody home."* (The teacher could not get the boy to answer. She said, "His attention is on something else.") **2** One is feebleminded or insane. *He pointed to the woman, tapped his head, and said, "Nobody home."* (He meant that the woman's mind was not normal; she was not able to think and act normally.)

nobody's fool *n. phr.* A smart person; a person who knows what he is doing; a person who can take care of himself. *In the classroom and on the football field, Henry was nobody's fool.* (He did good work in the classroom and on the football field. He was one of the best students and players.)

no deal *or* **no dice** *or* **no go** *or* **no sale** *or* **no soap** *slang* Not agreed to; refused or useless; without success or result; no; certainly not.—Used in the predicate or to refuse something. *Billy wanted to let Bob join the team but I said that it was no deal because Bob was too young.* (I said that Bob couldn't join the team.) *"Let me have a dollar." "No dice!" answered Joe.* ("Certainly not!" answered Joe.)

no doubt *adv.* Without doubt; doubtless; surely; certainly. *No doubt Susan was the smartest girl in her class.* (Susan was certainly the smartest girl in her class.)

no end *adv., informal* **1** Very much; exceedingly. *Jim was no end upset because he couldn't go swimming.* (Jim was very much upset because he couldn't go swimming.) **2** Almost without stopping; continually. *The baby cried no end.* (The baby cried without stopping.)

no end to *or informal* **no end of** So many, or so much of, as to seem almost endless; very many or very much. *There was no end to the letters pouring into the post office.* (So many letters were coming into the post office that they seemed to be without end.)

no great shakes *adj., informal* Mediocre, unimportant. *Joe is no great shakes.* (He is unimportant, mediocre.)

no love lost *n. phr.* Bad feeling; ill will. *Bob and Dick both wanted to be elected captain of the team, and there was no love lost between them.* (They did not like each other; they treated each other badly.) *There was no love lost between the sales and the accounting departments.* (There was bad feeling between the sales and the accounting departments.)

no matter **1** Not anything important. *I wanted to see him before he left, but it's no matter.* (It's not important.) **2** It makes no difference; regardless of. *She was going to be a singer no matter what difficulties she met.* (She meant to be a singer regardless of what difficulties she met.) *Mary wanted to get to school on time, no matter if she went without breakfast.* (She wanted to get to school on time, and she was willing to go without breakfast.)

nose about *or* **nose around** *v. phr., informal* To look for something kept private or secret; poke about; explore; inquire; pry. *In Grandmother's attic, Sally spent a while nosing about in the old family pictures.* (Sally looked among the old family pictures for

a while.) *The detective was nosing around in the crowd, looking for pickpockets.* (He moved about in the crowd, looking for pickpockets.)

nose down *v., of an aircraft* To head down; bring down the nose of. *The big airliner began to nose down for a landing.* (The airliner began to head down for a landing.)

nose in *informal* Prying or pestering interest in; unwelcome interest in; impolite curiosity. *He always had his nose in other people's business.* (He showed impolite curiosity in other people's business.)

nose out of *informal* Restraint from unwanted attention.—Usually used with a possessive and usually used with *keep*. *When Billy asked his sister where she was going, she told him to keep his nose out of her business.* (Billy's sister told him not to ask about things that were not his business.)

no-show *n., informal* A person who makes a reservation, e.g., at a hotel or at an airline, and then neither claims nor cancels the reservation. *The airlines were messed up because of a great number of no-show passengers.* (They had a large number of people who made reservations but never claimed nor canceled them.)

no sweat[1] *adj., slang, informal* Easily accomplished, uncomplicated. *That job was no sweat.* (That was an easy job.)

no sweat[2] *adv.* Easily. *We did it, no sweat.* (We did it easily.)

not a leg to stand on *n., phr., informal* No good proof or excuse; no good evidence or defense to offer. *The man with a gun and $300 in his pocket was ac-*

cused of robbing a gas station. He didn't have a leg to stand on. (The man could not explain why he had a gun and so much money in his pocket.)

not bad *or* **not so bad** *adj., informal* Pretty good; all right; good enough. *The party last night was not bad.* (The party last night was good.) *It was not so bad, as inexpensive vacations go.* (It was good enough, considering how little it cost.)

not for the world *or* **not for worlds** *adv. phr.* Not at any price; not for anything. *I wouldn't hurt his feelings for the world.* (I wouldn't hurt his feelings for any reason.)

nothing doing *adv. phr., informal* I will not do it; certainly not; no indeed; no. *"Will you lend me a dollar?" "Nothing doing!"* ("Will you lend me a dollar?" "Certainly not.")

nothing if not *adv. phr.* Without doubt; certainly. *With its bright furnishings, flowers, and sunny windows the new hospital dayroom is nothing if not cheerful.* (It is a very cheerful room.)

not on your life *adv. phr., informal* Certainly not; not ever; not for any reason.—Used for emphasis. *I wouldn't drive a car with brakes like that—not on your life.* (I would never drive that car, for any reason.) *Did he thank me for my advice? Not on your life.* (He certainly did not thank me.)

not to give one the time of day *v. phr., slang, informal* To dislike someone strongly enough so as to totally ignore him. *Sue wouldn't give Helen the time of day.* (She dislikes her so strongly that she totally ignores her.)

not to touch (something) with a ten-foot pole *v. phr.* To consider something completely undesirable or uninteresting. *Some people won't touch spinach with a ten-foot pole.* (Some people thoroughly dislike spinach.) *Kids who wouldn't touch an encyclopedia with a ten-foot pole love to find information with this computer program.* (They think the book dull; the computer, fun.)

number one *or* **Number One** *n. phr., informal* Oneself; one's own interests; one's private or selfish advantage. Usually used in the phrase *look out for number one*. *He was well known for his habit of always looking out for number one.* (He had a habit of thinking of himself first.)

number-one *adj. phr.* **1** Of first rank or importance; foremost; principal. *He is easily America's number-one golfer.* (He is the foremost American golfer.) **2** Of first grade; of top quality; best. *That is number-one western steer beef.* (That is the best western steer beef.)

nurse a grudge *v. phr.* To keep a feeling of envy or dislike towards some person; remember something bad that a person said or did to one, and dislike the person because of that. *Tom nursed a grudge against John because John took his place on the basketball team.* (Tom felt disappointed because John took his place, and he disliked and envied John.)

nutty as a fruitcake *adj. phr., slang* Very crazy; entirely mad. *He looked all right but when he began to talk, we saw that he was as nutty as a fruitcake.* (He seemed normal until he spoke; then we could tell that he was crazy.)

oddball n., slang, informal An eccentric person; one who doesn't act like everyone else. *John is an oddball—he never invites anyone.* (He acts strangely—he is a loner.)

of age adj. phr. **1a** Old enough to be allowed to do or manage something. *Mary will be of driving age on her next birthday.* (She will be 16, old enough to be allowed to drive a car.) **1b** Old enough to vote; having the privileges of adulthood. *The age at which one is considered of age to vote, or of age to buy alcoholic drinks, or of age to be prosecuted as an adult, varies within the United States.* (Statutes about these limits vary.) **2** Fully developed; mature. *Education for the handicapped came of age when special schools were accepted as a necessary part of the public school system.* (Schools for the blind, deaf, and other handicapped people developed when the public accepted responsibility for them.)

of course adv. phr. **1** As one would expect; naturally. *Bob hit Herman, and Herman hit him back, of course.* (As you would expect, Herman hit him back and the fight began.) **2** Without a doubt; certainly; surely. *Of course you know that girl; she's in your class.* (Surely you know that girl.)

off again, on again or **on again, off again** adj. phr., informal Not settled; changeable; uncertain. *John and Susan had an off-again, on-again romance.* (Sometimes they thought they were in love, and sometimes not.) *I don't like this off-again, on-again business. Are we going to have the party or not?* (I don't like not being sure if the party will be held or not.)

off and on, also **on and off** adv. Not regularly; occasionally; sometimes. *Joan wrote to a pen pal in England off and on for several years.* (Joan wrote to her friend in England occasionally.) *It rained off and on all day.* (Rain fell for a while, then stopped, then started, again and again.)

off balance adj. phr. Not prepared; unable to meet the unexpected. *The teacher's surprise test caught the class off balance, and nearly everyone got a poor mark.* (The surprise test caught the class unprepared.)

off base adj. phr., informal Not agreeing with fact; wrong. *The idea that touching a toad causes warts is off base.* (It is an old superstition that does not agree with fact.)

offbeat adj., informal Nonconventional, different from the usual, odd. *Linguistics used to be an offbeat field, but nowadays every self-respecting university has a linguistics department.* (It used to be an odd, unusual field; now that is no longer the case.)

off-center adj., informal Different from the usual pattern; not quite like most others; odd. *Roger's sense of humor was a bit off-center.* (It was a little odd. He didn't laugh at the things most people thought were funny.)

off-color adj., informal Not of the proper kind for polite society; in bad taste; dirty. *When Joe finished his off-color story, no one was pleased.* (He told an impolite joke, and nobody laughed. The group were offended.)

off duty adj Having free time; not working. *Sailors like to go sight-seeing when they are off duty in a foreign port.* (When sailors are not supposed to be at work on the ship, they go ashore and visit around town.)

off guard *adj.* Not alert to the unexpected. *Timmy's question caught Jean off guard, and she told him the secret before she knew it.* (Jean was so surprised by Timmy's question that she told him something that she had wanted to keep secret.)

off one's back *adj. phr. informal* Stopped from bothering one; removed as an annoyance or pest. *The singer was so popular with teenagers that he took a secret vacation, to keep them off his back.* (He had to keep his travels secret so that they could not bother him for autographs or souvenirs.)

off one's chest *adj. phr., informal* Told to someone and so not bothering one any more; not making one feel worried or upset, because one has talked about it. *After Dave told the principal that he had cheated on the test, he was glad because it was off his chest.* (He knew he had done wrong and it was bothering him. He wanted to tell someone.)

off one's hands *adv. phr.* No longer in one's care or possession. *Ginny was glad to have the sick dog taken off her hands by the doctor.* (She was glad to have the doctor take it out of her care.)

off one's high horse *adj. phr., informal* Not acting proud and scornful; humble and agreeable. *The girls were so kind to Nancy after her mother died that she came down off her high horse and made friends with them.* (She stopped being proud and acting important and became a good friend.)

off one's rocker *or* **off one's trolley** *adj. phr., informal* Not thinking correctly; crazy; silly; foolish. *Tom is off his rocker if he thinks he can run faster than Bob can.* (He is not thinking correctly; he is silly to think he is faster than Bob.)

off the beam *adv. or adj. phr., slang* Wrong; mistaken. *Maud was off the beam when she said that the girls didn't like her.* (Maud was wrong. The girls did like her.)

off the beaten track *adv. phr.* Not well known or often used; not gone to or seen by many people; unusual. *This feature is off the beaten track.* (This theatre is not well known. Not many people go to it.)

off the cuff *adv. phr., informal* Without preparing ahead of time what one will say; without preparation. *Some presidents like to speak off the cuff to newspaper reporters.* (Some presidents like to answer questions without careful preparation.)

off the hook *adv. phr.* Out of trouble; out of an awkward or embarrassing situation. *Thelma found she had made two dates for the same night; she asked Sally to get her off the hook by going out with one of the boys.* (Thelma asked Sally to get her out of an embarrassing situation by keeping one of the dates for her.)

off the record *adj. phr.* Not to be published or told; secret; confidential. *The President told the reporters his remarks were strictly off the record.* (He didn't want the reporters to tell people what he said.)

off the top of one's head *adv. or adj. phr., informal* Without thinking hard; quickly. *Vin answered the teacher's question off the top of his head.* (Vin answered the teacher's question without really thinking hard.)

off the wagon *adj. phr., slang* No longer refusing to drink whiskey or other alcoholic beverages; drinking liquor again, after stopping for a while. *When a heavy drinker quits, he must really quit. One little drink of whiskey is enough to drive him off the wagon.* (One drink can make a former heavy drinker start drinking too much again.)

old hat *adj. informal* Old-fashioned; not new or different. *By now, putting satellites in orbit is old hat to space scientists.* (They are used to it now because they have practiced often.)

on a dime *adv. phr., informal* In a very small space. *Bob can turn that car on a dime.* (Bob can turn his car in a very small space.) *Tom says his new sports car will stop on a dime.* (The new car will stop in a very short distance.)

on an even keel *adv. phr., informal* In a well-ordered way or condition; orderly. *When the football rally became unruly, the principal stepped to the platform and got things back on an even keel.* (He calmed the crowd and made things orderly again.)

on a shoestring *adv. phr.,* With little money to spend; on a very low budget. *The couple was seeing Europe on a shoestring.* (They were spending very little money.)

on board *prep.* On a ship, plane or similar form of transport. *Joan was not on board the ship when it sailed.* (Joan was not on the ship when it sailed.)

on call *adj. phr.* Ready and available. *This is Dr. Kent's day to be on call at the hospital.* (This is Dr. Kent's day to be ready and available to work at the hospital.)

once in a blue moon *adv. phr.* Very rarely; very seldom; almost never. *Coin collecting is interesting, but you find a valuable coin only once in a blue moon.* (Coin collecting is interesting, but you find a valuable coin only very rarely.)

once-over *n., slang* A quick look; a swift examination of someone or something.—Usually used with *give* or *get*. *The new boy got the once-over from the rest of the class when he came in.* (The class looked at the new boy to see what he was like.)

on cloud nine *adj. phr., slang* Too happy to think of anything else; very happy. *Ada has been on cloud nine since the magazine printed the story she wrote.* (Ada has been very happy since her story was printed in the magazine. She thinks of nothing but that.)

one-armed bandit *n., slang* A slot machine, like those used in Las Vegas and other gambling places. *Joe was playing the one-armed bandit all day—and he lost everything he had.* (He played the slot machines all day and he lost.)

on easy street *adj. phr., informal* Having enough money to live very comfortably; rather rich. *After years of hard work, the Grants found themselves on easy street.* (After years of hard work, the Grants found that they had plenty of money.)

on edge *adj. phr.* Excited or nervous; impatient. *He was on edge about the results of his test.* (He was worried and nervous about how he did on the test.)

one eye on *informal* Watching or minding (a person or thing) while doing something else; part of one's attention on.—Used after *have, keep,* or *with. Mother had one eye on the baby as she ironed.* (Mother ironed and minded the baby at the same time.)

one foot in the grave *n. phr.* Near death. *The dog is fourteen years old, blind, and feeble. He has one foot in the grave.* (The dog is old and weak. He will die soon.)

one for the books *n. phr., informal* Very unusual; a remarkable something. *The newspaper reporter turned in a story that was one for the books.* (The reporter wrote a story that was very unusual.)

on end *adj. phr.* Seemingly endless.—Used with plural nouns of time. *Judy spent hours on end writing and rewriting her essay.* (Judy spent seemingly endless hours writing and rewriting her essay.)

one on the city *n., slang* A glass of water (which is provided free of charge, as a free gift from the city.) *What will you have?—Oh, just give me one on the city.* (All I want is a glass of water.)

one-two *n.* **1** A succession of two punches, the first a short left, followed by a hard right punch, usually in the jaw. *Ali gave Fraser the one-two.* (He gave him the two classical punches.) **2** Any quick or decisive action that takes the opposition by surprise, thereby ensuring victory. *He gave us the old one-two and won the game.* (He took quick, decisive action and won.)

one up *adj. phr.* Having an advantage; being one step ahead. *John graduated from high school; he is one up on Bob, who dropped out.* (John graduated from high school; he has an advantage over Bob, who quit.)

one-upmanship *n., informal* The ability to keep ahead of others; trying to keep an advantage. *No matter what I do, I find that Jim has already done it better. He's an expert at one-upmanship.* (Jim does everything before I do it, and does it better. He keeps one step ahead of me.)

on faith *adv. phr.* Without question or proof. *He said he was twenty-one years old and the employment agency took him on faith.* (He said he was twenty-one years old and the employment agency accepted his word without question.)

on hand *adv. phr.* **1** Nearby; within reach. *Always have your dictionary on hand when you study.* (Always have your dictionary nearby when you study. Always have it within reach.) **2** Present. *Mr. Blake's secretary is always on hand when he appears in public.* (Mr. Blake's secretary is always present when he appears in public.) **3** In one's possession; ready. *The Girl Scouts have plenty of cookies on hand.* (The Girl Scouts have plenty of cookies in their possession.) *Jim had no cash on hand to pay for the gas.* (Jim had no money ready to pay for the gas.)

on ice *adv. or adj. phr., slang* Away for safekeeping or later use; aside. *You will have to put your vacation plans on ice until your debts are paid.* (You will have to suspend your vacation plans until you pay your debts.)

on one's back *adv. phr., informal* Making insistent demands of one; being an annoyance or bother. *My wife has been on my back for weeks to fix the front door screen.* (She has been making insistent demands of me for weeks to fix it. She bothers me about it.)

on one's chest *adv. phr., informal* Worrisome thoughts or feelings that one might need to share with someone else. *"Well, Dave," said the coach, "You look sad—what's on your chest?"* (The coach asked Dave what was making him feel disturbed. Did he want to talk it over?)

on one's coattails *adv. phr.* Along with someone else; as a result of someone else doing something. *Many people vote straight for all the candidates in the same political party. Most people voted for President K., so Governor B. rode in on K.'s coattails.* (Governor B. won because he was in the same political party as the popular President K.)

on one's feet *adv. phr.* Recovering; getting better from sickness or trouble. *Jack is back on his feet after a long illness.* (Jack is recovering after a long illness.)

on one's head *or* **upon one's head** *adv. phr.* On one's self. *Billy had been naughty all day, but he really brought his parents' anger down on his head by pushing his little sister into a mud puddle.* (His mischief was bad enough, but he really brought punishment on himself by pushing his sister.)

on one's high horse *adv. phr., informal* **1** Acting as if one is better than others; being very proud and scornful. *Martha was chairman of the picnic committee, and at the picnic she was on her high horse, telling everyone what to do.*

on one's last legs *adv. phr.* Failing; near the end. *The blacksmith's business is on its last legs.* (The blacksmith's business is failing.) *The dog is old and sick.*

He is on his last legs. (The dog is old and sick. He is near the end of life.)

on one's toes *adv. phr., informal* Alert; ready to act. *The successful ball player is always on his toes.* (A good ball player is alert.)

on pins and needles *adv. phr., informal* Worried; nervous. *Jane's mother was on pins and needles because Jane was very late getting home from school.* (Jane's mother was worried because Jane was so late.) *Many famous actors are on pins and needles before the curtain opens for a play.* (Many actors are nervous just before the show.)

on the air *adj. or adv. phr.* Broadcasting or being broadcast on radio or TV. *His show is on the air at six o'clock.* (The show starts at six.) *The ball game is on the air now.* (The game can be heard now.)

on the ball *adv. phr., informal* **1** Paying attention and doing things well. Used after *is* or *get*. *Ben is really on the ball in school.* (Ben pays attention and does well in school.) *The coach told Jim he must get on the ball or he cannot stay on the team.* (The coach told Jim he must watch more closely and play better.) **2** That which is a skill or ability; making one good at things. Used after *have*. *John will succeed in life; he has a lot on the ball.* (John has a lot of ability; he is good at many things.) *The coach was eager to try out his new team and see what they had on the ball.* (The coach wanted to see what the new team could do.)

on the bandwagon *adj. phr., informal* In or into the newest popular group or activity; in or into something one joins just because many others are joining it. Often used after *climb, get,* or *jump*. *When all George's friends decided to vote for Bill, George climbed on the bandwagon, too.* (George decided to join his friends and do the same thing.)

on the beam *adv. or adj. phr.,* slang Doing well; just right; good or correct. *Kenneth's answer was right on the beam.* (Kenneth answered the teacher's question correctly.)

on the blink *adv. phr., informal* Not working well; needing repair. *Bob's car went on the blink, so he rode to school with John.* (John gave Bob a ride because Bob's car was not working well.) *Mother called the repairman because her washing machine was on the blink.* (Mother's washing machine needs repairing.)

on the block *adv. phr.* To be sold; for sale. *The vacant house was on the block.* (The house was to be sold.) *Young cattle are grown and sent to market to be placed on the block.* (Cattle are sent to market to be sold.)

on the cuff *adj. or adv. phr., informal* Agreeing to pay later; to be paid for later; on credit. *Peter lost the money that Mother gave him to buy meat, and the store would not let him have meat on the cuff.* (The man who sold meat would not let Peter take it and pay later.) *Many people buy cars and television sets on the cuff.* (Many people get cars and television sets and pay a little each month until they are all paid for.)

on the dot *also* **on the button** *adv. phr., informal* Exactly on time; not early and not late. *Susan arrived at the party at 2:00 P.M. on the dot.* (Susan got to the party at exactly 2:00 P.M., just as she

had planned.) *Ben's plane arrived on the dot.* (The plane came in right on time.)

on the go *adj. phr., informal* Active and busy. *Successful people in business are on the go most of the time.* (Very often people in business take trips and move about in tending to their business.) *Healthy, happy people are usually on the go.* (People who are healthy and happy are usually active and busy.)

on the house *adj. phr., informal* Paid for by the owner. *At the opening of the new hotel, the champagne was on the house.* (The owners of the hotel paid for the drinks served at the opening of the hotel.) *Oscar was the first customer at the diner, so his lunch was on the house.* (Since he was the first customer to come into the diner, the owner paid for Oscar's lunch.)

on the level *adj. phr., informal* Honest and fair; telling the whole truth. *Our teacher respects the students who are on the level with her.* (The students who are honest gain the respect of our teacher.) *Joyce wondered if the fortune-teller was on the level.* (Joyce was not sure that the fortune-teller was honest.)

on the loose *adj. phr., informal* Free to go; not shut in or stopped by anything. *The zoo keeper forgot to close the gate to the monkey cage and the monkeys were on the loose.* (Because the zoo keeper forgot to close the gate, the monkeys were free to go all over the zoo.) *All of the seniors were on the loose on "Senior Skip Day."* (There was a special day for all seniors to go wherever they wanted.)

on the make *adj., slang* Promiscuous or aggressive in one's sexual advances. *I can't stand Murray; he's always on the make.* (He is always making aggressive sexual advances.)

on the mend *adj. phr.* Healing; becoming better. *John's broken leg is on the mend.* (John's broken leg is healing and will soon be well.) *Mary's relationship with Joan is on the mend.* (Mary and Joan had a disagreement, but their feelings toward each other are becoming better.)

on the move *adj. or adv. phr.* 1 Moving around from place to place; in motion. *It was a very cold day, and the teacher watching the playground kept on the move to stay warm.* (The teacher kept walking around to make himself warm.) *It was vacation time, and the highways were full of families on the move.* (The roads were full of families in cars and trailers going on their vacations.) 2 Moving forward; going somewhere. *The candidate promised that if people would make him President, he would get the country on the move.* (The man promised to make the country begin to do better; it would progress.)

on the nose *adv. phr., informal* Just right; exactly. *Stanley hit the ball on the nose.* (Stanley hit the ball just right.) *The airplane pilot found the small landing field on the nose.* (The pilot brought his plane into the airport just as planned; he did not need to look around for it.)

on the Q.T. *adv. phr., informal* Secretly, without anyone's knowing. *George and Paul formed a club on the Q.T.* (George and Paul formed a club, but they told no one.) *The teachers got the principal a present strictly on the Q.T.* (Secretly, the teachers got a present for the principal.)

on the sly *adv. phr.* So that other people won't know; secretly. *The boys smoked on the sly.* (The boys smoked when no one was looking.) *Mary's mother did not approve of lipstick, but Mary used it on the sly.* (She used lipstick but her Mother didn't know.)

on the spot *adv. or adj. phr.* 1 *or* **upon the spot** At that exact time and at the same time or place; without waiting or leaving. *The news of important events is often broadcast on the spot over television.* (We see and hear what happens then and there.) 2 *informal also* **in a spot.** In trouble, difficulty, or embarrassment. *Mr. Jones is on the spot because he cannot pay back the money he borrowed.* (Mr. Jones is in trouble because he cannot repay the money.) 3 *slang* In danger of murder; named or listed for death. *After he talked to the police, the gangsters put him on the spot.* (They decided to murder him.)

on the spur of the moment *adv. phr.* On a sudden wish or decision; suddenly; without thought or preparation. *John had not planned to take the trip; he just left on the spur of the moment.* (John had not planned the trip before; he just suddenly decided to go.) *Mary saw a help-wanted advertisement and applied for the job on the spur of the moment.* (She suddenly decided to try for the job.)

on the up and up *adj. phr., informal* Honest; trustworthy; sincere. *We felt that he was honest and could be trusted. This information is on the up and up.*

(This information can be believed.)

on top *adv. or adj. phr., informal* In the lead; with success; with victory. *The horse that everyone had expected would be on top actually came in third.* (The horse that was expected to win, didn't.) *Although John had been afraid that he was not prepared for the exam, he came out on top.* (John was successful on the exam.)

on top of *prep.* **1** *informal* Very close to. *The elevator was so crowded that everybody was on top of each other.* (People were crowded close together in the elevator.) **2** *informal* In addition to; along with. *Mrs. Lane had many expenses and on top of everything else, her baby became ill.* (In addition to all her other expenses, Mrs. Lane now needed a doctor for her baby.) **3** *informal* Managing very well; in control of. *Although his new job was very complicated, John was on top of it within a few weeks.* (John was managing his new job very well.) **4** Knowing all about; not falling behind in information about; up-to-date on. *Mary stays on top of the news by reading newspapers and magazines.* (Mary keeps up with the news.)

open one's heart *v. phr.* **1** To talk about one's feelings honestly; confide in someone. *After going around worrying, Mary opened her heart to her mother.* (Mary told her mother all about her worries.) **2** To be sympathetic to; give love or help generously. *Mrs. Smith opened her heart to the poor little boy.* (She loved him and was kind to him.)

open secret *n.* Something that is supposed to be a secret but that everyone knows. *It is an open secret that Mary and John are*

engaged. (Mary and John's engagement is supposed to be a secret but everyone knows about it.)

out cold *adv. or adj., informal* Unconscious; in a faint. *The ball hit Dick in the head and knocked him out cold for ten minutes.* (Dick was unconscious for ten minutes.) *They tried to lift Mary when she fell down, but she was out cold.* (Mary fainted after her fall.)

out for *prep.* Joining, or planning to join; taking part in; competing for a place in. *John is out for the basketball team.* (John is trying to get on the basketball team.)

out in left field *adj. phr., informal* **1** Far from the right answer. *Johnny tried to answer the teacher's question, but he was way out in left field.* (Johnny's answer was all wrong.) **2** Speaking or acting very queerly; crazy. *The girl next door was always peculiar, but after her father died, she was really out in left field and had to go to a hospital.*

out in the cold *adv. phr., informal* Alone; not included.—A cliché. *All the other children were chosen for parts in the play, but Johnny was left out in the cold.* (Johnny was not invited to take part in the play.)

out like a light *adv. phr., informal* **1** Fast asleep; to sleep very quickly. *As soon as the lights were turned off, Johnny was out like a light.* (Johnny fell asleep very quickly.) **2** In a faint; unconscious. *Johnny was hit by a ball and went out like a light.*

out of circulation *adj. phr., informal* Not out in the company of friends, other people, and groups; not active; not joining in what others are doing. *John has a job after school and is out of cir-*

culation with his friends. (He can't be with his friends so much.)

out of kilter   *adj. phr., informal* **1** Not balanced right; not in a straight line or lined up right. *The scale must be out of kilter because when I weighed myself on it, it said 300 pounds.* (The scale doesn't balance properly and doesn't indicate correct weight.)

out of line   *adv. phr.*   Not obeying or agreeing with what is right or usual; doing or being what people do not expect or accept. *Little Mary got out of line and was rude to Aunt Elizabeth.* (Mary broke the rules of politeness; she was naughty.)

out of one's element   *adv. phr.* Outside of one's natural surroundings; where one does not belong or fit in. *Wild animals are out of their element in cages.* (Wild animals are not happy in cages. They like to run free.) *Chris is out of his element in singing class.* (Chris can't sing and does not like to sing.)

out of one's hair   *adv. phr., informal*   Rid of as a nuisance; relieved of as an annoyance. *Harry got the boys out of his hair so he could study.* (Harry sent the boys away so they wouldn't bother him.)

out of one's shell   *adv. phr., informal*   Out of one's bashfulness or silence; into friendly conversation.—Usually used after *come*. *John wouldn't come out of his shell and talk to the boys and girls at the party.* (John was very bashful at the party.)

out of order   *adv. or adj. phr.* **1** In poor condition; not working properly. *Our television set is out of order.* (Our television set is not working properly.) **2** Against the rules; not suitable. *The judge told the people in the courtroom that*

they were out of order because they were so noisy. (The people were not obeying the rules of the court to be quiet.) *The children's whispering was out of order in church.* (The children's behavior was not suitable for church.)

out of place   *adv. phr.*   In the wrong place or at the wrong time; not suitable; improper. *Joan was the only girl who wore a long gown at the party, and she felt out of place.* (She felt embarrassed because her dress was not suitable for the party.) *It was out of place for Russell to laugh at the old lady.* (It was not proper; he should not have done it.)

out of sorts   *adj. phr.*   In an angry or unhappy mood; in a bad temper; grouchy. *Mary was out of sorts and wouldn't say good morning.* (Mary was grouchy and wouldn't talk to anyone.) *Bob was out of sorts because he didn't get a bicycle for his birthday.* (Bob was mad because he didn't get a bicycle for his birthday.)

out of step   *adv. or adj. phr.* **1** Not in step; not matching strides or keeping pace with another or others. *George always marches out of step with the music.* (George doesn't march in time to the music.) **2** Out of harmony; not keeping up.—Often followed by *with. Just because you don't smoke, it doesn't mean you are out of step with other boys and girls your age.* (Even if you don't smoke, it doesn't mean you are not keeping up with other boys and girls.)

out of the blue   *or* **out of a clear sky** *or* **out of a clear blue sky**   *adv. phr., informal*   Without any warning; by surprise; unexpectedly. *At the last minute Johnny came out of the blue to catch the pass and score a touchdown.* (No one expected him to catch the pass.) *The cowboy thought he was alone but suddenly out of a clear sky there were Indians all around him.* (The Indians were so quiet that they surprised the cowboy.)

out of the frying pan into the fire Out of one trouble into worse trouble; from something bad to something worse. *The movie cowboy was out of the frying pan into the fire. After he escaped from the robbers, he was captured by Indians.* (The cowboy got out of one danger into another.)

out of thin air *adv. phr.* Out of nothing or from nowhere. *The teacher scolded Dick because his story was concocted out of thin air.* (Dick's story was not based on facts or knowledge.)

out of tune *adv. or adj. phr.* Not in agreement; in disagreement; not going well together.—Often used with *with. What Jack said was out of tune with how he looked; he said he was happy, but he looked unhappy.* (His looks didn't agree with his words.)

out to lunch *adj., slang, informal* Inattentive, daydreaming, inefficient, stupid. *Neil Bender is just out to lunch today.* (He is very absent-minded.)

over one's head *adj. or adv. phr.* **1** Not understandable; beyond one's ability to understand; too hard or strange for one to understand. *Mary laughed just to be polite, but the joke was really over her head.* (Mary didn't understand the joke.) **2** To a more important person in charge; to a higher official. *When Mary's supervisor said no, Mary went over her head to the person in charge of the whole department.* (Mary went to a bigger boss.)

over the hill *adj., informal* Past one's prime, unable to function as one used to, senile. *Leo is sure not like he used to be; well, he's over the hill.* (He is getting old and weak.)

over with[1] *prep.* At the end of; finished with; through with. *They were over with the meeting by ten o'clock.* (They were finished by ten.) *By Saturday Mary will be over with the measles.* (Mary will be finished having the measles by Saturday; she will be well by then.)

over with[2] *adj., informal* At an end; finished. *John knew his mother would scold him for losing the money, and he wanted to get it over with.* (John wanted to be through with the scolding.) *After the hard test, Jerry said, "I'm glad that's over with!"* (Jerry felt glad that it was finished.)

own up *v., informal* To take the blame; admit one's guilt; confess. *When Mr. Jones asked who broke the window, Johnny owned up.* (Johnny confessed.)

P

paddy wagon *n.*, *informal* A police van used for transporting prisoners to jail or the police station. *The police threw the demonstrators into the paddy wagon.* (They were thrown into the police van.)

pain in the ass *or* **pain in the neck** *n.*, *slang*, *vulgar with "ass"* An obnoxious or bothersome person or event. *Eve is a regular pain in the neck/ass.* (She is a bothersome and obnoxious person.) (This expression is not vulgar when used with "neck.")

paint oneself into a corner *v. phr.* To get oneself into a bad situation that is difficult or impossible to get out of. *By promising both to lower taxes and to raise the defense budget, the President has painted himself into a corner.* (He has put himself into an impossible position.)

palm off *v.*, *informal* **1** To sell or give (something) by pretending it is something more valuable; to sell or give by trickery. *He palmed off freshly cut wood as seasoned firewood.* (The wood was too green to burn in a fireplace.) **2** To deceive (someone) by a trick or lie. *He palmed his creditors off with a false promise to sell some land to pay his debts.* (He didn't intend to sell any of his land.) **3** To introduce someone as a person he isn't; present falsely. *He palmed the girl off as a real Broadway actress.* (He got the girl the job by saying that she had acted on Broadway.)

pan out *v.*, *informal* To have a result, especially a good result; succeed. *Suppose the class tried to make money by selling candy. How would that pan out?* (How would that succeed? Would it

make money?) *Edison's efforts to invent an electric light bulb did not pan out until he used tungsten wires.* (He failed until he used tungsten wires.)

par for the course *n. phr.*, *informal* Just what was expected; nothing unusual; a typical happening. Usually refers to things going wrong. *When John came late again, Mary said, "That's par for the course."* (John was late, as usual.)

part and parcel *n. phr.* A necessary or important part; something necessary to a larger thing.— Usually followed by *of*. *Freedom of speech is part and parcel of the liberty of a free person.* (Freedom of speech is a necessary part of the liberty of a free person.)

pass away *v.* **1** To cease to exist; end; disappear; vanish. *When automobiles became popular, the use of the horse and buggy passed away.* (When automobiles were used by everyone, the horse and buggy disappeared.) **2** To have one's life stop; die. *He passed away at eighty.* (He died when he was eighty years old.)

pass muster *v. phr.*, *informal* To pass a test or checkup; be good enough. *After a practice period, Sam found that he was able to pass muster as a lathe operator.* (After training on the new job, he became a satisfactory lathe operator.) *His work was done carefully, so it always passed muster.* (He worked carefully, so everyone was satisfied with the work.)

pass off *v.* **1** To sell or give (something) by false claims; offer (something fake) as genuine. *The dishonest builder passed off a poorly built house by pretending it was well constructed.* (He sold the badly built house by saying it was good.) **2** To claim to be someone one is not; pretend to be someone else. *He passed himself off as a doctor until someone checked his record.* (He claimed to be a doctor until someone checked up.) **3** To go away gradually; disappear. *Mrs. White's morning headache had passed off by that night.* (Her morning headache had disappeared by evening.) **4** To reach an end; run its course from beginning to end. *The party passed off well.* (The party went well from beginning to end.)

pass on *v.* **1** To give an opinion about; judge; settle. *The college passed on his application and found him acceptable.* (The college examined his application and decided it was all right.) *The committee recommended three people for the job and the president passed on them.* (The president judged which one was best for the job.) **2** To give away (something that has been outgrown.) *As he grew up, he passed on his clothes to his younger brother.* (His clothes were given to his younger brother.) **3** To die. *Mary was very sorry to hear that her first-grade teacher had passed on.* (Mary's teacher died.)

pass the buck *v. phr., informal* To make another person decide something or accept a responsibility or give orders instead of doing it oneself; shift or escape responsibility or blame; put the duty or blame on someone else. *Mrs. Brown complained to the man who sold her the bad meat, but he only passed the buck and told her to see the manager.* (The man who sold the meat would not take the blame for the bad meat.)

pay dirt *n., slang* **1** The dirt in which much gold is found. *The man searched for gold many years*

before he found pay dirt. (After many years the man found much gold.) **2** *informal* A valuable discovery.—Often used in the phrase *strike pay dirt. When Bill joined the team, the coach struck pay dirt.* (The team became stronger, because Bill was a good player.)

pay off *v.* **1** To pay the wages of. *The men were paid off just before quitting time, the last day before the holiday.* (The men got their pay just before going home on the day before the holiday.) **2** To pay and discharge from a job. *When the building was completed, he paid off the laborers.* (When the building was finished he handed the workmen their wages and let them go.) **3** To hurt (someone) who has done wrong to one; get revenge on. *When Bob tripped Dick, Dick paid Bob off by punching him in the nose.* (Dick punished Bob by hitting him in the nose.) **4** *informal* To bring a return; make profit. *At first Mr. Harrison lost money on his investments, but finally one paid off.* (The investment made a profit.) **5** *informal* To prove successful, rewarding, or worthwhile. *Ben's friendship with the old man who lived beside him paid off in pleasant hours and broadened interests.* (The friendship gave him pleasure and widened his outlook.) *John studied hard before the examination, and it paid off. He made an A.* (John's studying was worthwhile. It was rewarded with a grade of A.)

pay-off *n., informal* (stress on *pay*) **1** Results of one's work. *"My pay-off is students who get good jobs,"* the teacher said. (Her reward is the success of her students.) **2** A bribe. *The crooked* *cops in Chicago took pay-offs from the mob.* (They accepted bribes.)

pay through the nose *v. phr., informal* To pay at a very high rate; pay too much. *He had wanted experience, but this job seemed like paying through the nose for it.* (This job seemed too hard for what experience he was getting.) *There was a shortage of cars; if you found one for sale, you had to pay through the nose.* (If you found a car for sale during the shortage, you had to pay too much for it.)

pecking order *n* The way people are ranked in relation to each other (for honor, privilege, or power); status classification, hierarchy. *After the President was in office several months, his staff developed a pecking order.* (There was a chain of command; staff members had influence according to the order of their authority.)

peeping Tom *n.* A man or boy who likes sly peeping. *He was picked up by the police as a peeping Tom.* (The police found him staring into a woman's window and arrested him.)

penny for one's thoughts Please tell me what you are thinking about; what's your daydream? *"A penny for your thoughts!" he exclaimed.* (He asked me to tell him what I was thinking about.)

penny-wise and pound-foolish Wise or careful in small things to the costly neglect of important things. *Mr. Smith's fence is rotting and falling down because he wouldn't spend money to paint it. He is penny-wise and pound-foolish.* (Mr. Smith would not spend money to buy paint, so he may have to spend more money to build a new fence.)

people who live in glass houses should not throw stones Do not complain about other people if you are as bad as they are. *Mary says that Betty is jealous, but Mary is more jealous herself. People who live in glass houses should not throw stones.* (Mary should not criticize Betty if she is just as bad.)

pep talk *n., informal* A speech that makes people feel good so they will try harder and not give up. *The football coach gave the team a pep talk.* (He encouraged them to keep trying.) *Mary was worried about her exams, but felt better after the teacher's pep talk.* (The teacher cheered Mary up.)

peter out *v., informal* To fail or die down gradually; grow less; become exhausted. *After the factory closed, the town pretty well petered out.* (After the factory shut down, the jobs were fewer and people began to move away from town.) *The mine once had a rich vein of silver, but it petered out.* (The mine once had a rich vein of silver, but it had all been dug out.)

pick-me-up *n. phr.* Food or a tonic one takes when one feels tired or weak. *John stopped at a drugstore for a pick-me-up after working three hours overtime.* (John was tired so he stopped and had a drink.) *Mary always carried a bar of chocolate in her pocketbook for a pick-me-up.* (Mary has a chocolate bar in case she feels tired.)

pick on *v.* **1** *informal* To make a habit of annoying or bothering (someone); do or say bad things to (someone). *Other boys picked on him until he decided to fight them.* (Other boys teased him until he began to defend himself.) **2** To single out; choose; select. *He visited a lot of colleges, and* *finally picked on Stanford.* (He visited a lot of colleges, and finally decided to go to Stanford.)

pick out *v.* **1** To choose. *It took Mary a long time to pick out a new dress at the store.* (It took her a long time to make up her mind and buy the one she wanted.) **2** To see among others; recognize; tell from others. *We could pick out different places in the city from the airplane.* (We could recognize places from high in the air.) **3** To find by examining or trying; tell the meaning. *The box was so dirty we couldn't pick out the directions on the label.* (We couldn't see what the directions were by looking very carefully at them.)

pick the brains of *v. phr.* To get ideas or information about a particular subject by asking an expert. *If you have time, I'd like to pick your brains about home computers.* (I'd like to get some facts and ideas from you.)

pick up *v.* **1** To take up; lift. *During the morning Mrs. Carter picked up sticks in the yard.* (She gathered sticks in the morning.) **2** *informal* To pay for someone else. *After lunch, in the restaurant, Uncle Bob picked up the check.* (He took the bill and paid for all the lunches.) **3** To take on or away; receive; get. *At the next corner the bus stopped and picked up three people.* (The bus stopped at the next corner and took on three people.) **4** To get from different places at different times; a little at a time; collect. *He had picked up rare coins in seaports all over the world.* (He had collected rare coins in seaports all over the world.) **5** To get without trying; get accidentally. *He picked up knowledge of radio just by*

staying around the radio station. (He learned a little about radio by listening to people at the radio station.) *Billy picked up a cold at school today.* (Billy caught a cold somehow.) **6a** To gather together; collect. *When the carpenter finished making the cabinet, he began picking up his tools.* (He began to get them together to take away with him.) **6b** To make neat and tidy; tidy up, put in order. *Pick up your room before Mother sees it.* (Make your room neater.) **6c** To gather things together; tidy a place up. *It's almost dinner time, children. Time to pick up and get ready.* (It's time to get your things together before dinner.) **7** To catch the sound of. *He picked up Chicago on the radio.* (He was able to hear a Chicago station on his radio.) **8** To get acquainted with (someone) without an introduction; make friends with (a person of the other sex.) *Mother told Mary not to walk home by herself from the party because some stranger might try to pick her up.* (Some stranger might try to make friends with her.) **9** *informal* To take to the police station or jail; arrest. *Police picked the man up for burglary.* (Police arrested him for stealing.) **10** To recognize the trail of a hunted person or animal; find. *State police picked up the bandit's trail.* (State police found the way the robber had gone.) *The dogs picked up the fox's smell.* (The dogs found the smell and were able to follow the fox by it.) **11** To make (someone) feel better; refresh. *A little food will pick you up.* (Something to eat will make you feel better.) **12a** To increase (the speed); make (the speed) faster. *The teacher told her singing class to pick up the tempo.*

(The teacher urged her class to sing faster.) *The car picked up speed.* (The car gathered speed.) **12b** To become faster; become livelier. *The speed of the train began to pick up.* (It began to go faster.) *After the band practiced for a while, the music began to pick up.* (The music got faster and more lively.) **13** To start again after interruption; go on with. *The class picked up the story where they had left it before the holiday.* (The class went on with the story from the place where they had stopped reading it before the holiday.) *They met after five years, and picked up their friendship as if there had been no interruption.* (After five years apart, they started their friendship again.) **14** *informal* To become better; recover; gain. *She picked up in her schoolwork.* (She began to do better in her schoolwork.) *He picked up gradually after a long illness.* (He regained his health slowly after a long illness.) *His spirits picked up as he came near home.* (He began to feel more cheerful.)

pickup *n.* (stress on *pick*) **1** Accosting, soliciting and/or befriending a member of the opposite sex. *They say that Sue is an easy pickup.* (It is easy to befriend her and take her to bed.) **2** Scheduled meeting in order to move merchandise, mostly illegally. *The gangsters made the pickup of heroin at 5 P.M.* (They took it into their possession at that time.) **3** A rugged, small truck. *The Subaru Brat is supposed to be a well-built small pickup (truck).*

piece of cake *n., informal* Any task easily accomplished for lack of resistance or challenge. *Writing a new program on this computer is a piece of cake.* (It's so easy that it is no challenge at all.)

piggyback *also* **pick-aback** *adj. or adv.* also Sitting or being carried on the back and shoulders. *Little John loved to go for a piggyback ride on his father's shoulders.* (Father carried little John on his shoulders.) *When Mary sprained her ankles, John carried her piggyback to the doctor.* (John carried Mary on his shoulders.)

piggy bank *n.* A small bank, sometimes in the shape of a pig, for saving coins. *John's father gave him a piggy bank.* (John's father gave him a little bank in the shape of a pig.)

pig in a poke *n. phr.* Something accepted or bought without looking at it carefully. *Buying land by mail is buying a pig in a poke: sometimes the land turns out to be under water.* (Buying land by mail is buying carelessly; sometimes agents may sell you part of the ocean bottom.)

pin down *v.* **1a** To keep (someone) from moving; make stay in a place or position; trap. *Mr. Jones' leg was pinned down under the car after the accident.* (His leg was under the car so that he couldn't move it.) **1b** To keep (someone) from changing what (he) says or means; make (someone) admit the truth; make (someone) agree to something. *I tried to pin Bob down to fix my bicycle tomorrow, but he wouldn't say that he could.* (He wouldn't agree to fix it tomorrow.) **2** To tell clearly and exactly; explain so that there is no doubt. *The police tried to pin down the blame for the fire in the school.* (They tried to find exactly who should be blamed for the fire.)

pipe dream *n., informal* An unrealizable, financially unsound, wishful way of thinking; an unrealistic plan. *Max went through the motions of pretending that he wanted to buy that $250,000 house, but his wife candidly told the real estate broker that it was just a pipe dream.* (Max's wife told the saleswoman that they couldn't really buy the house and were just wishfully toying with the idea.)

pipe up *v., informal* To speak up; to be heard. *Mary is so shy, everyone was surprised when she piped up with a complaint at the club meeting.* (Mary spoke up about what she didn't like.) *Everyone was afraid to talk to the police, but a small child piped up.* (A small child began to speak.)

pip-squeak *n., informal* A small, unimportant person. *If the club is really democratic, then every little pip-squeak has the right to say what he thinks.* (Everybody can talk, whether he is important or not.)

piss off *v., slang, vulgar, avoidable* To bother, annoy, irritate. *You really piss me off when you talk like that.* (What you say really irritates me.) **pissed off** *adj. Why act so pissed off just because I made a pass at you?* (Why are you acting so irritated just because I expressed a romantic interest in you?)

pitch in *v., informal* **1** To begin something with much energy; start work eagerly. *Pitch in and we will finish the job as soon as possible.* (Get to work and we will soon finish.) **2** To give help or money for something; contribute. *Everyone must pitch in and work together.* (Everyone must join together to work.) *We all pitched in a quarter to buy Nancy a present.* (We all gave a quarter.)

play ball *v. phr., informal* To join in an effort with others; cooperate. *It is often good business to play ball with a political machine.* (In business it often helps to be friends with the local political powers.)

play by ear *v. phr.* **1** To play a musical instrument by remembering the tune, not by reading music. *Mary does not know how to read music. She plays the piano by ear.* (Mary plays music on the piano by remembering how she heard it played before.) **2** *informal* To decide what to do as one goes along, to fit the situation.— Used with *it*. *John decided to play it by ear when he went for his interview.* (John didn't plan in advance what to say but improvised as he was asked questions.)

play cat and mouse with *v. phr.* To tease or fool (someone) by pretending to let him go free and then catching him again. *Joe's uncle had fun playing cat and mouse with him.* (Joe's uncle had fun pretending to let him go but not really letting him go.) *The policeman decided to play cat and mouse when he saw the woman steal the dress in the store.* (The policeman pretended to let the woman go, but he did not really let her go when he saw her steal the dress in the store.)

play down *v.* To give less emphasis to; make (something) seem less important; divert attention from; draw notice away from. *The newspaper stories played down the actor's unattractive past.* (The newspaper stories said little about the bad things in his past.)

played out *adj. phr.* Tired out; worn out; finished; exhausted. *It had been a hard day, and by night* *he was played out.* (It had been a tiring day, and by night he was worn out.)

play footsie *v. phr., slang, informal* **1** Touch the feet of a member of the opposite sex under the table as an act of flirtation. *Have you at least played footsie with her?* (Have you at least engaged in mild flirtation with her?) **2** To engage in any sort of flirtation or collaboration, especially in a political situation. *The mayor was suspected of playing footsie with the syndicate.* (They suspected the mayor of having underworld connections.)

play ———for *v., informal* To treat (someone) as; act toward (someone) as, handle (someone) as; handle as. *He played the man for a sucker.* (He treated the man as easy to fool.)

play hooky *v. phr., informal* To stay out of school illegally. *Carl is failing in school because he has played hooky so many times during the year.* (He often stayed out of school illegally during the year.)

play into one's hands *v. phr.* To be or do something that another person can use against one; help an opponent against oneself. *In the basketball game, Jerry's foul played into the opponents' hands.* (Jerry's foul gave the other team a free throw.)

play off *v.* **1** To match opposing persons, forces, or interests for one's own gain. *The girl played off her admirers against each other.* (She encouraged one man and then another so that they would do more to make her like them.) **2** To finish the playing of (an interrupted contest.) *The visitors came back the next Saturday to play off the game stopped by rain.* (They came back to finish the game stopped by rain.) **3** To settle (a tie score) between contestants by more play. *When each player had won two matches, the championship was decided by playing off the tie.* (They played another match to settle the tie; the winner of the extra match was the champion.)

play on *or* **play upon** *v.* **1** To cause an effect on; influence. *A heavy diet of television drama played on his feelings.* (Much watching of TV kept him excited and anxious.) **2** To work upon for a planned effect; excite to a desired action by cunning plans; manage. *The makeup salesman played on the woman's wish to look beautiful.* (He got her to buy his makeup by making her want to be beautiful.)

play one's cards right *or* **play one's cards well** *v. phr., informal* Make the best use of one's opportunities. *People liked Harold, and he played his cards well—and soon he began to get ahead rapidly.* (He was likeable and used his talents to good advantage and quickly succeeded.)

play the field *v. phr., informal* To date many different people; avoid steady dates with the same person. *Al had a steady girl friend, but John was playing the field.* (John dated many girls.)

play up *v.* To call attention to; talk more about; emphasize. *The coach played up the possibilities, and kept our minds off our weaknesses.* (The coach talked more about what could be done, and kept us from thinking about what we could not do.)

play up to *v. phr., slang* **1** To try to gain the favor of, especially for selfish reasons; act to win the approval of; try to please. *He played up to the boss.* (He tried to make the boss like him so that he would get more pay.) **2** To use (something) to gain an end; to attend to (a weakness). *He played up to the old lady's vanity to get her support.* (He flattered the old lady so she would support his plan.)

play with fire *v. phr.* To put oneself in danger; to take risks. *Leaving your door unlocked in New York City is playing with fire.* (It's dangerous not to lock your door in New York.)

plow into *v.* **1** To attack vigorously. *He plowed into his work and finished it in a few hours.* (He attacked his work with great energy.) **2** To crash into with force. *A truck plowed into my car and smashed the fender.* (A truck crashed into my car.)

pluck up *v.* **1** To have (courage) by one's own effort; make oneself have (courage). *In spite of failure, he plucked up heart to continue.* (Though he failed at first, he made himself brave enough to keep on.) *He plucked up courage when he saw a glimmer of hope.* (He was encouraged when he saw a little hope.) **2** To become happier; feel better; cheer up. *He plucked up when his wife recovered.* (He cheered up when his wife got well.)

point out *v.* To bring to notice; call attention to; explain. *The policeman pointed out that the law forbids public sale of firecrackers.* (He explained that the law forbids public sale of firecrackers.)

point up *v.* To show clearly; emphasize. *The increase in crime points up the need for greater police protection.* (The rise in crime shows that more police are needed.)

polish off *v., informal* **1** To defeat easily. *The Dodgers polished off the Yankees in four straight games in the 1963 World Series.* (The Dodgers won the Series easily in four straight games.) **2** To finish completely; finish doing quickly, often in order to do something else. *The boys were hungry and polished off a big steak.* (They ate up the steak hungrily.)

polish the apple *v. phr., slang* To try to make someone like one; to try to win favor by flattery. *Mary polished the apple at work because she wanted a day off.* (Mary tried to please her boss so he would give her a day off.)

pooped out *adj., slang* Worn out; exhausted. *Everyone was pooped out after the hike.* (Everyone was exhausted.) *The heat made them feel pooped out.* (They were worn out from the heat.)

pop up *or* **bob up** *v.* To appear suddenly or unexpectedly; show up; come out. *Just when the coach thought he had everything under control, a new problem bobbed up.* (Just when things seemed to be going smoothly, the coach ran into more trouble.)

pot call the kettle black *informal* The person who is criticizing someone else is as guilty as the person he accuses; the charge is as true of the person who makes it as of the one he makes it against. *Bill said John was cheating at a game but John replied that the pot was calling the kettle black.* (John meant that Bill was cheating too.)

pour oil on troubled waters *v. phr.* To quiet a quarrel; say something to lessen anger and bring peace. *The groups were nearing a bitter quarrel until the leader poured oil on the troubled waters.* (A bad quarrel seemed certain until the leader quieted the opposing groups.)

pour out v. **1** To tell everything about; talk all about. *Mary poured out her troubles to her pal.* (Mary told her friend all about her troubles.) **2** To come out in great quantity; stream out. *The people poured out of the building when they heard the fire alarm.* (All the people came out in a stream.)

powder room n. The ladies' rest room. *When they got to the restaurant, Mary went to the powder room to wash up.* (Mary went to the ladies' room.)

press one's luck or **push one's luck** v. phr. To depend too much on luck; expect to continue to be lucky. *When John won his first two bets at the race track, he pressed his luck and increased his bets.* (John expected to go on winning.) *If you're lucky at first, don't press your luck.* (Don't depend on being lucky all the time.)

prey on or **prey upon** v. **1** To habitually kill and eat; catch for food. *Cats prey on mice.* (Cats catch and eat mice.) **2** To capture or take in spoils of war or robbery. *Pirates preyed on American ships in the years just after the Revolutionary War.* (Pirates captured or robbed American ships for a while after the Revolutionary war.) **3** To cheat; rob. *Gangsters preyed on businesses of many kinds while the sale of liquor was prohibited.* (Gangsters robbed businesses of many kinds during the time when liquor could not be sold in America.) **4** To have a tiring and weakening effect on; weaken. *Ill health had preyed on him for years.* (Sickness had weakened his body for years.) *Business worries preyed on his mind.* (Business troubles tired and worried him.)

promise the moon v. phr. To promise something impossible. *A politician who promises the moon during a campaign loses the voters' respect.* (A politician who promises something impossible during a campaign loses the voters' respect.) *I can't promise you the moon, but I'll do the best job I can.* (I can't promise to do a perfect job, but I'll do my best.)

psyched up adj., informal Mentally alert, ready to do something. *The students were all psyched up for their final exams.* (They were all mentally alert and ready to take the exams.)

psych out v. phr., slang, informal **1** To find out the real motives of (someone). *Sue sure's got Joe psyched out.* (Sue has figured out what Joe's real motives are.) **2** To go berserk, to lose one's nerve. *Joe says he doesn't ride his motorcycle on the highway anymore because he's psyched out.* (He lost his courage.) *Jim psyched out and he robbed a liquor store, when he has all he needs and wants!* (He went berserk and committed a robbery when he had no need to do so.)

pull off v., informal To succeed in (something thought difficult or impossible); do. *Ben Hogan pulled off the impossible by winning three golf tournaments in one year.* (Ben Hogan succeeded in winning three golf tournaments in one year, although that seemed impossible.) *The bandits pulled off a daring bank robbery.* (The bandits succeeded in robbing a bank, despite the security system.)

pull one's leg v. phr., informal To try to get someone to accept a ridiculous story as true; fool someone with a humorous account of something; trick. *For a* *moment, I actually believed that his wife had royal blood. Then I realized he was pulling my leg.* (For a moment, I thought his wife was really a princess. Then I knew he was fooling me.)

pull one's weight *v. phr.* To do one's full share of work; do one's part. *In a small shop, it is important that each employee pull his weight.* (In a small shop, it is important for each worker to do his full share.)

pull out of a hat *v. phr., informal* To get as if by magic; invent; imagine. *When the introduction to a dictionary tells you how many hours went into its making, these figures were not pulled out of a hat.* (These figures were not invented or imagined.) *Let's see you pull an excuse out of your hat.* (Let's see you make up an excuse.)

pull over *v.* To drive to the side of the road and stop. *The policeman told the speeder to pull over.* (The policeman told the speeder to drive to the side of the road and stop.) *Everyone pulled over to let the ambulance pass.* (Everyone drove to the side of the road to let the ambulance go by.)

pull rank *v. phr., slang, informal* To assert one's superior position or authority on a person of lower rank, as in exacting a privilege or a favor. *"How come you always get night duty?"—"Norton pulled rank on me."* (He asserted his power and I got the worse assignment.)

pull strings *or* **pull wires** *v. phr., informal* To secretly use influence and power, especially with people in charge or in important jobs; make use of friends to gain one's wishes. *If you want to see the governor, Mr. Root can pull*

strings for you. (Mr. Root can help you because he knows the governor himself or he knows people who do.)

pull the plug on *v. phr., slang* To expose (someone's) secret activities. *The citizens' committee pulled the plug on the mayor, and he lost the election.* (The committee exposed the mayor's secret activities and this caused the mayor to lose the election.)

pull the rug out from under *v. phr., informal* To withdraw support unexpectedly from; to spoil the plans of. *Bill thought he would be elected, but his friends pulled the rug out from under him and voted for Vin.* (Bill's friends withdrew their support of him without warning.) *We were planning a vacation, but the baby's illness pulled the rug out from under us.* (The baby's illness spoiled our vacation plans.)

pull the wool over one's eyes *v. phr., informal* To fool someone into thinking well of one; deceive. *The florist had pulled the wool over his partner's eyes about their financial position.* (He had fooled his partner about money matters.) *Bob tried to pull the wool over his teacher's eyes, but she was too smart for him.* (Bob tried to make her think he was a good student but she knew he wasn't.)

pull through *v.* **1** To help through; bring safely through a difficulty or sudden trouble; save. *A generous loan showed the bank's faith in Father and pulled him through the business trouble.* (The bank had faith in Father and lent him money that saved his business.) **2** To recover from an illness or misfortune; conquer a disaster; escape death or failure. *By a near miracle, he pulled through* *after the smashup.* (He recovered after the car accident, although at first he wasn't expected to live.)

push around *v., informal* To be bossy with; bully. *Don't try to push me around!* (Don't try to be bossy with me.) *Paul is always pushing the smaller children around.* (Paul is always making the smaller children do what he wants.)

push off *or* **shove off** *slang* To start; leave. *We were ready to push off at ten o'clock, but had to wait for Jill.* (We were ready to start at ten o'clock, but had to wait for Jill.) *Jim was planning to stay at the beach all day, but when the crowds arrived he shoved off.* (Jim left the beach when the crowds arrived.)

push the panic button *v. phr., slang* To become very frightened; nervous, or excited especially at a time of danger or worry. *John thought he saw a ghost and pushed the panic button.* (John imagined he saw a ghost and was greatly scared.) *Keep cool; don't hit the panic button!* (Keep cool; don't get scared!)

put across *v.* **1** To explain clearly; make oneself understood; communicate. *He knew how to put his ideas across.* (He knew how to get his ideas understood.) **2** *informal* To get (something) done successfully; make real. *He put across a big sales campaign.* (He succeeded in a big selling plan.) *The new librarian put across a drive for a fine new library building.* (The new librarian persuaded people to raise the money and build a library building.)

put all one's eggs in one basket *v. phr.* To place all one's efforts, interests, or hopes in a single person or thing. *Going steady in high school is putting all your eggs in one basket too soon.* (A person who goes steady when he is young puts too much hope in one boy, or girl, too soon.)

put away *v.* **1** *informal* To put in a mental hospital. *He had to put his wife away when she became mentally ill.* (He had to put her in a mental hospital.) **2** To put to death for a reason; kill. *He had his dog put away when it became too old and sick.* (He had someone kill it because it was sick and weak.)

put down *v.* **1** To stop by force; crush. *In 24 hours the general had entirely put down the rebellion.* (He stopped the fighting in a day's time.) **2** To put a stop to; check. *She had patiently put down unkind talk by living a good life.* (She had ended unkind gossip by living a good life.) **3** To write a record of; write down. *He put down the story while it was fresh in his mind.* (He wrote down his account while he remembered the happenings.) **4** To write a name in a list as agreeing to do something. *The banker put himself down for $1,000.* (He agreed to give $1,000.) *Sheila put Barbara down for the decorations.* (Sheila made a list of helpers for the class party, and she wrote Barbara's name on the list as the person who would decorate the room.) **5** To decide the kind or class of; characterize. *He put the man down as a bum.* (He decided that the man was a bum.) *He put it down as a piece of bad luck.* (He blamed it on bad luck.) **6** To name as a cause; attribute. *He put the odd weather down to nuclear explosions.* (He blamed the odd weather on nuclear explosions.) **7** To dig; drill;

sink. *He put down a new well.* (He dug a new well.)

put in *v.* **1** To add to what has been said; say (something) in addition to what others say. *While the boys were discussing the car accident, Ben put in that the road was icy.* (Ben said that the road had been icy.) *My father put in a word for me and I got the job.* (My father said I was a good worker.) **2** To buy and keep in a store to sell. *He put in a full stock of drugs.* (He got all kinds of drugs to sell in his store.) **3** To spend (time.) *He put in many years as a printer.* (He worked as a printer for years.) *He put in an hour a day reading.* (He read about an hour every day.) **4** To plant. *He put in a row of radishes.* (He planted a row of radish seed.) **5** To stop at a port on a journey by water. *After the fire, the ship put in for repairs.* (It stopped at the next port.) **6** To apply; ask.—Used with *for*. *When a better job was open, he put in for it.* (When there was a better job, he asked for it.) *The sailor put in for time to visit his family before the ship went to sea.* (He asked permission to visit his family.)

put off *v.* **1** *informal* To cause confusion in; embarrass; displease. *I was rather put off by the shamelessness of his proposal.* (His suggestion was so boldly improper that I did not know what to say or do.) *The man's slovenliness put me off.* (The man's dirty condition displeased me.) **2** To wait and have (something) at a later time; postpone. *They put off the picnic because of the rain.* (They postponed the picnic because of the rain.) **3** To make (someone) wait; turn aside. *When he asked her to name a day for their wedding, she put him off.*

(When he asked her to name a day for their wedding, she made him wait for a decision.) **4** To draw away the attention; turn aside; distract. *Little Jeannie began to tell the guests some family secrets, but Father was able to put her off.* (Father was able to make her think and talk of something different.) **5** To move out to sea; leave shore. *They put off in small boats to meet the arriving ship.* (They rowed out in small boats to meet the arriving ship.)

put on *v.* **1** To dress in. *The boy took off his clothes and put on his pajamas.* (He dressed in his pajamas.) *Mother put a coat on the baby.* (She dressed the baby in a coat.) **2a** To pretend, assume, show. *Mary isn't really sick; she's only putting on.* (She's only pretending to be sick.) *He put on a smile.* (He pretended to smile.) *The child was putting on airs.* (The child showed a proud manner.) **2b** To exaggerate; make too much of. *That's rather putting it on.* (That's claiming more than is true.) **3** To begin to have more (body weight); gain (weight). *Mary was thin from sickness, and the doctor said she must put on ten pounds.* (She must gain ten pounds.) *Too many sweets and not enough exercise will make you put on weight.* (You will get fat.) **4a** To plan and prepare; produce; arrange; give; stage. *The senior class put on a dance.* (They held a dance.) *The actor put on a fine performance.* (He gave a fine show.) **4b** To make (an effort). *The runner put on an extra burst of speed and won the race.* (He made a last big effort.) **5** To choose to send; employ on a job. *The school put on extra men to get the new building ready.* (It employed more men to get the place ready.)

put one's foot in it *or* **put one's foot in one's mouth** *v. phr., informal* To get into trouble by unwittingly saying something embarrassing or rude. *She put her foot in her mouth with her joke about that church, not knowing that one of the guests belonged to it.* (She hurt one guest's feelings with her joke, because he was a member of the church she made fun of.)

put on one's thinking cap *v. phr.* To think hard and long about some problem or question. *Miss Stone told her pupils to put on their thinking caps before answering the question.* (She wanted them to take time to think hard before answering.)

put on the map *v. phr.* To make (a place) well known. *The first successful climb of Mount Matterhorn put Zermatt, Switzerland on the map.* (The first successful climb of Mt. Matterhorn made Zermatt very well known.) *Shakespeare put his hometown of Stratford-on-Avon on the map.* (People all over the world have heard of Stratford-on-Avon because it was Shakespeare's home.)

put out *v.* **1** To make a flame or light stop burning; extinguish; turn off. *Please put the light out when you leave the room.* (Please turn off the light when you leave the room.) *The firemen put out the blaze.* (The firemen extinguished the fire.) **2** To prepare for the public; produce; make. *For years he had put out a weekly newspaper.* (He had published a weekly newspaper for years.) *It is a small restaurant that puts out an excellent dinner.* (It is a small cafe that provides an excellent dinner.) **3** To invest or loan money. *He put out all his spare money at 10 per cent or better.* (He got 10 per cent

or more on all the money he had for lending.) **4** To make angry; irritate; annoy. *It puts the teacher out to be lied to.* (It angers him to be lied to.) *Father was put out when Jane spilled grape juice on his new suit.* (Father was angry.) **5** *informal* To cause inconvenience to; bother. *He put himself out to make things pleasant for us.* (He went to much trouble to make things pleasant for us.) *Will it put you out if I borrow your pen?* (Will it be difficult for you if I borrow your pen?) **6** To retire from play in baseball. *The runner was put out at first base.* (The runner was retired at first base.) **7** To go from shore; leave. *A Coast Guard boat put out through the waves.* (A small Coast Guard boat went out from shore through the waves.) **8** *vulgar, avoidable, said of women* To engage in promiscuous sexual intercourse. *Why do you think she puts out like that?* (Why is she promiscuous?)

put over *v., informal* To practice deception; trick; fool.—Used with *on*. *George thought he was putting something over on the teacher when he said he was absent the day before because his mother was sick and needed him.* (He thought he was fooling the teacher.) *Tom really put one over on us when he came to the Halloween party dressed as a witch.* (He fooled us; no one recognized him.)

put the bite on *v. phr., slang* To ask (for money, favors, etc.) *John put the bite on his friend for several tickets to the dance.* (John asked his friend to buy several tickets to the dance for him.) *The pitcher put the bite on his team for a large raise.* (The pitcher asked his team for a large increase in pay.)

put two and two together *v. phr.*
To make decisions from the seeming proofs; reason from the known facts; conclude; decide. *He had put two and two together and decided where they had probably gone.* (After weighing the various bits of evidence, he decided where they had probably gone.)

put up *v.* **1a** To make and pack (especially a lunch or medicine); get ready; prepare. *Every morning Mother puts up lunches for the three children.* (Every morning Mother makes sandwiches and packs lunches for the three children.) *The druggist put up the medicine that the doctor had prescribed.* (The druggist prepared the medicine that the doctor had advised.) **1b** To put food into jars or cans to preserve; can. *Mother is putting up peaches in jars.* (She is putting peaches in jars to preserve them.) **1c** To store away for later use. *The farmer put up three tons of hay for the winter.* (The farmer stored three tons of hay to feed to his animals.) **2** To put in place; put (something) where it belongs. *After he unpacked the car, Father put it up.* (Father put the car in the garage, where he kept it when he was not using it.) *After the hard ride, the doctor gave the horse to the stable boy to put up.* (The doctor gave the horse to the stable boy to put in the stable.) *After the battle, the knight put up his sword.* (The knight put his sword in its holder.) **3** To suggest that (someone) be chosen a member, officer, or official. *The club decided to take in another member, and Bill put up Charles.* (Bill suggested that Charles be chosen as a member of the club.)—Often used with *for. The Republicans put Mr. Williams up for mayor.* (The Repub-

licans nominated Mr. Williams mayor.) **4** To put (hair) a special way; arrange. *Aunt May puts up her hair in curlers every night.* (Aunt May winds her hair around curlers every night so that it will have a special wave.) *Sue put her hair up in a twist for the dance.* (Sue arranged her hair in a twist for the dance.) **5** To place on sale; offer for sale. *She put the house up for sale.* (She offered the house for sale.) **6a** To provide lodging for; furnish a room to. *The visitor was put up in the home of Mr. Wilson.* (The visitor was given a room in Mr. Wilson's home.) *They put Frank up at a good hotel.* (They got him a room at a good hotel.) **6b** To rent or get shelter; take lodging; stay in a place to sleep. *The traveler put up at a motel.* (He rented a room at a motel.) *We put up with friends on our trip to Canada.* (We stayed in the home of friends in Canada.) **7** To make; engage in. *He put up a good fight against his sickness.* (He fought bravely to get well.) **8** To furnish (money) or something needed; pay for. *He put up the money to build a hotel.* (He provided the money to build a hotel.)

put upon *v.* To use (someone) unfairly; expect too much from.— Used in the passive or in the past participle. *The bigger girls always put upon Martha.* (The bigger girls made Martha do things for them.)

put up or shut up *v. phr., informal* **1** To bet one's money on what one says or stop saying it.— Often used as a command; often considered rude. *The man from out of town kept saying their team would beat ours, and finally Father told him, "Put up or shut up."*

(Father told the man to make a bet on it with money, or else to be quiet.) **2** To prove something or stop saying it.—Often used as a command; often considered rude. *George told Al that he could run faster than the school champion, and Al told George to put up or shut up.* (Al told George to prove it.)

put up to *v. phr., informal* To persuade to; get to do. *Older boys put us up to painting the statue red on Halloween.* (Older boys told us we should do it.)

put up with *v.* To accept patiently; bear. *We had to put up with Jim's poor table manners because he refused to change.* (We had to accept Jim's poor table manners patiently, because he refused to change.) *The mother told her children, "I refuse to put up with your tracking in mud!"* (The mother said she refused to let her children track mud into the house any more.)

put wise *v., slang* To tell (someone) facts that will give him an advantage over others or make him alert to opportunity or danger. *The new boy did not know that Jim was playing a trick on him, so I put him wise.* (I told him that Jim was playing a trick on him.)—Often used with *to*. *Someone put the police wise to the plan of the bank robbers, and when the robbers went into the bank, the police were waiting to catch them.* (Someone told the police about the plan to rob the bank.)

put words into one's mouth *v. phr.* To say without proof that another person has certain feelings or opinions; claim a stand or an idea is another's without asking; speak for another without right. *When he said "John here is in favor of the idea," I told him not to put words in my mouth.* (I told him not to speak for me without asking me.)

R

rack one's brain *v. phr.* To try one's best to think; make a great mental effort; especially: to try to remember something one has known. *Bob racked his brain trying to remember where he left the book.* (He tried his best to think what he did with it.) *Susan racked her brain trying to guess whom the valentine came from.* (She made a great mental effort to guess who sent it.)

rain cats and dogs *or* **rain buckets** *or* **rain pitchforks** *v. phr., informal* To rain very hard; come down in torrents. *In the middle of the picnic it started to rain cats and dogs, and everybody got soaked.* (While people were busy eating, a storm cloud suddenly appeared and they got caught in a hard rain.)

rain check *n.* **1** A special free ticket to another game or show in place of one canceled because of rain. *When the drizzle turned into a heavy rain the manager announced that the baseball game would be replayed the next day. He told the crowd that they would be given rain checks for tomorrow's game as they went out through the gates.* (He said the special cards would be their free tickets for tomorrow's game.) **2** *informal* A promise to repeat an invitation at a later time. *Bob said, "I'm sorry you can't come to dinner this evening, Dave. I'll give you a rain check."* (Dave had other plans for the evening, so Bob promised to invite him to dinner some other time when he could come.)

raise eyebrows *v. phr.* To shock people; cause surprise or disapproval. *The news that the princess was engaged to a com-*moner raised eyebrows all over the kingdom. (Members of the royal family usually marry titled nobility, so people were shocked to learn that the princess was going to marry a commoner.)

rat out *or* **rat out on** *v. phr., slang* To desert or betray someone, to leave at a critical time. *Joe ratted out on Sue when she was 7-months pregnant.* (He deserted her.)

rat race *n., slang* A crowded, or disorderly rush; a confusing scramble, struggle, or way of living that does not seem to have a purpose. *The dance last night was a rat race. It was too noisy and crowded.* (The dance was noisy and there wasn't enough room to dance.) *School can be a rat race if you don't keep up with your studies.* (If you are always behind in your work and hurrying to catch up, school can be a confusing struggle.)

reach for the sky *v. phr., slang* To put one's hands high above one's head or be shot.—Usually used as a command. *A holdup man walked into a gas station last night and told the attendant "Reach for the sky!"* (He pointed a gun at the attendant and told him to put his hands high above his head.)

read between the lines *v. phr.* To understand all of a writer's meaning by guessing at what has been left unsaid. *Some kinds of poetry make you read between the lines.* (Some poets make a comparison in only a word or two and they leave their readers to guess at what they have left unsaid.) *A clever foreign correspondent can often avoid censorship by careful wording, leaving the audience to read between the lines.* (Experienced readers guess at all of a foreign correspondents' meaning by noticing what has not been said.)

read the riot act *v. phr.* To give someone a strong warning or scolding. *Three boys were late to class and the teacher read the riot act to them.* (He reminded them of the rules of the school and told them not to be late again or there would be serious trouble.)

regular guy *or* **regular fellow** *n., informal* A friendly person who is easy to get along with; a good sport. *You'll like Tom. He's a regular guy.* (He's a good sport, friendly and agreeable.)

rest on one's laurels *v. phr.* To be satisfied with the success one has already won; stop trying to win new honors. *Getting an A in chemistry almost caused Mike to rest on his laurels.* (He was almost satisfied with this one success in chemistry, but he wanted to do as well in other subjects.)

rest room *n.* A room or series of rooms in a public building, for personal comfort and grooming containing toilets, washbowls, mirrors, and often chairs or couches. *Sally went to the rest room to powder her nose.* (She used the things for comfort and personal grooming provided by the restaurant.)

rhyme or reason *n. phr.* A good plan or reason; a reasonable purpose or explanation.—Used in negative, interrogative, or conditional sentences. *Don could see no rhyme or reason to the plot of the play.* (He saw no well-organized plot in the play.) *It seemed to Ruth that her little brother had temper tantrums without rhyme or reason.*

ride herd on *v. phr., informal* To watch closely and control; take care of. *A special legislative assistant rides herd on the bills the*

President is anxious to have Congress pass. (The assistant watches closely, and if necessary urges Congress to act promptly on these bills.)

ride out *v.* To survive safely; endure. *The captain ordered all sails lowered so the ship could ride out the storm.* (He ordered the sails taken down so that the ship could withstand the storm and not sink.)

riding high *adj.* Attracting attention; enjoying great popularity. *After scoring the winning touchdown, John is riding high with his classmates.* (He is enjoying great popularity with them because of his winning play.)

rid of *adj. phr.* Free of; away from; without the care or trouble. *The puppy is finally rid of worms.* (The puppy is finally free of worms.) *If I could be rid of the children for the day, I would go.* (If I could be away from the children for the day, I would go.) *I wish you'd get rid of that cat!* (I wish you'd give away that cat!)

right on *adj., interj., slang, informal* **1** Exclamation of animated approval "Yes," "That's correct," "You're telling the truth," "We believe you," etc. *Orator: And we shall see the promised land! Crowd: Right on!* (That's true, that's what we want to hear!) **2** Correct, to the point, accurate. *The reverand's remark was right on!* (It was correct.)

right out *or* **straight out** *adv.* Plainly; in a way that hides nothing; without waiting or keeping back anything. *When Mother asked who broke the window, Jimmie told her right out that he did it.* (Jimmie told Mother that he broke the window; he did not try to hide the truth.) *When Ann entered the beauty contest, her* *little brother told her straight out that she was crazy.* (Ann's little brother was not polite; he told her she was crazy to think she could win a beauty contest.)

ring a bell *v. phr.* To make one remember something; sound familiar. *Not even the cat's meowing seemed to ring a bell with Judy. She still forgot to feed him.* (Even the meowing of the cat did not make Judy remember that it was time to feed him.)

ring up *v.* **1** To add and record on a cash register. *The supermarket clerk rang up Mrs. Smith's purchases and told her she owed $33.* (The clerk added up the prices of the things Mrs. Smith had bought and told her the total.) **2** *informal* To telephone. *Sally rang up Sue and told her the news.* (Sally telephoned Sue.)

rip off *v., slang* (Accent on *off*) Steal. *The hippies ripped off the grocery store.* (They burglarized the grocery store; they stole from it.)

rip-off *n., slang* (Accent on *rip*) An act of stealing or burglary. *Those food prices are so high, it's almost a rip-off.* (The prices are so high, it is almost like burglary.)

road hog *n., informal* A car driver who takes more than his share of the road. *A road hog forced John's car into the ditch.* (A selfish driver crowded John's car off the road.)

rob Peter to pay Paul *v. phr.* To trade one duty or need for another; take from one person or thing to pay another. *Bill owed Sam a dollar, so he borrowed another from Joe to pay Sam back. He robbed Peter to pay Paul.* (Bill still owes a dollar; he paid one debt by making another.) *Trying to study a lesson for one class* *during another class is like robbing Peter to pay Paul.* (You neglect one class when you are studying for another.)

rob the cradle *v. phr., informal* To have dates with or marry a person much younger than oneself. *When the old woman married a young man, everyone said she was robbing the cradle.* (The woman was criticized for marrying a man much younger than herself.)

rock the boat *v. phr., informal* To make trouble and risk losing or upsetting something; cause a disturbance that may spoil a plan. *The other boys said that Henry was rocking the boat by wanting to let girls into their club.* (The boys thought that girls might break up their club.)

roll around *v., informal* To return at a regular or usual time; come back. *When winter rolls around, out come the skis and skates.* (When winter returns at its regular point in the cycle of the year, people get out their skis and skates.)

rolling stone gathers no moss A person who often changes jobs or where he lives does not strike roots or accumulate property. *Uncle Willie was a rolling stone that gathered no moss. He worked in different jobs all over the country.* (Uncle Willie didn't stay in one place long enough to save money or buy property.)

roll out the red carpet *v. phr.* **1** To welcome an important guest by putting a red carpet down for him to walk on. *They rolled out the red carpet for the Queen when she arrived in Australia.* (They unrolled a red carpet on which she walked from her airplane.) **2** To greet a person with great respect and honor; give a hearty welcome. *Margaret's family rolled out the red carpet for her teacher when she came to dinner.* (They greeted her with great respect. They wore their best clothes and set the table with their best silver and china.)

roll up one's sleeves To get ready for a hard job; prepare to work hard or seriously. *When Paul took his science examination, he saw how little he knew about science. He rolled up his sleeves and went to work.* (He sat down and began to study hard.)

rope into *v., informal* **1** To trick into; persuade dishonestly. *Jerry let the big boys rope him into stealing some apples.* (The big boys tricked Jerry and made him steal apples.) **2** To get (someone) to join in; persuade to work at. *It was Sue's job to bathe the dog, but she roped Sam into helping her.* (She got Sam to help her.)

rough-and-ready *adj.* **1** Not finished in detail; not perfected; rough but ready for use now. *We asked Mr. Brown how long it would take to drive to Chicago and his rough-and-ready answer was two days.* (Mr. Brown didn't know exactly but gave us an answer that was good enough.) **2** Not having nice manners but full of energy and ability; unpolished. *Jim is a rough-and-ready character; he'd rather act than talk things over.* (Jim is always ready to act rather than argue or discuss a matter.)

rough-and-tumble *n.* **1** Very rough, hard fighting or arguing that does not follow any rules. *There was a rough-and-tumble on the street last night between some soldiers and sailors.* (The soldiers and sailors had a very rough fight.) *Many people don't like the rough-and-tumble of politics.* (Many people don't like the ar-

guing and name-calling in politics.) **2** *adj.* Fighting or arguing in a very rough and reckless way; struggling hard; not following rules or laws. *It took strong men to stay alive in the rough-and-tumble life of the western frontier.* (The men had to be tough and strong to live where there was a struggle to stay alive.)

rough up *v.* To attack or hurt physically; treat roughly; beat. *Three boys were sent home for a week because they roughed up a player on the visiting team.* (The boys beat a visiting player.) *While Pete was walking in a strange part of town, some boys roughed him up and told him to stay out of their territory.* (The boys pushed and hit Pete.)

round robin *n. phr.* **1** Something written, especially a request or protest that is signed by a group of people.—Often used like an adjective. *The people in our neighborhood are sending a round robin to the Air Force to protest the noise the jet planes make flying over our houses.* (The people in the neighborhood are sending a letter that many of the neighbors have signed, to complain to the Air Force.) **2** A letter written by a group of people, each writing one or two paragraphs and then sending the letter to another person, who adds a paragraph, and so on. *The class sent a round-robin letter to Bill in the hospital.* (The class sent a letter in which each member wrote something in the letter to Bill.) **3** A meeting in which each one in a group of people takes part; a talk between various members of a group.—Often used like an adjective. *There is a round-robin meeting of expert fishermen on the radio, giving advice on how to catch fish.* (Each one of the group of experts takes part in the talk and gives advice.) **4** A contest or games in which each player or team plays every other player or team in turn. *The tournament will be a round robin for all the high school teams in the city.* (Each team will play every other team.)

round up *v.* **1** To bring together (cattle or horses). *Cowboys round up their cattle in the springtime to brand the new calves.* (The cowboys bring the cattle together in one place.) **2** *informal* To collect; gather. *Dave rounded up many names for his petition.* (Dave got many people who were for his idea to sign their names on the paper.)

rub elbows *also* **rub shoulders** *v. phr.* To be in the same place (with others); meet and mix. *City people and country people, old and young, rub elbows at the horse show.* (People from different places and of different ages mix together at the horse show.)

rub it in *v. phr., slang* To remind a person again and again of an error or shortcoming; tease; nag. *Jerry was already unhappy because he fumbled the ball, but his teammates kept rubbing it in.* (Jerry's teammates were unkind; they reminded Jerry again and again of his error.) *I know my black eye looks funny. You don't need to rub it in.* (You don't need to tease me about my black eye.)

rub off *v.* **1** To remove or be removed by rubbing; erase. *The teacher rubs the problem off the chalkboard.* (The teacher erases the problem.) *After Ann shook hands with the President, she would not shake hands with anyone else, because she thought that the good luck would rub off.* (Pam thought that the President's touch

would bring her good luck and that if anyone else touched that hand, it would take away the good luck.) **2** To stick to something touched; come off. *Don't touch that charcoal; it will rub off.* (The black powder from the charcoal will stick to your hand.) *Mary's dress touched the door that Father was painting, and some paint rubbed off on her dress.* (Some paint stuck to her dress.) **3** To pass to someone near as if by touching. *Jimmy is very lucky; I wish some of his luck would rub off on me.* (I hope some of Jimmy's luck comes to me if I'm near him.)

rub out *v., slang* To destroy completely; kill; eliminate. *The gangsters rubbed out four policemen before they were caught.* (The gangsters killed four police officers before they were caught.)

rub the wrong way *v. phr., informal* To make (someone) a little angry; do something not liked by (someone); annoy; bother. *John's bragging rubbed the other boys the wrong way.* (John talked about the great things he did, and the other boys did not like it.) *Mother's friend called Harold a little boy, and that rubbed Harold the wrong way.* (Being called a little boy made Harold rather angry.)

run around *or* **chase around** *v., informal* To go to different places for company and pleasure; be friends. *Tim hasn't been to a dance all year; with school work and his job, he hasn't time to run around.* (Tim is too busy to go different places for company and pleasure.) *Chuck and Jim chase around a lot together.* (They often go places together; they are friends.)—Often used with *with*. *Ruth runs around with girls who* *like to go dancing.* (Ruth's friends are girls who like to dance.)

run away with *v.* **1a** To take quickly and secretly, especially without permission; steal. *A thief ran away with grandma's silver teapot.* (He stole it.) **1b** To go away with; elope. *Mary said that if her parents wouldn't let her marry Phil, she would run away with him.* (She said if they wouldn't let her marry, she would elope.) **1c** To take hold of; seize. *The boys thought they saw a ghost in the old house last night; they let their imagination run away with them.* (The boys became afraid and imagined they saw a ghost.) **2** To be much better or more noticeable than others in; win easily. *Our team ran away with the game in the last half.* (Our team beat the other team badly in the second half of the game.) *The fat comedian ran away with the TV show.* (The funny fat man was so good that he was noticed more than anyone else in the show.)

run down *v.* **1** To crash against and knock down or sink. *Jack rode his bicycle too fast and almost ran down his little brother.* (Jack went too fast and almost hit his brother with the bicycle.) *It was so foggy that the steamship almost ran down a small boat leaving port.* (The big ship almost hit the boat and sank it.) **2a** To chase until exhausted or caught. *The dogs ran down the wounded deer.* (They chased him until he was tired out.) **2b** To find by hard and thorough search; *also:* trace to its cause or beginning. *The policeman ran down proof that the burglar had robbed the store.* (He searched until he found proof that the burglar had robbed the store.) **2c** To catch (a base runner) between bases and tag out in baseball. *The*

pitcher saw that the base runner was not on base, so he surprised him by throwing the ball to the first baseman, who ran him down before he reached second base. (The runner was caught between first and second bases and the first baseman ran after him and tagged him with the ball.) **3** *informal* To say bad things about; criticize. *Suzy ran down the club because the girls wouldn't let her join.* (Suzy criticized the girls and their club because she couldn't be a member herself.) **4** To stop working; not run or go. *The battery in Father's car ran down this morning.* (The battery wouldn't work so the car wouldn't go.) *The kitchen clock ran down because we forgot to wind it.* (The clock stopped.) **5** To get into poor condition; look bad. *A neighborhood runs down when the people don't take care of their houses.* (The houses need paint and repairs; the whole street looks bad.)

run-down *adj.* In poor health or condition; weak or needing much work. *Father caught a cold because he was very run-down from loss of sleep.* (Father was weak and caught a cold.) *The houses near the center of the city get more run-down every year.* (The condition of the houses in the center of the city becomes worse every year.)

run for it *or* **make a run for it** *v. phr.* To dash for safety; make a speedy escape. *The bridge the soldiers were on started to fall down and they had to run for it.* (They had to dash for safety to the end of the bridge.) *The policeman shouted for the robber to stop but the robber made a run for it.* (The robber tried to escape by running away.)

run in *v.* **1** *informal* To take to jail; arrest. *The policeman ran the man in for peddling without a license.* (He arrested the peddler for not having a license.) **2** To make a brief visit. *The neighbor boy ran in for a minute to see Bob's newest model rocket.* (He made a brief visit to inspect it.)

run in the blood *or* **run in the family** *v. phr.* To be a common family characteristic; be learned or inherited from one's family. *A great interest in gardening runs in his family.* (Gardening is an interest many members of his family have had.) *Red hair runs in the family.* (It is a common family trait. Many members of the family have red hair.)

run into *v.* **1** To mix with; join with. *If the paint brush is too wet, the red paint will run into the white on the house.* (The red and the white colors will be mixed together on the house.) *This small brook runs into a big river in the valley below.* (The brook joins the big river.) **2** To add up to; reach; total. *Car repairs can run into a lot of money.* (Car repairs may cost many dollars.) *The number of people killed on the highways during holidays runs into hundreds.* (The total number of deaths reaches several hundred.) *A good dictionary may run into several editions.* (A good dictionary may be revised and printed again and again.) **3a** Bump; crash into; hit. *Joe lost control of his bike and ran into a tree.* (Joe hit a tree.) **3b** To meet by chance. *I ran into Joe yesterday on Main Street.* (I met Joe accidentally; I was not expecting to meet him.) **3c** Be affected by; get into. *I ran into trouble on the last problem on the test.* (I had trouble with the last problem.) *When I ran into a problem while making my model airplane, I asked Uncle Mark for help.* (When I was stopped by a problem, I got help.)

run into the ground *v. phr., informal* **1** To do or use (something) more than is wanted or needed. *It's all right to borrow my hammer once in a while, but don't run it into the ground.* (Don't try to borrow my hammer so much that you are a nuisance.) **2** To win over or defeat (someone) completely. *We lost the game today, but tomorrow we'll run them into the ground.* (We'll beat them badly tomorrow.) **3** to use without proper maintenance; to neglect. *He never gets his oil changed or brakes checked; he runs his car into the ground.* (He doesn't take care of his car.)

run off *v.* **1** To produce with a printing press or duplicating machine. *The print shop ran off a thousand copies of the newspaper.* (The print shop printed 1,000 copies of the newspaper.) **2** To drive away. *The boys saw a dog digging in mother's flower bed, and they ran him off.* (The boys chased the dog away.) *When the salesman tried to cheat the farmer, the farmer ran him off the farm.* (The farmer ordered the salesman off the property.)

run-of-the-mill *or* **run-of-the-mine** *adj.* Of a common kind; ordinary; usual. *Frank is a very good bowler, but Joe is just run-of-the-mill.* (Joe is no better than most bowlers.) *It was just a run-of-the-mine movie.* (There was nothing unusual about the movie. It was an average movie.)

run out *v.* **1a** To come to an end; be used up. *Jerry almost got across the brook on the slippery* stones but his luck ran out and he slipped and fell. (His luck ended and he fell into the brook.) We'd better do our Christmas shopping; time is running out. (There isn't much time left.) **1b** To use all of the supply; be troubled by not having enough. The car ran out of gas three miles from town. (It used all its gas and stopped.) Millie never runs out of ideas for clever party decorations. (She is never troubled by a lack of ideas. She has lots of them.) **2** informal To force to leave; expel. Federal agents ran the spies out of the country. (They made them leave.)

run over v. **1** To be too full and flow over the edge; spill over. Billy forgot he had left the water on, and the tub ran over. (Water filled up the tub and flowed over onto the floor.) **2** To try or go over (something) quickly; practise briefly. During the lunch hour, Mary ran over her history facts so she would remember them for the test. (Mary quickly looked again at her notes before the test.) The coach ran over the signals for the trick play with the team just before game time. (The coach reviewed the signals briefly.) **3** To drive on top of; ride over. At night cars often run over small animals that are blinded by the headlights. (Cars often crush small animals under their wheels.)

run scared v. phr. To use every means to avoid defeat, as in a political campaign. The one-vote defeat caused him to run scared in every race thereafter. (Since the close defeat, he has used every means to avoid losing, because he is afraid it might happen again.)

run short v. phr. **1** To not have enough. Bob asked Jack to lend him five dollars because he was running short. (Bob asked Jack to lend him five dollars because he did not have enough money.) We are running short of sugar. (We do not have very much sugar left.) **2** To be not enough in quantity. We are out of potatoes and the flour is running short. (We don't have enough flour to last us long.)

run the gauntlet v. phr. To face a hard test; bear a painful experience. Ginny had to run the gauntlet of her mother's questions about how the ink spot got on the dining room rug. (She had to bear the hard experience of her mother's questioning.)

run through v. **1** To make a hole through, especially with a sword; pierce. The pirate was a good swordsman, but the hero finally ran him through. (The hero finally pierced him with his sword and won the fight.) **2** To spend recklessly; use up wastefully. The rich man's son quickly ran through his money. (He spent it recklessly and was soon poor.) **3** To read or practice from beginning to end without stopping. The visiting singer ran through his numbers with the orchestra just before the program. (He sang them from beginning to end without a pause.)

run up v. **1** To add to the amount of; increase. Karl ran up a big bill at the bookstore. (He increased it by purchases from time to time until it was quite large.) **2** To put together or make hastily; sew quickly together. Jill ran up a costume for the party on her sewing machine. (She made it in a hurry.) **3** To pull (something) upward on a rope; put (something) up quickly. The pirates ran up the black flag. (They pulled it upward on a rope to the top of the mast.)

run wild *v. phr.* To be or go out of control. *The new supervisor lets the children run wild.* (The new supervisor lets the children do as they please. He cannot control them.) *The violets are running wild in the flower bed.* (The violet plants are spreading out of control.)

Russian roulette *n.* A game of chance in which one bullet is placed in a revolver, the cartridge cylinder is spun, and the player aims the gun at his own head and pulls the trigger. *Only a fool would risk playing Russian roulette.* (Only a fool would play a game in which he risks killing himself.)

S

sack in/out v., slang To go to sleep for a prolonged period (as from night to morning). *Where are you guys going to sack in/sack out?* (Where are you going to sleep?)

sacred cow n. A person or thing that is never criticized, laughed at, or insulted, even if it deserves such treatment. *Motherhood is a sacred cow to most politicians.* (Most politicians never criticize, laugh at, or insult the idea of motherhood.)

sail into v., informal **1** To attack with great strength; begin hitting hard. *George grabbed a stick and sailed into the dog.* (George began to hit the dog as hard and as fast as he could.) **2** To scold or criticize very hard. *The coach really sailed into Bob for dropping the pass.* (The coach scolded him hard for dropping the ball.)

save face v. phr. To save one's good reputation, popularity, or dignity when something has happened or may happen to hurt one; hide something that may cause one shame. *The policeman was caught accepting a bribe; he tried to save face by claiming it was money owed to him.* (He tried to hide his shame by saying it was the payment of a debt.) *The colonel who lost the battle saved face by showing his orders from the general.* (His orders showed that the general had made a mistake, not the colonel.)

save one's breath v. phr., informal To keep silent because talking will not help; not talk because it will do no good. *Save your breath; the boss will never give you the day off.* (Don't ask the

boss for a day off; he won't give it to you.)

save one's neck or **save one's skin** v. phr., slang To save from danger or trouble. *The fighter planes saved our skins while the army was landing from the ships.* (The air force kept us alive during that battle.) *Betty saved Tim's neck by typing his report for him; without her help he could not have finished on time.* (Betty saved Tim from getting in trouble with the teacher and making a bad grade.)

save the day v. phr. To bring about victory or success, especially when defeat is likely. *The forest fire was nearly out of control when suddenly it rained heavily and saved the day.* (The forest fire was nearly out of control when suddenly it rained heavily and brought us success in controlling the fire.) *The team was behind, but at the last minute Sam saved the day with a touchdown.* (Sam scored the winning points with a touchdown.)

say a mouthful v. phr., slang To say something of great importance or meaning; say more by a sentence than the words usually mean.—Usually in past tense. *Tom said a mouthful when he guessed that company was coming to visit. A dozen people came.* (Tom thought that only a few people would come, but twelve people were there.)

say one's piece or **speak one's piece** v. phr. To say openly what one thinks; say, especially in public, what one usually says or is expected to say. *John told the boss that he thought he was wrong and the boss got angry. He said, "You've said your little piece, so go on home."* (The boss said, "You've said that you think

233

I'm wrong; if that is what you think leave me alone.'')

say the word *v. phr., informal* To say or show that one wants something or agrees to something; show a wish, willingness, or readiness; give a sign; say yes; say so. *Just say the word and I will lend you the money.* (If you want me to lend you the money, you need only tell me.) *I will do anything you want; just say the word.* (Tell me if you want anything and I will do it.)

say uncle *also* **cry uncle** *v. phr., informal* To say that one surrenders; admit that one has lost; admit a defeat; give up. *The bully twisted Jerry's arm and said, "Cry uncle."* (The bully hurt Jerry's arm and commanded him to surrender.) *The other team was beating us, but we wouldn't say uncle.* (We wouldn't quit.)

scare out of one's wits *or* **scare stiff** *or* **scare the daylights out of** *v. phr., informal* To frighten very much. *The owl's hooting scared him out of his wits.* (The owl's cry frightened him very much.) *The child was scared stiff in the dentist's chair.* (The child was frightened at the thought of pain.) *Pete's ghost story scared the daylights out of the smaller boys.* (The ghost story frightened the smaller boys.)

scare up *or* **scrape up** *v., informal* To find, collect, or get together with some effort when needed. *"Will you stay for supper?" she asked. "I can scare up enough for us all."* (She said she could find and prepare enough food for them all.) *He managed to scrape up the money for his speeding fine.* (It wasn't easy, but he got the money.)

school of hard knocks *n. phr.* Life outside of school or college; life out in the world; the ordinary experience of learning from work and troubles. *He never went to high school; he was educated in the school of hard knocks.* (He never went to high school; he learned by life experience, working his way up to the position he now has.)

scrape the bottom of the barrel *v. phr., informal* To use or take whatever is left after the best has been taken; accept the poor ones. *The rural town had so few residents that they had to scrape the bottom of the barrel just to fill the posts of the town government.* (They had to chose even those who were poorly qualified.)

scratch one's back *v. phr., informal* To do something kind and helpful for someone or to flatter him in the hope that he will do something for oneself. Usually used in the expression *"You scratch my back and I'll scratch yours."* *Mary asked Jean to introduce her to her brother. Jean said, "You scratch my back and I'll scratch yours."* (Jean said that if Mary would help her she would help Mary.)

scratch the surface *v. phr.* To learn or understand very little about something.—Usually used with a limiting adverb (as *only, hardly*). *We thought we understood Africa but when we made a trip there we found we had only scratched the surface.* (We thought we understood Africa, but when we visited there we found we knew very little about it.)

screw around *v. phr., vulgar, avoidable* To hang around idly without accomplishing anything, to loaf about, to beat or hack around. *You guys are no longer welcome here; all you do is screw around all day.* (All you do is hang around idly without accomplishing anything.)

screw up *v. phr., slang, vulgar, best avoided* **1** To make a mess of, to make an error that causes confusion. *The treasurer screwed up the accounts of the Society so badly that he had to be fired.* (He made such a mess of the accounts that he had to be fired.) **2** To cause someone to be neurotic or maladjusted. *Her divorce screwed her up so badly that she had to go to a shrink.* (Her divorce caused her to be so maladjusted that she had to go to a psychiatrist.)

scrounge around *v. phr., slang* **1** To search for an object aimlessly without having one clearly in mind. *I don't know what's the matter with him; he is just scrounging around all day long.* (He is just looking around aimlessly.) **2** To look around for a way to get a free drink or a free meal. *Sue and her husband are so broke they never eat properly; they just scrounge around from one place to the next until someone offers them something.* (They just wander from one place to the next until someone offers them some food and drink.)

search me *slang* I don't know; how should I know?—May be considered rude. *When I asked her what time it was, she said, "Search me; I have no watch."* (When I asked her what time it was, she said, "I don't know.")

search one's heart *or* **search one's soul** *v. phr. formal* to study one's reasons and acts; try to discover if one has been fair and honest. *The teacher searched his heart trying to decide if he had* been unfair in failing Tom. (After the teacher failed Tom, the teacher thought he might have been unfair and asked himself if he had done the right thing.)

second-guess *v. phr.* **1** To criticize another's decision with advantage of hindsight. *The losing team's coach is always second-guessed.* (The losing team's coach is always criticized after the game.) **2** To guess what someone else intends or would think or do. *Television planners try to second-guess the public.* (They guess what people will like.)

second thought *n.* A change of ideas or opinions resulting from more thought or study. *Your second thoughts are very often wiser than your first ideas.* (Longer thought often shows the way to better judgment.) *We decided to climb the mountain, but on second thought realized that it was too dangerous.* (We thought it over and wisely decided not to risk the climb.)

second wind *also* **second breath** *n.* **1** The easier breathing that follows difficult breathing when one makes a severe physical effort, as in running or swimming. *After the first quarter mile, a mile runner usually gets his second wind and can breathe better.* (He gets used to running and his breath works harder.) **2** *informal* The refreshed feeling you get after first becoming tired while doing something and then becoming used to it. *Tom became very tired of working at his algebra, but after a while he got his second wind and began to enjoy it.* (Tom became tired of algebra, but after a while he got used to it and liked it.)

security blanket *n., slang, informal* An idea, person, or object that one holds on to for psychological reassurance or comfort as infants usually hang on to the edge of a pillow, a towel, or a blanket. *Sue has gone to Aunt Mathilda for a chat; she is her security blanket.* (Aunt Mathilda is the person Sue confides in when she has a problem.)

see about *v.* **1** To find out about; attend to. *If you are too busy, I'll see about the train tickets.* (If you are too busy, I'll take care of getting the train tickets.) **2** *informal* To consider; study. *I cannot take time now but I'll see about your plan when I have time.* (I cannot take time now, but I'll think over your plan when I have time.)

see eye to eye *v. phr.* To agree fully; hold exactly the same opinion. *Though we did not usually agree, we saw eye to eye in the matter of reducing taxes.* (Though we did not usually agree, we were in full agreement in the matter of reducing taxes.) *Mother did not see eye to eye with Father on where we would go for our vacation.* (Father and Mother did not agree; they had different ideas.)

see off *v.* To go to say or wave goodbye to. *His brother went to the train with him to see him off.* (His brother went to the train with him to say goodbye to him when he left.) *When Marsha flew to Cleveland, Flo saw her off at the airport.* (Flo went to the airport with Marsha and told her goodbye there.)

see out *v.* **1** To go with to an outer door. *A polite host sees his company out after a party.* (A gentleman goes to the door with his guests as they leave.) **2** To stay with and finish; not quit. *Pete's assignment was hard but he saw*

it out to the end. (His lesson was hard but he kept on and finished it.)

see red *v. phr., informal* To become very angry. *Whenever anyone teased John about his weight, he saw red.* (Whenever anyone teased John about being fat, he became very angry.)

see stars *v. phr., informal* To imagine one is seeing stars as a result of being hit on the head. *When Ted was hit on the head by the ball, he saw stars.* (He thought for a minute that he was seeing stars.) *The boxer's head hit the floor, making him see stars.* (He imagined he saw stars.)

see the light *v. phr., informal* To understand or agree, often suddenly; accept another's explanation or decision. *I did not approve of his action, but he explained his reason and then I saw the light.* (Then I understood and agreed with him.)

see the light of day *v. phr.* To be born or begun. *The children visited the old house where their great-grandfather first saw the light of day.* (They visited the house where their great-grandfather was born.) *The party was a failure, and Jean wished her plan had never seen the light of day.* (Jean wished that her plan for the party had never been made.)

see things *v. phr., informal* To imagine sights that are not real; think one sees what is not there. *I had not seen him for twenty years and when we met on the street I thought I was seeing things.* (I thought I was imagining things.) *She woke her husband to tell him she had seen a face at the window, but he told her she was seeing things.* (He told her she was dreaming.)

see to *also* **look to** *v.* To attend to; take care of; do whatever needs to be done about. *While Donna bought the theatre tickets, I saw to the parking of tne car.* (While Donna bought the theatre tickets, I took care of the parking of the car.)

see to it *v. phr.* To take care; take the responsibility; make sure.—Usually used with a noun clause. *We saw to it that the child was fed and bathed.* (We took care that the child was fed and bathed.)

sell out *v., informal* To be unfaithful to one's country for money or other reward; be disloyal; sell a secret; accept a bribe. *In the Revolutionary War, Benedict Arnold sold out to the British.* (He left the American army to help the British for a reward.)

sell-out *n., informal* (stress on *sell*) An act of treason. *Many people consider both Watergate and Chappaquiddick as equal sell-outs perpetrated on the American public.* (Many people regard Richard Nixon and Ted Kennedy as having betrayed the public.)

sell short *v.* To think (a person or thing) less good or valuable than is true; underestimate. *Don't sell the team short; the players are better than you think.* (Don't think the team is poor; you will be wrong.)

send up *v. phr., informal* To sentence (someone) to prison. *Did you know that Milton Shaeffer was sent up for fifteen years?* (Did you know he was sentenced to jail for 15 years?)

senior citizen *n.* An older person, often one who has retired from active work or employment. *Mrs. North, the history teacher, is a senior citizen.* (Mrs. North is

old enough to retire from teaching.)

serve one right *v. phr.* To be what (someone) really deserves as a punishment; be a fair exchange for what (someone) has done or said or failed to do or say. *He failed his exam; it served him right because he had not studied.* (He failed his exam; he really deserved to fail because he had not studied.)

set about *v.* To begin; start. *Benjamin Franklin set about learning the printer's trade at an early age.* (He began learning the printer's trade while young.)

set back **1** To cause to put off or get behind schedule; slow up; check. *The cold weather set back the planting by two weeks.* (The cold weather put off the planting by two weeks.) **2** *informal* To cause to pay out or to lose (a sum of money); cost. *His new car set him back over $8,000.* (His new car cost him over $8,000.)

set-back *n.* (stress on *set*) A hindrance, delay, or handicap. *The project suffered one setback after another.* (There were many obstacles to overcome.)

set foot *v. phr.* To step; walk; go.—Used with a negative. *She would not let him set foot across her threshold.* (She would not let him step through her door.)

set forth *v., formal* To explain exactly or clearly. *The President set forth his plans in a television talk.* (The President explained his plans in a talk on television.) **2** To start to go somewhere; begin a trip. *The troop set forth on their ten-mile hike early.* (The troop started on their ten-mile hike early.)

set in *v.* To begin; start; develop. *Before the boat could reach shore, a storm had set in.* (The storm began before the boat reached shore.) *He did not keep the cut clean and infection set in.* (Infection started because he did not keep the cut clean.)

set off *v.* **1** To decorate through contrast; balance by difference. *The bright colors of the birds were set off by the white snow.* (The whiteness made the colors seem brighter.) **2** To balance; make somewhat equal. *The comradeship of the group set off the dreary weather.* (The friendliness of the gathering made up for the disappointing weather.) **3** To cause to explode. *On July 4 we set off firecrackers in many places.* (We explode firecrackers on July 4.)

set one's heart on *v. phr., also* **have one's heart set on** To want very much. *He set his heart on that bike.* (He hoped very much to get that bike.) *also:* To be very desirous of; hope very much to succeed in.—Used with a verbal noun. *He had his heart set on winning the race.* (He really wanted to win the race.)

set out *v.* **1** To leave on a journey or voyage. *The Pilgrims set out for the New World.* (The Pilgrims began their voyage to the New World.) **2** To decide and begin to try, attempt. *George set out to improve his pitching.* (George decided to improve his pitching and began to try.) **3** To plant in the ground. *The gardener set out some tomato seedlings.* (He put some young tomato plants in the ground.)

set sail *v. phr.* To begin a sea voyage; start sailing. *The ship set sail for Europe.* (The ship began the voyage to Europe.)

set store by *v. phr., informal* To like or value; want to keep. Used with a qualifying word between *set* and *store*. *George sets great store by that old tennis racket.* (George really likes that old tennis racket.)

set the pace *v. phr.* To decide on a rate of speed of travel or rules that are followed by others. *The scoutmaster set the pace so that the smaller boys would not get tired trying to keep up.* (The scoutmaster hiked at a speed of march that was not too fast for the smaller boys.)

set the world on fire *v. phr., informal* To do something outstanding; act in a way that attracts much attention or makes one famous. *John works hard, but he will never set the world on fire.* (John works hard, but he will never be an outstanding success in his work.)

settle a score To hurt (someone) in return for a wrong or loss. *John settled an old score with Bob by beating him.* (Bob made trouble for John and at last John beat him in a fight.)

settle down *v.* **1** To live more quietly and sensibly; have a regular place to live and a regular job; stop acting wildly or carelessly, especially by growing up. *John will settle down after he gets a job and gets married.* (His conduct will improve.) **2** To become quiet, calm, or comfortable. *Father settled down with the newspaper.* (He made himself comfortable as he read the paper.)

settle for *v.* To be satisfied with (less); agree to; accept. *Jim wanted $200 for his old car, but he settled for $100.* (He wanted to sell it for $200, but at last agreed to a price of only $100.)

set up *v.* **1** To provide the money for the necessities. *When he was twenty-one, his father set*

him up in the clothing business.
(His father helped him with the
money to start a clothing store.)
2 To establish; start. *The government has set up many hospitals
for veterans of the armed forces.*
(The government built many hospitals for soldiers and sailors.)
3 to make ready for use by putting
the parts together or into their right
place. *The men set up the new
printing press.* (They put the parts
together so it would work.) **4** To
bring into being; cause. *Ocean
tides are set up partly by the pull
between earth and the moon.* (The
pull of the moon partly causes the
tides.) **5** To claim; pretend. *He
set himself up to be a graduate of
a medical school, but he was not.*
(He pretended to be a medical
school graduate.)

setup *n.* (stress on *set*) Arrangement; management; circumstances. *Boy, you really have
a wonderful setup in your office!*
(Your circumstances are enviably
good.) *I can't work in such a
sloppy setup.* (My environment
and circumstances are not conducive to work.) *It is a generous
setup, your sending $1,000 a
month to your sick, old father.* (It
is an advantageous arrangement
for him and generous of you to do
so.)

sewed up *adj. phr., informal*
Won or arranged as one wishes;
decided. *Dick thought he had the
job sewed up, but another boy got
it.* (Dick felt sure he would get the
job, but the man hired another
boy.)

shack up with *v. phr., slang* To
move in with (someone) of the
opposite sex without marrying the
person. *Did you know that Ollie
and Sue aren't married? They just
decided to shack up for a while.*
(They just decided to move in with
each other.)

shake a leg *v. phr., slang* To
go fast; hurry. *Shake a leg! The
bus won't wait.* (Hurry—the bus
is leaving!)

shake down *v., slang* To get
money by threats. *The gangsters
shook down the store owner every
month.* (They got money from the
owner by telling him they would
harm him.)

shake up *v., informal* To
bother; worry; disturb. *The notice
about a cut in pay shook up everybody in the office.* (They were all
worried by the news that they
would be paid less.)

shake-up *n., informal* (stress on
shake) Change in command or
leadership. *Rumor has it that there
will be a major cabinet-level
shake-up.* (It is believed that the
President will re-appoint some
cabinet posts.)

shape up *v., informal* **1** To begin to act or work right; get along
satisfactorily. *If the new boy
doesn't begin to shape up soon,
he'll have to leave school.* (He
will be expelled if he doesn't behave and do his work.) **2** To show
promise. *Plans for our picnic are
shaping up very well.* (The plans
look favorable for our picnic.)

shell out *v., informal* To pay or
spend. *Dick had to shell out a lot
of money for his new car.* (He
spent a large amount of money.)

shine up to *v., slang* To try to
please; try to make friends with.
*Smedley shines up to all the pretty
girls.* (He likes them and tries to
get them to like him.)

shoe on the other foot The opposite is true; places are changed.
*He was my captain in the army
but now the shoe is on the other*

foot. (Now I am his boss here in the factory.)

shoo-in *n.*, *informal* Someone or something that is expected to win; a favorite; sure winner. *Chris is a shoo-in to win a scholarship.* (Chris is sure to be a winner of a merit scholarship.)

shoot one's wad /*v. phr.*, *slang*, *informal* **1** To spend all of one's money. *We've shot our wad for the summer and can't buy any new garden furniture.* (We have spent all our money and cannot afford to buy anything new, such as garden furniture.) **2** To say everything that is on one's mind. *Also* **shoot one's load** *Joe feels a lot better now that he's shot his load at the meeting.* (He feels much better now that he said everything that was on his mind.)

shoot straight *or* **shoot square** *v.*, *informal* To act fairly; deal honestly. *You can trust that salesman; he shoots straight with his customers.* (That salesman deals honestly with his customers.)

shoot the breeze *or* **bat the breeze** *or* **fan the breeze** *or* **shoot the bull** *v. phr.*, *slang* To talk. *Father shot the breeze with his neighbor while the children were playing.* (They talked to each other while the children were playing.)

shoot the works *v. phr.*, *slang* **1** To spare no expense or effort; get or give everything. *Billy shot the works when he bought his bicycle; he got a bell, a light, a basket, and chrome trimmings on it, too.* (Billy got everything that could go on a bicycle.)

shoot up *v.* **1** To grow quickly. *Billy had always been a small boy, but when he was thirteen years old he began to shoot up.* (When he reached thirteen be began to grow quickly.) **2** To arise suddenly. *As we watched, flames shot*

up from the roof of the barn. (Flames arose suddenly from the roof of the barn.) **3** *informal* To shoot or shoot at recklessly; shoot and hurt badly. *The cowboys got drunk and shot up the barroom.* (They fired their guns wildly and damaged the barroom.) *The soldier was shot up very badly.* (He was badly wounded.) **4** *slang*, *drug culture* To take drugs by injection. *A heroin addict will shoot up as often as he can.* (A heroin addict will inject himself with the drug as often as possible.)

shore up *v.* To add support to (something) where weakness is shown; make (something) stronger where support is needed; support. *When the flood waters weakened the bridge, it was shored up with steel beams and sandbags until it could be rebuilt.* (The weakened bridge was made stronger for a while by putting steel beams and sandbags under it.) *The coach sent in a substitute guard to shore up the line when Fitchburg began to break through.* (The coach put a fresh player in the line to try to stop the Fitchburg team from breaking through.)

short end *n.* The worst or most unpleasant part. *The new boy got the short end of it because all the comfortable beds in the dormitory had been taken before he arrived.* (The new boy got the worst part of it, because the best beds had been taken.)

shot in the arm *n. phr.*, *informal* Something inspiring or encouraging. *We were ready to quit, but the coach's talk was a shot in the arm.* (We were ready to quit, but the coach's talk inspired us.)

shot in the dark *n. phr.* An attempt without much hope or chance of succeeding; a wild guess. *It was just a shot in the dark, but I got the right answer to the teacher's question.* (I answered correctly with a lucky guess.)

shove down one's throat *or* **ram down one's throat** *v. phr., informal* To force one to do or agree to (something not wanted or liked.) *The president was against the idea, but the club members rammed it down his throat.* (The members forced the president to accept the idea to which he was opposed.)

show-off *v.* **1** To put out nicely for people to see; display; exhibit. *The science fair gave Julia a chance to show off her shell collection.* (The fair gave Julia an opportunity to display her shell collection.) **2** *informal* To try to attract attention. *The children always show off when we have company.* (The children try to get the attention of our company.)

show-off *n.* (stress on *show*) An ostentatious person, a braggart. *Max talks big, but he's a stupid show-off.* (Despite his grandiloquence he is a shallow braggart.)

show one's colors *v. phr.* **1** To show what one is really like. *We thought Toby was timid, but he showed his colors when he rescued the ponies from the burning barn.* (Toby showed us that he was really brave by rescuing the ponies from the fire.) **2** To make known what one thinks or plans to do. *Mr. Ryder is afraid that he will lose the election if he shows his colors on civil rights.* (Mr. Ryder is afraid people won't elect him if he tells what he thinks about civil rights.)

show the door *v. phr.* To ask (someone) to go away. *Ruth was upsetting the other children, so I showed her the door.* (Ruth was disturbing the other children, so I asked her to go away.)

show up *v.* **1** To make known the real truth about (someone). *The man said he was a mind reader, but he was shown up as a fake.* (The man claimed to be a mind reader, but the truth that he was a fake was made known.) **2** To come or bring out; become or make easy to see. *The detective put a chemical on the paper, and the fingertips showed up.* (They became easy to see.) **3** *informal* To come; appear. *We had agreed to meet at the gym, but Larry didn't show up.* (Larry didn't come to the gym to meet me.)

shut off *v.* **1** To make (something like water or electricity) stop coming. *Please shut off the hose before the grass gets too wet.* (Please turn off the hose before the grass gets too wet.) **2** to be apart; be separated from; *also* to separate from. *Our camp is so far from the highway we feel shut off from the world when we are there.* (Our camp is so far from the road that we feel apart from the world when we are there.)

shut-off *n.* (stress on *shut*) A cessation, a stoppage. *There was a water shut-off in several Chicago suburbs yesterday.* (Running water had to be temporarily stopped.)

shut out *v.* **1** To prevent from coming in; block. *During World War II Malta managed to shut out most of the Italian and German bombers by throwing up an effective anti-aircraft screen.* (Malta managed to prevent most of the Italian and German bombers from coming in.) **2** To prevent (an opposing team) from scoring throughout an entire game. *The Dodgers shut out the Reds, 5–0.*

(The Dodgers didn't let the Reds score and won the game 5–0.)

shut up v. **1** *informal* To stop talking. *Little Ruthie told Father about his birthday surprise before Mother could shut her up.* (Before Mother could make Ruthie stop talking, Ruthie had told the secret.)—Often used as a command; usually considered rude. *Shut up and let Joe say something.* (Stop talking and let Joe say what he thinks.) **2** To close the doors and windows of. *We got the house shut up only minutes before the storm hit.* (We got the doors and windows of the house closed just before the storm hit.) **3** To close and lock for a definite period of time. *The Smiths always spend Labor Day shutting up their summer home for the year.* (The Smiths always close and lock their summer home on Labor Day.) **4** To confine. *That dog bites. It should be shut up.* (That dog should be confined because it bites.)

sick and tired adj. **1** Feeling strong dislike for something repeated or continued too long; exasperated; annoyed. *Jane was sick and tired of always having to wait for Bill.* (Jane was annoyed at always being kept waiting.)

side with v. To agree with; help. *Adam always sides with Johnny in an argument.* (Adam always agrees with Johnny in an argument.)

sight unseen adv. phr. Before seeing a thing or a person. *Tom read an ad for a garden cart and sent the money for it sight unseen.* (He paid the money for the cart before he had ever seen it.)

sign over v. To give legally by signing one's name. *He signed his house over to his wife.* (He gave his wife the house by sign-

ing a doument prepared by his lawyer.)

sign up v. **1** To promise to do something by signing one's name; join; sign an agreement. *We will not have the picnic unless more people sign up.* (More people must sign their names on the paper promising to come to the picnic.) **2** To write the name of (a person or thing) to be in an activity; also, to persuade (someone) to do something. *Betty decided to sign up her dog for obedience training.* (Betty decided to put her dog's name on the list for obedience school.)

simmer down v., *informal* To become less angry or excited; become calmer. *Tom got mad, but soon simmered down.* (He became angry, but soon grew calmer.)

sing a different tune or **whistle a different tune** also **sing a new tune** v. phr., *informal* To talk or act in the opposite way; contradict something said before. *Charles said that all smokers should be expelled from the team, but he sang a different tune after the coach caught him smoking.* (After the coach saw him smoking, Charles said that no players should be expelled from the team for smoking.)

sink in or **soak in** v., *informal* To be completely understood; be fully realized or felt. *Everybody laughed at the joke but Joe; it took a moment for it to sink in before he laughed too.* (Joe didn't understand the meaning of the joke at first.)

sit back v. **1** To be built a distance away; stand away (as from a street). *Our house sits back from the road.* (Our house is not on the road.) **2** To relax; rest, often while others are working; take time out.

Sit back for a minute and think about what you have done. (Relax for a minute and think about what you have done.)

sit by *v.* **1** To stay near; watch and care for. *The nurse was told to sit by the patient until he woke up.* (The nurse was told to stay near the patient until he woke up.) **2** To sit and watch or rest especially while others work. *Don't just sit idly by while the other children are all busy.* (Don't sit and do nothing.)

sit in *v.* **1** To be a member; participate. *We're having a conference and we'd like you to sit in.* (We want you to be there and to talk and vote.) *also* **sit in on:** To be a member of; participate in. *We want you to sit in on the meeting.* (We want you to participate in the meeting.) **2** To attend but not participate. Often used with *on. Our teacher was invited to sit in on the conference.* (He could not talk or vote because he was not a member.)

sit-in *n.* (stress on *sit*) A kind of political demonstration during which students or workers refuse to leave their classrooms or posts through the night. *There were many sit-ins all over America during the Vietnam era.* (Many such demonstrations took place.)

sit on *v.* **1** To be a member of (a jury, board, commission, etc.) *Mr. Brown sat on the jury at the trial.* (He was a member of the jury at the trial.) **2** *informal* To prevent from starting or doing something; squelch. *The teacher sat on Fred before he could get started with the long story.* (Fred was stopped as soon as he began his long story.)

sit tight *v. phr., informal* To make no move *or* change; stay where one is.—Often used as a

command. *Sit tight; I'll be ready to go in a few minutes.* (Wait while I get ready to go.) *The doctor said to sit tight until he arrived.* (The doctor said to do nothing but wait until he arrived.)

sitting duck *n., informal* **1** An immobile target more easily hit with arrows or bullets than one in motion. *Shoot at the ping pong balls bouncing on the water stream, not these little sitting ducks!* (Choose a mobile target.) **2** An unsuspecting or naive person easily fooled or taken in, as if waiting to be attacked. *The poor old lady was a sitting duck for the robbers.* (She was an unsuspecting, easy target.) *Uncle Joe is a sitting duck for conniving, catty females.* (He is easily fooled by flattering women who have ulterior or motives.)

sit up *v.* **1** To stay awake instead of going to bed. *Mrs. Jones will sit up until both of her daughters get home from the dance.* (Mrs. Jones won't go to bed until her daughters come home.) **2** *informal* To be surprised. *Janice really sat up when I told her the gossip about Tom.* (Janice was surprised by the gossip.)

sit-up *n.* (stress on *sit*) A kind of exercise done in order to reduce one's waistline and tighten the abdominal muscles. *How many sit-ups can you do without stopping?* (What's your limit on raising your torso?)

sit well (with) *v.* Find favor with; please. *The reduced school budget did not sit well with the teachers.* (They did not like it.)

six of one and half-a-dozen of the other *n. phr.* Two things the same; not a real choice; no difference. *Which coat do you like better, the brown or the blue? It's six of one and half-a-dozen of the* *other*. (The two coats are equally attractive.)

size up *v., informal* To decide what one thinks about (something); to form an opinion about (something). *Give Joe an hour to size up the situation and he'll tell you what to do next*. (Let Joe have an hour to decide what he thinks and then he will tell you what to do.)

skate on thin ice *v. phr*. To take a chance; risk danger, disapproval or anger. *You'll be skating on thin ice if you ask Dad to increase your allowance again*. (You'll be taking a chance if you ask Dad for more money.)

skeleton in the closet *n. phr*. A shameful secret; someone or something kept hidden, especially by a family. *The skeleton in our family closet was Uncle Willie. No one mentioned him because he drank too much*. (No one in the family talked about Uncle Willie or his drinking.)

skid lid *n., slang* A crash helmet worn by motorcyclists and race drivers. *How much did you pay for that handsome skid lid?* (How much did your crash helmet cost?)

skid row *n*. The poor part of a city where people live who have no jobs and drink too much liquor. *That man was once rich, but he drank and gambled too much, and ended his life living on skid row*. (The man became a heavy drinker, lost everything, and died in the poorest part of the city.) *The Bowery is New York City's skid row*. (Drunks and vagrants live on the Bowery.)

skin alive *v. phr*. **1** *informal* To scold angrily. *Mother will skin you alive when she sees your torn pants*. (Mother will scold you angrily when she sees your torn

pants.) **2** *informal* To spank or beat. *Dad was ready to skin us alive when he found we had ruined his saw*. (Dad was ready to spank us when he discovered we had ruined his saw.) **3** *slang* To defeat. *We all did our best, but the visiting gymnastic team skinned us alive*. (We all tried to win, but the visiting team defeated us.)

skin and bones *n*. A person or animal that is very thin; someone very skinny. *The puppy is healthy now, but when we found him he was just skin and bones*. (When we found the puppy, he was very thin.) *Have you been dieting? You're nothing but skin and bones!* (Have you been trying to lose weight? You are very skinny!)

skin-deep *adj*. Only on the surface; not having any deep or honest meaning; not really or closely connected with what it seems to belong to. *Mary's friendliness with Joan is only skin-deep*. (Mary pretends to be Joan's friend, but she really is not.)

skin off one's nose *n. phr., slang* Matter of interest, concern, or trouble to one. *Go to Jake's party if you wish. It's no skin off my nose*. (Go to Jake's party if you want to; it doesn't concern me.)

skip it *v. phr., informal* To forget all about it. *When Jack tried to reward him for returning his lost dog, the man said to skip it*. (The man told Jack to forget all about the reward.)

sleep around *v. phr., slang, vulgar, avoidable* To be free with one's sexual favors; to behave promiscuously. *Sue is nice, but she sleeps around an awful lot with all sorts of guys*. (She is nice but too promiscuous.)

sleep a wink *v. phr*. To get a moment's sleep; enjoy a bit of sleep.—Used in negative and conditional statements and in questions. *I didn't sleep a wink all night.* (I went without sleep the whole night.)

sleep on *v.* To postpone a decision about. *We asked Judy if she would join our club and she answered that she would sleep on it.* (Judy said she would think about joining our club and decide later.)

slip of the pen *n. phr.* The mistake of writing something different from what one should or what one planned. *That was a slip of the pen. I meant to write September, not November.* (That was a mistake. I meant to write ''September'' and wrote ''November'' by mistake.)

slip of the tongue *n. phr.* The mistake of saying something one had not wanted or planned to say; an error of speech. *No one would have known our plans if Kay hadn't made a slip of the tongue.* (No one would have known if Kay had not made the mistake of mentioning it.)

slip up *v.* To make a mistake. *Someone at the bank slipped up. There are only 48 pennies in this 50¢ roll of coins.* (Someone at the bank made a mistake and put only 48 pennies in the roll.)

slip-up *n.* (stress on *slip*) A mistake. *I'm sorry sir, it was an unintentional slip-up.* (It was an unintentional author error.)

slow down *v.* To go more slowly than usual. *The road was slippery, so Mr. Jones slowed down the car.* (Mr. Jones drove his car more slowly than usual because the road was slippery.)

slow-down *n.* (stress on *slow*) A form of striking without coming to a complete halt in production. *The workers voted not to walk out but to stage a slow-down*

instead. (It was decided to put on a mild strike in protest.)

small fry *n.* **1** Young children. *In the park, a sandbox is provided for the small fry.* (There is a sandbox for the little children.) **2** Something or someone of little importance. *Large dairies ignore the competition from the small fry who make only a few hundred pounds of cheese a year.* (The activities of the small producers are of no concern to the big businesses.)

smash hit *n., informal* A very successful performance, song, play, movie, or opera. *The school play was a smash hit.* (The school play was a great success.)

smell a rat *v. phr., informal* To be suspicious; feel that something is wrong. *Every time Tom visits me, one of my ashtrays disappears. I'm beginning to smell a rat.* (I'm starting to suspect that Tom is stealing my ashtrays.)

smoke out *v.* **1** To force out with smoke. *The boys smoked a squirrel out of a hollow tree.* (The boys made a fire and sent smoke into the hollow tree, forcing the squirrel out.) **2** *informal* To find out the facts about. *It took the reporter three weeks to smoke out the whole story.* (It took the reporter three weeks to find the facts of the story.)

smooth over *v.* To make something seem better or more pleasant; try to excuse. *Bill tried to smooth over his argument with Mary by making her laugh.* (He tried to make her forget the argument.)

snail's pace *n.* A very slow movement forward. *Time moved at a snail's pace before the holidays.* (Time passed very slowly just before the holidays.) *The donkey on which he was riding* *moved at a snail's pace*. (The donkey walked very slowly.)

snap up *v., informal* To take or accept eagerly. *Eggs were on sale cheap, and the shoppers snapped up the bargain.* (The shoppers quickly bought all of the cheap eggs.) *Mr. Hayes told Bob that he would take him skiing, and Bob snapped up the offer.* (Bob quickly said he would go.)

sneeze at *v., informal* To consider unimportant.—Used with negative. *John finished third in a race with twenty other runners. That is nothing to sneeze at.* (John did not win the race, but he ran faster than most of the runners. That is no small thing. He deserves praise for that.)

snow job *n., slang, informal* **1** Insincere or exaggerated talk designed to gain the favors of someone. *Joe gave Sue a snow job and she believed every word of it.* (He flattered her in exaggerated terms, but she believed it.) **2** The skillful display of technical vocabulary and prestige terminology in order to pass oneself off as an expert in a specialized field without really being a knowledgeable worker in that area. *That talk by Nielsen on pharmaceuticals sounded very impressive, but I will not hire him because it was essentially a snow job.* (It was essentially an artificial display of prestige terminology covering up a gap in actual knowledge.)

snow under *v., informal* To give so much of something that it cannot be taken care of; to weigh down by so much of something that one cannot do anything about it.—Usually used in the passive. *The factory received so many orders that it was snowed under with work.* (The factory got so many orders that they could not fill all of them quickly.)

soak up *v., informal* To take up into oneself in the way a sponge takes up water. *Mary was lying on the beach soaking up the sun.* (Mary was taking the hot rays of the sun into her skin in the form of a tan.) *Charles soaks up facts as fast as the teacher gives them.* (Charles understands and remembers facts quickly.)

sob story *n.* A story that makes one feel pity or sorrow; a tale that makes one tearful. *The beggar told us a long sob story before he asked for money.* (The beggar told us a long story that made us feel sorry for him before he asked for money.)

sock it *v. phr., also interj., slang, informal* To give one's utmost; everything one is capable of; to give all one is capable of. *Right on, Joe, sock it to 'em!* (We agree with you, Joe, you are correct; let them have it; do your best to convince them.) *I was watching the debate on television and more than once Bill Buckley really socked it to them.* (He more than once really let them have it, as a clever debater.)

so far, so good *informal* Until now things have gone well. *So far, so good; I hope we keep on with such good luck.* (Up until now, we have done well. I hope we keep on doing well.)

so help me *interj., informal* I promise; I swear; may I be punished if I lie. *I've told you the truth, so help me.* (I swear that I have told you the truth.)

so long *interj., informal* Good-bye.—Used when one is leaving someone or he is leaving one. *So long, I will be back tomorrow.* (Good-bye, I am leaving now, but I will be back tomorrow.)

somebody up there loves/hates me *slang* An expression intimating that an unseen power in heaven, such as God, has been favorable or unfavorable to the one making the exclamation. *Look at all the money I won! I say somebody up there sure loves me!* (I am so fortunate that it must be because of divine help.) *Look at all the money I've lost! I say somebody up there sure hates me!* (I am so unfortunate that it must be that I am under divine punishment).

something else *adj., slang, informal* So good as to be beyond description; the ultimate; stupendous. *Janet Hopper is really something else* (She is indescribably beautiful and striking.)

something else again *n. phr.* A different kind of thing; something different. *I don't care if you borrow my dictionary sometimes, but taking it without asking and keeping it is something else again.* (Taking and keeping my dictionary is different from borrowing and returning it; I don't like that.)

song and dance *n., informal* **1** Foolish or uninteresting talk; dull nonsense. Usually used with *give*. *I met Nancy today and she gave me a long song and dance about her family.* (She talked for a long time foolishly about her family and it was very uninteresting.) **2** A long lie or excuse, often meant to get pity. Usually used with *give*. *Billy gave the teacher a song and dance about his mother being sick as an excuse for being late.* (He told the teacher a long lie.)

son of a bitch, sunuvabitch, S.O.B. *n. phr., vulgar, avoidable, becoming informally more acceptable if spoken with friendly intonation to someone the speaker knows well* Fellow, character, guy, individual. (negatively) *Get out of here, you filthy sunuvabitch!* (Leave, you filthy character!) *So you won a million dollars at the Irish sweepstakes, you lucky son of a bitch!* (I lovingly envy you, you lucky fellow.)

son of a gun *n. phr., slang* **1** A bad person; a person not liked. *I don't like Charley; keep that son of a gun out of here.* (Keep that fellow Charley away from me.) **2** A mischievous rascal; a lively guy. *The farmer said he would catch the son of a gun who let the cows out of the barn.* (The farmer said he would catch the mischief maker.) **3** Something troublesome; a hard job. *The test today was a son of a gun.* (It was very hard.) **4**—Used as an exclamation, usually to show surprise or disappointment. *Son of a gun! I lost my car keys.* (I'm surprised to have lost my keys.)

sound off *v., informal* To tell what one knows or thinks in a loud clear voice, especially to brag or complain. *If you don't like the way we're doing the job, sound off!* (If you don't approve, say so.)

sound out *v.* To try to find out how a person feels about something usually by careful questions. *Alfred sounded out his boss about a day off from his job.* (Alfred tried to find out how his boss felt about giving him a day off from work.)

souped-up *adj., informal* More powerful or faster because of changes and additions. *Many teenaged boys like to drive souped-up cars.* (Many teenaged boys like to drive cars that have been made more powerful by making changes in the motor.)

spaced out *adj., slang, informal* Having gaps in one's train of thought, confused, incoherent; resembling the behavior of someone who is under the influence of drugs. *Joe's been acting funny lately—spaced out, you might say.* (He has been incoherent and his thoughts and sentences were gappy as if under the influence of drugs.)

speak for *v.* **1** To speak in favor of or in support of. *At the meeting John spoke for the change in the rules.* (John told the meeting why he thought the rules should be changed.) **2** To make a request for; to ask for. *The teacher was giving away some books. Fred and Charlie spoke for the same one.* (Fred and Charlie asked for the same book.) **3** To give an impression of; be evidence that (something) is or will be said.—Used with the words *well* or *ill*. *It seems that it will rain today. That speaks ill for the picnic this afternoon.* (It may rain. If it rains we cannot have the picnic.)

speak of the devil and he appears A person comes just when one is talking about him. *We were just talking about Bill when he came in the door. Speak of the devil and he appears.* (Bill came when we were talking about him and did not expect him.)

speak out *or* **speak up** *v.* **1** To speak in a loud or clear voice. *The trucker told the shy boy to speak up.* (The trucker told him to speak loudly and clearly. He was afraid to speak.) **2** To speak in support of or against someone or something. *Willie spoke up for Dan as club president.* (Willie said Dan would make a good president for the club.) *Ed spoke up against letting girls join the club.* (Ed said he didn't want girls in the club.)

spell out *v., informal* To explain something in very simple words; explain very clearly. *The class could not understand the problem, so the teacher spelled it out for them.* (The teacher explained the problem again slowly and in simple words.)

spill the beans *v. phr., informal* To tell a secret to someone who is not supposed to know about it. *John's friends were going to have a surprise party for him, but Tom spilled the beans.* (Tom told John about the party, so John was not surprised.)

spitting image *or* **spit and image** *n., informal* An exact likeness; a duplicate. *John is the spitting image of his grandfather.* (John is an exact likeness of his grandfather. He looks exactly like his grandfather.)

split hairs *v. phr.* To find and argue about small and unimportant differences as if the differences are important. *John is always splitting hairs; he often starts an argument about something small and unimportant.* (John is always arguing about differences that do not really matter.)

split the difference *v. phr., informal* To settle a money disagreement by dividing the difference, each person giving up half. *Bob offered $25 for Bill's bicycle and Bill wanted $35; they split the difference.* (They agreed on $30, which is halfway between $25 and $35.)

split ticket *n.* A vote for candidates from more than one party. *Mr. Jones voted a split ticket.* (He voted for candidates from more than one party.) *An independent voter likes a split ticket.* (He likes voting for some candidates from one party and some from another party.)

spoon-feed v. To make (something) too easy for someone. *Some students want the teacher to spoon-feed them the lessons.* (Some students want the teacher to make the lesson very easy and do all their thinking for them.)

spread oneself too thin v. phr. To try to do too many things at one time. *As the owner, chef, waiter, and dishwasher of his restaurant, Pierre was spreading himself too thin.* (He could not manage so many jobs.)

spring chicken n., slang A young person.—Usually used with no. *Mr. Brown is no spring chicken, but he can still play tennis well.* (He is not a young person, but he can still play tennis well.)

square away v. phr., informal To put right for use or action.—Often used in the passive or participle. *The living room was squared away for the guests.* (The living room was arranged for the comfort of the visitors.) *Harry got into trouble, but his scoutmaster talked with him and got him squared away.* (The scoutmaster helped Harry to do better.)

square peg in a round hole n., informal A person who does not fit into a job or position; someone who does not belong where he is. *Arthur is a square peg in a round hole when he is playing ball.* (Arthur isn't at all good at playing ball.)

stab in the back[1] v. phr., slang To say or do something unfair that harms (a friend or someone who trusts you). *Owen stabbed his friend Max in the back by telling lies about him.* (Max and Owen were friends but Owen lied about Max and hurt him unfairly.)

stab in the back[2] n. phr., slang An act or a lie that hurts a friend or trusting person; a promise not kept, especially to a friend. *When John stole from his friend, it was a stab in the back.* (He injured his friend.)

stack the cards v. phr. To arrange things (unfairly) for or against a person; have things so that a person has an (unfair) advantage or disadvantage; make sure in an unfair way that things will happen.—Usually used in the passive with ''in one's favor'' or ''against one.'' *A tall basketball player has the cards stacked in his favor.* (If a basketball player is tall, he can do better than a shorter player.)

stamping ground n., informal A place where a person spends much of his time. *Pete's soda fountain is an after-school stamping ground.* (They usually go to Pete's soda fountain after school.) *When John returned to his home town many years later, he visited all of his old stamping grounds.* (When John came back to his home town, he visited the places he used to go to often.)

stamp out v. To destroy completely and make disappear. *In the last few years, we have nearly stamped out polio by using vaccine.* (In recent years, we have given people polio shots, and now almost nobody catches polio.) *The police and judges are trying to stamp out crime.* (They try to stop murder, robbery, and other law-breaking.)

stand by v. 1 To be near, waiting to do something when needed. *The policeman in the patrol car radioed the station about the robbery, and then stood by for orders.* (He stayed where he was and waited.) 2 To follow or keep (one's promise). *He is a boy who always stands by his promises.* (He does what he promises to do.)

3 To be loyal to; support; help. *When three big boys attacked Bill, Ed stood by him.* (Ed helped Bill fight the big boys.)

stand for *v.* **1** To be a sign of; make one think of; mean. *The letters "U.S.A." stand for "United States of America"* ("U.S.A." means "United States of America.") *The written sign "=" in an arithmetic problem stands for "equals."* ("=" means "equals.") *Our flag stands for our country.* (It makes us think of our country.) *The owl stands for wisdom.* (The owl is a symbol of wisdom.) **2** To speak in favor of something, or show that one supports it. *The new president stood for honest government.* (The new president made speeches saying he was in favor of honest government.) *John always stands for what is right.* (John always tries to do what is right.) **3** *informal* To allow to happen or to be done; permit.—Usually used in the negative. *The teacher will not stand for fooling in the classroom.* (The teacher will not allow foolishness in the classroom.)

stand in awe of *v. phr.* To look upon with wonder; feel very respectful to. *Janet always stands in awe of the superintendent.* (She always looks upon him with respect.) *The soldier stood in awe of his officers.* (He was very respectful to them.)

stand off *v.* **1** to stay at a distance; stay apart. *At parties, Mr. Jones goes around talking to everyone, but Mrs. Jones is shy and stands off.* (Mrs. Jones is not friendly.) **2** To keep (someone or something) from coming near or winning. *The soldiers defending the fort stood off a large band of Indians.* (The soldiers kept the In-

dians from coming into the fort.) *The other schools wanted to beat our team and win the championship, but our boys stood them all off.* (Our team kept the other teams from taking the championship away from us.)

stand out *v.* To be more noticeable in some way than those around one; be higher, bigger, or better. *Fred was very tall and stood out in the crowd.* (He was so tall that it was easy to see him in the crowd.) *John stood out as a track star.* (John was a track star and better than others.)

stand over *v.* **1** To watch closely; keep checking all the time. *Ted's mother had to stand over him to get him to do his homework.* (She had to watch him closely to make sure that he did it.) **2** To be held over for later action; be postponed; wait. *The committee decided to let the proposal stand over until its next meeting.* (They decided to delay action on it until their next meeting.)

stand pat *v., informal* To be satisfied with things and be against a change. *Bill had made up his mind on the question and when his friends tried to change his mind, he stood pat.* (Bill liked things as they were, and was against any change.)

stand to reason *v. phr.* To seem very likely from the known facts. *If you have a driver's license, it stands to reason you can drive.* (If you have a driver's license, you are almost sure to know how to drive.) *Joe is intelligent and studies hard; it stands to reason that he will pass the examination.* (Being smart and a good student, Joe is almost sure to pass the examination.)

stand up v. **1** To be strong enough to use hard or for a long time. *A rocket must be built strongly to stand up under the blast-off.* (A rocket must be built strongly so that it does not break under the force of the blast off.) **2** *informal* To make a date and then fail to keep it. *June cried when Bill stood her up on their first date.* (June cried when Bill did not meet her after he had invited her on a date.)

stand up and be counted v. phr. To be willing to say what one thinks in public; let people know that one is for or against something. *The equal rights movement needs people who are willing to stand up and be counted.* (The equal rights movement needs people who are willing to publicly support it.)

stand up for or *informal* **stick up for** v. To defend against attack; fight for. *John always stands up for his rights.* (John always claims what he has a right to do or have.)

stand up to v. To meet with courage. *Mary stood up to the snarling dog that leaped toward her.* (Mary bravely faced the dog.) *A soldier must stand up to danger.* (A soldier must be brave in a dangerous situation.)

stand up with v., *informal* To be best man or maid of honor at a wedding. *A groom often chooses his brother to stand up with him.* (He often asks his brother to be best man when he gets married.)

stars in one's eyes n. phr. **1** An appearance or feeling of very great happiness or expectation of happiness. *Mary gets stars in her eyes when she thinks of her boyfriend.* (Mary feels and looks very happy; her eyes sparkle.) **2** A belief in

the possibility of quick and lasting reforms in people and life and can eagerness to make such changes. *Some inexperienced people get stars in their eyes when they think of improving the world.* (They are sure they can improve the world and are eager to try.)

start in v., *informal* **1** To begin to do something; start. *Fred started in weeding the garden.* (Fred began to weed the garden.) **2** To begin a career. *Bob started in as an office boy and became president.* (Bob first worked as an office boy, but at last he became president.) **3** To give a first job to. *The bank started him in as a clerk.* (The bank gave him a job as clerk first.)

start up v. **1** To begin operating. *The driver started up the motor of the car.* (The driver started the motor running.) **2** To begin to play (music). *The conductor waved his baton, and the band started up.* (The conductor waved his baton, and the band started playing.) **3** To rise or stand suddenly. *When he heard the bell, he started up from his chair.* (He stood up suddenly.)

stay put v. phr. To stay in place; not leave. *Harry's father told him to stay put until he came back.* (His father told him not to leave until he came back.)

steal a march on v. phr. To get ahead of someone by doing a thing unnoticed; get an advantage over. *The army stole a march on the enemy by marching at night and attacking them in the morning.* (The army marched at night and surprised the enemy.)

steal one's thunder v. phr. To do or say something, intentionally or not, that another person had planned to say or do. *Fred* *intended to nominate Bill for president, but John got up first and stole Fred's thunder.* (John nominated Bill himself, so Fred had nothing to say.)

steal the show *v. phr.* To act or do so well in a performance that one gets most of the attention and the other performers are unnoticed. *Mary was in only one scene of the play, but she stole the show from the stars.* (Mary's acting was so good that the audience paid more attention to her than to the stars.)

steer clear of *v., informal* To stay away from; keep from going near. *Fred was angry at Bill, and Bill was steering clear of him.* (Because Fred was angry, Bill was trying not to meet him.)

step down *v.* 1 To decrease speed little by little. *The train was approaching the station, so the engineer stepped it down.* (The engineer decreased the speed of the train because it was nearing the station.) 2 To leave an important position. *When the judge became ill, he had to step down.* (When the judge became ill, he had to resign.)

step on it *or* **step on the gas** *v. phr., informal* To go faster; hurry. *Step on it, or we'll be late for school.* (Move faster or we will be late for school.) *John is a slow starter, but he can step on the gas when it looks as if he might lose the race.* (John can run faster when he must win.)

step on one's toes *or* **tread on one's toes** *v. phr.* To do something that embarrasses or offends someone else. *If you break in when other people are talking, you may step on their toes.* (If you interrupt other people, you may embarrass them or make them angry.)

step up *v.* 1 To go or to make (something) go faster or more actively. *When John found he was going to be late, he stepped up his pace.* (When John found he was going to be late, he walked faster.) 2 To rise to a higher or more important position; be promoted. *This year Mary is secretary of the club, but I am sure she will step up to president next year.* (Mary is secretary this year, but I am sure she will be promoted to president next year.)

stepped up *adj.* Carried on at a faster or more active rate; increased. *To fill the increase in orders, the factory had to operate at a stepped-up rate.* (To fill the orders, the factory had to work faster.)

stew in one's own juice *v. phr., informal* To suffer from something that one has caused to happen oneself. *John lied to Tom, but Tom found out. Now Tom is making John stew in his own juice.* (Since Tom found that John had lied to him, he has been making John suffer.)

stick around *v., informal* To stay or wait nearby. *John's father told him to stick around and they would go fishing.* (John's father told him to wait nearby and they would go fishing.)

stick-in-the-mud *n., informal* An over-careful person; someone who is old-fashioned and fights change. *Mabel said her mother was a real stick-in-the-mud to make a rule that she must be home by 10 o'clock on week nights and 11:30 Saturdays.* (She said her mother was very old-fashioned to make such rules.)

stick one's neck out *or* **stick one's chin out** *v. phr., informal* To do something dangerous or risky. *When I was in trouble, Paul was* *the only one who would stick his neck out to help me.* (When I was in trouble, Paul was the only one who would put himself in danger to help me.)

stick up *v., informal* To rob with a gun. *When the messenger left the bank, a man jumped out of an alley and stuck him up.* (A man jumped out of the alley and pointed a gun at the messenger to rob him.) *In the old West, outlaws sometimes stuck up the stage coaches.* (Outlaws sometimes robbed the coaches with guns.)

stick-up *n., informal* (stress on *stick*) A robbery by a person with a gun. *Mr. Smith was the victim of a stick-up last night.* (Mr. Smith was robbed by a man with a gun last night.)

stick with *or* **stay with** *v., informal* **1** To continue doing; not quit. *Fred stayed with his homework until it was done.* (Fred spent a long time on his homework, but he finished it.) *Practicing is tiresome, but stick with it and some day you will be a good pianist.* (Practice constantly, and some day you will be a good pianist.) **2** To stay with; not leave. *Stick with me until we get out of the crowd.* (Stay with me. Do not leave me.) **3** To sell (someone) something poor or worthless; cheat. *Father said that the man in the store tried to stick him with a bad TV set.* (The man tried to sell Father a set that was no good.) **4** To leave (someone) with (something unpleasant); force to do or keep something because others cannot or will not.—Usually used in the passive. *When Harry and I went to the store to buy ice-cream cones, Harry ran out with his cone without paying and I was stuck with paying for it.* (I was left to pay because Harry was gone.)

sticky fingers *n. phr., slang* **1** The habit of stealing things one sees and wants. *Don't leave money in your locker; some of the boys have sticky fingers.* (Don't leave money in your locker because some of the boys are easily tempted to steal.)

stir up *v.* **1** To bring (something) into being, often by great exertion or activity; cause. *It was a quiet afternoon, and John tried to stir up some excitement.* (John tried to bring about something exciting that would get rid of his boredom.) *Bob stirred up a fight between Tom and Bill.* (Bob caused a fight between Tom and Bill.) **2** To cause (someone) to act; incite to action or movement; rouse. *The coach's pep talk stirred up the team to win.* (The coach kindled the team's desire to win.)

stir up a hornet's nest *v. phr.* To make many people angry; do something that many people don't like. *The principal stirred up a hornet's nest by changing the rules at school.* (He changed the rules and many pupils and teachers got angry.)

stone-broke *or* **dead broke** *or* **flat broke** *adj., informal* having no money; penniless. *Jill wanted to go to the movies but she was stone-broke.* (She had no money with which to buy a ticket.) *The man gambled and was soon flat broke.* (He gambled and was soon penniless.)

stop cold *or* **stop dead** *or* **stop in one's tracks** *v. phr., informal* To stop very quickly or with great force. *The hunter pulled the trigger and stopped the deer cold.* (The hunter shot the deer and the deer dropped right there.)

stop off *v.* To stop at a place for a short time while going somewhere. *We stopped off after school* *at the soda fountain before going home.* (We stopped at the soda fountain and then went home.)

stop over *v.* (stress on *over*) To stay at a place overnight or for some other short time while on a trip elsewhere. *When we came back from California, we stopped over one night near the Grand Canyon.* (We stayed one night near the Grand Canyon.)

stop-over *n.* (stress on *stop*) A short stay at one place while on a trip to another. *We had a brief stop-over at the Grand Canyon.* (They visited it for a short time.)

straight from the horse's mouth *slang* Directly from the person or place where it began; from a reliable source or a person that cannot be doubted. *They are going to be married. I got the news straight from the horse's mouth—their minister.* (I heard it from a person who can't be doubted—their minister.)

straw in the wind *n. phr.* A small sign of what may happen. *The doctor's worried face was a straw in the wind.* (His worried face was a sign that something serious might happen.) *The quickly-called meeting of the President and his cabinet was a straw in the wind.* (It was a sign that something might happen.)

strike it rich *v. phr., informal* To become rich or successful suddenly or without expecting to. *Everyone wanted to buy one of the new gadgets, and their inventor struck it rich.* (The inventor sold very many gadgets and became rich from the sales.) *John did not know that he had a rich uncle in Australia. John struck it rich when his uncle left his money*

to John. (John became rich when his uncle died and left his money to John.)

strike out *v., informal* To be put out of action through one's own errors. *The novice actor wanted the part, but he struck out at the audition.* (When he read the part at the tryouts, he wasn't good enough to get the part.)

string along *v., informal* **1** To deceive; fool; lead on dishonestly. *Mary was stringing John along for years but she didn't mean to marry him.* (She fooled him for years but didn't mean to marry him.) **2** To follow someone's leadership; join his group. *Those of you who want to learn about wildflowers, string along with Jake.* (Follow Jake's leadership. He will show you where they grow and tell you what they are.)

string out *v.* To make (something) extend over a great distance or a long stretch of time. *The telephone poles were strung out along the road as far as we could see.* (The telephone poles were set one after another as far as we could see.)

stuck on *slang* Very much in love with, crazy about. *Judy thinks she is very pretty and very smart. She is stuck on herself.* (Judy is very vain. She is proud of her good looks and her intelligence.) *Lucy is stuck on the football captain.* (Lucy is very fond of the football captain.)

stuck-up *adj., informal* Acting as if other people are not as good as one is; conceited; snobbish. *Mary is very stuck-up, and will not speak to the poor children in her class.* (Mary feels that she is better than the poor children, so she will not speak to them.)

sucker list *n., slang* A list of easily-fooled people, especially people who are easily persuaded to buy things or give money. *The crook got hold of a sucker list and started out to sell his worthless stock.* (He got a list of easily fooled people.)

sugar daddy *n., slang, semi-vulgar, avoidable* An older, well-to-do man, who gives money and gifts to a younger woman, usually in exchange for sexual favors. *Betty Morgan got a mink coat from her sugar daddy.* (The older man who keeps her bought her a mink coat.)

sum up *v.* To put something into a few words; shorten into a brief summary; summarize. *The teacher summed up the lesson in three rules.* (The teacher gave all of the important material from her lesson again in three rules.)

sunbelt *n., informal* A portion of the southern United States where the winter is very mild in comparison to other states. *The Smiths left Chicago for the sunbelt, because of poor health.* (They left the harsh climate of Chicago for a warmer place.)

sunny-side up *adj.* Eggs fried on one side only. *Barbara likes her eggs sunny-side up.* (She likes them fried on one side only, so that the yolk is not flattened by being turned over.)

sure thing **1** *n., informal* Something sure to happen; something about which there is no doubt. *It's no fun betting on a sure thing.* (It's no fun to bet on something about which there is no doubt.)—**sure thing** **2** *adv.* Of course; certainly. *Sure thing, I'll be glad to do it for you.* (Of course, I'll be glad to do it for you.)

swallow one's pride *v. phr.* To bring one's pride under control; humble oneself. *After Bill lost the race, he swallowed his pride and shook hands with the winner.* (After Bill lost the race he brought his pride under control and shook hands with the winner.)

swallow one's words To speak unclearly; fail to put enough breath into one's words. *Phyllis was hard to understand because she swallowed her words.* (She was hard to understand because she didn't speak clearly.)

swear by *v.* **1** To use as the support or authority that what one is saying is truthful; take an oath upon. *A witness swears by the Bible that he will tell the truth.* (A witness promises to tell the truth with his hand on the Bible.) **2** To have complete confidence in; be sure of; trust completely. *When John has to go somewhere fast, he swears by his bike to get there.* (John knows that his bike will get him where he has to go.) *We can be sure that Fred will come on time, since his friend Tom swears by him.* (We can be sure that Fred will come, since Tom tells us he is sure Fred will come.)

swear in *v.* To have a person swear or promise to do his duty as a member or an officer of an organization, government department, or similar group. *At the inauguration, the Chief Justice swore in the new President.* (The Chief Justice asked the new President to take an oath that he would faithfully do his duty.)

swear off *v., informal* To promise to give up something one is in the habit of using. *Mary swore off candy until she lost ten pounds.* (Mary promised herself she would not eat candy until she lost ten pounds.) *John has sworn off dessert for Lent.* (John promised not to eat dessert during Lent.)

swear out *v.* To get (a written order to do something) by swearing that a person has broken the law. *The policeman swore out a warrant for the suspect's arrest.* (The policeman swore that, as far as he knew, the suspect had committed the crime; so that the judge would give him a legal order to arrest the suspect.) *The detectives swore out a search warrant.* (The detectives got a legal order to search a house by swearing that in the house there was evidence of a crime.)

sweat blood *v. phr., slang* **1** To be very much worried. *The engine of the airplane stopped, and the pilot sweated blood as he glided to a safe landing.* (The pilot was badly worried until he landed the plane.) **2** To work very hard. *Jim sweated blood to finish his composition on time.* (Jim worked very hard to finish his composition on time.)

sweat out *v., informal* To wait anxiously; worry while waiting. *Karl was sweating out the results of the college exams.* (He was waiting anxiously to hear how well he did on them.) *The search plane signaled that help was on the way. The men in the lifeboat just had to sweat it out.* (They had to worry while waiting for the rescue ship to come.)

sweep off one's feet *v. phr.* To make (someone) have feelings (as love or happiness) too strong to control; overcome with strong feeling. *The handsome football captain swept Joan off her feet.* (The football captain quickly won her love.)

sweep under the rug *v. phr.* To hide or dismiss casually (something one is ashamed of or does not know what to do about). *In many places, drug abuse by school children is swept under the rug.* (People refuse to admit that their students abuse drugs.)

sweetie pie *n., informal* A person who is loved; darling; sweetheart. *Arnold blushed with pleasure when Annie called him her sweetie pie.* (He blushed when she called him her darling.)

sweet on *adj. phr., informal* In love with; very fond of. *John is sweet on Alice.* (John is in love with Alice.)

sweet talk **1** *n., informal* Too much praise; flattery. *Sometimes a girl's better judgment is overcome by sweet talk.* (Her better judgment is overcome by flattery.) **2** *v., informal* To get what one wants by great praise; flatter. *Polly could sweet talk her father into anything.* (She could get him to do anything she wanted to by flattering him.)

swelled head *n., informal* A feeling that one is very important or more important than one really is. *When John won the race, he got a swelled head.* (When John won the race, he became very conceited.)

swim against the current *or* **swim against the stream** *v. phr.* To do the opposite of what most people want to do; go against the way things are happening; struggle upstream. *The boy who tries to succeed today without an education is swimming against the stream.* (Today you need an education for most jobs, and without education you will have a hard struggle.)

switched on *adj., slang* **1** In tune with the latest fads, ideas, and fashions. *I dig Sarah; she is really switched on.* (I like her because she knows the current fads and fashions.) **2** Stimulated; as if under the influence of alcohol or drugs. *How come you're talking so fast? Are you switched on or something?* (Why do you speak so rapidly? Are you under the influence of alcohol or some drug?)

tail between one's legs *n. phr.* State of feeling beaten, ashamed, or very obedient, as after a scolding or a whipping. *The boys on the team had boasted they would win the tournament, but they went home with their tails between their legs.* (They lost the tournament and were disappointed and ashamed.) [So called because a beaten dog usually puts his tail down between his legs and slinks away.]

take a back seat *v. phr., informal* To accept a poorer or lower position; be second to something or someone else. *She does not have to take a back seat to any singer alive.* (No other singer is any better than she.)

take a bath *v. phr., informal* To come to financial ruin. *Boy, did we ever take a bath on that merger in Philadelphia!* (Speaker says that the merger caused them financial ruin.)

take a dim view of *v. phr.* **1** To have doubts about; feel unsure or anxious about. *Tom took a dim view of his chances of passing the exam.* (Tom was afraid he would not pass the exam.) **2** To be against; disapprove. *John's father took a dim view of his wanting to borrow the car.* (John's father didn't want him to use the car.) *The teacher took a dim view of the class's behavior.* (The teacher didn't like the class's behavior.)

take after *v.* To be like because of family relationship; to have the same looks or ways as (a parent or ancestor.) *He takes after his father in mathematical ability.* (He is like his father in mathematical skill.) *She takes after her father's side of the family in looks.* (She looks like her father's people.)

take a leak *v. phr., vulgar, avoidable* To urinate. *"I'm gonna hit the can to take a leak,"* Joe said. (He says he is going to the bathroom to urinate.)

take a shine to *v. phr., slang* To have or show a quick liking for. *He took a shine to his new teacher the very first day.* (He liked his teacher the very first day.)

take back *v.* To change or deny something offered, promised, or stated; admit to making a wrong statement. *I take back my offer to buy the house, now that I've had a good look at it.* (I will change my offer and refuse to buy the house.)

take by storm *v. phr.* **1** To capture by a sudden or very bold attack. *The army did not hesitate. They took the town by storm.* (They marched right in and captured it.) **2** To win the favor of; make (a group of people) like or believe one. *The comic took the audience by storm.* (He made everyone laugh and like him.)

take care of *v. phr.* **1** To attend to; supply the needs of. *She stayed home to take care of the baby.* (She stayed home to keep the baby safe, clean, warm, and fed.) **2** *informal* To deal with; do what is needed with. *I will take care of that letter.* (I will write an answer to that letter and mail the answer.) *The coach told Jim to take care of the opposing player.* (He told Jim to keep the opposite player away from the ball carrier.)

take down *v.* **1** To write or record (what is said). *I will tell you how to get to the place; you had better take it down.* (I will give you directions to reach the place; you should write them now.) **2** To pull to pieces; take apart. *It* will be a big job to take that tree down. (It will take much time and work to cut and pull the tree down.) *In the evening the campers put up a tent, and the next morning they took it down.* (The next morning they took it apart and folded it up again.) 3 *informal* To reduce the pride or spirit of; humble. *Bob thought he was a good wrestler, but Henry took him down.* (Bob was proud of his wrestling but Henry humbled him by beating him.)

take down a notch *or* **take down a peg** *v. phr., informal* To make (someone) less proud or sure of himself. *The team was feeling proud of its record, but last week the boys were taken down a peg by a bad defeat.* (Losing the game last week made the boys feel less proud.)

take effect *v. phr.* 1 To have an unexpected or intended result; cause a change. *It was nearly an hour before the sleeping pill took effect.* (It was nearly an hour before the sleeping pill caused the sick person to go to sleep.) 2 To become lawfully right, or operative. *The new tax law will not take effect until January.* (The new law will not be enforced until January 1.)

take exception to *v. phr.* To speak against; find fault with; be displeased or angered by; criticize. *There was nothing in the speech that you could take exception to.* (There was nothing in the speech for you to criticize or oppose.)

take for *v.* To suppose to be; mistake for. *Do you take me for a fool?* (Do you suppose I am a fool?) *At first sight you would take him for a football player, not a poet.* (At first sight you would

mistakenly think he was a football player, not a poet.)

take for a ride *v. phr., slang* 1 To take out in a car, intending to murder. *The gang leader decided that the informer must be taken for a ride.* (The gang leader ordered the death of the man who told the police.) 2 To play a trick on; fool. *The girls told Linda that a movie star was visiting the school, but she did not believe them; she thought they were taking her for a ride.* (She thought they were trying to fool her.) 3 To take unfair advantage of; fool for one's own gain. *His girl friend really took him for a ride until he stopped dating her.* (She was interested in him only for the entertainment and gifts he gave her.)

take for granted *v. phr.* 1 To suppose or understand to be true. *Mr. Harper took for granted that the invitation included his wife.* (He supposed that the invitation was for both him and his wife.) *A teacher cannot take it for granted that students always do their homework.* (A teacher cannot suppose that students always do their homework.) 2 To accept or become used to (something) without noticing especially or saying anything. *George took for granted all that his parents did for him.* (George accepted their help and care without really noticing it or thanking them.) *No girl likes to have her boyfriend take her for granted; instead, he should always try to make her like him better.* (No girl wants her boyfriend to suppose that he is the only boy she could be interested in.)

take heart *v. phr.* To be encouraged; feel braver and want to try. *The men took heart from their leader's words and went on to win* *the battle*. (They felt braver and won the battle.)

take ill *or* **take sick** *v.* To become sick. *Father took sick just before his birthday.* (He became sick just before his birthday.)—Used in the passive with the same meaning.

take in *v.* **1** To go and see; visit. *The students decided to take in a movie while they were in town.* (They decided to go to see a movie while they were in town.) **2** To make smaller. *This waist band is too big; it must be taken in about an inch.* (The waist must be made smaller.) **3** To grasp with the mind; understand. *He didn't take in what he read because his mind was on something else.* (He didn't understand what he read because he was thinking of something else.) **4a**—In the passive: To be deceived, cheated, fooled. *The teacher was taken in by the boy's innocent manner.* (The teacher was fooled by the boy's acting as if he had done nothing.) **4b**—In the passive: To accept without question; believe. *The magician did many tricks, and the children were taken in.* (They believed that the magician really made things disappear.) **5a** To receive; get. *The senior class held a dance to make money and took in over a hundred dollars.* (The class earned more than a hundred dollars.) **5b** Let come in; admit. *The farmer took in the lost travelers for the night.* (He let the lost travelers stay in his house for the night.) *When her husband died, Mrs. Smith took in boarders.* (To make money, she had paying guests.) **6** To see or hear with interest; pay close attention to. *When Bill told about his adventures, the other boys took it all in.* (They listened with great interest.)

take in stride *v. phr.* To meet happenings without too much surprise; accept good or bad luck and go on. *He learned to take disappointments in stride.* (He learned to meet disappointments without being greatly upset or discouraged by them.)

take it *v. phr.* **1** To get an idea or impression; understand from what is said or done.—Usually used with *I. I take it from your silence that you don't want to go.* (Your silence makes me think you don't want to go.) **2** *informal* To bear trouble, hard work, criticism; not give up or weaken. *Henry could criticize and tease other boys, but he couldn't take it himself.* (Henry teased other boys, but could not accept teasing himself.)

take it easy *v. phr., informal* **1** *or* **go easy** *or* **take things easy** To go or act slowly, carefully, and gently. *Take it easy. The roads are icy.* (Drive slowly and carefully.) **2** *or* **take things easy** To avoid hard work or worry; have an easy time; live in comfort. *The doctor said that Bob would have to take things easy for awhile after he had his tonsils out.* (He would have to rest and not work or play.) *Mr. Wilson has just made a lot of money and can take things easy now.* (He won't have to work hard any more, because he has enough money.)

take it on the chin *v. phr., informal* **1** To be badly beaten or hurt. *Our football team really took it on the chin today. They are all bumps and bruises.* (They are all sore from the beating they got on the football field.) *Mother and I took it on the chin in the card game.* (We lost the card game by a very great amount.) **2** To accept without complaint something bad that happens to one; accept trouble or defeat calmly. *A good football player can take it on the chin when his team loses.* (A good player will not be discouraged or upset or angry when his team loses.)

take it out on *v. phr., informal* To be unpleasant or unkind to (someone) because one is angry or upset; get rid of upset feelings by being mean to. *The teacher was angry and took it out on the class.* (He was angry but didn't know whom to blame, so he punished the whole class.)

take its toll *v. phr.* To cause loss or damage. *The bombs had taken their toll on the little town.* (The bombs had ruined much of the little town.) *The budget cut took its toll of teachers.* (The cut in funds caused some teachers to be discharged.)

take kindly to *v.* To be pleased by; like.—Usually used in negative, interrogative, and conditional sentences. *He doesn't take kindly to any suggestions about running his business.* (He doesn't like to be advised about managing his business.)

take leave of *v. phr.* 1 To abandon, go away from, or become separated from.—Usually used in the phrase *take leave of one's senses. Come down from the roof, Billy! Have you taken leave of your senses?* (Come down or you'll fall. Have you gone crazy?)

take liberties *v. phr.* To act toward in too close or friendly a manner; use as one would a close friend or something of one's own. *She took liberties rearranging her friend's furniture.* (She moved it around as if it were her own.)

taken aback *also* **taken back** *adj.* Unpleasantly surprised; suddenly puzzled or shocked. *When he came to pay for his dinner he was taken aback to find that he had left his wallet at home.* (He was confused and embarrassed.)

take off *v.* **1a** To leave fast; depart suddenly; run away. *The dog took off after a rabbit.* (The dog ran after a rabbit.) **1b** *informal* To go away; leave. *The six boys got into the car and took off for the drugstore.* (They left to go to the drugstore.) **2** To leave on a flight; begin going up. *A helicopter is able to take off and land straight up or down.* (A helicopter can go straight up and come straight down.) **3** **do a takeoff** *v. phr., informal* To imitate amusingly; copy another person's habitual actions or speech. *At the party, Charlie did a takeoff on the principal and some of the teachers.* (He imitated them.) **4** To take (time) to be absent from work. *When his wife was sick he took off from work.* (When his wife was sick, he did not go to his job.) *Bill was tired out, so he took the day off.* (He was very tired and didn't go to work that day.)

take-off *n., informal* (stress on *take*) **1** Departure of an airplane. *We had a smooth take-off.* (The departure went well.) **2** Imitation as parody or jest. *Joe can do a perfect take-off on any politician's speech.* (He is an accomplished mimic.)

take off one's hat to *v. phr.* To give honor, praise, and respect to. *He is my opponent, but I take off my hat to him for his courage.* (I honor and respect his bravery.)

take on *v.* **1** To receive for carrying; be loaded with. *A big ship was at the dock taking on automobiles in crates to carry overseas for sale.* (A ship was being loaded with automobiles.) **2** To begin to have (the look of); take (the appearance of). *Others joined the fist fight until it took on the look of a riot.* (Others got into the fight and it began to look like a riot.) **3a** To give a job to; hire, employ. *The factory has opened and is beginning to take on new workers.* (The factory is open and is beginning to hire new workers.) **3b** To accept in business or a contest. *The big man took on two opponents at once.* (He fought with two men at one time.) *After his father died, Bill took on the management of the factory.* (After his father died, Bill became the manager of the factory.) **4** *informal* To show great excitement, grief, or anger. *At the news of her husband's death she took on like a mad-woman.* (At the news of her husband's death she began to scream and cry as if she were crazy.)

take one's medicine *v. phr.* To accept punishment without complaining. *The boy said he was sorry he broke the window and was ready to take his medicine.* (He was ready to accept punishment without complaining or excusing himself.)

take one's time *v. phr.* To avoid haste; act in an unhurried way. *He liked to take his time over breakfast.* (He liked to eat breakfast without hurrying.)

take out *v. phr.* **1** To ask for and fill in. *Mary and John took out a marriage license.* (Before their marriage, Mary and John filled out the necessary legal forms at the town hall.)

take over *v.* **1a** To take control or possession of. *He expects to take over the business when his father retires.* (He expects to own and run the business.) **1b** To take

charge or responsibility. *The airplane pilot fainted and his copilot had to take over.* (His copilot had to become the pilot and commander of the airplane.) **2** To borrow, imitate, or adopt. *The Japanese have taken over many European ways of life.* (The Japanese have begun to do things the way Europeans do them.)

take-over *n.. informal* (stress on *take*) A forceful seizure of power; a coup. *There was a military take-over in the Near East.* (There was a coup there.)

take place *v. phr.* To happen; occur. *The accident took place only a block from his home.* (The accident happened only a block from his home.)

take sides *v. phr.* To join one group against another in a debate or quarrel. *Switzerland refused to take sides in the two world wars.* (Switzerland stayed out of the wars.)

take steps *v. phr.* To begin to make plans or arrangements; make preparations; give orders.—Usually used with *to* and an infinitive. *The city is taking steps to replace its street cars with buses.* (The city is making arrangements to change street cars for buses.)

take stock *v. phr.* **1** To count the items of merchandise or supplies in stock; take inventory. *The grocery store took stock every week on Monday mornings.* (They counted up all the things they had in the store.) **2** To study carefully a situation, or a number of possibilities or opportunities. *Before deciding to buy a house, Jane took stock of her financial situation.* (She reviewed her economic assets to see if she could afford a house.)

take stock in *v. phr., informal* To have faith in; trust; believe.— Usually used in the negative. *He took no stock in the idea that women were better cooks than men.* (He did not believe that women were better cooks than men.)

take the bull by the horns *v. phr., informal* To take definite action and not care about risks; act bravely in a difficulty. *He decided to take the bull by the horns and demand a raise in salary even though it might cost him his job.* (He decided to act directly and decisively in spite of the risk.)

take the edge off *also* **take off the edge** *v. phr.* To lessen, weaken, soften, or make dull. *Eating a candy bar before dinner has taken the edge off Becky's appetite.* (She had eaten a candy bar before dinner so that she was not very hungry for dinner.)

take the Fifth *v. phr., informal* 1 Taking refuge behind the Fifth Amendment of the Constitution of the United States, which guarantees any witness the right not to incriminate himself while testifying at a trial. *Alger Hiss took the Fifth when asked whether he was a member of the Communist Party.* (He declined to answer the question on grounds of possible self-incrimination.) 2 Not to answer any question in an informal setting. *Have you been married before? — I take the Fifth.* (I am not telling you—it's none of your business.)

take the rap *v. phr., slang* To receive punishment; to be accused and punished. *All of the boys took apples, but only John took the rap.* (John was the only boy punished for taking apples.)

take the words out of one's mouth *v. phr.* To say what another was just going to say; to put another's thought into words. *"Let's go to the beach tomorrow." "You took the words right out of my mouth."* ("You said what I was going to say.")

take to *v.* 1 To go to or into; get oneself quickly to.—Often used in the imperative. *This summer let's take to the hills.* (Let's go for a mountain vacation.) 2 To begin the work or job of; make a habit of. *He took to repairing watches in his spare time.* (He did the job of repairing watches when he wasn't on his regular job.) 3 To learn easily; do well at. *Father tried to teach John to swim, but John didn't take to it.* (John didn't learn easily; swimming was hard for him.) 4 To like at first meeting; be pleased by or attracted to; accept quickly. *Our dog always takes to children quickly.* (He always likes children.)

take to task *v. phr.* To reprove or scold for a fault or error. *The President took Congress to task for cutting the defense budget.* (He expressed his disapproval.) *The principal took Bill to task for breaking the window.* (He scolded Bill.)

take to the cleaners *v. phr., slang* 1 To win all the money another person has (as in poker). *Watch out if you play poker with Joe; he'll take you to the cleaners.* (He will win all your money.) 2 To cheat a person out of his money and possessions by means of a crooked business transaction or other dishonest conduct. *I'll never forgive myself for becoming associated with Joe; he took me to the cleaners.* (I lost all I had because of working with him.)

take to the woods *v. phr., informal* To run away and hide. *When John saw the girls coming, he took to the woods.* (When John saw the girls, he hid from them.)

take turns *v. phr.* To do something one after another. *In class we should not talk all at the same time; we should take turns.* (First one person should talk, then another.)

take up *v.* **1** To fill (a place or time); occupy. *All his evenings were taken up with study.* (He was busy every evening studying.) **2** To gather together; collect. *We are taking up a collection to buy flowers for John, because he is in the hospital.* (We are collecting money for flowers.) **3** To take away. *John had his driver's license taken up for speeding.* (He lost his license because he was speeding. It was taken away.) **4a** To begin; start. *The teacher took up the lesson where she left off yesterday.* (She started where she stopped yesterday.) **4b** To begin to do or learn; go into as a job or hobby. *He recently took up gardening.* (He started to learn about gardening.) **5** To pull and make tight or shorter; shorten. *The tailor took up the legs of the trousers.* (He shortened the legs.) *Take up the slack on the rope!* (Pull the rope tighter so it won't be so loose.) **6** To take or accept something that is offered. *I'll take you up on your offer to drive me home.* (I accept your offer of a ride.)

take up arms *v. phr., literary* To get ready to fight; fight or make war. *The people were quick to take up arms to defend their freedom.* (They were quick to fight.)

take with a grain of salt *also* **take with a pinch of salt** *v. phr.* To accept or believe only in part; not accept too much. *A politician who says he is not a candidate for President should usually have his statement taken with a grain of salt.* (His denial should not be believed completely.) *We took Uncle George's stories of the war with a pinch of salt.* (We believed them in part, but not entirely.)

talk back *also* **answer back** *v., informal* To answer rudely. *When the teacher told the boy to sit down, he talked back to her and said she couldn't make him.* (The teacher told the boy to sit down, but he was disrespectful.)

talk big *v., informal* To talk boastfully; brag. *He talks big about his pitching, but he hasn't won a game.* (He tries to make people believe that he is a very good pitcher.)

talk down *v.* **1** To silence someone by talking louder or longer. *Sue tried to give her ideas, but the other girls talked her down.* (Sue stopped talking because the other girls spoke so loud and long.) **2** To use words or ideas that are too simple. *The speaker talked down to the students, and they were bored.* (He used words that were oversimple, and told them things they had known before.)

talk into *v.* **1** To get (someone) to agree to; make (someone) decide on (doing something) by talking; persuade to.—Used with a verbal noun. *Bob talked us into walking home with him.* (Bob made us agree to go home with him.) **2** To cause to be in or to get into by talking. *You talked us into this mess. Now get us out!* (Your talking got us into this trouble.)

talk out *v.* To talk all about and leave nothing out; discuss until everything is agreed on; settle. *After their quarrel, Jill and John talked things out and reached full agreement.* (They talked about things until everything was understood.)

talk out of v. **1** To persuade not to; make agree or decide not to.— Used with a verbal noun. *Mary's mother talked her out of quitting school.* (Mary's mother talked to her and persuaded her not to quit.) **2** To discourage punishment or blame by talking; to dissuade. *Johnny is good at talking his way out of trouble.* (Johnny is a good talker and people believe him.)

talk over v. **1** To talk together about; try to agree about or decide by talking; discuss. *Tom talked his plan over with his father before he bought the car.* (Tom talked with his father and got his advice.) **2** To persuade; make willing; talk and change the mind of. *Fred is trying to talk Bill over to our side.* (Fred is trying to make Bill agree with us.)

talk shop v. phr., informal To talk about things in one's work or trade. *Two chemists were talking shop, and I hardly understood a word they said.* (The chemists were talking about their work and they used many words I did not know.)

talk through one's hat v. phr., informal To say something without knowing or understanding the facts; talk foolishly or ignorantly. *John said that the earth is nearer the sun in summer, but the teacher said he was talking through his hat.* (The teacher meant that John didn't know the truth; he was wrong.)

talk up v. **1** To speak in favor or support of. *Let's talk up the game and get a big crowd.* (Let's tell people the game is important, so that they will come.) **2** To speak (more) distinctly. *The teacher asked the student to talk up.* (The teacher asked the student to speak

more loudly and clearly.) **3** informal To say what one wants or thinks; say what someone may not like. *Talk up if you want more pie.* (If you want pie, say so; don't be shy.)

tan someone's hide v. phr., informal To give a beating to; spank hard. *Bob's father tanned his hide for staying out too late.* (Bob's father gave him a beating because he stayed out too late.)

taper off v. **1** To come to an end little by little: become smaller toward the end. *The heavy downpour of rain tapered off to a drizzle.* (The rain gradually diminished to a fine sprinkle.) **2** To stop a habit gradually; do something less and less often. *Ruth tapered off her use of sugar by taking her coffee without sweetening.* (She began to reduce sugar in her diet by eliminating it in her coffee.)

tar and feather v. **1** To pour heated tar on and cover with feathers as a punishment. *In the Old West bad men were sometimes tarred and feathered and driven out of town.* (In the Old West men sometimes put warm tar and feathers on bad men and ran them out of town.) **2** To punish severely. *The School Board wanted to tar and feather the principal when he went over the budget.* (They wanted to punish him.)

tear down v. **1** To take all down; destroy. *The workmen tore down the old house and built a new house in its place.* (The old house was destroyed and the parts were taken away to make a place for the new house.) **2** To take to pieces or parts. *The mechanics had to tear down the engine, and fix it, and put it together again.* (They took the engine apart to repair it.) **3** To say bad things about; criticize. *Why do you always tear people down? (Why do you always say bad things about people? Why not praise them instead?)*

tell it like it is *v. phr., slang, informal* To be honest, sincere; to tell the truth. *Joe is the leader of our commune; he tells it like it is. (He tells the truth without subterfuge.)*

tell it to the marines *or* **tell it to Sweeney** *slang* I don't believe you; stop trying to fool me. *John said, "My father knows the President of the United States." Dick answered, "Tell it to the marines." (Dick did not believe John; Dick thought John was trying to fool him.)*

tell off *v., informal* To speak to angrily or sharply; attack with words; scold. *Mr. Black got angry and told off the boss. (Mr. Black angrily told his boss that he was wrong.)*

tell on *v., informal* To tell someone about another's wrong or naughty acts.—Used mainly by children. *Andy hit a little girl and John told the teacher on Andy. (John told the teacher that Andy hit a little girl.)*

tempest in a teapot *n. phr.* Great excitement about something not important. *The debate over the naming of the new town park was a tempest in a teapot. (It was not an earthshaking issue.)*

ten-four *n., slang, citizen's band radio jargon* An acknowledgment of understanding. *Is that a ten-four? (Do you understand me?) Yes, that's a ten-four, good buddy. (Yes, I understand you.)*

that'll be the day *informal* That will never happen. *Joe wanted me to lend him money.*

That'll be the day! (I will never do that.)

the creeps *n., informal* **1** An uncomfortable tightening of the skin caused by fear or shock. *Reading the story of a ghost gave Joe the creeps. (Joe felt uncomfortable while reading the story.)* **2** A strong feeling of fear or disgust. *The cold, damp, lonely swamp gave John the creeps. (The swamp filled John with horror and fear.)*

the lid *n., slang* Something that holds back or holds out of sight. *The police blew the lid off the gambling operations. (The police discovered and made public the gambling operations.)*

the pits *n.* **down in the pits** *adv. phr.* A low class, blighted place; to be in such a place or in a mood suggested by such a place. *Joe, I'm not going to sleep in this motel; this is the pits! (This is such a poor and dirty place that I won't stay here.) Poor Marcy is down in the pits over her divorce. (She is depressed because of her divorce.)*

the ropes *n. plural, informal* Thorough or special knowledge of a job; how to do something; the ways of people or the world. *On a newspaper a cub reporter learns his job from an older reporter who knows the ropes. (The older reporter knows people and he knows his job very well.)*

the score *n., slang* The truth; the real story or information; what is really happening; the way people and the world really are. *Very few people know the score in politics. (Few people know what goes on in politics.)*

the tracks *n.* The line between the rich or fashionable part of town and the poor or unfashionable part of town. *The poor children knew* *they would not be welcome on the other side of the tracks*. (The poor children knew that the rich people did not want them to come to their neighborhood.)

the works *n., plural, slang* **1** Everything that can be had or that one has; everything of this kind, all that goes with it. *When the tramp found $100, he went into a fine restaurant and ordered the works with a steak dinner.* (He wanted everything he could possibly eat.) **2** Rough handling or treatment; a bad beating or scolding; killing; murder.—Usually used with *get* or *give*. *The boy said that Joe was going to get the works if he ever came back to that neighborhood again.* (He said that Joe would get a beating.)

think aloud *or* **think out loud** *v.* To say what one is thinking. *"I wish I had more money for Christmas presents,"* Father thought aloud. (He was saying the things he was thinking.)

think better of *v.* To change one's mind about; to consider again and make a better decision about. *John told his mother he wanted to leave school, but later he thought better of it.* (John changed his mind.)

think little of *v. phr.* Think that (something or someone) is not important or valuable. *John thought little of Ted's plan for the party.* (John didn't like Ted's plan.)

think nothing of *v. phr.* To think or consider easy, simple, or usual. *Jim thinks nothing of hiking ten miles in one day.* (Jim thinks it is easy to hike ten miles in one day.)

think out *v.* **1** To find out or discover by thinking; study and understand. *Andy thought out a way of climbing to the top of the*

pole. (He studied it and found out how to do it.) **2** To think through to the end; to understand what would come at last. *Bill wanted to quit school, but he thought out the matter and decided not to.* (Bill thought about the future and felt he would have trouble without a good education.)

think over *v.* To think carefully about; consider; study. *When Charles asked Betty to marry him, she asked him for time to think it over.* (Betty wanted time to think carefully about marrying Charles before she said yes or no.)

think piece *n., slang* **1** The human brain. *Lou's got one powerful think piece, man.* (Lou is really smart.) **2** Any provocative essay or article that, by stating a strong opinion, arouses the reader to think about it and react to it by agreeing or disagreeing. *That article by Charles Fenyvesi on Vietnamese refugees in the Washingtion Post sure was a think piece!* (It certainly was an article that challenged the readers intellectually.)

think twice *v.* To think again carefully; reconsider; hesitate. *The teacher advised Lou to think twice before deciding to quit school.* (Lou should not make a quick decision.)

think up *v.* To invent or discover by thinking; have a new idea of. *Mary thought up a funny game for the children to play.* (She had never seen or heard of the game; she invented it.)

third world *n.* The underdeveloped nations of the world; the countries not aligned with either the Communist or non-Communist bloc. *Africa and the rest of the third world must be freed from poverty.* (The countries that have not shared in the prosperity of industrial development must be freed from poverty.)

three sheets to the wind *adj. phr., informal* Unsteady from too much liquor, drunk. *The sailor came down the street, three sheets to the wind.* (The drunken sailor staggered down the street.)

through the mill *adv. phr., informal* Through real experience of the difficulties of a certain way of life. *He won't be surprised by anything on the new job. He's been through the mill.* (He has had enough experience in that line not to be surprised by anything on the new job.)

through thick and thin *adv. phr.* Through all difficulties and troubles; through good times and bad times. *The friends were faithful through thick and thin.* (The friends were faithful in good times and bad.)

throw a curve *v. phr., slang, informal* 1 To mislead or deceive someone, to lie. *John threw me a curve about the hiring.* (John lied to me about the hiring.) 2 To take someone by surprise in an unpleasant way. *Mr. Weiner's announcement threw the whole company a curve.* (It took the whole company by surprise in an unpleasant manner.)

throw a monkey wrench or **throw a wrench** *v. phr., informal* To cause something that is going smoothly to stop. *The game was going smoothly until you threw a monkey wrench into the works by fussing about the rules.* (We were having fun playing the game until you spoiled it by fussing about the rules.)

throw away *v.* To fail to make use of. *She threw away a good chance for a better job.* (She had a chance for a better job, but didn't take it.)

throw down the gauntlet *v. phr.* To challenge, especially to a fight. *Another candidate for the presidency has thrown down the gauntlet.* (Another person has entered the fight to become president.)

throw in *v.* 1 To give or put in as an addition; to give to or with something else. *John threw in a couple of tires when he sold Bill his bicycle.* (John gave Bill a couple of tires with the bicycle he sold him.) 2 To push into operating position. *Mr. Jones threw in the clutch and shifted gears.* (Mr. Jones pushed the clutch pedal to the floor so that he could shift gears.)

throw in one's lot with or literary **cast in one's lot with** *v. phr.* To decide to share or take part in anything that happens to; join. *The thief decided to throw in his lot with the gang when he heard their plans.* (The thief decided to join the gang when he heard their plans.)

throw in the sponge or **throw in the towel** *v. phr., informal* To admit defeat; accept loss. *After taking a beating for five rounds, the fighter threw in the sponge.* (After the fighter had been badly beaten for five rounds, he stopped fighting.)

throw off *v.* 1 To get free from. *He was healthy enough to throw off his cold easily.* (He was healthy enough to free himself of the cold easily.) 2 To mislead; confuse, fool. *They went by a different route to throw the hostile Indians off their track.* (They went a different way to fool the enemy Indians.) 3 To produce easily or as if without effort. *She could throw off a dozen poems in a night.* (She could produce a dozen poems in one night with no trouble at all.)

throw one's weight around *v. phr., informal* To use one's influence or position in a showy or noisy manner. *John was the star of the class play, and he was throwing his weight around telling the director how the scene should be played.* (John was using his position as the star to tell the director what to do.)

throw out *or* **toss out** *v.* To force to leave; dismiss. *When the baseball manager complained too loudly, the umpires threw him out.* (The umpires ordered the manager to leave the game when he complained too loudly.)

throw the baby out with the bath (*or* **bathwater**) *v. phr.* To reject all of something because part is faulty. *There are weaknesses in the program, but if they act too hastily they may cause the baby to be thrown out with the bathwater.* (They may reject a good program just because part of it hasn't worked.)

throw the book at *v. phr., informal* To give the most severe penalty to (someone) for breaking the law or rules. *Because it was the third time he had been caught speeding that month, the judge threw the book at him.* (Because it was his third speeding arrest that month, the judge gave him the greatest penalty.)

throw together *v.* **1** *also* **slap together** To make in a hurry and without care. *Bill and Bob threw together a cabin out of old lumber.* (Bill and Bob built a cabin without paying attention to the way a strong building should be built.) *The party was planned suddenly, and Mary threw together a meal out of leftovers.* (Mary made a meal quickly out of whatever she could find in the house.) **2** —In the passive. To be grouped with

other people by chance. *The group of strangers was thrown together when the storm trapped them on the highway.* (The strangers became grouped together when the storm caught them.)

throw to the wolves *v. phr.* To send into danger without protection. *The general knew the attack was doomed, but he threw his men to the wolves anyway.* (He sent his men into battle although he knew they would be killed.)

throw up *v.* **1** *informal or slang* **heave up** To vomit. *The heat made him feel sick and he thought he would throw up.* (The heat made him sick and he thought he would vomit.) *He took the medicine but threw it up a minute later.* (He took the medicine but vomited it a minute later.) **2** *informal* To quit; leave; let go; give up. *When she broke their engagement he threw up his job and left town.* (When their engagement was broken he left his job and went elsewhere.) **3** To build in a hurry. *The contractor threw up some temporary sheds to hold the new equipment.* (The contractor hurriedly built sheds for the new equipment to be kept in for a while.) **4** To mention often as an insult. *His father threw up John's wastefulness to him.* (John's father often mentioned his wastefulness.)

throw up one's hands *v. phr.* To give up trying; admit that one cannot succeed. *Mrs. Jones threw up her hands when the children messed up the living room for the third time.* (Mrs. Jones stopped trying to keep the living room clean.)

thumb a ride *v. phr., informal* To get a ride by hitchhiking; hitchhike. *Not having much money, Carl decided to thumb a ride to New York.* (Since Carl was low on money he decided to hitch-hike to New York.)

thumb one's nose *v. phr.* **1** To hold one's open hand in front of one's face with one's thumb pointed at one's nose as a sign of scorn or dislike. *After Bob ran into the house he thumbed his nose at Tom through the window.* (Bob made an impolite gesture at Tom when he knew he was safe.) **2** *informal* To look with disfavor or dislike; regard with scorn; refuse to obey.—Used with *at*. *Betty thumbed her nose at her mother's command to stay home.* (Betty went out although her mother ordered her to stay home.) *Mary thumbed her nose at convention by wearing odd clothes.* (Mary wore odd clothes to show she didn't care about what other people thought was proper.)

thus and so *also* **thus and thus** *adv. phr.* In a particular way; according to directions that have been given. *The teacher is very fussy about the way you write your report. If you don't do it thus and so, she gives you a lower mark.* (If you don't write your report just the way the teacher tells you, she gives you a lower mark.)

tickle pink *v. phr., informal* To please very much; thrill; delight.—A trite expression, usually used in the passive participle. *Nancy was tickled pink with her new dress.* (Nancy was delighted with her new dress.)

tick off *v.* **1** To mention one after the other; list. *The teacher ticked off the assignments that Jane had to do.* (The teacher listed one assignment after the other.) **2** To scold; rebuke. *The boss ticked off the waitress for dropping her tray.* (He criticized her harshly.) **3** To anger or upset. Usually used as *ticked off*. *She was ticked off at*

him for breaking their dinner date again. (She was angry at him because he again cancelled their date to go to dinner.)

tide over *v.* To carry past a difficulty or danger; help in bad times or in trouble. *He was out of work last winter but he had saved enough money to tide him over until spring.* (He had enough money to live on until spring although he didn't work all winter.) *An ice cream cone in the afternoon tided her over until supper.* (The ice cream cone satisfied her hunger until it was time for supper.)

tie down *v.* To keep (someone) from going somewhere or doing something; prevent from leaving; keep in. *Mrs. Brown can't come to the party. She's tied down at home with the children sick.* (Mrs. Brown can't leave her sick children and come to the party.) *The navy tied the enemy down with big gun fire while the marines landed on the beach.* (The navy used big guns to keep the enemy from attacking the marines who were landing.) *I can't help you with history now! I'm tied down with these algebra problems.* (I can't help you now with your history because I must do my algebra problems.)

tied to one's mother's apron strings Not independent of one's mother; not able to do anything without asking one's mother. *Even after he grew up he was still tied to his mother's apron strings.* (Even after he grew up he was unable to make any decisions without asking his mother what to do.)

tie in *v.* To connect with something else; make a connection for.—Often used with *with*. *The teacher tied in what she said with* *last week's lesson.* (The teacher showed the connection between what she said today and last week's lesson.) *The English teacher sometimes gives compositions that tie in with things we are studying in other classes.* (The English assignment is sometimes about the same subject as the history or science assignment.) *The detectives tied in the fingerprints on the man's gun with those found on the safe, so they knew that he was the thief.* (The detectives connected the fingerprints on the gun with those found on the safe.)

tie in knots *v. phr.* To make (someone) very nervous or worried. *The thought of having her tooth pulled tied Joan in knots.* (Joan was made very nervous by the thought of having her tooth pulled.) *The little boy's experience with the kidnapper tied him in knots and it was hard for him to sleep well for a long time.* (His memories of the kidnapping made him nervous for a long time.)

tie into See LACE INTO.

tie one's hands *v. phr.* To make (a person) unable to do anything.—Usually used in the passive. *Since Mary would not tell her mother what was bothering her, her mother's hands were tied.* (Since Mary would not tell what her trouble was, her mother could do nothing to help her with it.) *Charles wanted to help John get elected president of the class, but his promise to another boy tied his hands.* (Charles could not help John, because his help was promised to another boy.) *Father hoped Jim would not quit school, but his hands were tied; Jim was old enough to quit if he wanted to.* (Father could not make Jim stay in school because the law did not make a son obey at his age.)

tie the knot *v. phr., informal* To get married; *also* to perform a wedding ceremony. *Diane and Bill tied the knot yesterday.* (Diane and Bill were married yesterday.) *The minister tied the knot for Diane and Bill yesterday.* (The minister married Diane and Bill yesterday.)

tie up *v.* **1** To show or stop the movement or action of; hinder; tangle. *The crash of the two trucks tied up all traffic in the center of town.* (The accident stopped traffic in the center of town.) *The strike tied up the factory.* (The strike slowed down—sometimes even stopped—the work done in the factory.) **2** To take all the time of. *The meeting will tie the president up until noon.* (The meeting will take all of the president's time until noon.) *The Senate didn't vote because a debate on a small point kept it tied up all week.* (A debate on a small point kept the Senate from voting.) *He can't see you now. He's tied up on the telephone.* (He can't see you now because he can't leave the telephone call he is making.) **3** To limit or prevent the use of. *His money is tied up in a trust fund and he can't take it out.* (His money has been put in a trust fund so he can't take it out all at once.) *Susan tied up the bathroom for an hour.* (She used it for an hour and nobody else could use it.) **4** To enter into an association or partnership; join. *Our company has tied up with another firm to support the show.* (Our company has joined with another to put the show on.) **5** To dock. *The ships tied up at New York.* (The ships docked at New York.) **6** *slang* To finish; complete. *We've talked long enough; let's tie up these* *plans and start doing things.* (Let's finish making these plans.)

tight end *n.* An end in football who plays close to the tackle in the line. *The tight end is used to catch passes but most often to block.* (The end that plays close to the tackle is used mostly as a blocker although he does catch passes.)

tighten one's belt *v. phr.* To live on less money than usual; use less food and other things.—A trite phrase. *When father lost his job we had to tighten our belts.* (When father lost his job we had to do without many things.) Often used in the expression tighten one's belt another notch. *Father lost his job and we had to do without many things, but when our savings were all spent, we had to tighten our belts another notch.* (We learned to use even less food and other things than before.)

tighten the screws *v. phr.* To try to make someone do something by making it more and more difficult not to do it; apply pressure. *When many students still missed class after he began giving daily quizzes, the teacher tightened the screws by failing anyone absent four times.* (The teacher put more pressure on students to come to class by adding a more severe punishment.)

Tijuana taxi *n., slang, citizen's band radio jargon* A police car. *I've got a Tijuana taxi in sight.* (I have spotted a police car.)

till the last gun is fired *or* **until the last gun is fired** *adv. phr.* Until the end; until everything is finished or decided. *Fred always liked to stay at parties until the last gun was fired.* (He wanted to stay until the very end.) *The candidate didn't give up hope of being elected until the last gun was*

fired. (He didn't give up until it was clearly over.)

time and again *or* **time and time again** *adv.* Many times; repeatedly; very often. *I've told you time and again not to touch the vase!* (I've told you many many times not to touch the vase!) *Children are forgetful and must be told time and time again how to behave.* (Children must be told many times before they will remember.)

time and a half *n. phr.* Pay given to a worker at a rate half again as much as he usually gets. *John got time and a half when he worked beyond his usual quitting time.* (John got paid his usual rate plus half of it besides for working late.) *Tom gets one dollar for regular pay and a dollar and a half for time and a half.* (Tom gets a dollar plus half of a dollar when he works late.)

time is ripe The best time has come for doing something. *The Prime Minister will hold elections when the time is ripe.* (The Prime Minister will call for elections when he thinks he will win.) *Lee saw his mother was upset, so he decided the time was not ripe to tell her about the broken window.* (Lee decided that it was not a good time to tell his mother that he had broken the window.)

time of one's life *n. phr.* A very gay or wonderful time. *John had the time of his life at the party.* (John had a wonderful time at the party.) *I could see that she was having the time of her life.* (It was plain that she was enjoying herself greatly.)

time out *n. phr.* Time during which a game or other activity is stopped for a while for some reason. *He took a time out from studying to go to a movie.* (He interrupted his studying to go to a movie.) *The player called time out so he could tie his shoe.* (The player stopped the game so he could tie his shoe.)

tip off *v., informal* To tell something not generally known; tell secret facts to; warn. *The class president tipped off the class that it was the superintendent's birthday.* (The class president informed the class in private that it was the superintendent's birthday.) *The thieves did not rob the bank as planned because someone tipped them off that it was being watched by the police.* (Someone warned them that the bank was being watched.)

tip the scales *v. phr., informal* **1** To weigh. *Martin tips the scales at 180 pounds.* (Martin weighs 180 pounds.) **2** *or* **tip the balance** To have important or decisive influence; make a decision go for or against you; decide. *John's vote tipped the scales in our favor, and we won the election.* (John's vote gave us the most votes, and we won.)

tit for tat *n. phr.* Equal treatment in return; a fair exchange. *Billy hit me, so I gave him tit for tat.* (Billy hit me, so I hit him back.) *I told him if he did me any harm I would return tit for tat.* (I said I would return harm for harm.) *They had a warm debate and the two boys gave each other tit for tat.* (Each boy answered the other with good points.)

to a degree *adv. phr.* **1** *Chiefly British* Very; to a large extent. *In some things I am ignorant to a degree.* (In some things I am very ignorant.) **2** Somewhat; slightly; in a small way; rather. *His anger was, to a degree, a confession of defeat.* (His anger gave a hint that he was defeated.) *To a degree,*

Mary was to blame for Bob's failing mathematics, because he spent much time with her when he should have been studying. (Mary was a little to blame for John's failure.)

to advantage *adv. phr.* So as to bring out the good qualities of; favorably; in a flattering way. *The jeweler's window showed the diamonds to advantage.* (The jeweler's window brought out the beauty in the diamonds.) *The green dress showed up to advantage with her red hair.* (The green dress and her red hair went well together.)

to a fault *adv. phr.* So very well that it is in a way bad; to the point of being rather foolish; too well; too much. *Aunt May wants everything in her house to be exactly right; she is neat to a fault.* (Aunt May is really too neat; she makes other people uncomfortable.) *Mary acts her part to a fault.* (Mary acts her part very well, but she acts so realistically that she draws attention to herself.) *John carries thoroughness to a fault; he spends many hours writing his reports.* (John is too thorough; he spends more time than is helpful in writing his reports.)

to all intents and purposes *adv. phr.* In most ways; in fact. *The president is called the head of state, but the prime minister, to all intents and purposes, is the chief executive.* (The prime minister is the one who really does most of the administrative work.)

to a man *adv. phr.* Without exception; with all agreeing. *The workers voted to a man to go on strike.* (Every single worker voted to go on strike.) *To a man John's friends stood by him in his trouble.* (They all were loyal to him.)

to and fro *adv.* *phr.* Forward and back again and again. *Father pushed Judy in the swing, and she went to and fro.* (Judy swung forward and back, again and again.) *Buses go to and fro between the center of the city and the city limits.* (Buses go from the center of the city to the city limits and back, again and again.) *The man walked to and fro while he waited for his phone call.* (The man walked away and came back many times while he was waiting for his phone call.)

to a T *or* **to a turn** *adv.* *phr.* Just right; to perfection; exactly. *The roast was done to a turn.* (The roast was done just right.) *His nickname, Tiny, suited him to a T.* (He was so small that "Tiny" fitted him.)

to-be *adj.* That is going to be; about to become.—Used after the noun it modifies. *Bob kissed his bride-to-be.* (Bob kissed the girl who is going to marry him.) *The principal of the high school greeted the high school students-to-be on their last day in junior high.* (The principal spoke to the junior high students who will be in high school next year.)

to be sure *adv.* *phr.* Without a doubt; certainly; surely. *"Didn't you say Mr. Smith would take us home?" "Oh, yes. To be sure, I did."* (That's right. I did say that.)—Often used before a clause beginning with *but*. *He works slowly, to be sure, but he does a good job.* (No doubt he works slowly, but he does a good job.) *To be sure, Jim is a fast skater, but he is not good at doing figures.* (It is true that Jim is a good skater, but he is not good at figure-skating.)

to blame *adj.* *phr.* Having done something wrong; to be blamed; responsible. *John was to blame for the broken window.* (John broke the window.) *The teacher tried to find out who was to blame in the fight.* (The teacher tried to find out who started the fight.)

to boot *adv.* *phr.* In addition; besides; as something extra. *He not only got fifty dollars, but they bought him dinner to boot.* (He was given the fifty dollars and in addition they paid for his dinner.)

to date *adv.* *or adj.* *phr.* Up to the present time; until now. *To date twenty students have been accepted into the school.* (Up to now, twenty students have been accepted into the school.) *The police have not found the runaway to date.* (The police have not found the runaway yet.) *Jim is shoveling snow to earn money, but his earnings to date are small.* (Jim has earned only a little money up to the present time.)

to death *adv. phr., informal* To the limit; to the greatest degree possible.—A trite phrase used for emphasis with verbs such as *scare, frighten, bore. Cowboy stories bore me to death, but I like mysteries.* (I don't like cowboy stories because I find them dull.) *Sara is scared to death of snakes.* (Sara is very much afraid of snakes.) *John is tickled to death with his new bike.* (John likes his new bike very much.)

toe the line *or* **toe the mark** *v. phr.* To be very careful to do just what you are supposed to do; obey the rules and do your duties. *The new teacher will make Joe toe the line.* (The new teacher will make Joe behave and do his work.) *Bill's father is strict with him and he has to toe the mark.* (Bill's father expects him to obey him and do right.)

together with *prep.* In addition to; in the company of; along with. *John, together with his brother, has gone to the party.* (John has gone to the party with his brother.) *The police found a knife, together with the stolen money, hidden in a hollow tree.* (The police found a knife, besides the stolen money, in a hollow tree.)

to heel *adj. phr.* **1** Close behind. *The dog ran after a rabbit, but Jack brought him to heel.* (Jack made the dog stay just behind him.) **2** Under control; to obedience. *When Peter was sixteen, he thought he could do as he pleased, but his father cut off his allowance, and Peter soon came to heel.* (Peter soon began to obey his father again.)

Tom, Dick, and Harry *n. phr.* People in general; anyone; everyone.—Usually preceded by *every* and used to show scorn or disrespect. *The drunk told his troubles to every Tom, Dick and Harry who passed by.* (The drunk told his troubles to anyone who happened to pass by.)

tone down *v.* To make softer or quieter; make less harsh or strong; moderate. *He toned down the sound of the TV.* (He made the sound softer and quieter.) *She wanted the bright colors in her house toned down.* (She wanted softer colors, not too bright.) *When the ladies arrived, he toned down his language.* (He talked more quietly and politely.) *The strikers were asked to tone down their demands for higher pay so that there might be a quicker agreement and an end to the strike.* (The strikers were asked to reduce their demands so the company would accept them.)

tongue-lashing *n.* A sharp scolding or criticism. *Jim's*

mother gave him a tongue-lashing for telling family secrets. (Jim's mother scolded him very much for telling secrets.)

tongues wag *informal* People speak in an excited or gossipy manner; people spread rumors. *If married women go out with other men, tongues will wag.* (People will talk about them.) *When the bank clerk showed up in an expensive new car, tongues wagged.* (They began to wonder where the clerk got the money to buy such an expensive car.)

to no avail *or* **of no avail**[1] *adj. phr., formal* Having no effect; useless, unsuccessful. *Tom's practicing was of no avail. He was sick on the day of the game.* (Tom's practicing for the game was useless because he couldn't play.) *Mary's attempts to learn embroidery were to no avail.* (Mary couldn't learn embroidering.)

to no avail[2] *adv. phr., formal* Without result; unsuccessfully. *John tried to pull the heavy cart, but to no avail.* (John tried to pull the cart but he couldn't.) *Mary studied hard for the test but to no avail.* (Mary studied hard, but she failed the test.)

too bad *adj.* To be regretted; worthy of sorrow or regret; regrettable.—Used as a predicate. *It is too bad that we are so often lazy.* (It is to be regretted that we are so often lazy.) *It was too bad Bill had measles when the circus came to town.* (It was bad luck for Bill to have measles so he missed the circus.)

too big for one's breeches *or* **too big for one's boots** *adj. phr.* Too sure of one's own importance; feeling more important than one really is. *That boy had grown too big for his breeches. I'll have* *to put him back in his place.* (That boy is acting much more important than he is. I'll have to make him less proud.) *When the teacher made Bob a monitor, he got too big for his boots and she had to warn him.* (He got too proud of himself and too rough with the other pupils.)

too ——— by half *adj.* *(princ. British)* Much too; excessively. *The heroine of the story is too nice by half; she is not believable.* (The reader cannot believe anyone would be that nice.)

to oneself[1] *adv. phr.* **1** Silently; in the thoughts; without making a sign that others can see; secretly. *Tom thought to himself that he could win.* (Tom thought he could win, but he told no one so.) *Mary said to herself that Joan was prettier than Ann.* (Mary judged that Joan was prettier, but she didn't tell Joan.) *Bill laughed to himself when John fell down.* (Bill laughed silently and did not let John see he was laughing.) **2** Without telling others; in private; as a secret.—Used after *keep.* *Mary keeps her affairs to herself.* (Mary doesn't tell others about what she is doing.) *John knew the answer to the problem, but he kept it to himself.* (John didn't tell anyone the answer to the problem.)

to oneself[2] *adj. phr.* **1** Without company; away from others; alone; deserted. *The boys went home and John was left to himself.* (The boys went home and left John alone.) *When Mary first moved to her new neighborhood she was very shy and kept to herself.* (Mary did not mix with other people; she stayed alone.) **2** Following one's own beliefs or wishes; not stopped by others. *When John insisted on going,*

Fred left him to himself. (When John insisted, Fred gave up trying to stop him from going.) *The teacher left Mary to herself to solve the problem.* (The teacher didn't help Mary, but let her solve the problem in her own way.)

to one's face *adv. phr.* Directly to you; in your presence. *I told him to his face that I didn't like the idea.* (I told him directly that I didn't like the idea.) *I called him a coward to his face.* (I told him plainly that he was a coward.)

to one's feet *adv. phr.* To a standing position; up. *After Henry had been tackled hard by four big players, he got to his feet slowly and painfully.* (Henry stood up slowly and painfully.) *When Sally saw the bus coming, she jumped to her feet and ran out.* (Sally stood up quickly.)

to one's heart's content *adv. phr.* As much as you want. *She told them they could eat cake to their heart's content.* (She told them they could eat all the cake they wanted.) *There was even a place where he could dig to his heart's content.* (There was a place where he could dig as much as he wanted.)

to one's name *adv. phr.* In your ownership; of your own; as part of your belongings. *David did not have a book to his name.* (David owned no books.) *Ed had only one suit to his name.* (He owned only one suit.)

to order *adv. phr.* According to directions given in an order in the way and size wanted. *The manufacturer built the machine to order.* (The manufacturer made the machine in the style and size asked for in the customer's order.) *A very big man often has his suits made to order.* (He orders suits made in his size and as he wants them.)

tooth and nail *adv. phr.* With all weapons or ways of fighting as hard as possible; fiercely.—Used after *fight* or a similar word. *The farmers fought tooth and nail to save their crops from the grasshoppers.* (They did everything they could to kill and drive off the grasshoppers and save their crops.) *His friends fought tooth and nail to elect him to Congress.* (They tried very hard to help him win.)

top banana or **top dog** *n., informal* The head of any business or organization; the most influential or most prestigious person in an establishment. *Who's the top banana/dog in this outfit?* (Who is the boss in the place?)

top-drawer *adj., informal* Of the best; or most important kind. *Mary's art work was top-drawer material.* (Her work was the best among the artists.) *Mr. Rogers is a top-drawer executive and gets a very high salary.* (Mr. Rogers is an important boss in his company.)

to pieces *adv. phr.* **1** Into broken pieces or fragments; destroyed. *The cannon shot the town to pieces.* (The cannon destroyed the town.) *The vase fell to pieces in Mary's hand.* (The vase broke in Mary's hand.) **2** *informal* So as not to work; into a state of not operating. *After 100,000 miles the car went to pieces.* (After 100,000 miles the car wouldn't run any more.) *When Mary heard of her mother's death, she went to pieces.* (When Mary heard the news, she became so upset she could do nothing.) **3** *informal* Very much; greatly; exceedingly.—A hackneyed phrase. *Joan was thrilled to pieces to see*

Mary. (Joan was very glad to see Mary.) *The noise scared Bob to pieces.* (The noise scared Bob very much.)

top off *v.* To come or bring to a special or unexpected ending; climax. *John batted three runs and topped off the game with a home run.* (John completed his good day by hitting a home run.) *Mary hadn't finished her home work, she was late to school, and to top it all off she missed a surprise test.* (Mary had a lot of trouble, but missing the test was the worst trouble of all.) *George had steak for dinner and topped it off with a hot fudge sundae.* (George brought a good dinner to a special ending with a hot fudge sundae.)

to scale *adv. phr.* in the same proportions as in the true size; in the same shape, but not the same size. *The statue was made to scale, one inch to a foot.* (The statue was one-twelfth full size.) *He drew the map to scale, making one inch represent fifty miles.* (One inch on the map was fifty miles in real length.)

to speak of *adj. phr., informal* Important; worth talking about; worth noticing.—Usually used in negative sentences. *Did it rain yesterday? Not to speak of.* (Did it rain? Very little.) *What happened at the meeting? Nothing to speak of.* (Nothing very important happened.) *Judy's injuries were nothing to speak of; just a few scratches.* (Judy was not hurt much.)

toss off *v.* **1** To drink rapidly; drain. *He tossed off two drinks and left.* (He quickly drank two drinks and left.) **2** To make or say easily without trying or thinking hard. *She tossed off smart remarks all during dinner.* (She made many witty remarks all through dinner.) *He thinks a re-porter should be able to toss off an article every few hours.* (He thinks a news writer should be able to write many articles quickly and without any trouble.)

to that effect *adj.* or *adv. phr.* With that meaning. *She said she hated spinach, or words to that effect.* (She said she hated spin-ach, or said something that meant she hated spinach.) *When I leave, I will write you to that effect so you will know.* (When I leave, I will write and tell you that I have left.)

to the best of one's knowledge As far as one knows; to the extent of one's knowledge. *He has never won a game, to the best of my knowledge.* (If he has won a game, I don't know about it.) *To the best of my knowledge he is a college man, but I may be mis-taken.* (I think he is a college man.)

to the bitter end *adv. phr.* To the point of completion or conclu-sion. *Although Mrs. Smith was bored by the lecture, she stayed to the bitter end.* (Although bored by the lecture, Mrs. Smith stayed un-til it was over.) *They knew the war would be lost, but the men fought to the bitter end.* (They kept on fighting though they knew it was no use.)

to the bone *adv., slang, informal* Thoroughly, entirely, to the core, through all layers. *I am dreadfully tired; I've worked my fingers to the bone.* (I've worked so hard that it almost eroded the flesh off my hands—an obvious exaggera-tion.)

to the contrary *adv.* or *adj. phr.* With an opposite result or effect; just the opposite; in disagreement; saying the opposite. *Although Bill was going to the movies, he told*

Joe to the contrary. (Bill was go-ing but he said he was not.) *We will expect you for dinner unless we get word to the contrary.* (We will expect you for dinner unless you send us a message saying you cannot come.) *School gossip to the contrary, Mary is not engaged to be married.* (Mary isn't en-gaged, but the gossip say she is.)

to the effect that *adj. phr.* With the meaning or purpose; to say that. *He made a speech to the effect that we would all keep our jobs even if the factory were sold.* (He made a speech to say that we would all keep our jobs even if the factory were sold.) *The new governor would do his best in the office to which he had been elected.* (He made a few remarks with the meaning that he would do his best.)

to the eye *adv. phr.* As it is seen; as a person or thing first seems; apparently. *That girl looks to the eye like a nice girl to know, but she is really rather mean.* (That girl appears at first to be a nice girl, but she isn't.) *That suit appears to the eye to be a good buy, but it may not be.* (The suit may not be as it appears.)

to the fore *adv.* or *adj. phr.* Into leadership; out into notice or view; forward. *The hidden skill of the lawyer came to the fore during the trial.* (The lawyer's abilities had not been noticed before, but everyone saw them during the trial.) *In the progress of the war some new leaders came to the fore.* (Men who were not known before were noticed and promoted to leadership.)

to the full *adv. phr.* Very much; fully. *The campers enjoyed their trip to the full.* (The campers enjoyed their trip very much.) *We appreciated to the full the* *teacher's help*. (We were very grateful for the teacher's help.)

to the good *adv. phr.* On the side of profit or advantage; in one's favor; to one's benefit; ahead. *After I sold my stamp collection, I was ten dollars to the good.* (I made ten dollars profit when I sold my stamp collection.) *The teacher did not see him come in late, which was all to the good.* (Luckily, the teacher did not see him come in late.)

to the hilt *or* **up to the hilt** *adv. phr.* To the limit; as far as possible; completely. *The other boys on the team told Tom he couldn't quit. They said, "You're in this to the hilt."* (The boys told Tom that he had promised his complete loyalty to the team.) *The Smith's house is mortgaged up to the hilt.* (The Smith's house is mortgaged as much as it can be mortgaged; they can not borrow any more money on it.)

to the king's taste *or* **to the queen's taste** *adv. phr.* Perfectly; just as anyone could want it; very satisfactorily. *The rooms in their new home were painted and decorated to the queen's taste.* (The rooms could not be more perfectly decorated.) *The soldiers dressed and marched to the king's taste.* (Even a king couldn't expect better dressed or trained soldiers.)

to the letter *adv. phr.* With nothing done wrong or left undone; exactly; precisely. *He carried out his orders to the letter.* (He did everything exactly as he was told.) *When writing a test you should follow the instructions to the letter.* (You should follow them exactly.)

to the manner born *adj. phr.* At ease with something because of lifelong familiarity with it. *She says her English is the best because she is to the manner born.* (She claims that hers is the most correct English because she grew up among people who spoke only correct English, so it comes naturally.)

to the nth degree *adv. phr.* To the greatest degree possible; extremely; very much so. *Scales must be accurate to the nth degree.* (Scales must be as exact as possible.) *His choice of words was exactly to the nth degree.* (He always used his words in exactly the right way and place.)

to the tune of *adv. phr., informal* To the amount or extent of; in the amount of. *He had to pay to the tune of fifty dollars for seeing how fast the car would go.* (It cost him fifty dollars for speeding because he wanted to see how fast his car would go.) *When she left the race track she had profited to the tune of ten dollars.* (She won ten dollars.)

to the wall *adv. phr.* Into a place from which there is no escape; into a trap or corner. *John's failing the last test drove him to the wall.* (By failing the last test, John no longer had a chance of passing the course.) *The score was 12–12 in the last minute of play, but a touchdown forced the visitors to the wall.* (Our side won the game in the last minute of play.) *Bill had to sell his five Great Danes. The high cost of feeding them was driving him to the wall.* (He had to sell the dogs because he could not afford to keep on feeding them.)

touch and go *adj. phr.* Very dangerous or uncertain in situation. *Our team won the game, all right, but it was touch and go for a while.* (Our team won, but for a while it looked like we wouldn't win.) *At one time while they were climbing the cliff it was touch and go whether they could do it.* (They were in a dangerous place and might have fallen.)

touch off *v.* **1** To cause to fire or explode by lighting the priming or the fuse. *The boy touched off a firecracker.* (The boy lit the fuse of a firecracker, and it exploded.) **2** To start something as if by lighting a fuse. *The coach's resignation touched off a quarrel.* (The coach's resignation started a quarrel.)

touch on *or* **touch upon** *v.* To speak of or write of briefly. *The speaker touched on several other subjects in the course of his talk but mostly kept himself to the main topic.* (The speaker kept mostly to his topic although he did mention briefly several other topics.)

touch up *v.* **1** To paint over (small imperfections.) *I want to touch up that scratch on the fender.* (I want to paint over the scratch on the fender.) *The woodwork is done, but there are a few places he has to touch up.* (The woodwork has been done but there are still a few places that need a little more paint.) **2** To improve with small additions or changes. *He touched up the photographic negative to make a sharper print.* (He made small improvements in the negative so that the picture would be sharper.) *It's a good speech, but it needs a little touching up.* (It's a good speech, but it needs a few small improvements.) **3** *slang* To talk into lending; wheedle from. *He touched George up for five bucks.* (He talked George into lending him five dollars.)

tough cat *n., slang* A man who is very individualistic and, as a result, highly successful with women. *Joe is a real tough cat, man.* (He is highly individualistic and succeeds easily with women.)

track down *v.* To find by or as if by following tracks or a trail. *The hunters tracked down game in the forest.* (The hunters found animals in the forest by following the animals' trails.) *She spent weeks in the library tracking the reference down in all their books on the subject.* (She spent weeks in the library hunting through books to find the reference.)

trade in *v.* To give something to a seller as part payment for another thing of greater value. *The Browns traded their old car in on a new one.* (The Browns gave their old car to the dealer as part payment for the new one.)

trade-in *n.* Something given as part payment on something better. *The dealer took our old car as a trade-in.* (The dealer took our old car as part payment on a new one.)—Often used like an adjective. *We cleaned up the car at trade-in time.* (We cleaned up the car when it was time to trade it in.)

trade on *v.* To use as a way of helping yourself. *The coach traded on the pitcher's weakness for left-handed batters by using all his southpaws.* (The coach used his own left-handers because in that way he could best take advantage of the other side's weakness. *The senator's son traded on his father's name when he ran for mayor.* (The son was unknown, but his father was famous. So the son made sure that everyone knew whose son he was.)

travel light *v. phr.* To travel with very little luggage or with very little to carry. *Plane passengers must travel light.* (Plane passengers cannot take very much baggage.) *Tom and Fred traveled light on their camping trip.* (Tom and Fred carried small packs and no tents.)

tread water *v. phr.* To keep the head above water with the body in an upright position by moving the feet as if walking. *He kept afloat by treading water.* (He kept his head above water by moving his feet up and down.)

trial and error *n.* A way of solving problems by trying different possible solutions until you find one that works. *John found the short circuit by trial and error.* (John kept testing different wires until he found the one that was causing the short circuit.) *The only way Tom could solve the algebra problem was by the method of trial and error.* (Tom had to solve the problem by guessing at possible answers and then seeing if they would satisfy the problem.)

trial balloon *n.* A hint about a plan of action that is given out to find out what people will say. *John mentioned the class presidency to Bill as a trial balloon to see if Bill might be interested in running.* (John mentioned the presidency to see if Bill might make some remarks about the job.) *The editorial was a trial balloon to test the public's reaction to a change in the school day.* (The editorial was designed to get the public to write letters in support of, or against changing the school day.)

trick of the trade *n. phr.; usually in plural, informal* **1** A piece of expert knowledge; a smart, quick, or skillful way of working at a trade or job. *Mr. Olson spent years learning the tricks of the trade as a carpenter.*

(He spent years learning to do the work quickly and well.) *Anyone can learn how to hang wallpaper, but only an expert can show you the tricks of the trade.* (An expert can show you the quickest way to do it.) **2** A smart and sometimes tricky or dishonest way of doing something in order to succeed or win. *The champion knows all the tricks of the boxing trade; he knows many ways to hurt his opponent and to get him mixed up.* (The champion knows many tricks and unfair ways to beat his opponents.)

trick or treat *n.* The custom of going from house to house on Halloween asking for small gifts and playing tricks on people who refuse to give. *When Mrs. Jones answered the doorbell, the children yelled "Trick or treat." Mrs. Jones gave them all some candy.* (Mrs. Jones gave the children candy so they would not play a trick on her.) *On Halloween Bill and Tom went out playing trick or treat.* (Bill and Tom went out begging food and threatening to play tricks if they were refused.)

triple threat *n.* A football player who is able to pass, kick, and run all very well. *The triple threat halfback was the star of the team.* (Because he could do all these things well, he was the most valuable offensive player on the team.)

tripped out *adj., slang, informal* Incoherent, confused, faulty of speech, illogical; as if under the influence of drugs or alcohol. *It was hard to make sense of anything Max said yesterday; he sounded so tripped out.* (People had difficulty understanding Max, for he was so confused and illogical.)

trip up *v.* **1** To make (someone) unsteady on the feet; cause to miss a step, stumble, or fall. *A root tripped Billy up while he was running in the woods, and he fell and hurt his ankle.* (The root of a tree caught Billy's foot while he was running.) **2** To cause (someone) to make a mistake. *The teacher asked tricky questions in the test to trip up students who were not alert.* (The teacher put tricky questions in the test to catch those students who were not giving careful attention.)

trump card *n.* Something kept back to be used to win success if nothing else works. *The coach saved his star pitcher for a trump card.* (The coach kept his star pitcher in reserve in case he was needed later in the game to stop the other team.) *Mary had several ways to get Joan to come to her party. Her trump card was that the football captain would be there.* (Mary would use all her other reasons before she told Joan about the football captain, but then Joan would be sure to come.)

trump up *v.* To make up (something untrue); invent in the mind. *Every time Tom is late getting home he trumps up some new excuse.* (He makes up an untrue story to explain his being late.) *The Russians were afraid he was a spy, so they arrested him on a trumped-up charge and made him leave the country.* (The Russians arrested him on false accusations and made him leave the country.)

try on *v.* To put (clothing) on to see if it fits. *She tried on several pairs of shoes before she found one she liked.* (She put on several pairs of shoes before she found a comfortable pair.) *The clerk told him to try the coat on.* (The clerk told him to put on the coat and see how he liked it.)

try one's hand *v. phr.* To make an inexperienced attempt (at something unfamiliar.) *I thought I would try my hand at bowling, although I had never bowled before.* (I thought I would give bowling a try although I had never bowled before.)

try out *v.* **1** To test by trial or by experimenting. *He tried golf out to see if he would like it.* (To see if he would like golf, he tried playing the game.) *The scientists tried out thousands of chemicals before they found the right one.* (The chemists tested thousands of chemicals before they found the one they needed.) *The coach wants to try the new play out in the first game.* (The coach wants to see if the new play will work.) **2** To try for a place on a team or in a group. *Tom tried out for the basketball team.* (Tom went to basketball practice and tried to be chosen as a member of the team.) *Shirley will try out for the lead in the play.* (Shirley will practice the leading part in the play and hopes she will be selected to play it.)

tug-of-war *n.* **1** A game in which two teams pull on opposite ends of a rope, trying to pull the other team over a line marked on the ground. *The tug-of-war ended when both teams tumbled in a heap.* (Both teams fell down together and neither side won.) **2** A contest in which two sides try to defeat each other; struggle. *A tug-of-war developed between the boys who wanted to go fishing and those who wanted to go hiking.* (The boys who wanted to go fishing started arguing with those who wanted to go hiking.) *Betty felt a tug-of-war between her wish to go to the movies and her realizing* she had to do her homework. (Betty felt pulled to one side by her wishes and to the other side by her duty.) *The tug of war between the union men and management ended in a long strike.* (The meetings between the Union and the company failed to settle the problem.

tune in To adjust a radio or television set to pick up a certain station. *Bob tuned in his portable radio to a record show.* (Bob set his radio to a station playing records.) *Tom tuned in to Channel 11 to hear the news.* (Tom got Channel 11 on the television so that he could hear the news.)

tune up v. **1a** To adjust (a musical instrument) to make the right sound. *Before he began to play, Harry tuned up his banjo.* (Harry put his banjo in tune by tightening the strings to the proper sound.) **1b** To adjust a musical instrument or a group of musical instruments to the right sound. *The orchestra came in and began to tune up for the concert.* (The members of the orchestra adjusted their instruments so they could play together.) **2** To adjust many parts of (car engine) which must work together so that it will run properly. *He took his car to the garage to have the engine tuned up.* (He took the car to the garage so that the mechanics could adjust the parts of the engine to run properly.)

tune-up n. **1** The adjusting or fixing of something (as a motor) to make it work safely and well. *Father says the car needs a tune-up before winter begins.* (Things wrong with the car's motor must be fixed or corrected before winter starts.) **2** Exercise or practicing for the purpose of getting ready; a trial before something.

The team went to the practice field for their last tune-up before the game tomorrow. (The team will have exercise and practice for the last time before their game.)

turn a blind eye v. phr. To pretend not to see; not pay attention. *The corrupt police chief turned a blind eye to the open gambling in the town.* (The police chief pretended not to know there was gambling in the town.) *Bob turned a blind eye to the "No Fishing" sign.* (Bob pretended not to see the "No Fishing" sign.)

turn a deaf ear to v. phr. To pretend not to hear; refuse to hear; not pay attention. *Mary turned a deaf ear to Lois's asking to ride her bicycle.* (Mary paid no attention when Lois asked to ride her bicycle.) *The teacher turned a deaf ear to Bob's excuse.* (The teacher would not listen to Bob's excuse.)

turn a hand v. phr. To do anything to help.—Usually used in the negative. *When we were all hurrying to get the house ready for company, Mary sat reading and wouldn't turn a hand.* (Mary refused to help.)

turn color v. phr. To become a different color. *In the fall the leaves turn color.* (In the fall the leaves turn from green to red and brown.) *When the dye was added the solution turned color.* (The dye changed the color of the solution.)

turn down v. **1** To reduce the loudness, brightness, or force of. *The theater lights were turned down.* (The lights were dimmed.) *Turn down that radio, will you?* (Please make the radio play more quietly.) *The hose was throwing too much water so I turned down the water a little bit.* (I reduced the pressure of the water in the hose.) **2** To refuse to accept; reject. *His request for a raise was turned down.* (He asked for a raise but it was refused.) *If she offers to help, I'll turn her down.* (I won't accept any help from her.) *Many boys courted Lynn, but she turned them all down.* (Many boys courted Lynn, but she wouldn't marry any of them.)

turn in *v.* **1** *or* **hand in** To give to someone; deliver to someone. *I want you to turn in a good history paper.* (I want you to give me a good history paper.) *When the football season was over, we turned in our uniforms.* (At the end of the season we returned our uniforms.) **2** To inform on; report. *She turned them in to the police for breaking the street light.* (She reported them to the police for breaking the street light.) **3** To give in return for something. *They turned in their old money for new.* (They gave their old money in exchange for new.) *We turned our car in on a new model.* (We gave our old car as part payment for a new one.) **4** *informal* To go to bed. *We were tired, so we turned in about nine o'clock.* (We went to bed at about nine o'clock.)

turn in one's grave *or* **turn over in one's grave** *v. phr.* To be so grieved or angry that you would not rest quietly in your grave. *If your grandfather could see what you're doing now, he would turn over in his grave.* (Your grandfather would be so angry with what you're doing he wouldn't be able to lie still in his grave.)

turn off *v.* **1** To stop by turning a knob or handle or by working a switch; to cause to be off. *He turned the water off.* (He stopped the water by turning the handle.) *He turned off the light.* (He made

the light go off by working the switch.) **2** To leave by turning right or left onto another way. *Turn off the highway at exit 5.* (Leave the highway at exit 5.) *The car turned off on Bridge Street.* (The car went off the street it was on and turned and went along Bridge Street.) *slang* **3** To disgust, bore, or repel (someone) by being intellectually, emotionally, socially, or sexually unattractive. *I won't date Linda Bell anymore—she just turns me off.* (I am repelled by her.)

turn of the century *n. phr.* The time at the end of one century and the beginning of the next century; *especially:* The time when the 1800's became the 1900's; the early 1900's. *Automobiles were strange things to see at the turn of the century.* (About the year 1900 people were surprised to see automobiles.)

turn on *v.* **1** To start by turning a knob or handle or working a switch; cause to be on. *Jack turned on the water.* (Jack started the water running by turning the handle.) *Who turned the lights on?* (Who switched the lights on?) **2** *informal* To put forth or succeed with as easily as turning on water. *She really turns on the charm when that new boy is around.* (She makes herself charming when the new boy is around.) **3** To attack. *The lion tamer was afraid the lions would turn on him.* (The lion tamer was afraid the lions would attack him.) *After Joe fumbled the ball and lost the big game, his friends turned on him.* (Even his friends said bad things about him because he lost the game.) **4** *slang* The opposite of turning someone off; to become greatly interested in an idea, person, or undertaking; to arouse the senses pleasantly. *Mozart's music always turns me on.* (I always derive a pleasant sensation by listening to Mozart.) **5** Introducing someone to a new experience, or set of values. *Benjamin turned me on to transcendental meditation, and ever since I've been feeling great!* (He introduced me to meditation.)

turn one's back on *v. phr.* To refuse to help (someone in trouble or need.) *He turned his back on his own family when they needed help.* (He would not help his family when they needed it.) *The poorer nations are often not grateful for our help, but still we can not turn our back on them.* (We cannot refuse to help them.)

turn one's head *v. phr., informal* To make you lose your good judgment. *The first pretty girl he saw turned his head.* (The first pretty girl he saw made him act foolishly.) *Winning the class election turned his head.* (Winning the class election made him too proud of himself.)

turn one's stomach *v. phr., informal* To make you feel sick. *The smell of that cigar was enough to turn your stomach.* (The smell of that cigar was enough to make you sick.) *The sight of blood turns my stomach.* (I feel sick when I see blood.)

turn on one's heel *v. phr.* To turn around suddenly. *When John saw Fred approaching him, he turned on his heel.* (When John saw Fred, he turned around quickly so as not to have to speak to him.) *When little Tommy's big brother showed up, the bully turned on his heel.* (When the bully saw Tommy's brother, he ran away.)

turn out *v.* **1** To make leave or go away. *His father turned him out of the house.* (His father made him leave the house.) *If you don't behave, you will be turned out.* (If you don't behave, you will have to leave.) **2** To turn inside out; empty. *He turned out his pockets looking for the money.* (He turned his pockets inside out looking for the money.) **3** to make; produce. *The printing press turns out a thousand books an hour.* (The printing press prints a thousand books an hour.) **4** *informal* To get out of bed. *At camp the boys had to turn out early and go to bed early too.* (At camp they got up early.) **5** *informal* To come or go out to see or do something. *Everybody turned out for the big parade.* (Everybody came to watch the big parade.) **6** To prove to be; be in the end; be found to be. *The noise turned out to be just the dog scratching at the door.* (The noise proved to be just the dog scratching at the door.) **7** To make (a light) go out. *Please turn out the lights.* (Please switch the lights off.)

turn over *v.* **1** To roll, tip, or turn from one side to the other; overturn; upset. *He's going to turn over the page.* (He's going to turn the page from one side to the next.) **2** To think about carefully; to consider. *He turned the problem over in his mind for three days before he did anything about it.* (He thought about the problem three days before he did anything.) **3** To give to someone for use or care. *I turned my library books over to the librarian.* (I gave my library books to the librarian.) **4** Of an engine or motor; to start. *The battery is dead and the motor won't turn over.* (The battery is dead and the motor won't start.) **5a** To buy and then sell to customers. *The store* *turned over $5,000 worth of skiing equipment in January.* (The store sold $5,000 worth of things for skiing to customers after buying them from the makers.) **5b** To be bought in large enough amounts; sell. *In a shoe store, shoes of medium width turn over quickly, because many people wear that size, but a pair of narrow shoes may not be sold for years.* (A shoe store may buy and sell several pairs of shoes of medium width before it sells a pair of narrow width.)

turn over a new leaf *v. phr.* To make a sudden change for the better in conduct. *George turned over a new leaf and stopped disturbing the class.* (George suddenly began behaving much better in class.) *Julie decided to turn over a new leaf and study harder.* (Julie suddenly decided to be a better student.)

turn tail *v. phr., informal* To run away from trouble or danger. *When the bully saw my big brother, he turned tail and ran.* (The bully was scared and ran away from my big brother.)

turn the clock back *v. phr.* To return to an earlier period. *Mother wished she could turn the clock back to the days before the children grew up and left home.* (Mother wished to live again in the time when the children were living at home.) *Will repealing the minimum wage for workers under age eighteen turn the clock back to the abuses of the last century?* (Will the unfair practices of a hundred years ago come again?)

turn the other cheek *v. phr.* To let someone do something to you and not to do it in return; not hit back when hit; be patient when injured or insulted by someone; not try to get even. *Joe turned the*

other cheek when he was hit with a snowball. (He did not throw a snowball back at the person who hit him with one.)

turn the tables *v. phr.* To make something happen just the opposite of how it is supposed to happen. *The boys turned the tables on John when they took his squirt gun away and squirted him.* (John was going to squirt the boys, but they got his squirt gun and squirted him instead.)

turn the tide *v. phr.* To change what looks like defeat into victory. *We were losing the game until Jack got there. His coming turned the tide for us, and we won.* (We were losing the game until Jack came. He helped us turn the defeat into victory.)

turn the trick *v. phr., informal* To bring about the result you want; succeed in what you plan to do. *Jerry wanted to win both the swimming and diving contests, but he couldn't quite turn the trick.* (Jerry wanted to win both contests but he could only win one of them.)

turn thumbs down *v. phr.* To disapprove or reject; say no.— Usually used with *on*. *The company turned thumbs down on Mr. Smith's sales plan.* (The company refused to accept his sales plans.) *The men turned thumbs down on a strike at that time.* (They didn't approve of a strike at that time.)

turn turtle *v. phr.* To turn upside down. *The car skidded on the ice and turned turtle.* (The car skidded on the ice and turned upside down.)

turn up *v.* **1** To find; discover. The police searched the house hoping to turn up more clues. (The police searched the house hoping to find more things that would help explain what happened.) **2** To appear or be found suddenly or unexpectedly. *The missing boy turned up an hour later.* (The boy was found an hour later.) *A man without training works at whatever jobs turn up.* (He works at whatever jobs happen to come along.)

turn up one's nose at *v. phr.* To refuse as not being good enough for you. *He thinks he should only get steak, and he turns up his nose at hamburger.* (He thinks hamburger isn't good enough for him.)

turn up one's toes *v. phr., slang* To die. *One morning the children found that their pet mouse had turned up his toes, so they had a funeral for him.* (The mouse died.)

twiddle one's thumbs *v. phr.* To do nothing; be idle. *I'd rather work than stand around here twiddling my thumbs.* (I'd rather work than stand around doing nothing.)

twist——around one's little finger *also* **turn——around one's little finger** *or* **wrap ——around one's finger** *v. phr.* To have complete control over; to be able to make (someone) do anything you want. *Sue can twist any of the boys around her little finger.* (She can get any of the boys to do what she wants them to.)

twist one's arm *v. phr., informal* To force someone; threaten someone to make him do something.—Usually used jokingly. *Will you dance with the prettiest girl in school? Stop, you're twist-*ing my arm! (Don't worry, I don't have to be forced to dance with the pretty girl!) *I had to twist Tom's arm to make him eat the candy!* (Tom had to be forced to eat candy!)

two bits *n., slang* Twenty-five cents; a quarter of a dollar. *A haircut only cost two bits when Grandfather was young.* (You paid the barber only twenty-five cents for a haircut then.)

two cents *n., informal* **1** Something not important or very small; almost nothing. *Paul was so angry that he said for two cents he would quit the team.* (It would not take much to make Paul quit.) *When John saw that the girl he was scolding was lame, he felt like two cents.* (He was ashamed to be scolding a lame girl and felt very small.) **2** *or* **two cents worth** Something you want to say; opinion.—Used with a possessive. *The boys were talking about baseball, and Harry put in his two cents worth, even though he didn't know much about baseball.* (Harry said what he thought about it.) *If we want your two cents, we'll ask for it.* (If we want your opinion, we'll ask for it.)

two-time *v., slang* To go out with a second boy or girl friend and keep it a secret from the first. *Joan was two-timing Jim with Fred.* (Joan was Jim's girl, but she was going out with Fred without telling Jim.) *Mary cried when she found that Joe was two-timing her.* (Mary cried when she found out that Joe was dating another girl.)

U

ugly duckling *n.* An ugly or plain child who grows up to be pretty and attractive. *Mary was the ugly duckling in her family, until she grew up.* (Mary is pretty now but she was not a pretty child.)

under a cloud *adj. phr.* **1** Under suspicion; not trusted. *Joyce has been under a cloud since her roommate's bracelet disappeared.* (Joyce has been under suspicion of stealing her roommate's bracelet.) *The butcher is under a cloud because the inspectors found his scales were not honest.* (The butcher is not trusted because the inspectors found his scales did not weigh correctly.) **2** Depressed, sad, discouraged. *Joe has been under a cloud since his dog died.* (Joe has been very sad since his dog died.)

under age *adj. phr.* Too young; not old enough; below legal age. *He could not enlist in the army because he was under age.* (He could not enlist in the army because he was below age 18.) *Rose was not allowed to enroll in the Life Saving Course because she was under age.* (Rose was not permitted to take the Life Saving Course because she was not old enough.)

under arrest *adj. phr.* Held by the police. *The man believed to have robbed the bank was placed under arrest.* (The man was held by the police.) *The three boys were seen breaking into the school building and soon found themselves under arrest.* (The boys were seen breaking into the school building and soon found themselves held by the police.)

under cover *adv. or adj. phr.* Hidden; concealed. *The prisoners escaped under cover of darkness.* (The prisoners escaped, hidden by the darkness.) *He kept his invention under cover until it was patented.* (He concealed his invention until it was patented.)

under fire *adv. phr.* Being shot at or being attacked; hit by attacks or accusations; under attack. *The soldiers stood firm under fire of the enemy.* (The soldiers did not retreat when the enemy shot at them.) *The principal was under fire for not sending the boys home who stole the car.* (The principal was accused of being too easy.)

under one's belt *adv. phr., informal* **1** In your stomach; eaten; or absorbed. *Once he had a good meal under his belt, the man loosened his tie and fell asleep.* (When he had eaten a good meal, the man loosened his tie and fell asleep.) *Jones is talkative when he has a few drinks under his belt.* (Jones talks a lot when he has absorbed a few drinks.) **2** In your experience, memory or possession; learned or gotten successfully; gained by effort and skill. *Jim has to get a lot of algebra under his belt before the examination.* (Jim has to learn a lot of algebra before the examination.) *With three straight victories under their belts, the team went on to win the championship.* (After they won three games, the team kept winning until they were champions.)

under one's breath *adv. phr.* In a whisper; with a low voice. *The teacher heard the boy say something under his breath and she asked him to repeat it aloud.* (The teacher heard the boy whisper something and she asked him to say it aloud.) *I told Lucy the news under my breath, but Joyce overheard me.* (I told Lucy the news with a low voice, but Joyce heard what I said.)

under one's nose   *or*   **under the nose of**   *adv. phr., informal*   In sight of; in an easily seen or noticeable place. *The thief walked out of the museum with the painting, right under the nose of the guards.* (The thief walked out of the museum with the painting in sight of the guards.) *When Jim gave up trying to find a pen, he saw three right under his nose on the desk.* (When Jim gave up trying to find a pen, he saw three very close and in plain sight on the desk.)

under one's own steam   *adv. phr., informal*   By one's own efforts; without help. *The boys got to Boston under their own steam and took a bus the rest of the way.* (The boys got to Boston by their own efforts and took a bus the rest of the way.) *We didn't think he could do it, but Bobby finished his homework under his own steam.* (We didn't think he could do it, but Bobby finished his homework without help.)

under one's thumb   *or*   **under the thumb**   *adj. or adv. phr.*   Obedient to you; controlled by you; under your power. *The Jones family is under the thumb of the mother.* (Mrs. Jones makes her family obey her.) *Jack is a bully. He keeps all the younger children under his thumb.* (Jack is a bully. He controls all the younger children.) *The mayor is so popular that he has the whole town under his thumb.* (The mayor is so well-liked that he has the town under his influence.)

under one's wing   *adv. phr.*   Under the care or protection of. *Helen took the new puppy under her wing.* (Helen took care of the new puppy.) *The boys stopped teasing the new student when Bill took him under his wing.* (The boys stopped teasing the new student when Bill took him under his protection.)

under the circumstances   *also in the circumstances*   *adv. phr.*   In the existing situation; in the present condition; as things are. *In the circumstances, Father couldn't risk giving up his job.* (He couldn't take a chance on getting along without steady income because we needed the money.) *Under the circumstances, the stagecoach passengers had to give the robbers their money.* (The robbers had them at gunpoint and they could not refuse.)

under the counter   *adv. phr., informal*   Secretly (bought or sold). *That book has been banned, but there is one place you can get it under the counter.* (That book has been forbidden, but there is one place where you can buy it secretly.) *The liquor dealer was arrested for selling beer under the counter to teenagers.* (The liquor dealer was arrested for unlawfully selling beer to teenagers.)—Also used like an adjective, with hyphens. *During World War II, some stores kept scarce things hidden for under-the-counter-sales to good customers.* (Stores sold scarce things secretly only to good customers.)

under the hammer   *adv. phr.*   Up for sale at auction. *The Brights auctioned off the entire contents of their home. Mrs. Bright cried when her pewter collection went under the hammer.* (Mrs. Bright cried when her pewter collection was sold at auction.) *The picture I wanted to bid on came under the hammer soon after I arrived.* (The picture I wanted to bid on was sold at auction soon after I arrived.)

under the sun *adj. or adv. phr.* On earth; in the world. —Used for emphasis. *The President's assassination shocked everyone under the sun.* (The President's murder shocked everyone on earth.) *Where under the sun could I have put my purse?* (Where in the world could I have put my purse?)

under wraps *adv. or adj. phr.* Not allowed to be seen until the right time; not allowed to act or speak freely; in secrecy; hidden. *We have a new player, but we are keeping him under wraps until the game.* (We won't let him be seen or known before.) *What the President is planning will be kept under wraps until tomorrow. The spy was kept under wraps and not allowed to talk to newspapermen.* (The police did not let the spy tell anything he knew.)

unknown quantity *n.* Someone or something whose value and importance are not known, especially in a certain situation, time or place; a new and untested person or thing. *What we would find if we could fly to the moon is an unknown quantity.* (No one knows what is on the moon.) *The new player is still an unknown quantity. We'll find out how good he is in the game.* (The player hasn't been tried out yet. He will be tested in the game.)

until hell freezes over *Adv. phr., slang* Forever, for an eternity. *He can argue until hell freezes over; nobody will believe him.* (He can talk forever, nobody will be convinced.)

up against *prep. phr.* Blocked or threatened by. *When she applied to medical school, the black woman wondered whether she was up against barriers of sex and race prejudice.* (She wondered whether she had to overcome prejudice in the admissions committee in order to be accepted.)

up against it *adj. phr., informal* Faced with a great difficulty or problem; badly in need. *The Smith family is up against it because Mr. Smith cannot find a job.* (The Smith family does not have enough money to buy what they need to live.) *You will be up against it if you don't pass the test. You will probably fail arithmetic.* (You will be almost sure to fail arithmetic if you don't pass the test.)

up a tree *adv. or adj. phr.* **1** Hunted or chased into a tree; treed. *The dog drove the coon up a tree so the hunter could shoot him.* (The coon was caught in the tree and couldn't get away.) **2** *informal* In trouble; having problems; in a difficulty that it is hard to escape or think of a way out of. *John's father has him up a tree in the checker game.* (John is trapped and it will be hard for him to win the game.)

up for grabs *adj. phr., informal* Available for anyone to try to get; ready to be competed for; there for the taking. *When the captain of the football team moved out of town, his place was up for grabs.* (The other players could compete to become captain.)

up front¹ *n., slang, informal* The managerial section of a corporation or firm. *Joe Catwallender finally made it (with the) up front.* (He became a member of the managerial section of the firm.)

up front² *adj., slang, informal* Open, sincere, hiding nothing. *Sue was completely up front about why she didn't want to see him anymore.* (She told the truth about

up in arms *adj. phr.* **1** Equipped with guns or weapons and ready to fight. *All of the colonies were up in arms against the Redcoats.* (All of the people had their guns ready to fight against the Redcoats.) **2** Very angry and wanting to fight. *Robert is up in arms because John said he was stupid.* (Robert is insulted and wants to fight.) *The students were up in arms over the new rule against food in the dormitory.* (The students were angry and ready to fight against the new rule.)

up in the air *adj. or adv. phr.* **1** *informal* In great anger or excitement. *My father went straight up in the air when he heard I damaged the car.* (He was very angry at me.) *The Jones family are all up in the air because they are taking a trip around the world.* (They are very excited and mixed up.) **2** *also* **in midair** Not settled; uncertain; undecided. *Plans for the next meeting have been left up in the air until Jane gets better.* (It isn't sure when or where the meeting will be, or even if it will be held until Jane is better.) *The result of the game was left hanging in midair because it rained before the finish.* (The game was not finished, and will have to be continued before we know who won.)

up one's sleeve *or* **in one's sleeve** *adv. phr.* **1** Hidden in the sleeve of one's shirt or coat and ready for secret or wrongful use. *The crooked gambler hid aces up his sleeve during the card game so that he would win.* (He hid the cards to use secretly during the game.) **2** *informal* Kept secretly ready for the right time or for a time when needed. *Jimmy knew that his father had some trick up*

his sleeve because he was smiling to himself during the checker game. (His father had some secret trick planned and would use it at the right time.)

upper crust *n., informal* The richest, most famous, or important people in a certain place; the highest class. *It is a school that only the children of the upper crust can afford.* (The school is expensive and only rich people can afford to send their children there.)

upper hand *or* **whip hand** *n.* Controlling power; advantage. *In the third round the champion got the upper hand over his opponent and knocked him out.* (The champion began to win the fight in the third round.) *The cowboy trained the wild horse so that he finally got the whip hand and tamed the horse.* (The cowboy could finally control the horse.)

upper story *n.* **1** A floor or level of a building above the first floor. *The apartment house where Gene lives is five stories high and he lives in one of the upper stories.* (Gene lives in one of the floors above the ground.) **2** *slang* A person's head or brain. *Lulu has nobody home in the upper story.* (She is crazy or very silly.) *Bill's sister says he is weak in the upper story.* (Bill's brain is weak; he is not smart.)

upset the applecart *or* **upset one's applecart** *v. phr., informal* To ruin a plan or what is being done, often by surprise or accident; change how things are or are being done, often unexpectedly; ruin or mix up another person's success or plan for success. *John upset the other team's applecart by hitting a home run in the last inning and we won the game.* (John ruined the other team's hope that they would win.) *We are planning a surprise party for Bill, so don't let Mary upset the applecart by telling him before the party.* (Don't let her spoil our plan.) *Frank thinks he is going to be the boss, but I'll upset his applecart the first chance I get.* (I won't let him be boss.)

up the creek *or* **up the creek without a paddle** *adj. phr., informal* In trouble or difficulty and unable to do anything about it; stuck. *Father said that if the car ran out of gas in the middle of the desert, we would be up the creek without a paddle.* (We would be in serious trouble because we couldn't get any gas there.) *I'll be up the creek if I don't pass this history test.* (I may not pass the course in history.)

uptight *adj., slang, informal* Worried, irritated, excessively eager or anxious. *Why are you so uptight about getting that job? The more you worry, the less you'll succeed.* (Why are you so excessively concerned about it?)

up to *prep.* **1** As far as, as deep, or as high as. *The water in the pond was only up to John's knees.* (The water was as high as his knees.) **2** Close to; approaching. *The team did not play up to its best today.* (They didn't play nearly as well as they could.) **3** As high as; not more than; as much or as many as. *Pick any number up to ten.* (Pick a number lower than ten.) **4** *or* **up till** *or* **up until**— Until; till. *Up to her fourth birthday, the baby slept in a crib.* (She slept in the crib till she was four years old.) **5** Capable of; fit for; equal to; strong or well enough for. *We chose Harry to be captain because we thought he was up to the job.* (We thought Harry was able to be a good captain.) *Mother*

is sick and not up to going out to the store.* (Mother is not strong or well enough to go there.) **6** Doing or planning secretly; ready for mischief. *What are you up to with the matches, John?* (You are going to start a fire with the matches?) *Mrs. Watson was sure that the boys were up to no good, because they ran when they saw her coming.* (She knew they were doing something naughty.) **7** Facing as a duty; to be chosen or decided by; depending on. *It's up to you to get to school on time.* (You're responsible. It's your duty.)

up to par *or informal* **up to scratch** *or informal* **up to snuff** **1** In good or normal health or physical condition. *I have a cold and don't feel up to par.* (I don't feel well.) *The boxer is training for the fight but he isn't up to scratch yet.* (He still is not in his best and strongest condition to fight.) **2** *or* **up to the mark** As good as usual; up to the usual level or quality. *The TV program was not up to par tonight.* (The program wasn't as good as usual.) *John will have to work hard to bring his grades up to snuff.* (He will have to work to raise his marks so that he will pass.)

up to the chin in *or* **in———up to the chin** *adj. phr., informal* —A trite expression used also with *ears, elbows, eyes* or *knees* instead of *chin,* and with a possessive instead of *the.* **1** Having a big or important part in; guilty of; not innocent of; deeply in. *Was Tom mixed up in that trouble last night? He was up to his ears in it.* (He was very much mixed up in it.) *Mr. Johnson is up to the eyes in debt.* (He is deeply in debt.) *Mrs. Smith is in debt up to her chin.* (She is heavily in debt.)

2 Very busy with; working hard at. *Bob is up to his neck in homework.* (He is very busy.) *They are up to their elbows in business before Christmas.* (They are extremely busy.) **3** Having very much or many of; flooded with. *Mary was up to her knees in invitations to go to parties.* (She had very many invitations.)

used to[1] *adj. phr.* In the habit of or familiar with. *People get used to smoking and it is hard for them to stop.* (They get the habit of smoking.) *Farmers are used to working outdoors in the winter.* (Farmers often work outdoors in the winter cold and are not bothered by it as much as people who don't work outdoors.) *After my eyes became used to the dim light in the cave, I saw an old shovel on the ground.* (After I was able to see in the poor light. I saw a shovel.) *On the hike Bob soon got tired, but Dick did not because he was used to walking.* (Dick was in the habit of walking, so it did not bother him.)

used to[2] *or* **did use to** *v. phr.* Did formerly; did in the past.— Usually used with an infinitive to tell about something past. *Uncle Henry used to have a beard, but he shaved it off.* (Uncle Henry once had a beard.) *Did your father use to work at the bank?* (Did your father work at the bank for a while?) *People used to say that tomatoes were poison.* (Years ago people said tomatoes were poison.)—Sometimes used without the infinitive. *I don't go to that school any more, but I used to.* (Now I don't go to that school, but before, I did.) *We don't visit Helen as much as we used to.* (We don't visit Helen as much as we did before.) *I used to go to the movies often. Did you use to?*

(Did you go often, too?)

used to be *or* **did use to be** *v. phr.* Formerly or once was. *Mary used to be small; but she has grown up.* (Mary was small but she is bigger now.) *Dick used to be the best pitcher on the team last year; now two other pitchers are better than he is.* (Last year Dick was the best pitcher.)

use one's head *or* slang **use one's bean** *or* slang **use one's noodle** *or* slang **use one's noggin** *v. phr.* To use one's brain or mind; think; have common sense.— Often used as a command. *If you used your bean you wouldn't be in trouble now.* (If you acted with good sense, you would not be in trouble.) *Never point a gun at anybody, John. Use your head!* (Don't be so stupid as to point a gun at anybody!)

use up *v.* **1** To use until nothing is left; spend or consume completely. *Don't use up all the soap. Leave me some to wash with.* (Don't use all of the soap.) *Jack used up his last dollar to see the movies.* (Jack spent his last dollar.) **2** *informal* To tire completely; make very tired; exhaust; leave no strength or force in.— Usually used in the passive. *After rowing the boat across the lake, Robert was used up.* (Robert's strength was all gone because he was very tired.)

utility room *n.* A room in a house or building for machinery and other things important in the daily use of the building and the work of the people in it. *There is a utility room upstairs where Mother does the laundry.* (The machines for washing clothes are in the room.) *The oil burner is kept in the utility room in the basement.* (The oil furnace for heat is there.)

V

vanishing cream *n*. A cosmetic cream for the skin that is used chiefly before face powder. *Mrs. Jones spread vanishing cream on her face before applying her face powder.* (She used a cosmetic cream before face powder.)

vanity case *n*. **1** A small case containing face powder, lipstick, and other things and usually carried in a woman's handbag; a compact. *She took out her vanity case and put lipstick on.* (She took out her small case which had cosmetics in it and used the lipstick.) **2** A handbag or a small bag carried by a woman and holding various toilet articles. *She had the porter carry her big bags and she herself carried her vanity case.* (The porter carried her heavy bags, but she kept her small one.)

variety show *n*. A program that includes several different kinds of entertainment (as songs, dances, comic skits and little dramas). *Jane's father was the master of ceremonies of a variety show on TV.* (Jane's father introduced people who did different things to entertain on TV.)

variety store *n*. A store that sells many different kinds of things, especially items that are fairly small and in everyday use. *I went into a variety store and bought some paint.* (The store sold many different small things.) *Five-and-ten cent stores are a kind of variety store.* (Five-and-ten cent stores sell many kinds of things.)

very well *interj., formal* Agreed; all right.—Used to show agreement or approval. *Very well. You may go.* (All right, I approve. You may go.) *Very well, I will do as you say.* (All right, I agree to do as you say.)

vibrations *or* **vibes** *n*. Psychic emanations radiating from an object, situation, or person. *I don't think this relationsip will work out—this guy has given me bad vibes.* (I have the sensation that we will not get along well.)

visiting nurse *n*. A nurse who goes from home to home taking care of sick people or giving help with other health problems. *After John returned home from the hospital, the visiting nurse came each day to change his bandages.* (She stopped at his home every day on her way to different homes.)

voice box *n*. The part of the throat where the sound of your voice is made; the larynx. *Mr. Smith's voice box was taken out in an operation, and he could not talk after that.* (The doctor cut out the part of Mr. Smith's throat that made noise when he talked.)

voiceprint *n., technological, colloquial* The graphic pattern derived from converting an individual's voice into a visible graph used by the police for identification purposes, much as fingerprints. *They have succeeded in identifying the murderer by using a voiceprint.* (They identified the murderer by studying a visible graphic pattern of his voice.)

vote down *v*. To defeat in a vote. *Congress voted the bill down.* (Congress defeated the proposed law when a majority of its members voted against it.)

W

wade in or **wade into** v., informal **1** To go busily to work. *The house was a mess after the party, but Mother waded in and soon had it clean again.* (The house was a mess after the party, but Mother went busily to work and soon had it clean again.) **2** To attack. *When Bill had heard Jim's argument, he waded in and took it apart.* (When Bill had heard Jim's argument, he attacked and showed it was wrong.) *Jack waded into the boys with his fists flying.* (Jack attacked the boys with his fists.)

wait at table or **wait on table** or **wait table** v. phr. To serve food. *Mrs. Lake had to teach her new maid to wait on table properly.* (Mrs. Lake had to teach her new maid to serve food properly.) *The girls earn spending money by waiting at table in the school dining rooms.* (The girls earn money by serving food in the school dining rooms.)

waiting list n. A list of persons waiting to get into something (as a school). *The nursery school enrollment was complete, so the director put our child's name on the waiting list.* (The nursery school was full, so the director put our child's name on the list of persons waiting to get in. If another child does not come, our child will take his place.) *The landlord said there were no vacant apartments available, but that he would put the Rogers' name on the waiting list.* (The landlord said he would put the Rogers' name on the list of persons waiting for apartments.)

wait on or **wait upon** v. **1** To serve. *Sue has a summer job waiting on an invalid.* (She has a summer job serving a sick person.) *The clerk in the store asked if we had been waited upon.* (The clerk asked if we had been served.) **2** formal To visit as a courtesy or for business. *We waited upon the widow out of respect for her husband.* (We visited the widow as a courtesy, to show our respect for her husband.) *John waited upon the President with a letter of introduction.* (John visited the President to give him a letter introducing John.) **3** To follow. *Success waits on hard work.* (Success follows hard work.)

wait on hand and foot v. phr. to serve in every possible way; do everything for (someone). *Sally is spoiled because her mother waits on her hand and foot.* (Sally is spoiled because her mother serves her in every possible way.) *The gentleman had a valet to wait on him hand and foot.* (The gentleman had a servant to do everything for him.)

walk away with or **walk off with** v. **1** To take and go away with; take away; often: steal. *When Father went to work, he accidentally walked off with Mother's umbrella.* (Father was not paying attention and took Mother's umbrella.) *How can a thief walk off with a safe in broad daylight?* (How can a thief steal a safe in the daytime?) **2** To take, get, or win easily. *Jim walked away with all the honors on Class Night.* (Jim got all the honors on Class Night.) *Our team walked off with the championship.* (Our team easily won the championship.)

walking papers or **walking orders** also **walking ticket** n., informal A statement that you are fired from your job; dismissal. *The boss was not satisfied with*

Paul's work and gave him his walking papers. (The boss was not satisfied with Paul's work and dismissed him from the job.) *George is out of work. He picked up his walking ticket last Friday.* (George is out of work. He was told last Friday that he was fired from his job.)

walk of life *n. phr.* Way of living; manner in which people live. *Many rich people have yachts; people in their walk of life can afford them.* (People of their kind who have wealth, can own yachts.) *The banker did not want his son to marry a girl in a different walk of life.* (The banker was wealthy and did not want his son to marry a poor girl.) *People from every walk of life enjoy television.* (All kinds of people enjoy television.)

walk on air *v. phr., informal* To feel happy and excited. *Sue has been walking on air since she won the prize.* (Sue has felt happy and excited since she won the prize.) *His father's compliment left Jed walking on air.* (His father's praise left Jed feeling happy and excited.)

walk out *v.* **1** To go on strike. *When the company would not give them higher pay, the workers walked out.* (When the company refused to raise their pay, the workers went on strike.) **2** To leave suddenly; especially to desert. *He didn't say he wasn't coming back; he just walked out.* (He didn't say he wasn't coming back; he just left suddenly.)— Often used informally with *on*. *The man walked out on his wife and children.* (The man deserted his family.)

walk over or **walk all over** or **step all over** *v. phr., informal* To make (someone) do whatever one wishes; make selfish use of; treat like a slave; impose upon. *Jill is so friendly and helpful that people walk all over her.* (Jill is so friendly and helpful that people make her help them too much.) *We wanted the man's business, so we let him step all over us.* (We wanted the man's business, so we let him treat us like slaves.)

walk the floor *v. phr.* To walk one direction and then the other across the floor, again and again; pace. *Mr. Black walked the floor, trying to reach a decision.* (Mr. Black walked across the floor and back many times, trying to decide what to do.) *The sick baby had his mother walking the floor all night.* (The baby's mother walked back and forth carrying him and trying to make him sleep.) *Mrs. Black's toothache hurt so much that she got up and walked the floor.* (She couldn't sleep or read, and walking one way and then the other, again and again, seemed to help.)

walk the plank *v. phr.* **1** To walk off a board extended over the side of a ship and be drowned. *The pirates captured the ship and forced the crew to walk the plank.* (The pirates captured the ship and forced the crew to walk over the side of the ship and be drowned.) **2** *informal* To resign from a job because someone makes you do it. *When a new owner bought the store, the manager had to walk the plank.* (When a new owner took control of the store, the manager was forced to resign from his job.)

war baby *n., informal* A person born during a war. *War babies began to increase college enrollments early in the 1960s.* (Persons born during World War II began to enlarge college enrollments early in the sixties.) *The* *war babies forced many towns to build new schools.* (The large number of children born during World War II forced many towns to build more schools.)

warm one's blood *v. phr.* To make one feel warm or excited. *When the Bakers came to visit on a cold night, Mr. Harmon offered them a drink to warm their blood.* (He offered them a drink to make them feel warm.)

warm the bench *v. phr., informal* To act as a substitute on an athletic team. *Bill has been warming the bench for three football seasons; he hopes that the coach will let him play this year.* (Bill has been acting as a substitute for three seasons.)—**bench warmer** *n., informal* A substitute player. *Last year Ted was only a bench warmer, but this year he is the team's star pitcher.* (Last year Ted was only a substitute, pitching when the regular pitchers were out of the game.)

warm up *v.* **1** To reheat cooked food. *Mr. Jones was so late that his dinner got cold; his wife had to warm it up.* (Mr. Jones was so late that his wife had to heat his dinner again.) *When the children had left for school, their mother warmed up the breakfast coffee.* (When the children had left, their mother reheated the breakfast coffee.) **2** To become friendly or interested. *It takes an hour or so for some children to warm up to strangers.* (It takes an hour or so for some children to become friendly with strangers.) *As he warmed up to his subject, Tom forgot his bashfulness.* (As he became more interested in his subject, Tom forgot his shyness.) **3** To get ready for a game or other event by exercising or practicing. *The dancers began to warm up fifteen minutes before*

the performance. (The dancers exercised for fifteen minutes before the performance to loosen their muscles.) *The coach told us to warm up before entering the pool.* (The coach told us to exercise briefly before entering the pool.)

warm-up *n.* A period of exercise or practice in preparation for a game or other event. *During the warm-up the baseball players were throwing the ball around and running up and down the side of the field.* (During the period of getting ready to play, the players were practicing and exercising.) *Before the television quiz program, there was a warm-up to prepare the contestants.* (Before the program, the people in the quiz practised what they would do.)

wash and wear *adj.* Not needing to be ironed.—Refers especially to synthetic and synthetic blend fabrics. *Dick bought three wash and wear shirts to take on his trip.* (Dick bought three shirts that do not need ironing to take on his trip.) *Sally's dress is made of a wash and wear fabric.* (Sally's dress is made of a fabric that can be laundered and worn without ironing.)

wash one's hand of *v. phr.* To withdraw from or refuse to be responsible for. *We washed our hands of politics long ago.* (We quit politics a long time ago.) *The school washed its hands of the students' behavior during spring recess.* (The school refused to be responsible for things that the students did during spring vacation.)

waste away *v.* To become more thin and weak every day. *Jane is wasting away with tuberculosis.* (Jane is becoming thin and weak from tuberculosis.) *After Mrs.*

Barnes died, her husband wasted away with grief. (Her husband lost interest in life and became more and more thin and weak.)

waste one's breath *v. phr.* To speak or to argue with no result; do nothing by talking. *The teacher saw that she was wasting her breath; the children refused to believe her.* (The teacher realized that she was talking in vain; the children could not accept what she said.) *I know what I want. You're wasting your breath.* (I will not change my ideas. You are gaining nothing by talking to me.)

watch it *v. phr., informal* To be careful.—Usually used as a command. *You'd better watch it. If you get into trouble again, you'll be expelled.* (You'd better be careful not to get into trouble again.) *Watch it—the bottom stair is loose!* (Be careful where you step—the bottom stair is loose.)

watch one's dust *or* **watch one's smoke** *v. phr., slang* To notice your quick action; watch you do something quickly. *Offer Bill a dollar to shovel your sidewalk, and watch his smoke!* (Offer to pay Bill a dollar to shovel your sidewalk and see how quickly he will do it.) *"We'll have your yard cleaned in a jiffy,"* the Boy Scouts told Mr. Truitt.* *"Watch our smoke!"* (The Boy Scouts told Mr. Truitt that they would have his yard cleaned up quickly.) *"I can go to the store and be back in five minutes,"* bragged Tom. *"Just watch my dust."* (Tom said to see how quickly he could go to the store and return.)

water down *v.* To change and make weaker; weaken. *The Senator argued that the House should water down the bill before passing it.* (The senator argued that the bill

was too strong and that the House should weaken it before making it a law.) *After talking with the management about their demands, the workers agreed to water them down.* (After talking with the management, the workers agreed to ask for less.) *The teacher had to water down the course for a slow-learning class.* (The teacher had to simplify the lessons for a slow-learning class.)

water over the dam *or* **water under the bridge** *n. phr.* Something that happened in the past and cannot be changed. *Since the sweater is too small already, don't worry about its shrinking; that's water over the dam.* (Since the sweater is too small already, don't worry about its shrinking because it can't be changed back into the right size.)

way the wind blows *or* **how the wind blows** *n. phr.* The direction or course something may go; how things are; what may happen. *Most senators find out which way the wind blows in their home state before voting on bills in Congress.* (The senators find out if the people want the bill or not before voting.)

ways and means *n. plural* Methods of getting something done or getting money; how something can be done and paid for. *The boys were trying to think of ways and means to go camping for the weekend.* (They were thinking how to go camping and pay for it.) *The United States Senate has a committee on ways and means.* (The Senate has a committee which studies how to raise money through taxes.)

wear down *v.* **1** To make or become smaller, weaker, or less by use or wear; make or become useless or less useful by wearing or aging. *My pencil is so worn down, it is too small to write with.* (The pencil has become too short from writing and sharpening.) *The heels of my shoes are wearing down.* (The shoes are becoming damaged from so much wear.) **2** To exhaust; tire out, win over or persuade by making tired. *Mary wore her mother down by begging so that she let Mary go to the movies.* (Mary tired her mother out by asking her over and over.)

wear off *or* **wear away** *v.* **1** To remove or disappear little by little through use, time, or the action of weather. *Time and weather have worn off the name on the gravestone.* (Long exposure to weather has removed the letters of the name.) *The eraser has worn off my pencil.* (Much use has removed the eraser.) *The grass has worn away from the path near the house.* (People have walked on the path so much that there is now no grass on it.) **2** To lessen; become less little by little. *The people went home as the excitement of the fire wore off.* (They went home as the excitement passed.) *John could feel the pain again as the dentist's medicine wore away.* (John felt the pain as the effect of the medicine lessened.)

wear on *v.* **1** To anger or annoy; tire. *Having to stay indoors all day long is tiresome for the children and wears on their mother's nerves.* (It makes their mother tired and nervous.) **2** To drag on; pass gradually or slowly; continue in the same old way. *Johnny tried to wait up for Santa Claus, but as the night wore on, he couldn't keep his eyes open.* (Time went by very slowly because it was Christmas Eve.) *As the years wore on, the man in prison grew old.* (The time in prison passed very slowly.) *The boys' quarrel wore on all afternoon.* (The boys continued to quarrel all afternoon in the same old way.)

wear one's heart on one's sleeve *also* **pin one's heart on one's sleeve** *v. phr.* To show one's feelings openly; show everyone how one feels; not hide one's feelings. *She wears her heart on her sleeve. It's easy to see if she is sad or happy.* (Everyone can see if she feels sad or happy.) *Sometimes it is better not to pin your heart on your sleeve.* (Sometimes it is better to hide how you feel.)

wear out *v.* **1a** To use or wear until useless. *Bobby got a toy truck that would run on a battery, and he used it so much that he soon wore it out.* (Bobby ran the new truck until the parts became worn and broken, and the truck would not go anymore.) *The stockings are so worn out that they can't be mended any more.* (The stockings have been worn to pieces.) **1b** To become useless from use or wear. *The old clock finally wore out.* (The clock was so old it wouldn't run any more.) *One shoe wore out before the other.* (One shoe got a hole in the sole, but the other was still good.) **2** *or* **tire out** To make very tired; weaken. *The children played inside when it rained, and they soon wore out their mother.* (The children made their mother very tired.) *When Dick got home from the long walk, he was all worn out.* (He was weak; he felt that he could not walk any more.)— Often used with *oneself. Don't wear yourself out by playing too hard.* (Don't make yourself too tired.) **3** To make by rubbing, scraping, or washing. *The waterfall has worn out a hole in the* *stone beneath it.* (The water falling on the stone has made a hole in it.)

wear out one's welcome *v. phr., informal* To visit somewhere too long or come back too often so that one is not welcome any more. *The Smith children have worn out their welcome at our house because they never want to go home.* (The Smith children always stay too long and are a nuisance.) *This hot weather has worn out its welcome with us.* (We are tired of its lasting so long.)

wear the pants *v. phr., informal* To have a man's authority; be the boss of a family or household. *Mr. Wilson is henpecked by his wife; she wears the pants in that family.* (Mrs. Wilson tells Mr. Wilson and their family what to do.) *Mrs. Jones talks a lot but Mr. Jones wears the pants in their house.* (Mr. Jones is the real boss in their house.)

wear thin *v.* **1** To become thin from use, wearing, or the passing of time. *My old pair of pants has worn thin at the knees.* (The cloth is thin from wear.) *This old dime has worn very thin.* (It has become thin from being handled so much.) **2** To grow less, or less interesting; decrease. *The joke began to wear thin when you heard it too many times.* (The joke was not so funny when you heard it too often.) *The teacher's patience began to wear thin when he saw that no one knew the lesson.* (His patience was less and he became angry.)

wear well *v.* **1** To continue to be satisfactory, useful, or liked for a long time. *My old overcoat has worn very well.* (It has lasted a long time and is still useful.) *Their marriage has worn well.* (Their marriage has continued to be sat-

isfactory and successful.) *That author wears well.* (His books are still liked and widely read.) **2** To carry, accept, or treat properly or well. *Grandfather wears his years well.* (He does not act like an old man but still acts much the same.) *Tommy has won many honors, but he wears them well.* (Tommy accepts his honors in the right way, modestly and pleasantly.)

weasel word *n., informal* A word which has more than one meaning and may be used to deceive others. *When the thief was being questioned by the police, he tried to fool them with weasel words.* (He would not give plain answers.)

weather eye *n.* **1** Eyes that can tell what the weather will be. *Grandfather's weather eye always tells him when it will rain.* (Grandfather knows when it will rain.) **2** Eyes ready or quick to see; careful watch.—Usually used in phrases like *keep a weather eye on, open,* or *out for. Mrs. Brown kept a weather eye on the children so they wouldn't hurt each other.* (She watched them carefully.) *Keep a weather eye out for Uncle George at the store.* (Try to see him at the store among the other people.) *Keep a weather eye open for deer.* (Be ready to see them if they are near.) *The police have a weather eye out for the robbers.* (They are watching carefully.)

weed out *v.* **1** To remove what is unwanted, harmful, or not good enough from. *Mother weeded out the library because there were too many books.* (She removed the unwanted books from the library.) *Many colleges and universities weed out their freshman classes to make room for better students.* (The colleges drop the poorer students to make room for better ones.) **2** To take (what is not wanted) from a collection or group; remove (a part) for the purpose of improving a collection or group; get rid of. *The coach is weeding out the weak players this week.* (The coach is letting the poor players go and keeping the good ones.) *The teacher told Elizabeth to read over her English composition and weed out every sentence that was not about the subject.* (The teacher told her to take out every part of the composition that was not needed, to make it better.)

wee folk *or* **little folk** *or* **little people** *n. pl.* Fairy people; brownies; elves; fairies; or goblins. *Mother read me a story about the wee folk who lived in the forest and came out at night.* (Mother read me a fairy story.) *There are many stories about little people dancing in the moonlight.* (There are many stories about fairies and elves who dance in the moonlight.)

weigh down *also* **weight down** **1** To make heavy; cause to go down or bend with weight; overload. *The evergreens are weighed down by the deep snow.* (The evergreen trees' branches are pushed down by the snow.)—Often used with *with* or *by*. *There are so many children in the back seat that they are weighing down the back of the car.* (The weight of the children is making the back of the car sink down.) **2a** To overload with care or worry; make sad or low in spirits. —Usually used in the passive. *The family is weighed down by sorrow.* (The hearts of the family are heavy. They are very sad.) *The company is weighed down by debt.* (The company is having trouble because it owes much

money.) **2b** To make heavy, hard, or slow; make dull or uninteresting.—Often in the passive used with *by* or *with*. *The book is weighted down with footnotes.* (Too many notes at the bottom of the pages make the book hard to read.) *The TV program is weighed down by commercials.* (The program is made slow and boring by too many commercials.)

weigh in *v.* **1a** To take the weight of; weigh. *The man at the airport counter weighed in our bags and took our plane tickets.* (Before we got on the plane the man weighed our bags.) *A doctor weighed in the wrestlers.* (The doctor found out their weights.) **1b** To have oneself or something that one owns weighed.—Often used with *at*. *I weighed in at 100 pounds on the scale today.* (I weighed 100 pounds on the scale.) *We took our bags to the airport counter to weigh in.* (We had our bags weighed.) **1c** To have oneself weighed as a boxer or wrestler by a doctor before a match.—Often used with *at*. *The champion didn't want to weigh in at more than 160 pounds.* (He wanted to weigh under 160 pounds.) **2** *slang* To join or interfere in a fight, argument, or discussion. *We told Jack that if we wanted him to weigh in with his opinion, we would ask him.* (We told Jack to mind his own business and not give his opinion until we asked for it.)

weigh on *or* **weigh upon** *v.* **1** To be a weight or pressure on; be heavy on. *The pack weighed heavily on the soldier's back.* (The load of the pack was heavy.) **2** To make sad or worried; trouble; disturb; upset. *Sadness weighed on Mary's heart when* *her kitten died.* (Mary felt very sad.) *John's wrong-doing weighed upon his conscience.* (John was sorry he had done wrong.) *The teacher's advice weighed upon Tom's mind.* (The teacher's advice troubled him.)

weigh one's words *v. phr.* To choose one's words carefully; be careful to use the right words. *When a teacher explains about religion, he must weigh his words because his pupils may be of several different faiths.* (The teacher must choose his words carefully so that no student will misunderstand or be offended.) *When old Mr. Jones talked to the students about becoming teachers, he spoke slowly, weighing his words.* (He chose strong words to make some students want to become teachers.) *In a debate, a political candidate has little time to weigh his words, and may say something foolish.* (He hasn't time to think about his words before he speaks.)

weight of the world on one's shoulders *or* **world on one's shoulders** *or* **world on one's back** *n. phr.* A very heavy load of worry or responsibility; very tired or worried behavior, as if carrying the world; behavior as if one is very important. *Don't look as if you had the weight of the world on your shoulders, Henry, just because you have to mow the lawn.* (Don't act as if you had to carry the world.) *John acts as if he were carrying the world on his back because he has a paper route.* (John tries to act very important.)

welcome mat *n.* **1** A mat for wiping one's shoes on, often with the word *welcome* on it, that is placed in front of a door. *Mother bought a welcome mat for our new house.* (Mother bought a mat to put in front of our front door.) **2** *informal* A warm welcome; a friendly greeting.—Used in such phrases as *the welcome mat is out* and *put out the welcome mat. Our welcome mat is always out to our friends.* (We are always ready to welcome friends who come to visit us.) *Spread out the welcome mat, children, because Uncle Bill is visiting us tonight.* (Get ready to welcome Uncle Bill.)

well and good *adj. phr.* Good; satisfactory. *If my daughter finishes high school, I will call that well and good.* (I will be satisfied if she finishes high school.)—Often used without a verb to show agreement or understanding. *Well and good; I will come to your house tomorrow.* (The plans are satisfactory; I will come to your house.)

well-heeled *adj., slang* Wealthy; having plenty of money. *Bob's father, who is well-heeled, gave him a sports car.* (Bob's father is rich. He gave Bob a sports car.)

well-to-do *adj.* Having or making enough money to live comfortably; prosperous. *John's father owns a company and his family is well-to-do.* (The family has enough money and lives well.)—Often used with *the* like a plural noun. *This is the part of town where the well-to-do live.* (People with money live here.)

wet behind the ears *adj. phr., informal* Not experienced; not knowing how to do something; new in a job or place. *The new student is still wet behind the ears; he has not yet learned the tricks that the boys play on each other.* (The new boy does not know what to expect.)

wet blanket *n., informal* A person or thing that keeps others from enjoying life. *The teenagers don't invite Bob to their parties because he is a wet blanket.* (Bob just sits in a corner when he comes to a party, so he is never invited.) *The weatherman throws a wet blanket on picnic plans when he forecasts rain.* (The weatherman discourages picnic plans when he says it will rain.)

wet one's whistle *v. phr., slang* To have a drink, especially of liquor. *Uncle Willie told John to wait outside for a minute while he went in to the cafe to wet his whistle.* (He had a drink in the cafe.)

whale away *v., informal* **1** To beat or hit hard; strike again and again.—Often used with *at. The boxer is whaling away at his opponent with both fists.* (He is hitting him hard and often.) **2** To attack severely or again and again; go on without stopping or with great force; pound away. *Mary has been whaling away on the typewriter for an hour.* (Mary has been working hard on the typewriter.)—Often used with *at. During the election the Mayor whaled away at the other party in his speeches.* (He attacked and criticized the other party.)

what about *interrog.* About or concerning what; in connection with what.—Often used alone as a question. *"I want to talk to you." "What about?"* (Why? What do you want to talk to me about?)

what for[1] *interrog.* For what reason; why? *I told Mary what I was going to town for.* (I told her the reason.) *What are you running for?* (What is the purpose of your running?)—Often used alone as a question. *Billy's mother told him to wear his hat. "What for?" he asked.* (Why should I wear a hat?)

what for[2] *n. phr., informal* A scolding, or other punishment.— Usually used with *get* or *give. Tom got what for from his father for answering me rudely, and I heard him crying in the house.* (Tom got a spanking.) *The teacher gave me what for because I was late.* (The teacher gave me a strong scolding.)

what have you or **what not** *n. phr., informal* Whatever one likes or wants; anything else like that. *The store sells big ones, small ones, medium ones, or what have you.* (The store sells any size you want.) *We found suits, coats, hats and what not in the closet.* (We found suits, coats, hats, and other clothing in the closet.)

what if What would, or will, happen if, what is the difference if, suppose that. *What if you go instead of me?* (What would happen if you went in my place?) *What if we paint it red. How will it look?* (If we paint it red, how will it look?) *"You can't go now," said mother. "What if I do?" Dick asked.* (What's the difference, or what do you care, if I do?) *What if Jack scores a touchdown?* (Just suppose that Jack scores a touchdown.)

what of it or **what about it** *interj., informal* What is wrong with it; what do you care. *Martha said, "That boy is wearing a green coat." Jan answered, "What of it?"* (What is wrong with a green coat?) *"John missed the bus." "What of it?"* (What do you care?)

what's the big idea or **what's the idea** *informal* What is the purpose; what do you have in mind; why did you do that; what are you doing; how dare you.—Often used to question someone or something that is not welcome. *The Smith family painted their house red, white, and blue. What's the big idea?* (What was the reason for doing that?) *What's the idea of coming in here after I told you not to?* (How dare you come in here again?) *I heard you are spreading false rumors about me, what's the big idea?* (Why are you spreading rumors about me?)

what's up *or* **what's cooking** *also* **what's doing** *slang* What is happening or planned; what is wrong.—Often used as a greeting. *"What's up?" asked Bob as he joined his friends. "Are you going to the movies?"* (What are you going to do?) *What's cooking? Why is the crowd in the street?* (What is happening that so many people are in the street?) *What's doing tonight at the club?* (What is planned?) *Hello Bob, what's up?* (How are you and what are you doing?)

what's what *or* **what is what** *n. phr., informal* **1** What each thing is in a group; one thing from another. *The weeds and the flowers are coming up together, and we can't tell what is what.* (We can't tell what plants are weeds and what plants are flowers.) **2** All that needs to be known about something; the important facts or skills. *Richard did the wrong thing, because he is new here and doesn't yet know what's what.* (Richard doesn't yet know what we do and how we do it and who is in charge.) *When Bob started his new job, it took him several weeks to learn what was what.* (He was new on the job and it took him a few weeks to learn about it.) *When it comes to cooking, Jenny knows what's what.* (Jenny knows all about cooking.) *Harold began*

to tell the teacher how to teach the class, and the teacher told him what was what. (The teacher told Harold the important factors about who was boss in the classroom.)

what's with *or* **what's up with** *also* **what's by** *slang* What is happening to; what is wrong; how is everything; what can you tell me about. *Mary looks worried. What's with her?* (What's wrong with her?) *What's with our old friends?* (What are our old friends doing?) *I'm fine. What's with you?* (I'm fine. How are you?)

what with *prep.* Because; as a result of. *I couldn't visit you, what with the snowstorm and the cold I had.* (I couldn't visit you because there was a snowstorm and I had a cold.) *What with dishes to wash and children to put to bed, mother was late to the meeting.* (Because she had much to do, mother was late.)

wheel and deal *v. phr., slang* To make many big plans or schemes; especially with important people in government and business; in matters of money and influence; handle money or power for one's own advantage; plan important matters in a smart or skillful way and sometimes in a tricky, or not strictly honest way. *Mr. Smith made a fortune by wheeling and dealing on the stock market.* (Mr. Smith invested his money cleverly on the stock market and became rich.) *The senator got this law passed by wheeling and dealing in Congress.* (He made plans and arrangements with other people to pass the law in Congress.)—**wheeler-dealer** *n. phr., slang* A person with power and control. *The biggest wheeler-dealer in the state has many friends in high places in business and government and is a rich man*

·himself. (The man has much money and power, and can influence much that happens in the business and government of the state.)

when hell freezes over *adv. phr., slang* Never. *I'll believe you when hell freezes over.* (I will never believe you.)

when the chips are down *adv. cl., informal* When the winner and loser of a bet or a game are decided; at the most important or dangerous time. *Tom hit a home run in the last inning of the game when the chips were down.* (Tom hit a home run at the most important time and decided the game.) *When the chips were down, the two countries decided not to have war.* (When there was the greatest danger of war, the countries decided not to start a war.) [From the facts that in gambling games, a person puts chips or money down in front of him to show that he is willing to risk an amount in a bet.]

where it's at *adv. phr., informal* That which is important; that which is at the forefront of ongoing social, personal, or scientific undertakings. *We send sophisticated machines to Mars instead of people; that's where it's at.* (The important thing is to send sophisticated machinery rather than people to Mars.)

where the shoe pinches *n. phr., informal* Where or what the discomfort or trouble is. *Johnny thinks the job is easy, but he will find out where the shoe pinches when he tries it.* (He will learn by experience that the job isn't easy.) *The coach said he wasn't worried about any position except quarterback; that was where the shoe pinched.* (His trouble was that he

didn't have an experienced quarterback.)

whether——or *or* whether ——or whether 1 *coord. conj.* Used to introduce an indirect question. *You must decide whether you should go or stay.* (You must answer the question: Shall I go or stay?) *I don't know whether Jack or Bill is a better player.* (I don't know which boy is a better player.) **2** Used to show a choice of things, or that different things are possible. *Whether the bicycle was blue or red, it didn't matter to Frank.* (Frank didn't care if it was a blue or a red bicycle.)

which is which *n. phr.* Which is one person or thing and which is the other; one from another; what the difference is between different ones; what the name of each one is. *Joe's coat and mine are so nearly alike that I can't tell which is which.* (Our coats are so nearly alike that I can't tell which one is mine and which one is Joe's.) *Mr. Hadley hadn't seen his friend's daughters in such a long time that he couldn't remember which was which.* (He hadn't seen the girls in a long time, and he couldn't remember which one was Sally and which one was Jane.)

while ago *adv.* At a time several minutes in the past; a few minutes ago; a short time ago.— Used with *a. I laid my glasses on this table a while ago, and now they're gone.* (I put my glasses on this table only a short time ago, and they have already been taken away.) *A while ago, Mary was tired and wanted to go home; now she's dancing with Bob as if she could dance all night.* (A few minutes ago, Mary felt very tired; now she feels like dancing.)

while away v. To make time go by pleasantly or without being bored; pass or spend. *We whiled away the time that we were waiting by talking and playing cards.* (We spent the time pleasantly.) *We whiled away the summer swimming and fishing.* (We used our time this summer for swimming and fishing.)

while back adv. At a time several weeks or months in the past.—Used with a. *We had a good rain a while back, but we need more now.* (We had rain several weeks ago.) *Grandfather is well now, but a while back he was in the hospital for three weeks.* (Several months ago Grandfather was sick for three weeks.)

whip up v., informal **1** To make or do quickly or easily. *Mary whipped up a lunch for the picnic.* (She prepared the lunch quickly.) *The reporter whipped up a story about the fire for his paper.* (He wrote the story fast and easily.) **2** To make active; stir to action; excite. *The girls are trying to whip up interest for a dance Saturday night.* (The girls are trying to interest the boys in having a dance.)

whispering campaign n. The spreading of false rumors, or saying bad things, about a person or group, especially in politics or public life. *A bad man has started a whispering campaign against the mayor, saying that he isn't honest.* (The bad man has told lies about the mayor because he doesn't like him or because he wants a new mayor.)

whistle for v., informal To try to get (something) but fail; look for (something) that will not come. *Mary didn't even thank us for helping her, so the next time she needs help she can whistle for*

it. (The next time, she can ask us but we won't help.)

whistle in the dark v. phr., informal To try to stay brave and forget one's fear. *Tom said he could fight the bully with one hand, but we knew that he was just whistling in the dark.* (We knew that he was really scared, and trying to keep up his courage by bragging.) [From the fact that people sometimes whistle when walking in a dark, scary place to keep up their courage.]

white sale n. The selling, especially at lower prices, of goods or clothing usually made of white cloth. *Mother always buys many things at the January white sale to save money.* (By buying sheets, towels, and other white goods at a sale, she doesn't have to buy them at higher prices later.)

whitewash n., informal A soothing official report that attempts to tranquilize the public. *Some people believe that the Warren Commission's report on the Kennedy assassination was a whitewash.* (Some people think that the Warren Commission's report is a document meant to soothe the masses.)

whitewash something v., informal To explain a major, national scandal in soothing official terms so as to assure the public that things are under control and there is no need to panic. *Many people in the United States believe that President Kennedy's assassination was whitewashed by the Warren Commission.* (Many people believe that the true facts weren't told and that the Commission's long report was meant to tranquilize the public.)

whole cheese slang or informal **whole show** n., informal The only important person; big boss.

Joe thought he was the whole cheese in the game because he owned the ball. (Joe owned the ball so he thought he could tell everyone else what to do.) *You're not the whole show just because you got all A's.* (You're not the only one who is important in school.)

whoop it up *v. phr., slang* **1** To make a loud noise; have a noisy celebration; enjoy yourself noisily. *The team whooped it up after winning the game.* (The team cheered and shouted happily.) **2** To praise something enthusiastically; encourage enthusiasm or support.—Often used with *for*. *Father wanted to go to the country, but the children whooped it up for the beach.* (The children enthusiastically tried to make Father go to the beach instead of the country.)

who's who *or* **who is who** *informal* **1** Who this one is and who that one is; who the different ones in a group of people are or what their names or positions are. *It is hard to tell who is who in the parade because everyone in the band looks alike.* (It is hard to tell if you know any of them.) *It took the new teacher a few days to remember who was who in the class.* (She could not remember the names and faces of everyone right away.) **2** Who the important people are. *John didn't recognize the champion on television. He doesn't know who is who in boxing.* (He doesn't know who the important people in boxing are.) *After about a year, Mr. Thompson had lived in this town long enough to know who was who.* (He had lived there long enough to know who the important people were.)

why and wherefore *n.* The answer to a question or problem; usually used in the plural. *Father told him not to always ask the whys and wherefores when he was told to do something.* (His father told him not to always ask why he had to do something, but to do it.)

wide of the mark *adv. or adj. phr.* **1** Far from the target or the thing aimed at. *James threw a stone at the cat but it went wide of the mark.* (The stone didn't come near to hitting the cat.) **2** Far from the truth; incorrect. *You were wide of the mark when you said I did it, because Bill did it.* (You were not right at all.)

wiener roast *or* **hot dog roast** *n.* A party where frankfurters are cooked and eaten over an outdoor fire. *For his birthday party, John had a wiener roast in his back yard.* (John had a hot dog party for his birthday.) *Mary's Girl Scout troop had a hot dog roast on their overnight hike.* (The girls cooked frankfurters outdoors.)

wild cat strike *n., informal* A strike not ordered by a labor union; a strike spontaneously arranged by a group of workers. *The garbage collectors have gone on a wild cat strike, but the union is going to stop it.* (They started a spontaneous strike, but the union will make them go back to work.)

wild pitch *n.* A pitch in baseball that is so high, so low, or so far from the plate that the catcher cannot catch it and a base runner can move to the next base. *The runner went to second base on a wild pitch.* (The runner went to second base when the pitcher threw the ball over the catcher's head.)

will not hear of *v. phr.* Will not allow or consider; refuse attention to or permission for. *I want to* *go to the show tonight, but I know my mother will not hear of it.* (I want to go to the show, but I know she will not let me.) *Mary needs another day to finish her book report, but the teacher won't hear of any delay.* (The teacher will not allow any delay.) *John's father told him he would not hear of his having a car.* (His father told John he wouldn't let him have a car.)

wind up *v.* **1** To tighten the spring of a machine; to make it work or run. *Mary wound up the toy car and let it run across the room.* (She tightened the spring so the toy would run.) *He doesn't have to wind up his watch because it is run by a battery.* (He doesn't have to tighten the spring in his watch; it has no mainspring.) **2** To make very excited, nervous, upset. —Usually used in the past participle. *The excitement of her birthday party got Jane all wound up so she could not sleep.* (The party made her feel excited.) **3** *informal* To bring or come to an end; finish; stop. *John got two hits and wound his afternoon up with a home run.* (He made two base-hits and finished the game with a home run.) *Before Jim knew it, he had spent all his money and he wound up broke.* (He ended his trip to the big city with no money.) *The boys followed the path to the left and wound up where they started.* (The boys followed the path to the left, and ended where they started.) **4** To put (one's business or personal affairs) in order; arrange; settle. *Fred wound up his business and personal affairs before joining the Navy.* (He got everything in order before going into the Navy.) **5** To swing one's arm with the ball just before pitching to a batter. *The pitcher wound up quickly and then*

threw a curve. (He swung his arm to throw the ball harder and faster.)

win in a walk *or* **win in a breeze** *v. phr., informal* To win very easily; win without having to try hard. *Joe ran for class president and won in a walk.* (No one else was close to winning.) *Our team won the game in a breeze.* (They won very easily.)

wink at *v.* To allow and pretend not to know about (a rule or law being broken). *John was not allowed to stay out late at night, but his parents winked at his being five minutes late.* (They kept quiet about his coming in only a little late.) *A judge shoud never wink at any law-breaking.* (A judge should never allow the law to be broken if he knows about it.)

winning streak *n.* A series of several wins one after the other. *The team extended their winning streak to ten.* (They won ten games one right after the other.)

win one's spurs *v. phr.* **1** In old times, to be named a knight with the right to wear little sharp spikes on your heels. *A young squire won his spurs in battle.* (He fought bravely and the king made him a knight.) **2** To win fame or honor. *The young lieutenant won his spurs by leading an attack on enemy machine guns.* (He won notice and honor by leading his men bravely.) *Edison won his spurs as an inventor while rather young.* (Edison was young when he first won fame and honor as an inventor.) *He has yet to win his spurs as a big league ball player.* (He is not famous yet.)

win out *v.* To be victorious or successful after hard work or difficulty; win or succeed; in the end. *Half way through the race Tom* *was last, but in the end he won out.* (Tom was far behind, but he ran hard and won the race.) *Jack won out over the giant because he was smarter than the giant.* (He finally beat the huge giant.) *Frank was a poor boy but he won out and became rich by hard work.* (He succeeded and made money.)

wipe out *v.* **1** To remove or erase by wiping or rubbing. *The teacher wiped out with an eraser what she had written on the board.* (The teacher erased what she had written.) **2** *informal* To remove, kill, or destroy completely. *The earthquake wiped out the town.* (The earthquake destroyed all of the town.) *Doctors are searching for a cure that will wipe out cancer.* (Doctors are hunting for a cure that will end all cancer.)

wipe-out *n., informal* (stress on *wipe*) A disaster, a calamity or an unexpectedly huge success. *The Bay of Pigs invasion in Cuba under President Kennedy was a total wipe-out for the Americans.* (It was a complete failure.) *Mme. Chantal Cinquin is so beautiful that when she appears at a party it's a total wipe-out.* (Everybody stares at her, she is so beautiful.)

wise guy *n. phr., informal* A person who acts as if he were smarter than other people; a person who jokes or shows off too much. *Bill is a wise guy and displeases others by what he says.* (Bill thinks he is very smart and says things he shouldn't.)

wise up to *v. phr., slang* To finally understand what is really going on after a period of ignorance. *Joe immediately quit his job when he wised up to what was really going on.* (As soon as he realized what was happening, he quit his job.)

wish on *v.* **1** To use as a lucky charm while making a wish. *Mary wished on a star that she could go to the dance.* (Mary wished that she could go to the dance and called on a star to make her wish come true.) *Bob wished on his lucky rabbit's foot that he could pass the test.* (Bob held his rabbit foot and wished.) **2** *or* **wish off on** *informal* To get rid of (something unwanted) by passing it on to someone else. *Martha did not like to do the dishes and wished the job on to her little sister.* (Martha got her little sister to wash the dishes so she didn't have to.) *Tom got a very ugly tie for his birthday and when Billy's birthday came, Tom wished the tie off on Billy.* (Tom gave the ugly tie to Billy as a birthday present because he did not want it.)

with a whole skin *also* **in a whole skin** *adv. phr.* With no injury; unhurt; safely.—A trite expression. *The boy was lucky to escape with a whole skin when the car went off the road.* (He was not hurt in the accident.) *Jack came through the game with a whole skin.* (He was not hurt in the game.) *The horse threw him off, but he got away in a whole skin.* (He was not hurt when the horse threw him off.)

with bad grace *or* **with a bad grace** *adv. phr.* In an unpleasant or discourteous way; unwillingly. *Fred takes defeat with bad grace.* (When Fred is beaten he accepts it angrily; he is not a good sport.) *Tom shouted "Hello" to Bill. Bill was in a sour mood and replied with a bad grace.* (Tom shouted "Hello," and Bill answered crossly.)

with bells on *adv. phr., informal* With enthusiasm; eager or ready and in the best of spirits for an event. *"Will you come to the farewell party I'm giving for Billy?" asked Jerry. "I'll be there with bells on," replied Ed.* (Ed said he would be there and all ready to enjoy it.)

with child *adv. phr., literary* Going to have a baby; pregnant. *The angel told Mary she was with child.* (The angel told Mary she was going to have a baby.)

with flying colors *adv. phr.* With great or total success; victoriously. *Tom finished the race with flying colors.* (Tom won the race way in front of the other runners.) *Mary came through the examination with flying colors.* (Mary did well in the examination.)

with good grace *adv. phr.* With pleasant and courteous behavior; politely; willingly; without complaining. *The boys had been well-coached; they took the loss of the game with good grace.* (They were not cross or impolite about the loss.) *The principal scolded Nora, who accepted his criticism with good grace.* (Nora did not talk back or get angry; she was polite about it.)

within an ace of *informal or* **within an inch of** *adv. phr.* Almost but not quite; very close to; nearly. *Tim came within an ace of losing the election.* (Tim almost lost the election, but he did win.) *John was within an inch of drowning before he was pulled out of the water.* (John nearly drowned before he was rescued from the water.)

within an inch of one's life *adv. phr.* Until one is almost dead; near to dying. *The bear clawed the hunter within an inch of his*

life. (The bear clawed the hunter almost to death.)—Often used after *to*. *The prize fighter was beaten to within an inch of his life.* (The fighter was in danger of death.)

within bounds *adv. or adj. phr.* **1** Inside of the boundary lines in a game; on or inside of the playing field. *You must hit the ball inside the lines of the tennis court or it will not be within bounds.* (If the ball goes outside of the lines of the court, you will lose the point.) *If you kick the football over a side-line, it will not be in bounds.* (The ball will be off the playing field.) **2** Inside of a place where one is allowed to go or be. *The soldiers are within bounds on one side of the city, but are out of bounds on the other side.* (The soldiers are allowed to go into one side of the city, but not the other.) **3** Inside of safe or proper limits; allowable. *If you ask Father for a quarter, he might give it to you, but a dollar would not be within bounds.* (A dollar would be too much, and Father wouldn't allow you to have it.) *He succeeded in keeping his temper within bounds.* (He was angry but controlled himself.)

within call *adv. phr.* **1** *or* **within hail** Near enough to hear each other's voices. *When the two ships were within hail, their officers exchanged messages.* (When the ships were near enough, their officers talked to each other.) *Billy's mother told him to stay within call because supper was nearly ready.* (She told Billy to stay near enough to hear her when she called him to supper.) **2** In a place where you can be reached by phone, radio, or TV and be called. *The sick man was very low and the doctor stayed within call.* (He stayed where he could be called on the phone or by a messenger.) *The soldiers were allowed to leave the base by day, but had to stay within call.* (They had to stay in places where they could be called over the phone, radio, or TV if needed.

within reason *adv. or adj. phr.* Within the limits of good sense; in reasonable control or check; moderate. *I want you to have a good time tonight, within reason.* (I want you to have a good time, but not to do anything foolish.) *If Tom wants to go to the fair, he must keep his expenses within reason.* (If Tom wants to go to the fair, he must spend only a reasonable amount of money.) *Jean's plans are quite within reason.* (Jean's plans are very sensible.)

with might and main *adv. phr.* With full strength or complete effort. *The sailors pulled the rope with might and main.* (The sailors pulled the rope with their full strength.) *John tried with all his might and main to solve the problem.* (John tried as hard as he could to solve the problem.)

with open arms *adv. phr.* **1** With the arms spread wide for hugging or catching. *When Father came home from work, little Sally ran out to meet him with open arms.* (Sally ran out ready to hug her father.) *Dick stood under the window with open arms, and Jean dropped the bag of laundry down to him.* (Dick stretched out his arms to catch the bag of laundry.) **2** With words or actions showing that you are glad to see someone; gladly, warmly, eagerly. *When Grandmother came to visit us at Christmas, we welcomed her with open arms.* (We were very happy that Grandmother had come and greeted her warmly.) *After his pioneering flight in the Friendship*

VII, Col. John Glenn was welcomed with open arms by the people of his home town. (Col. Glenn's friends and neighbors turned out to welcome him warmly after his historic flight.)

without fail *adv. phr.* Without failing to do it or failing in the doing of it; certainly, surely. *Be here at 8 o'clock sharp, without fail.* (Be sure to be here at exactly 8 o'clock. You must be here by then.) *Ben promised to return the bike at a certain time without fail.* (Ben promised to return the bike on time no matter what might happen.)

with the best *or* **with the best of them** *adv. phr.* As well as anyone. *Bob could horseback ride with the best of them, but he never boasted about it.* (Bob never bragged about being a good horseback rider.) *John can bowl with the best of them.* (John is an excellent bowler.)

wolf in sheep's clothing *n. phr.* A person who pretends to be good but really is bad. *Mrs. Martin trusted the lawyer until she realized that he was a wolf in sheep's clothing.* (She realized that he was really dangerous.) *Mr. Black was fooled by the salesman's manners until he showed that he was really a wolf in sheep's clothing, by selling Mr. Black a car that was falling apart.* (When the salesman cheated him, Mr. Black knew that his nice ways were just hiding his mean character.)

word for word *adv. phr.* In exactly the same words. *Mary copied Sally's composition word for word.* (Mary and Sally's compositions were exactly the same. Mary copied every word of Sally's story.) *Joan repeated the conversation word for word.* (Joan told exactly what everyone had said.)

She learned the poem many years ago but she recited it word for word. (She remembered every word of the poem.)

words of one syllable　*n. phr.* Language that makes the meaning very clear; simple, or frank language.—Usually used after *in*. *Mary explained the job to Ann in words of one syllable so that she would be sure to understand.* (Mary spoke in very simple language.) *Some people say that John is cute and mischievous, but in words of one syllable, he's just a brat.* (If you want to be honest, you have to call John a brat.)

worked up *also* **wrought up** *adj., literary* Feeling strongly; excited; angry; worried. *Mary was all worked up about the exam.* (Mary was worried and nervous.) *John got worked up when they blamed him for losing the game.* (John was angry and troubled.)

work in *v.* **1** To rub in. *The nurse told Mary to put some cream on her skin and to work it in gently with her fingers.* (The nurse told Mary to rub some cream on her skin.) **2** To slip in; mix in; put in. *When Mary was planning the show, she worked a part in for her friend Susan.* (Mary included Susan in the show.)

working girl *n., slang* **1** (*vulgar, avoidable*) A prostitute. *I didn't know Roxanne was a working girl.* (I didn't know Roxanne was a prostitute.) **2** A girl, usually single, who supports herself by working in an honest job, such as in an office, etc. *The average working girl can't afford such a fancy car.* (A self-supporting young woman earning an office salary cannot pay for such an expensive car.)

work into *v.* **1** Force into little by little. *John worked his foot into the boot by pushing and pulling.* (John forced his foot into the boot.) **2** Put into; mix into. *Mary worked some blue into the rug she was weaving.* (Mary mixed blue into the color pattern of the rug.)

work off *v.* To make (something) go away, especially by working. *John worked off the fat around his waist by doing exercise every morning.* (John got rid of some extra weight.) *Mr. Smith worked off his anger by chopping wood.* (Mr. Smith made his angry feelings go away by keeping himself busy with hard physical work.)

work on *also* **work upon** *v.* **1** Have an effect on; influence. *Some pills work on the nerves and make people feel more relaxed.* (Some pills cause the nerves to relax.) **2** To try to influence or convince. *Senator Smith worked on the other committee members to vote for the bill.* (Senator Smith tried to convince the others to vote for the bill.)

work one's fingers to the bone *v. phr.* To work very hard. *Mary and John worked their fingers to the bone to get the house ready for the party.* (They worked very hard so that the house would be ready on time.) *Mr. Brown worked his fingers to the bone to make enough money to buy a new car.* (He worked very hard.)

work out *v.* **1** To find an answer. *John worked out his math problems all by himself.* (John solved his problems without help.) *Mary had trouble getting along with her roommate, but they worked it out.* (Mary and her roommate found a way to live together without fighting.) **2** To plan; develop. *Mary worked out a* beautiful design for a sweater. (Mary designed a plan for making a sweater.) *Alice worked out a new hair-do.* (Alice developed a new hair-style.) **3** To accomplish; arrange. *The engineers worked out a system for getting electricity to the factory.* (They arranged it so that the factory would have electricity.) **4** To be efficient; get results. *If the traffic plan works out, it will be used in other cities too.* (If the plan does what it is supposed to, other people will use it too.) **5** To exercise. *John works out in the gym two hours every day.* (John does exercises.)

work over *v. phr., slang* To beat someone up very roughly in order to intimidate him or extort payment, etc. *Matthew was worked over by the hoodlums in the park right after midnight.* (He was beaten up very badly.)

work up *v.* **1** To stir up; arouse; excite. *I can't work up any interest in this book.* (I can't make myself be interested in this book.) *He worked up a sweat weeding the garden.* (The work in the garden made him sweat.) **2** To develop; originate. *He worked up an interesting plot for a play.* (He made up a good story.)

world is one's oyster Everything is possible for you; the world belongs to you; you can get anything you want. *When John won the scholarship, he felt as though the world was his oyster.* (John felt as though he had won the whole world for himself.) *The rich girl acts as though the world is her oyster.* (She acts as though she could have anything she wanted.)

world without end *adv. phr., literary* Endlessly; forever; eternally. *Each human being has to die, but mankind goes on world without end.* (Life goes on forever.)

worse for wear *adj. phr.* Not as good as new; worn out; damaged by use. —Used with *the. Her favorite tablecloth was beginning to look the worse for wear.* (It was getting worn out.) —Often used with *none* to mean: as good as new. *The doll was Mary's favorite toy but it was none the worse for wear.* (Mary played with the doll often but it was not worn out.)

worth a cent *adj. phr.* Worth anything; of any value. —Used in negative, interrogative, and conditional sentences. *The book was old and it was not worth a cent.* (The book was old and hadn't any value.)

worth one's salt *adj. phr.* Being a good worker, or a productive person; worth what you cost. *Mr. Brown showed that he was worth his salt as a salesman when he got the highest sales record for the year.* (Mr. Brown earned his salary by getting more sales than any other salesman.) —Often used with *not* or *hardly. When the basketball team did so poorly, people felt that the coach was hardly worth his salt.* (The coach did not do a good job with the team.)

would that *or* **I would that** *or* **would God** *or* **would heaven** *literary* I wish that. —Used at the beginning of a sentence expressing a wish; followed by a verb in the subjunctive; found mostly in poetry and older literature. *Would that I could only drop everything and join you.* (I wish that I were free to go with you.) *Would that my mother were alive to see me married.* (I wish that my mother were still living so that she could come to my wedding.)

wrapped up in *adj. phr.* Thinking only of; interested only in. *John has no time for sports because he is all wrapped up in his work.* (John is so busy in his work that he has no time for play.) *Mary was so wrapped up in her book, she didn't hear her mother calling her.* (Mary was very much interested in her book.) *Jean is so wrapped up in herself, she never thinks of helping others.* (Jean thinks only of herself.) *Mrs. Brown gave up her career because her life was all wrapped up in her children.* (Everything Mrs. Brown did was for her children.)

wrap up *or* **bundle up** *v. phr.* **1** To put on warm clothes; dress warmly. *Mother told Mary to wrap up before going out into the cold.* (Mother told Mary to put on warm clothing.) **2** *informal* To finish (a job). *Let's wrap up the job and go home.* (Let's finish.) **3** *informal* To win a game. *The Mets wrapped up the baseball game in the seventh inning.* (They really won the game in the seventh inning.)

wringing wet *adj.* Wet through and through; soaked, dripping. *He was wringing wet because he was caught in the rain without an umbrella.* (His clothes were all wet from the rain.) *He was wringing wet after working in the fields in the hot sun.* (He was wet with perspiration.)

write home about *v. phr.* To become especially enthusiastic or excited about; boast about. *Mary's trip to the World's Fair was something to write home about.* (She had a very exciting time and saw many new and interesting things.) *Joe did a good enough job of painting but it was nothing to write home about.* (Joe's painting was fair but nothing to boast about.) *"That was a dinner worth writing home about!" said Bill, coming out of the restaurant.* (That was really a good dinner!)

write off *v. phr.* **1** To remove (an amount) from a business record; cancel (a debt); accept as a loss. *If a customer dies when he owes the store money, the store must often write it off.* (The store must cancel the debt since the man is dead and can't pay what he owes.) **2** To accept (a loss or trouble) and not worry any more about it; forget. *Mr. Brown had so much trouble with the new TV set that he finally wrote it off and bought a new one.* (Mr. Brown realized that the TV set was no good and that he had lost the money he paid for it.) *Jim's mistake cost him time and money, but he wrote it off to experience.* (He accepted losing the time and money as an experience that taught him something.) **3** To say that (something) will fail or not be good; believe worthless. *Just because the boys on the team are young, don't write the team off.* (Don't think the team is not good, or too young to play well.)

writer's cramp *n.* Pain in the fingers or hand caused by too much writing. *Holding your pencil too tightly for too long often gives you writer's cramp.* (If you write a great deal and hold the pencil too hard, your hand may ache.)—Often used humorously to stress the idea that you have been doing a lot of writing. *By the time Mary finished her Christmas cards she complained of writer's cramp.* (Mary pretended that she had so many cards to write that her hand ached from doing it.)

write up *v.* **1** To write the story of; describe in writing; give a full account of. *Reporters from many* newspapers are here to write up the game. (Reporters will write all about the game for their newspapers.) *The magazine is writing up the life of the President.* (The magazine is telling the story of the President's life.) **2** To put something thought or talked about into writing; finish writing (something). *John took notes of what the teacher said in class and he wrote them up when he got home.* (John wrote short notes so he could remember what the teacher said and write it all down later.) *The author had an idea for a story when he saw the old house, and he wrote it up later.* (He wrote a whole story from the idea he had when he saw the house.)

write-up *n.* A report or story in a newspaper or magazine. *There was a write-up of the accident in the newspaper.* (The accident was reported in the newspaper.) *I read an interesting write-up about the President in a new magazine.* (I read an interesting article.)

X

x-double minus *adj., slang, informal* Extremely poorly done, bad, inferior (said mostly about theatrical or musical performances). *Patsy gave an x-double minus performance at the audition and lost her chance for the lead role.* (Patsy gave an unusually bad performance and will not be selected for a role in the play.)

x-rated *adj. slang, informal* Pertaining to movies, magazines, and literature judged pornographic and therefore off limits for minors. *My son celebrated his 21st birthday by going to an x-rated movie.* (My son celebrated his birthday by going to a pornographic movie reserved for those over 21.)

x-raying machine *n., slang, citizen's band radio jargon* Speed detection device by radar used by the police. *The smokies are using the x-raying machine under the bridge!* (There is a police radar unit under the bridge.)

Y

yak-yak *or* **yakety-yak** *or* **yakity-yak** *n., slang* Much talk about little things; talking all the time about unimportant things. *Tom sat behind two girls on the bus, and he got tired of their silly yak-yak.* (The two girls talked all the time about silly things and Tom got tired of it.)

year-round *or* **year-around** *adj.* Usable, effective, or operating all the year. *In New England an outdoor pool can be used only in the summer but an indoor pool makes swimming a year-round sport.* (An indoor swimming pool can be used all year.) *Colorado is a year-around resort; there is fishing in the summer and skiing in the winter.* (People visit Colorado both in summer and in winter.)

yellow-bellied *adj., slang* Extremely timid, cowardly. *Joe Bennett is a yellow-bellied guy, don't send him on such a tough assignment!* (He is too timid and cowardly to handle such a difficult job.)

yes-man *n., informal* A person who tries to be liked by agreeing with everything said; especially, someone who always agrees with a boss or the one in charge. *John tries to get ahead on his job by being a yes-man.* (He agrees with everyone because he wants everyone to like him.) *Nobody respects the boss's helper because he is just a yes-man.* (He always agrees with his boss and never says what he really thinks.)

yoo-hoo *interj.* —Used as an informal call or shout to a person to attract his attention. *Louise opened the door and called, "Yoo-hoo, Mother—are you home?"*

you bet *or* **you bet your boots** *or* **you bet your life** *informal* Most certainly; yes, indeed; without any doubt.—Used to declare with emphasis that a thing is really so. *Do I like to ski? You bet your life I do.* (I like to ski very much.) *You bet I will be at the party.* (I will surely be there.) *You can bet your boots that Johnny will come home when his money is gone.* (You can be sure.)

you don't say *interj., informal* —Used to show surprise at what is said. *Your ring is a real diamond? You don't say!* (Although I know you are telling the truth, I am surprised.) *"Bill and Jean are going to get married." "You don't say!"* (I am surprised to hear it.)

you're telling me *interj., informal* —Used to show that a thing is so clear that it need not be said, or just to show strong agreement. *"You're late." "You're telling me!"* (I know very well that I'm late. You don't have to tell me.)

you said it *or* **you can say that again** *interj., slang* —Used to show strong agreement with what another person has said. *"That sure was a good show." "You said it!"* (I agree with you wholeheartedly when you say that was a good show.) *"It sure is hot!" "You can say that again!"* (I agree perfectly that it is really hot!)

you tell 'em *interj., slang* —Used to agree with or encourage someone in what he is saying. *The drunk was arguing with the bartenders and a man cried, "You tell 'em!"* (He wanted the drunk to keep on arguing.) *The speaker said his party would win the election and the crowd shouted, "You tell 'em!"* (The crowd agreed with the speaker.)

317

yum-yum *interj., informal* — Used usually by or to children, to express great delight, especially in the taste of food. *"Yum-Yum! That pie is good!"* (That pie tastes very good.)

Z

zero hour *n.* **1** The exact time when an attack or other military action is supposed to start. *Zero hour for the bombers to take off was midnight.* (The air force planned to have the bombers leave exactly at midnight.) **2** The time when an important decision or change is supposed to come; the time for a dangerous action. *It was zero hour and the doctor began the operation on the man.* (It was the dangerous time for the man.) *On the day of the championship game, as the zero hour came near, the players grew nervous.* (As the time for the important game came near, the players were nervous.)

zero in on *v.* **1** To adjust a gun so that it will exactly hit (a target); aim at. *Big guns were zeroed in on the enemy fort.* (The big guns were aimed exactly to hit the fort.) *American missiles have been zeroed in on certain targets, to be fired if necessary.* (American missiles have aimed at and are ready to hit certain marks.) **2** *slang* To give one's full attention to. *The Senate zeroed in on the Latin-American problems.* (The Senate gave its full attention to matters connected with South and Central America.) *Let's zero in on grammar tonight.* (Let's really study our grammar lessons tonight.)

zone defense *n.* A defense in a sport (as basketball or football) in which each player has to defend a certain area. *The coach taught his team a zone defense because he thought his players weren't fast enough to defend against individual opponents.* (Instead of telling each of his players to defend against one particular player on the other team, the coach taught his players to defend a certain part of the basketball floor.)

zonk out *v. phr., slang* **1** To fall asleep very quickly. *Can I talk to Joe?—Call back tomorrow, he zonked out.* (He fell asleep.) **2** To pass out from fatigue, or alcohol. *You won't get a coherent word out of Joe, he has zonked out.* (He has collapsed and is unconscious.)